EXPLORING MUSIC LITERATURE

EXPLORING MUSIC LITERATURE

Michael Fink

THE UNIVERSITY OF TEXAS AT SAN ANTONIO

SCHIRMER ™
THOMSON LEARNING

Australia • Canada • Mexico • Singapore • Spain • United Kingdom • United States

Wadsworth is an imprint of the Wadsworth Group,
a division of Thomson Learning, Inc.
Thomson Learning™ is a trademark
used herein under license.

Wadsworth Group/Thomson Learning
10 Davis Drive
Belmont CA 94002-3098
USA

For information about our products, contact us:
Thomson Learning Academic Resource Center
1-800-423-0563
http://www.wadsworth.com

For permission to use material from this text, contact us by
Web: http://www.thomsonrights.com
Fax: 1-800-730-2215
Phone: 1-800-730-2214

Printed in the United States of America
10 9 8 7 6 5 4 3 2

BOOK DESIGN BY KEVIN HANEK

Library of Congress Cataloging-in-Publication Data

Fink, Michael, 1939-
        Exploring music literature / by Michael Fink.
            p.   cm.
        Intended as an introductory text for college-level music majors.
        Includes index.
        ISBN   0-02-864844-7 (alk. paper)
        1. Music appreciation.   I. Title.
    MT90   .F56   1999
    780—dc21

                                                                98-33452
                                                                    CIP
                                                                    MN

to the glory of God

Contents

Keyboard Music

Song

CHAPTER FIVE   120

Chamber Music

CHAPTER SIX   156

Orchestral Music

CHAPTER SEVEN   199

The Concerto

CHAPTER EIGHT   225

Opera

CHAPTER NINE   254

Choral Music

Preface

USIC HISTORY and music literature are central subjects in the study of music on the college level. The history of music, organized in a chronological survey ranging from Greek music theory to 20th-century music, is the mainstay of this inquiry—a cycle course usually taught at the upper division. For an in-depth understanding of the principles behind the development of musical style, students of these courses have prerequisite courses in music theory and usually also in music literature.

A problem in music history and music literature is how to organize a music literature course that will (1) introduce the lower-division music student to historical studies, (2) prepare that student for the more advanced music history survey courses, and (3) not be redundant. At some campuses, the preparatory course is treated merely as another historical survey. Not only is this approach redundant, but it usually also necessitates using an elementary music-appreciation textbook inappropriate for music majors. *Exploring Music Literature* takes a different, fresher approach:

- The study is organized by *performance genres* rather than chronologically, as in a big historical survey.
- The study focuses in moderate depth on a few representative works in each genre.
- Biographical sketches of composers provide essential literature-oriented material.
- Source-reading quotations draw the reader into the composer's milieu.
- Studies in style analysis, both with and without score, help the student to understand the nature of each work.

The rationale behind the genre organization relates to how the student listener experiences live music. Most live performances focus on just one musical genre: a solo recital, chamber music concert, orchestral concert, choral concert, or an evening of opera. Thus, the listener experiences the literature of a single performance genre: solo piano, song, chamber music, orchestral/concerto, choral music, or opera. For the time frame of a given performance, performing artists and audience have carved a particular musical literature out of the whole body of music. This makes sense to the listener and provides a satisfying, unified experience. We follow that model here in studying music literature.

To gain the full value of *Exploring Music Literature*, the reader must use the main text, score anthology, and recordings together. The subsections on each work in the textbook titled "Exploring [Title of Work]" develop musicianly listening skills and provide some analytic work without reference to a printed score. However, subsections titled "[Title of Work]: A Closer Look" require the score anthology for a sequence of tasks that make close and frequent references to the printed music.

The study of music history and music literature can be exciting if we approach it as an exploration of known and unknown territory. I hope that *Exploring Music Literature* will be just such an adventure for you.

MICHAEL FINK

EXPLORING MUSIC LITERATURE

𝄢 C H A P T E R   O N E

Music Literature and Style Periods

This chapter begins our study of music literature. In order to understand what we're hoping to accomplish, we must first define exactly what music literature is. We will then discuss how music literature has been studied—by historical period, by countries or culture, and by genre—and identify the approach we will take here. A brief overview of musical periods follows, with key genres/forms/trends and composers listed. Finally, some innovations in music itself—including the development of music printing and traditional patronage—are discussed because of their impact on the study of music literature.

THE STUDY OF MUSIC LITERATURE

What is music literature? Because we often call music a "language," extending the analogy is natural. Most written languages also have a "literature," a body of writings in prose or verse. By analogy, written music can be considered the literature of music.

Merriam-Webster's Collegiate Dictionary (tenth edition) gives as one definition of literature: "writings in prose or verse; *esp[ecially]*: writing having excellence of form or expression and expressing ideas of permanent or universal interest"; and further, "the body of written works produced in a particular subject, language, country, or age." By analogy, we expect that any music literature worth hearing or studying possesses "excellence of form or expression." Despite changes in fashions and tastes, these **works** are musical expressions of relatively "permanent or universal interest."

Merriam-Webster's final definition of literature reads, "the aggregate of a usu[ally] specified type of musical compositions." Here, the dictionary both legitimizes "literature" as a musical term and defines it as a way of organizing an aggregate (or group) of compositions (or works). We can usefully subdivide music as literature, therefore, into "aggregates": groups of literature or various "literatures" of music.

We need to distinguish music literature from musical repertoire. As we have defined it, music literature is written, notated music. There are, however, aggregates of music—some of a very high quality in "form or expression"—conveyed mainly through performance and *not* usually notated. Some types of folk and world music, ancient religious liturgies, and jazz are examples. We are fortunate that audio recordings have preserved parts of some important repertoires. Thus, the recorded jazz of Miles Davis is part of a *repertoire*, while the printed piano music of Chopin is part of a *literature*.

The chief ways of grouping music into its literatures are by:

1. Historical style periods

2. Countries or cultures

3. Genres

art music The cultivated composed music of a culture, as distinct from folk, vernacular, or popular music.

Many introductory music courses are organized chronologically, tracing the history of music through major "style periods": Middle Ages, Renaissance, Baroque, Classical, Romantic, Modern, and so forth. Many world music courses are organized around culture or country, such as Polynesia or India. However, in studying European-American **art music** literature, the genre organization is a flexible means of gaining grounding in some basics of music study.

The organization of this book is by genre. To begin, Chapter 2 introduces some Early Music forms to lay the groundwork for the rest of our study. Each of the remaining chapters addresses a single genre or "aggregate" of music literature:

- Chapter 3: Keyboard music
- Chapter 4: Song
- Chapter 5: Chamber music
- Chapter 6: Orchestral music
- Chapter 7: Concertos
- Chapter 8: Opera
- Chapter 9: Choral music

You will study representative musical works from a genre's literature in several ways:

- Background on the genre around that time
- The composer's biography
- The composer's other music in the genre
- Background on the work under study
- Introductory exploration of the work
- In-depth exploration of the work using the score

THE MUSICAL STYLE PERIODS

The major thrust of this text is the study of music literature by genres. However, each of those genres has its own history that has spanned several centuries. Over time, musical styles have changed, and certain major trends have taken hold. In their works, the most important composers have interacted with these style trends, sometimes pioneering a trend, helping it to develop, or bringing it to a point of perfection. Historians of Western culture have observed major shifts in human history and have given labels to the periods defined by these changes. Thus, we speak of the Renaissance or the Romantic period, for example, to identify events and developments within a period in all areas of human activity, including the arts.

In studying music literature, we can describe every composer and every work in the context of one (or sometimes more than one) historical style period. Music history study has adopted some of general Western history's period labels but has added one or two of its own. Thus, general Western history might mention "The Age of Enlightenment," meaning the entire eighteenth century, while in music, that time period spans the end of the Baroque period and most of the Classical period. For the study of music history and literature, knowing "where you are" among the style periods is vital. A knowledge of some fundamental characteristics of each period is also very helpful as a basis of understanding music literatures that fall within a period.

These are the six style periods in Western art/religious music since antiquity:

- Middle Ages (6th–14th centuries)

- Renaissance (15th–16th centuries)

- Baroque period (17th to early 18th centuries)

- Classical period (late 18th to early 19th centuries)

- Romantic period (19th century)

- Modern and Postmodern periods (20th century)

Over the next few pages, you will see a series of time-line charts and tables giving a general overview of the important genres and forms and key composers for each musical style period. Many terms and names may be new to you. However, you will encounter several of these throughout the text, so it is important to place them in their historical context.

Middle Ages (6th–14th centuries)

IMPORTANT GENRES AND FORMS	IMPORTANT COMPOSERS
Gregorian chant	Early: mostly anonymous
Notre Dame polyphony	Léonin
Medieval motet	Pérotin
Courtly French vocal music of the:	Guillaume de Machaut
Troubadours	Francesco Landini
Trouvères	
Minnesinger	
Courtly Italian vocal music forms	
(Italian Ars Nova):	
Ballata	
Madrigal	
Caccia	
Dance music: the estampie	

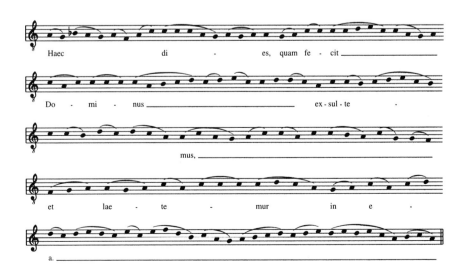

Ex. 1-1 Gregorian Chant: Part of the Easter service. Text is Psalm 118:24, "This is the day which the Lord has made; Let us rejoice and be glad in it."

Earlier Middle Ages

——————— Charlemagne (742–814)
• Election of Pope Gregory I (590)
• End of Roman Empire (476)

500	600	700	800	900	1000

• Boethius, *de institutione musica* (c. 500)
———— — — Gregorian Chant codified
accretions to liturgy — — ——————————— — —
(trope, sequence, liturgical drama)
Musica enchiriadis (c. 900) •
(birth of polyphony)

Later Middle Ages

Papal schism (1378–1417) ————
Papacy moved to Avignon (1309) •
• Dante, The Divine Comedy (1307)
• Magna Carta (1215)
• Richard Coeur-de-Lion King of England (1189)

⌐ Ars Nova ¬

1000	1100	1200	1300	1400

————— — — Notre Dame polyphony
—— Leonin at Notre Dame (1163–1190)
———— — — School of Perotin, Notre Dame
(1180–c. 1207)
Troubadours and Trouvères — — ——————— — — —
Roman de Fauvel (c. 1314) •
Philippe de Vitry, *Ars nova* (c. 1323) •
Guillaume de Machaut (c. 1300–1377) —————
Francesco Landini (c. 1325–1397) —————

_____ William Shakespeare
                (1564–1616)
_____ Council of Trent (1545–1563)
• Martin Luther's Ninety-five Theses (1517)
• da Vinci paints *Mona Lisa* (1503)
• Columbus's first voyage to America (1492)
• Gutenberg prints Bible from movable type (ca. 1454)
• End of Hundred Years' War (1453)
• End of Papal Schism (1417)

1400   1500   1600

_____ Josquin des Prez (c. 1440–1521)
• Petrucci prints music from movable type (1501)
_____ Giovanni Pierluigi da Palestrina
                (1524/26–1594)
_____ Orlando di Lasso (1532–1594)
_____ William Byrd
                (1543–1623)
_____ Giovanni Gabrieli
                (1554/57–1612)

Ill. 1-1 A woodcut from *The Tri-umphs of Maximilian I* (c. 1512), displaying Renaissance instruments. This grouping was unlikely to have actually played together. At the left are a bass viol, a harp (played by the image of Emperor Maximilian himself), and a treble viol. In front are large and small **lutes**. Behind them are two **shawms**, and at the far right a musician plays a **pipe and tabor**.

lute A plucked string instrument popular from the Middle Ages through the Baroque period. It was one of the forerunners of the guitar.

shawm A double-reed wood-wind instrument used in Europe during the 13th–17th centuries; forerunner to the oboe.

pipe and tabor A pair of instru-ments for one player. The **recorder**-like pipe had only three holes and, thus, a limited range. While the left hand played the pipe the right would tap out rhythms on the tabor, a cylindri-cal drum.

NEW MUSICAL GENRES AND FORMS	*IMPORTANT COMPOSERS*
Mass	Josquin des Prez
Lutheran chorale	Giovanni Pierluigi da Palestrina
Renaissance motet	Orlando di Lasso
Renaissance madrigal	William Byrd
Chanson	Giovanni Gabrieli
Dances, dance groupings	
Canzona	
Ricercar	
Toccata	

Baroque Period (17th to Early 18th Centuries)

George I King of England (1714) •
• Milton, *Paradise Lost* (1667)
• Galileo, *Dialogue on the Two Chief Systems* (1632)
• Shakespeare, *First Folio* (1623)
_____ Thirty Years' War (1618–1648)
• Kepler, *Astronomia nova* (1609)

1600	1625	1650	1675	1700	1725	1750

• Peri, *Euridice* (1600)
• Monteverdi, *Orfeo* (1607)
• Monteverdi in Venice (1613)
• L. Rossi, *Orfeo* staged in Paris (1647)
Purcell, *Dido and Aeneas* (1689) •
Bach in Weimar (1708–1717) ____
Handel arrives in London (1710) •
Handel, *Water Music* (c. 1717) •
Bach in Leipzig (1723–1750) _____
Vivaldi, *The Four Seasons* (1726) •
Bach, Cantata No. 140 (1731) •
Handel, *Messiah* (1742) •
— — ____ Giovanni Gabrieli (1554/1557–1612)
— — _____ Claudio Monteverdi (1567–1643)
— — _____ Heinrich Schütz (1585–1672)
_____ Jean Baptiste Lully (1632–1687)
Arcangelo Corelli (1653–1713) _____
Henry Purcell (1659–1695) _____
Antonio Vivaldi (1678–1741) _____
J. S. Bach (1685–1750) _____
G. F. Handel (1685–1759) _____

NEW MUSICAL GENRES AND FORMS	IMPORTANT COMPOSERS
Opera	Giovanni Gabrieli
Sacred vocal concerto	Claudio Monteverdi
Concerto grosso	Heinrich Schütz
Solo concerto	Jean Baptiste Lully
Oratorio	Arcangelo Corelli
Passion	Alessandro Scarlatti
Cantata (sacred or secular)	Henry Purcell
Fugue	Antonio Vivaldi
Variations	Johann Sebastian Bach
Ensemble sonata	George Frideric Handel
Dance suite	
French overture	

Ill. 1-2 Opening of Corelli's Violin Sonata in F Major, Op. 5, No. 4, in an English edition from the early 18th century. Above the violin part is a heavily ornamented version attributed to Corelli himself. The line for "Violone e Cimbalo" is the ***basso continuo***.

bass continuo A style of accompaniment employed in most music of the Baroque period. It consists of a bass line and chords built up from the bass line. The chords are usually symbolized by numbers and other signs, collectively called "figured bass." Technically at least two players are required to "realize" a basso continuo: (1) a single-line bass instrument such as a viol or cello and (2) a harmony instrument such as a lute or keyboard instrument. In certain situations, such as early monodies and operas or organ continuo playing, a single instrument suffices.

Classical Period (Late 18th to Early 19th Centuries)

NEW MUSICAL GENRES AND FORMS	IMPORTANT COMPOSERS
Symphony	Domenico Scarlatti
String quartet	Carl Philip Emanuel Bach
Chamber music with piano	Christoph Willibald Gluck
Serenade/divertimento	Joseph Haydn
Keyboard sonata	Wolfgang Amadeus Mozart
Comic opera	Ludwig van Beethoven
Lied	

Napoleon's first campaign (1796) •

Fall of the Bastile (1789) •

Kant, *Critique of Pure Reason* (1781) •

Declaration of Independence (1776) •

Louis XIV King of France (1774) •

George III King of England (1760) •

Voltaire, *Candide* (1759) •

1700	1725	1750	1775	1800

• Scarlatti arrives in Portugal (c. 1720)

• Rousseau, *Treatise on Harmony* (1722)

• Pergolesi, *La serva padrona* (1729)

"War of the Buffoons" in Paris (1752) •

Haydn hired by the Esterházys (1761) •

Mozart's first journey (1763) •

Mozart, *Marriage of Figaro* (1786) •

Haydn in London (1791) •

Beethoven in Vienna (1792) •

Haydn completes *The Creation* (1798) •

Domenico Scarlatti (1685–1757)

C. P. E. Bach (1714–1788)

C. W. Gluck (1714–1787)

Joseph Haydn (1732–1809)

Wolfgang Amadeus Mozart (1756–1791)

Ludwig van Beethoven (1770–1827)

Ill. 1-3 Performance of a harpsichord concerto in Zürich during 1777. The accompanying instruments include two flutes, two violins, two horns, and a cello. From the Department of Prints and Drawings of the Zentralbibliothek Zürich.

Romantic Period (19th Century)

NEW MUSICAL GENRES AND FORMS	IMPORTANT COMPOSERS
Song cycle	Franz Schubert
Grand opera	Hector Berlioz
Operetta	Felix Mendelssohn
Short piano pieces	Robert Schumann
Concert overture	Frédéric Chopin
Symphonic poem	Franz Liszt
Program symphony	Richard Wagner
Nationalistic music	Giuseppe Verdi
	Johannes Brahms
	Peter I. Tchaikovsky
	Antonín Dvořák
	Richard Strauss

Metropolitan Opera opened (1883) •

Edison invents the incandescent light (1879) •

Franco-Prussian War (1870–71) •

Lincoln assassinated (1865) •

Tolstoy, *War and Peace* (1864) •

• Revolutions in Germany (1848)

• New York Philharmonic Society founded (1842)

• Congress of Vienna (1814)

• Goethe, *Faust,* Part I (1808)

1800	1825	1850	1875	1900

• Weber, *Der Freischütz* (1821)

• Beethoven, Ninth Symphony (1823)

• Berlioz, *Symphonie fantastique* premiered (1830)

• Chopin, Etudes, Op. 10, published (1832)

Verdi, *Rigoletto* (1851) •

Wagner, *Tristan and Isolde* (1859) •

Brahms, Piano Quintet in F Minor (1864) •

Verdi, *Requiem* (1874) •

R. Strauss, Don Juan (1889) •

Puccini, *La Bohème* (1896) •

———————————— Franz Schubert (1797–1828)

———————————— Hector Berlioz (1803–1869)

———————————— Fanny Mendelssohn Heusel (1805–1857)

———————————— Robert Schumann (1810–1856)

———————————— Frédéric Chopin (1810–1849)

———————————— Franz Liszt (1811–1886)

———————————— Guiseppe Verdi (1813–1901)

———————————— Richard Wagner (1813–1883)

———————————— Johannes Brahms (1833–1897)

———————————— Peter I. Tchaikovsky (1840–1893)

Antonín Dvořák (1841–1904) ————————————

Gabriel Fauré (1845–1924) ————————————

Claude Debussy (1862–1918) ————————————

Richard Strauss (1864–1949) ————————————

Arnold Schoenberg (1874–1951) ————————————

Charles E. Ives (1874–1954) ————————————

Satyrisches Bild.

Ein Concert im Jahre 1846!

Ill. 1-4 Cartoon of Hector Berlioz conducting an orchestral concert (1846). The artist is satirizing bombastic orchestral effects by including many brass instruments, percussion, and even a cannon. © Negative, Bibliothèque Nationale de France, Paris.

Modern and Postmodern Periods (20th Century)

NEW MUSICAL TRENDS	IMPORTANT COMPOSERS
Impressionism	Claude Debussy
Expressionism	Arnold Schoenberg
Neo-Classicism	Charles E. Ives
Atonality	Béla Bartók
Polytonality	Igor Stravinsky
12-Tone Method/Serialism	Anton Webern
Indeterminacy/Chance Music	Alban Berg
Electronic music	Paul Hindemith
Minimalism	George Gershwin
Jazz influences	Aaron Copland
	John Cage
	Karlheinz Stockhausen
	Krysztof Penderecki
	George Crumb

Early 20th Century

World War II (1939–1945) _____

Adolf Hitler chancellor of Germany (1933) •

New York stock market crash (1929) •

• T. S. Eliot, *The Waste Land* (1922)

• Einstein's general theory of relativity (1916)

_____ World War I (1914–1918)

• Freud, *The Interpretation of Dreams* (1900)

1900	1910	1920	1930	1940	1950

• Debussy, *Nocturnes* (1900)

• Schoenberg, *Pierrot Lunaire* (1912)

• Stravinsky, *Le Sacre du Printemps* (1913)

• Berg, *Wozzeck* premiered (1925)

• Weill, *Threepenny Opera* (1928)

Hindemith, *Mathis der Maler* (1933) •

Gershwin, *Porgy and Bess* (1935) •

Copland, *Appalachian Spring* (1944) •

Claude Debussy (1862–1918)

Richard Strauss (1864–1949)

Arnold Schoenberg (1874–1951)

Charles E. Ives (1874–1954)

Béla Bartók (1881–1945)

Igor Stravinsky (1882–1971)

Anton Webern (1883–1945)

William Grant Still (1895–1978)

Paul Hindemith (1895–1963)

George Gershwin (1898–1937)

Aaron Copland (1900–1990)

Dissolution of U.S.S.R. (1991) •
Ellen Taafe Zwilich wins Pulitzer Prize (1983) •
Compact disc (CD) introduced (1983) •
• Watergate investigation (1973)
• Astronauts walk on Moon (1969)
• John F. Kennedy assassinated (1963)
• Vatican Council II (1962)
Korean War (1950–1953)

1950	1960	1970	1980	1990	2000

• Columbia-Princeton Electronic Music Center opens (1951)
• Bernstein, *West Side Story* (1957)
• Penderecki, *Threnody for the Victims of Hiroshima* (1960)
• Riley, *In C* (1964)
• Crumb, *Ancient Voices of Children* (1970)
Adams, *Nixon in China* (1987) •
Corigliano, *The Ghosts of Versailles* (1991) •

Igor Stravinsky (1882–1971)
Aaron Copland (1900–1990)
John Cage (1912–1992)
Leonard Bernstein (1918–1990)
Karheinz Stockhausen (1928–)
George Crumb (1929–)
Krysztof Penderecki (1933–)
Ellen Taafe Zwilich (1939–)
John Adams (1947–)

Ill. 1-5 First page of George Crumb's choral-orchestral work *Star Child* (1977). The score illustrates **fermatas** measured in seconds and, below, circular notation. © 1977 by C.F. Peters Corporation. Reproduced by special permission. All rights reserved.

fermata A symbol placed over a note or chord to show that it is to be held longer than normal. A *fermata lunga* (long fermata) in 20th-century music may appear between notes and may be measured in seconds.

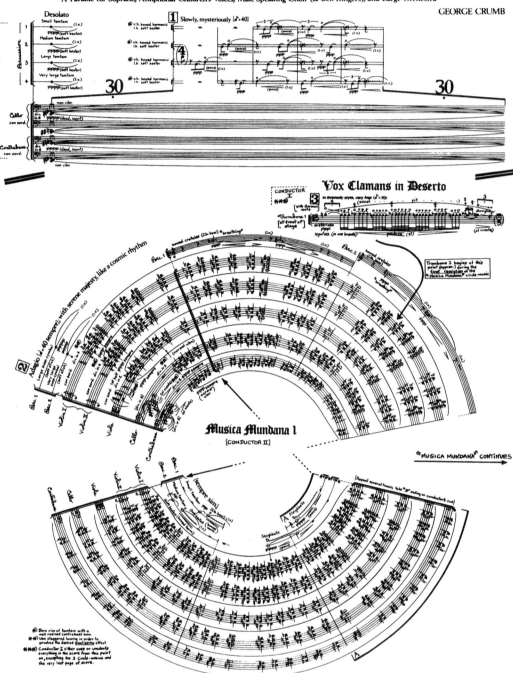

Many events, issues, and developments have influenced the growth of music through the ages. Not only have these determined changes in style, but many of them have had a bearing on the various music literatures themselves. In fact, developments in notation and printing have determined the very *existence* of music literature and its communication among musicians. First we will survey two technical developments than enabled music literature to develop: (a) staff notation, and (b) **rhythmic** organization and notation. Then we will briefly address two sociological developments that fostered the development of music literature: (a) the invention of music printing, and (b) traditional patronage systems.

Two Technical Developments

STAFF NOTATION   In the earlier Middle Ages, music was conveyed orally with little written down. As late as the 9th century, scribes began writing out a liturgical text, placing *neumes* above the words. Neumes were little shapes and marks to remind singers of the general contour of the chant **melody** (see Ill. 1-6 [a]). About the year 900, instruction manuals attempted to represent a primitive staff, locating **pitch** with text syllables instead of notes, but this method did not last. Not until the 12th century did music writers begin to add lines to staffless neumes to indicate their pitches a little more accurately. Middle C was sometimes the only line, but two lines sometimes surrounded that pitch, such as the A and E lines (see Ill. 1-6 [b]). By the 13th century, the staff had increased to four or more lines, and a more accurate square notation had replaced the old neumes. A clef representing middle C could be placed on any line, depending on the range of the music (Ill. 1-6 [c]). Thus, from that time, the pitch of every note in a composition could be accurately notated.

RHYTHMIC ORGANIZATION AND NOTATION   The majority of scholars hold that Gregorian chant had no prescribed rhythmic values but that longer or shorter notes could have resulted from the natural, speechlike patterns of accentuation. In the late 12th century (chiefly at Notre Dame, Paris), composers began applying written rhythmic values consistently to their music. At first these were in "rhythmic modes," which were repeated patterns derived from the feet of Latin poetry (iambic, trochaic, etc.). The use of rhythmic modes resulted in a type of musical triple **meter** called a "perfection" (the three beats symbolizing the Holy Trinity).

About the middle of the 13th century, Franco of Cologne codified a freer system of rhythm derived from the modes. In it, any of the three beats could be subdivided. The following century, the Ars Nova endorsed duple meter as the ideological equal of triple meter and halved the note values previously used. Notation now began to look more modern, mostly like double whole notes and diamond-shaped whole notes and half notes, all with their centers blackened.

The organization and notation of rhythm became codified throughout the late Ars Nova and the Renaissance. Although rhythmic patterns were very flexible within any part, metric organization fell strictly into one of the four "prolations," what we would call the symmetrical meters. In modern terms, these were determined by (a) whether a measure had two or three beats and (b) whether each beat contained two or three subdivisions. Ex. 1-2 is a table of the four prolations. Based on these, music in the Baroque period merely used smaller note values at times and often doubled the length of a measure to create a newly designated meter. For example, one measure of 4/4 is analogous to two measures of 2/4.

rhythm The aspect of music related to time; specifically, the durations of sounds and silences in relation to the pulse (beat) of the music. Adj.: rhythmic.

melody A succession of single tones, usually expressing a musical idea. Adj.: melodic.

pitch Any point on the continuum of our perception of the relative depth or height of a sound. Pitch is a function of frequency, usually measured in Hertz (Hz), meaning vibrations per second.

meter The division of musical time into groups of pulses (beats). Simple meters (2/4, 3/4, and 4/4) and compound meters (6/8, 9/8, and 12/8) are divisible into groups of two or three pulses. Asymmetrical meters (e.g., 5/4 or 7/8) combine groups of two and three pulses. Adj.: metric, metrical.

Ill. 1-6 Evolution of pitch notation in the Middle Ages: (a) staffless neumes above a text (late 9th century); (b) two-line "staff" representing A below middle C and E above it (12th century); (c) later copy of a Gregorian chant using a 4-line staff and square notation (13th century). Sources: (a) Stiftsbibliothek St. Gallen, Cod. Sang. 359, p. 125; (b) and (c) Bibliothèque Nationale de France Paris: Lat. 10.508, fol. 32v; and Lat. 1107, fol. 19v. © Negatives, Bibliothèque Nationale de France, Paris.

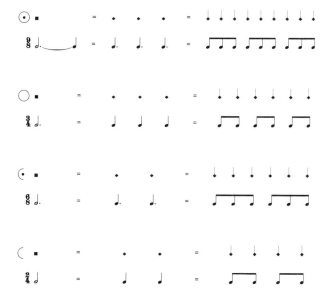

Ex. 1-2. The four prolations of the Ars Nova and Renaissance (14th–16th centuries) with their signatures and usual interpretation in modern transcriptions. Notice that the symbol "C" (actually a half circle) survived into modern notation.

Two Sociological Developments

THE INVENTION OF MUSIC PRINTING Although Johannes Gutenberg (c. 1397–1468) had developed practical movable-type text printing by the 1450s, it would be nearly another fifty years before a technique for music printing by this method would evolve. In the meantime, printers in Germany and Italy produced a few successful collections of Gregorian chant using woodblock technique. First the staves would be printed, then the paper would be overprinted using a block containing notes and text.

Between about 1490 and 1501, Ottaviano Petrucci (1466–1539), working in Venice, developed practical music printing. He used metallic movable type for the world's first music books. His was a three-pass method. The first impression placed staves on the page. The second pass printed the text (though vocal texts were abbreviated and not usually underlaid below the music). Finally, all the notes for that page were imprinted, carefully aligned with the staves. On May 25, 1501, Petrucci released his first publication, *Harmonice musices odhecaton* (translated "One hundred polyphonic songs," although it contained 96 compositions). The book consisted mostly of French chansons in three or four parts, chiefly by composers of Josquin des Prez's generation. Petrucci quickly followed the *Odhecaton* with two more volumes (1501 and 1503). Soon he also published **tablature** for the **lute** using movable type as well as *frottole* (forerunners to the Italian **madrigal**). Altogether, Petrucci produced 43 titles by 1509.

tablature A type of graphic notation for lute or guitar in which letters, numbers, or symbols show fingering positions rather than pitches.

madrigal Renaissance secular vocal ensemble genre popular in Italy and England.

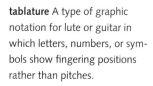

Ill. 1-7 Facing pages (17–18) from Petrucci's *Harmonice musices odhecaton* (1501), showing its choirbook layout. Superius and tenor parts appear on the left, while altus and bassus parts are on the right. The work is a chanson, "Pourquoy non," by Pierre de la Rue, a contemporary of Josquin des Prez.

Soon other printers established music presses, and music publishing fairly exploded during the 16th century. Prominent music publishers could be found in Venice, Rome, London, Paris, and in several German and Flemish towns. Before the mid-16th century, publishers had developed a one-pass printing system, in which each piece of type consisted of a particular note on a particular line or space. Other single pieces of type set along the line might be clefs, signatures, rests, and accidentals. Vocal text appeared as a line of type under the musical type.

It is difficult to imagine the huge impact of music publishing on the development of music. Musical communication now became far more widespread than before, allowing for musicians of one locale (or country) to study and perform the music of another. Also, much of the rise and spread of instrumental music is attributable to the flourishing music-publishing industry.

During the following century, printed music began to be prepared using engraved plates of copper or pewter; and later music printers used punches to impress notes, musical symbols, and signs. Music engraving remained the method of choice until photography, lithography, and photo-offset methods made possible music preparation on plain white paper during the 19th and 20th centuries. The musical typewriter, introduced in 1955, has since given way to the personal computer as the principle means of preparing music for printing.

TRADITIONAL PATRONAGE SYSTEMS. Through the ages, church and art music (and hybrids of the two) have been the highest expressions of music in the Western world. Support for the work of composers in these fields has come from different sources at different times. Traditional patrons of music have been the church (Catholic or Protestant), the noble courts, and lastly the public. In our times, patronage also comes from government, foundations and trusts, and higher education.

It may not be altogether proper to think of the church of the early Middle Ages as a "patron" of the arts, especially music. That is because, as far as we know, its composers were all members of the clergy. Working on liturgical music was their sacred vocation. Yet church leaders in many locales recognized that calling and the need for an increasing repertoire of sacred music. Thus, composing and revising church music was the "job" of certain church musicians. The church supported their lives while they created. Thus, the church was the first patron of Western music.

The goliards in medieval universities and the troubadours and trouvères of medieval courts were composers of **secular** music. However, they were not professionals. The goliards were students; the troubadours and trouvères were courtiers in Provençe and northern France, respectively. Although each of these groups produced a high quality of music, they worked at it as an avocation and were, therefore, on the periphery of the patronage system. At that time, church musicians were generally the best educated, leading the newer trends in music, notably Franco of Cologne and Philippe de Vitry. Not until the time of Guillaume de Machaut (a poet as well as a composer) did courts foster the work of professional composers. Machaut worked first for the King of Bohemia and later for the French nobility, including the future King Charles V. In Italy, Machaut's counterpart Francesco Landini was a church organist, but his large output of courtly vocal music strongly suggests additional patronage from the nobility of Florence, where he lived.

In the Renaissance, wealthy Italian courts rivaled the church in musical patronage. However, a court musician's job was closely church-related. Throughout the period, singers and other musicians were invariably placed on the payroll of the court's private "chapel" (meaning

secular Worldly, rather than sacred.

the religious staff). However, in addition to singing and playing for services, a composer of the chapel was expected to supply secular music for the court's pleasure. In the 16th century, new secular, rather than sacred, music became even more important in courtly patronage. Thus, at the end of the Italian Renaissance and early Baroque period, entire operas were mounted at court expense. Also, a new publication of music was usually funded by a composer's noble patron, to whom the work would be dedicated.

In the field of Renaissance church music, only the biggest cathedrals could afford to attract fine composers as their music directors and organists. Many composers divided their careers between court and church. Josquin des Prez and Cipriano de Rore are examples. A few devoted their lives exclusively to church work, notably Giovanni Palestrina and Giovanni Gabrieli. The Protestant Reformation (from the 1520s) changed the role of music in German churches, but the church/court patronage system remained essentially the same in the North. On the other hand, Calvinism (from the 1540s) in Switzerland and, later, France and Scotland placed severe restrictions on music, but these, in turn, prompted new Calvinist musical publications.

The structure of the Renaissance's church/court patronage system continued during the Baroque era. Entire bodies of music literature sometimes resulted from courtly patronage. For example, French lute and **harpsichord** music developed almost exclusively at the royal court, where composer-performers competed for attention. Church patronage, too, provided environments where new genres could be developed. The Roman Catholic Church sponsored Latin **oratorios**, and the Lutheran Church developed sacred **cantatas**, culminating in the works of J.S. Bach. By Bach's time, the most important Lutheran Church musicians' jobs were controlled by city councils of middle-class citizens. Thus, church music patronage began to shift to the public sector.

Music was going public outside the church as well. The first public opera house opened in Venice in 1637, and subsequent public support made Italian opera the most popular type of music in Europe. Courtly music patronage in most of Europe continued through the 18th century and into the 19th, but a rising middle class led to an increasing number of public musical concerts. For example, in Leipzig during the 1730s, Bach led a series of weekly concerts at a local coffeehouse. Public patronage in England and Ireland determined the two phases of Handel's career there: as an opera composer and as a composer of oratorios.

Thus, musical patronage systems in the Middle Ages, Renaissance, and Baroque period experienced shifts of emphasis from the church to the court, and then to the public. By Mozart's and Beethoven's time in the Classical period, many court and church positions were still available, but musical society also had room for the freelance, entrepreneurial composer. A freelance composer could (a) place music with a publisher for a fee; (b) execute paid commissions from wealthy patrons; and (c) organize concerts of his own music, paying expenses from the proceeds and keeping the remainder as compensation.

harpsichord The most popular Baroque keyboard instrument. Pressing a key causes a plectrum to pluck one or more of its strings.

oratorio A quasidramatic, unstaged, vocal-choral work. Originating in the Baroque period, oratorios were usually based on stories from the Old Testament.

cantata A composition for soloists or chorus or both with instrumental participation. In the Baroque period, chamber cantatas contained recitatives and arias for one or two soloists. Sacred cantatas contained these and chorus movements.

Three Baroque Forms

In Chapter 1 we discussed some technical and sociological trends that had an impact on the growth of music literature. Besides these trends, several key developments in composition occurred in the Baroque period, which influenced later music. Three of them were:

- Fugue (the epitome of **counterpoint**)
- Recitative and aria (an early development in opera)
- Binary form (dance-suite **movement**)

To better understand our discussion of musical genres in subsequent chapters, we will study these developments first. In each case, we will discuss the background and characteristics of the development and then examine a specific musical **score**.

FUGUE:
J.S. BACH'S ORGAN FUGUE IN G MINOR (BWV 578)

One of the most important developments in composition in early music was the evolution of the *fugue*, an advanced technique of counterpoint. **Polyphony** is a **texture**, and counterpoint is the body of techniques for composing music in that texture. In the earliest centuries of polyphony, only very basic technique was necessary: composing one new melody to go with an existing melody. A composer merely layered the new melody over the old one. Even with the development of the Gothic and Ars Nova **motets** in the 13th–14th centuries, the instrumental **tenor** part was written out first and each of the two vocal parts was layered over it. Double texts reinforced this compositional method (see Ex. 2-1).

---

counterpoint The craft of composing in polyphony. The principal techniques of the craft include imitation, canon, and fugue. Adj.: contrapuntal.

movement A comparatively independent portion of a larger instrumental composition such as a sonata, symphony, or suite. In performance, movements are usually separated by brief pauses (during which the audience does not applaud).

score A musical work in visible, notated form, thus, the basic material of music literature.

polyphony A musical texture consisting of two or more melodies heard simultaneously. Adj.: polyphonic.

texture (1) The pattern of sound created by the interplay of the music's constituents, such as melody, rhythm, and tone color; (2) one of the common textures of music: monophony, polyphony, homophony, or heterophony.

motet In sacred music of the Renaissance and later, an individual polyphonic choral piece, usually a setting of a Biblical passage.

tenor A high men's vocal range. In the Middle Ages, the term "tenor" or "contratenor" referred to instrumental parts roughly in that range but usually extended downward into the baritone range.

Ex. 2-1 Gothic motet, c. 1250. The first text reads: "Fair maiden, pleasing and personable, Pretty, polite and pleasant, The delightful one whom I so desire . ..." The second text reads: "I languish, sullen from love. I would sooner that it kill me . ...." The instrumental part below is based on a segment of a Gregorian chant setting of "Benedicamus Domino" (Let us praise the Lord) from the Mass.

Development of the Fugue before Bach

FUGUE: J.S. BACH'S ORGAN FUGUE IN G MINOR (BWV 578)

The Renaissance, the age of polyphony, became the age of consummate counterpoint. By the 15th century, composers had begun to write polyphonic parts simultaneously. In this music, the ideal sound was homogeneous and all parts were of potentially equal importance. Counterpoint advanced during the central Renaissance (c. 1450–c. 1520), when composers developed the technique of **imitation**, also called imitative counterpoint.

Imitation worked this way: For each phrase of text, the composer would write a unique melody. One *voice* (the contrapuntal term for "part") would introduce the melody with its text. Then, in turn, each of the other voices would present the melody and text in "imitation" of the preceding voice (see Ex. 2-2).

imitation A technique of counterpoint wherein a short melody stated in one part is restated (imitated) after a brief time interval in another part. Adj.: imitative.

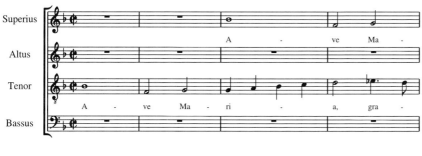

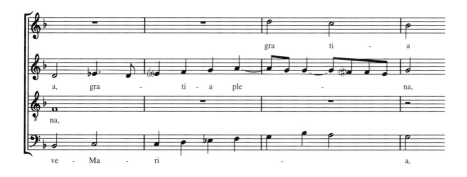

Ex. 2-2 Opening of the Renaissance motet "Ave Maria" by Josquin des Prez. The music displays the central Renaissance's balanced four-part choral sound and imitation among the parts.

Phrase by phrase, these complexes of imitative counterpoint would unfold, often continuing with free material, once all voices had presented the new melody, until the next **cadence**.

Imitation could, hypothetically, occur at any interval away from the original pitch. However, in the Des Prez motet opening of Ex. 2-2, the imitating voices follow at these intervals:

Superius: Octave above
Altus: Unison
Bassus: Fourth below

phrase Part of a melody that conveys a partial or whole musical thought, analogous to a clause or sentence in prose.

cadence A melodic or harmonic formula at the end of a phrase, section, or movement that conveys the feeling of momentary or permanent repose.

Mass Service in the Roman Catholic Church commemorating the Last Supper. In music, usually a setting of the text to the sections of the sung "ordinary," those performed daily. These sections include Kyrie, Gloria, Credo, Sanctus, and Agnus Dei.

Renaissance music theorists recognized a tendency toward imitation at the unison, octave, fourth, or fifth. In 1558 the Italian theorist Gioseffo Zarlino distinguished *fuga* from free imitation based on strict adherence to these intervals (*fuga* meant "flight" or "chase"). Thus, fugal procedure began in Renaissance vocal music. One example is the Palestrina **Mass** excerpt in Ex. 2-3. After the initial entrance in the Quintus (Tenor II), fugal imitations occur at these intervals:

Bassus:	Fifth below
Altus:	Fourth above
Tenor I:	Fourth above
Cantus:	Octave above

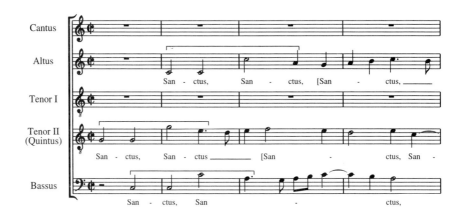

Ex. 2-3 Opening of the Sanctus from Palestrina's *Missa Ascendo ad Patrem*. The fugal entrance of each voice is bracketed.

In 16th-century vocal music, free imitation and *fuga* became standard compositional tools for composing Masses, motets, madrigals, and chansons. Fugal procedure was not limited to vocal music, however. In newly emerging instrumental music, ensemble canzonas and ricercars (modeled on chansons and motets, respectively) were constructed largely on fugal procedure. The Renaissance and Baroque ricercar was especially important as the most direct forerunner to the Baroque fugue. At first, ensemble ricercars—the instrumental parallels of motets—were constructed as a series of phrases, each based on a unique melody and usually developed as a series of fugal entries among the voices. Toward the end of the 16th century, the *monothematic* ricercar appeared: an entire movement built on continuing fugal presentations of a single **theme**, or "subject."

In the early Baroque period, the ensemble ricercar disappeared, but the form thrived in organ music. Girolamo Frescobaldi (1583–1643), the leading organ composer of his time, defined the organ ricercar as a fugal composition steeped in abstract, learned counterpoint. Both Frescobaldi and the Dutch organist Jan Pieterszoon Sweelinck (1562–1621) also composed fugal **pieces** called "**fantasias**," another Renaissance term for contrapuntal movements.

theme A musical idea used as a basis for a composition or a movement within a multi-movement composition. A composition, movement, or song may employ more than one theme.

piece An individual movement, song, or aria that is part of a larger work, or a work written as a single movement.

fantasy, fancy, fantasia, fantaisie, phantasy (1) A Renaissance-Baroque contrapuntal form, forerunner to the fugue; (2) A free, rhapsodic, improvisatory-style movement of the 18th-20th century.

Ex. 2-4 Beginnings of two fugue-type organ works of the early 17th century: (a) Frescobaldi, *Ricercar dopo il Credo;* (b) Sweelinck, Fantasia.

An important feature to notice in both of the openings in Ex. 2-4 is the tonal pattern of subject entries. In the Frescobaldi (a), the first subject entrance on the note G, the *tonic*, is "answered" by the subject on the note D, the *dominant*, then another G subject and another answer on D:

Soprano:	Answer (dominant), m. 7
Alto:	Subject (tonic), m. 5
Tenor:	Answer (dominant), m. 3
Bass:	Subject (tonic), m. 1

In the Sweelinck (b), the first subject's triadic outline defines its **tonality**; thus, the entries are:

Soprano: Subject (tonic), m. 1

Alto: Answer (dominant), m. 5

Tenor: Subject (tonic), m. 9

Bass: Answer (dominant), m. 13

These examples show the norm for an opening "exposition" of the subject in a ricercar or fugue: alternating the starting points on the notes of the tonic (subject) and dominant (answer) of the piece's key. This procedure, *fugal imitation*, also parallels the transition from the older **modality** to the newer tonality (and its system of major-minor keys).

Ricercar subjects were usually abstract and mostly in even note values, a throwback to the restrained Renaissance motet style. During the 17th century, however, German organist-composers began writing fugal works using subjects that were more lively, containing true rhythmic character. They now distinguished these works by a designation of *fuga* (fugue) rather than ricercar. An example of the distinction is a pair of organ pieces by Johann Philipp Krieger (1649–1725). As one of the last appearances of the title *ricercar*, Krieger composed a severe fugal movement based on a typically abstract subject (Ex. 2-5a). By contrast, he invented a subject for a *fuga* that contains repeated eighth notes and angular leaps (Ex. 2-5b), giving the subject a character of its own that permeates the entire movement.

tonality, key Nearly synonymous terms. A system in which one pitch class at a time (called the "tonic") is central or nuclear to the music. The system has dominated Western music from the Middle Ages to the present, with a system of tonal harmonic "common practice" prevalent from the late 17th to the early 20th century. Adj., tonal.

mode, modality (1) A diatonic scale, such as one of the eight Church modes used in the Middle Ages. (2) A major or minor scale.

(a)

(b)

Ex. 2-5 Beginnings of (a) Ricercar and (b) Fuga, both by Johann Philipp Krieger and published in the same 1698 collection.

Two important German organ composers of the generation before Bach were Johann Pachelbel (1653–1706) and Johann Caspar Ferdinand Fischer (1665–1746). Pachelbel composed many fugues, ninety-four of them on the traditional Magnificat tune (associated with Vespers) to be played in alternation with choral verses. In 1702, Fischer published *Ariadne musica*, an organized cycle of fugues in twenty different keys, each preceded by a short **prelude**. This publication was a model to Bach for each book of *The Well-Tempered Clavier* (see below). Bach even borrowed Fischer's ricercar-style E major subject for his own E Major fugue in *WTC II*.

Johann Sebastian Bach was born in Eisenach, Germany, on March 21, 1685, the youngest of four surviving siblings. Part of a long family line of musicians, Bach probably received training in string instruments from his father, but we know only that he attended a Latin school in town. By 1695, both of Bach's parents had died, and he went to live with his brother, Johann Christoph, organist at Ohrdruf. There he continued his schooling at the Lyceum, and under his brother's guidance, he began to study the keyboard. Apparently he began to compose about this time, teaching himself by copying the music of other composers.

In 1700, Bach moved to Lüneberg, where he continued his schooling and became a professional musician, playing and singing. He probably began organ study under a famous organist of the time, Georg Böhm (1661–1733). During 1702–1703, Bach spent a brief period as a musician at the minor court of Weimar before being appointed to his first full-time position as a church organist in Arnstadt. During 1704, he took a three-month leave of absence to travel to Lübeck (purportedly on foot) to hear the famous organist, Dietrich Buxtehude (1637–1707). Bach returned, inspired to play in a new, highly ornamented style that displeased the conservative churchgoers of Arnstadt. In 1707, he relocated to Mühlhausen, which was delighted to have the young organist-composer.

Possibly he composed his masterpiece *Christ lag in Todesbanden* (Cantata No. 4) in Mühlhausen, among other early cantatas. Bach married for the first time in October 1707. His bride was a cousin, Maria Barbara. Together, they would have seven children, among them two of Bach's famous sons, Wilhelm Friedeman (1710–1784) and Carl Philipp Emanuel (1714–1788). Bach's lifelong vocation as an educator began in Mühlhausen, as he taught his first organ students there.

The move to Weimar in 1708 was an important one in Bach's career. Duke Wilhelm Ernst had hand-picked Bach to be his court organist, grooming him also for future musical leadership. Most of Bach's organ music undoubtedly came from the Weimar period, although these works are difficult to date with certainty. Besides several sacred cantatas written for the ducal chapel, Bach **arranged** for keyboard solo or organ 22 Italian **concertos**—nine by Antonio Vivaldi (1678–1741)—which may be a sign of his first major exposure to those works. It was not until 1712 that the court's pay records mentioned Bach as a "chamber musician" besides his job as court organist. Then, in 1713, he was promoted to *Concertmeister* (first violinist) working under the *Capellmeister* (music director). About that time, Bach began to be noticed outside Weimar, notably in Halle (Handel's birthplace), which offered him an organist's position. The next job offer came from Prince Leopold of Anhalt-Cöthen, who wanted the composer as

(continued)

prelude A piece of music originally intended to introduce one or more other movements, such as a fugue or a suite. Later, an independent movement.

JOHANN SEBASTIAN BACH

Painting by Elias Gottlib Haussmann, 1748. Stadtgeschichtliches Museum, Leipzig.

arrangement (1) Elaboration of a simple melody resulting in a full composition; (2) adaptation or transcription of a composition for a performance medium different from the one originally intended. "Transcription" is sometimes a synonym. Adj.: arranged. Verb: arrange.

JOHANN SEBASTIAN BACH *(continued)*

his *Capellmeister*. Bach jumped at the chance, and he must have resigned from Weimar on poor terms, because the record reads:

> On November 6 [1717] … concertmeister and organist Bach was confined to the County Judge's place of detention for too stubbornly forcing the issue of his dismissal, and finally on December 2 was freed from arrest with notice of his unfavorable discharge.

Maria Barbara and the children had gone ahead to Cöthen, and Johann Sebastian was settled there by Christmas.

Bach's life at Cöthen was entirely different from his life at Weimar. His new position was strictly as a secular court musician. Apart from the secular cantatas Bach wrote for birthdays and similar events, his compositions during the Cöthen period were almost exclusively instrumental music: keyboard, chamber, and **orchestral**. He wrote the first book of *The Well-Tempered Clavier*, the 15 two-part inventions, and 15 three-part sinfonias. From that time also come his collections of works for unaccompanied violin, unaccompanied cello, and pairings of violin, flute, and **viola da gamba** with keyboard. Violin concertos, the "Brandenburg" Concertos, and two of the overture-suites suggest an energetic musical life in Bach's orchestra. The prince, his patron, was an amateur musician himself and a connoisseur of fine music. In 1720, he took Bach with him to Carlsbad. Bach returned to find that his wife Maria Barbara had died and had already been buried. About one and one-half years later, the composer remarried. His new wife was Anna Magdalena, a "chamber musician" (possibly a singer), 15 years younger than he. Soon he began to compose/compile the famous *Clavierbüchlein (Little Keyboard Book)* to teach her to play. Bach's Cöthen period ended as a result of the prince's marriage in 1721. His new wife was "not interested in the Muses" and was probably jealous of her husband's friendship with the composer. By 1722, Bach's popularity at court had cooled considerably.

The post of Cantor in the St. Thomas Church of Leipzig became vacant in 1722 with the death of Johann Kuhnau (1660–1722). After several other prominent musicians turned the position down, Bach was called in 1723, tested, and hired. Although the position placed him in charge of music in four churches and for civic affairs, it was a step down from being a court *Capellmeister*. However, Leipzig had a first-rate university, and Bach had sons to educate. Seven years after coming to Leipzig, Bach wrote to an old schoolmate:

> Though at first it did not seem at all proper to me to change my position of Capellmeister for that of Cantor. Wherefore, then, I postponed my decision for a quarter of a year; but this post was described to me in such favorable terms that finally (particularly since my sons seemed inclined toward [university] studies) I cast my lot, in the name of the Lord, and made the journey to Leipzig, took my examination, and then made the change of position.
>
> [Hans T. David and Arthur Mendel, eds., *The Bach Reader: A Life of Johann Sebastian Bach in Letters and Documents*, rev. ed. (New York: W.W. Norton, 1966), p.125.]

Bach was again a church musician and would remain so until the end of his life. His principal duties were composing and directing music for Sunday services and church feasts, but he was also expected to participate in weddings and funerals (for a fee). In his first years at Leipzig, Bach composed mainly cantatas. By 1725, he had completed two complete cantata cycles (about 60 cantatas in each) for the church year, and over the next 15 years he wrote an additional three cycles: about 300 in all (of which about 200 have survived). Besides cantatas, the

orchestra A large ensemble of instruments, as distinct from a small chamber music group. In an orchestra, more than one player performs each string part. Adj.: orchestral.

viola da gamba Bass member of the family of viols, held between the legs; often employed in a Baroque *basso continuo*.

earlier years of Bach's Leipzig period also saw the creation of two larger masterpieces, the *St. John Passion* and the *St. Matthew Passion*.

Despite being recognized as an excellent musician and educator, Bach went unappreciated and underpaid most of the time. Repeatedly he wrangled with the town council over his low salary, insufficient musicians, lack of recognition, and outright personal abuse. The situation reached a crisis state by 1730, and Bach strongly considered leaving Leipzig. However, he decided to stay; part of the reason may have been his recent (1729) involvement as director of Leipzig's Collegium Musicum, a volunteer instrumental ensemble of professional musicians and university students. Here was a refreshingly new activity reminiscent of his happy years at Cöthen. The Collegium performed weekly public concerts. For the organization, Bach revised a few of his Cöthen works and composed/arranged new chamber and orchestral music, notably two overture-suites and seven harpsichord concertos (history's first keyboard concertos).

Bach continued to work as a pedagogue. Part of his duties at the St. Thomas Church was to give music lessons in its school. In addition, the keyboard and organ music he composed during the Leipzig years leaned strongly in instructional directions. These works offered practical pedagogy to the keyboardist and technical-artistic examples to the aspiring composer. The second book of *The Well-Tempered Clavier* (1738–1742) is an example, as is his last work left unfinished, *The Art of the Fugue* (c. 1745–1750). Equally didactic-artistic are the four parts of a series Bach published between 1731 and 1742, under the general title, *Clavierübung (Keyboard Practice)*. Part I consists of the six Partitas, incomparable examples of the keyboard **suite**. Part II (1735) includes adaptations for keyboard of the leading orchestral forms originating in Italy and France: the *Concerto in the Italian Style* ("Italian Concerto") and the *Ouverture in the French Manner*. The third part (1739), sometimes called the "German Organ Mass," is a compendium of chorale preludes for organ. And Part IV (1742) is the monumental "Goldberg" Variations for harpsichord.

In 1733, Bach presented a choral-orchestral *Kyrie* and *Gloria* to the Elector of Saxony in Dresden (a Roman Catholic stronghold), hoping to use the Elector's favor for a little leverage against the Leipzig town council. Instead, he eventually received only an honorary title of Court Composer. Of greater significance, however, is that those two movements became the opening of the Mass in B Minor, Bach's great musical testament. About 1748, he finished assembling this musical monument, adapting some movements from cantatas and composing others anew. There was no known performance of the B Minor Mass during Bach's lifetime.

Bach composed **canons** intensively during the 1740s. Several of the "Goldberg" Variations and the fourteen canons in manuscript Bach attached to them vividly show this tendency, as do the Canonic Variations on the hymn *Vom Himmel hoch* (1747). His culminating work in this genre is the *Musical Offering* (1747), consisting of canonic movements and **fugues** based on a melody by Frederick the Great of Prussia, given to Bach during a visit to the royal court.

During 1749, Bach's health became unstable, and he developed severe eye problems. By March 1750, he underwent eye surgery, which had to be repeated the following month. These procedures weakened the 65-year-old composer, and on July 28 he died following a stroke. Bach left a modest estate, divided between Anna Magdalena and the nine surviving children (out of 20) from both marriages.

As a church composer, Bach was almost immediately forgotten. He continued to be revered as a contrapuntist, but chiefly by composers and students of counterpoint. Until the 19th century, *The Well-Tempered Clavier* was almost the only music by Bach generally known.

suite A loosely organized series of movements related either by key or by subject matter (as in a ballet suite).

canon (1) A technique of counterpoint wherein an extended melody stated in one part is restated (imitated) in its entirety after a time interval in another part; (2) a more complex contrapuntal puzzle in which one part is given and other parts must be deduced from it. Adj.: canonic.

fugue A contrapuntal form or procedure involving statements of a subject, called "expositions" alternating with relatively free sections called "episodes." Adj.: fugal.

(continued)

JOHANN SEBASTIAN BACH (*continued*)

Johann Nicolaus Forkel's 1802 biography of Bach and other writings stimulated some interest. However, a true Bach revival had to wait until Felix Mendelssohn (1809–1847) conducted the Berlin Singakademie in the complete *St. Matthew Passion* in 1829. An avalanche of interest followed, leading to the establishment of a Bach-Gesellschaft (Bach Society) in 1850, the centennial of Bach's death. The society sponsored the first publication of his complete works. Between that time and ours, recognition of Bach's greatness in Western culture has grown exponentially. His place in music has been compared with Aristotle's in philosophy and da Vinci's in art. In his article on J.S. Bach in *The New Grove Dictionary of Music and Musicians* (1980), Walter Emery summarizes Bach's universal significance:

> His art was of an encyclopedic nature, drawing together and surmounting the techniques, the styles and the general achievements of his own and earlier generations and leading on to new perspectives which later ages have received and understood in a great variety of ways.

Bach as a Fugue Composer

The study of counterpoint occupied J.S. Bach all his life, and his mastery of the fugue may be found in many of his works, vocal and instrumental. Here we are concerned with his instrumental fugues. Bach's fugue writing is tied closely to his activities as an organist, for which he was famous. As we have observed, the development of ricercars and fugues in the Baroque period had been mainly the work of organists, and Bach inherited that responsibility. He brought the fugue to a height never to be exceeded, only to be imitated.

For the "keyboard" (usually meaning *harpsichord*), Bach composed several independent fugues, mostly on his own subjects, but some as studies on the subjects of other composers. More usually, he preceded a fugue with a prelude in the same key. Bach's monumental contribution to the prelude-fugue genre was his two-volume work *The Well-Tempered Clavier* (Book I: 1722; Book II: 1738–1742). For each book, Bach composed a prelude and fugue in each of the 24 possible major and minor keys. Beginning with C major, he went on to the parallel C minor. Then he moved up to C-sharp major and minor for Preludes and Fugues Nos. 3 and 4. The rest of the book continues in that manner: moving up a half-step for the next major-mode prelude and fugue, then a prelude-fugue pair in the parallel minor—until the cycle concluded with a prelude and fugue in B minor. Because Bach cycled through the 24 keys twice, the two books of *The Well-Tempered Clavier* are sometimes called "The 48."

The last project in Bach's life was a great cycle of fugues titled *The Art of the Fugue* (c. 1745–1750). Its purpose was didactic, to demonstrate all the possible techniques of fugue composition. All the fugues are in D minor, and all contain a "motto" subject. Bach died before he could complete this monumental cycle.

As in his *clavier* music, Bach's works for the organ include many fugues, usually preceded by a prelude, **toccata**, or fantasia (by then a free, virtuosic piece similar to the toccata). In addition, the modern *Bach-Werke-Verzeichnis* ("BWV," Bach Works Catalog) lists four independent fantasias, two independent preludes, and four independent fugues, including the Organ Fugue in G Minor (BWV 578).

toccata A piece for keyboard (organ or harpsichord) in a free, quasi-improvisatory style. Around 1600, the term was also applied to fanfares.

Ill. 2-1 Printed ticket to an English concert in the early 18th century. Engraving by William Hogarth (1697–1764).

Exploring the G Minor Organ Fugue

We often call the Organ Fugue in G Minor (BWV 578) the "Little" G Minor Fugue. This is to distinguish it from the "Great" G Minor Fugue (BWV 542) that Bach composed in Weimar, later preceding it with a fantasia composed at Cöthen. We do not know exactly when the early, independent "Little" Organ Fugue in G Minor was composed. However, noted Bach scholar Albert Schweitzer wrote, "So vigorously and broadly laid out a subject as that of the G minor fugue is not to be met with in previous organ music—to say nothing of the rapid and weighty development of the fugue. …" Then, referring to both this fugue and the famous Toccata and Fugue in D Minor (BWV 565), probably composed about the same time, Schweitzer writes:

> The peculiar charm of these works comes from their spontaneous freshness of invention. They affect the hearer almost more powerfully than any other of Bach's organ works, and to play them is always to experience something of what the master himself must have felt when, for the first time, he exploited the full possibilities of the organ with regard to wealth of tone and variety of combination.

Schweitzer's remark about the broadness and vigor of the fugue's subject (Ex. 2-6a) is illuminating. Its mere length accounts for a "broadness" that also carries an aspect of grandeur. We can account for the "vigor" by observing how the subject's rhythm accelerates. Interestingly, the subject begins in fairly even note values (mostly quarter notes), in the manner of an old ricercar-type subject (Ex. 2-6b). Continuing, the subject develops "character" as the rhythm speeds up to mostly eighth notes (Ex. 2-6c), then further increasing to a steady pattern of an eighth and two sixteenths (Ex. 2-6d), and, finally, becoming running sixteenth notes (Ex. 2-6e).

(a)

(b)

(c)

(d)

(e)

Ex. 2-6 Analysis of the subject of Bach's Organ Fugue in G Minor. (a) is the full subject; (b)–(e) show the subject broken apart, demonstrating rhythmic acceleration.

WHAT IS A FUGUE? As discussed above, fugue is both a procedure and a form. Fully developed *fugal procedure* consists simply of an alternation between two elements:

Exposition A formal presentation of a subject either with or without an answer (a subject presentation on the dominant, following a presentation on the tonic). The subject or subject-answer combinations may occur more than once in an exposition.

Episode A passage that does not include a formal presentation of the subject. Episodes occur between expositions and have three functions (used individually or in combination):

1. giving the listener a *respite* from hearing the subject, so that the subject will sound fresh in the next exposition;

2. *modulating* (at the composer's option) so that expositions can occur in different keys; and

3. *developing* (at the composer's option) a **motive** drawn from the subject. This is done chiefly by (a) using it in **sequences**, (b) passing it between voices, or (c) altering the motive slightly. These are usually combined in some way.

development (1) The application of various techniques to exploit musical material already exposed (chiefly, themes or motives), also termed "working out"; (2) the central section of a sonata form, where these techniques are commonly found.

motive A short melodic/rhythmic idea, sometimes constructed from shorter figures. Motives are sometimes derived from longer themes or fugue subjects.

sequence The immediate repetition of a figure or motive at another pitch.

Listen to the Organ Fugue in G Minor. Be aware of when an exposition begins and when an episode occurs. Listen to the fugue again. On paper, keep track of each exposition, noting whether the subject is heard high in the texture, in the middle, or low. Also note whether the subject is in the major or minor mode.

The fugue begins with four statements of the subject, the first exposition:

1. High   Minor
2. Middle   Minor
3. Middle (lower)   Minor
4. Low   Minor

After the first episode, an exposition begins in the middle. Soon it seems to dissolve, but the subject is quickly picked up in a higher part.

5. Middle/high   Minor

The second episode leads to a major key.

6. Middle   Major

Episode three digresses slightly but returns to the same key.

7. Low   Major

The fourth episode immediately prepares for a minor mode exposition.

8. High   Minor

The longest episode in the fugue returns to the original G minor in preparation for the final exposition.

9. Low   Minor

THE OPENING EXPOSITION. Now let us examine the score of the fugue and identify precisely where each exposition and each episode begins. Initially, we expect to hear the subject in each entering voice, until the four-voice texture of this piece is complete. The **soprano** enters first with the subject.

Locate the second appearance. Is it an "answer"? The second appearance occurs in m. 6 (alto) and is on D, the dominant of G minor. Therefore, this is the answer to the first entry.

The full subject is shown in Ex. 2-6a. *Notice the absence of the subject in m. 5 (beats 3–4), and from m. 10 (beat 3) to m. 12 (beat 2).* Technically, we could label each of these passages an episode or "mini"-episode. However, some theorists say that a real episode cannot occur until all voices have sounded the subject or its answer.

Locate the next subject and answer. The subject appears in m. 12 (beat 3, tenor), and its answer (on D) occurs in m. 17 (beat 3, **bass**). The answer's ending is slightly simplified, probably because it must also be the music's bass **line**. Its last note is the downbeat of m. 22. This completes the first exposition.

A "FALSE" ENTRY Find the next subject and follow it for two measures. It begins at the outset of m. 25 in the tenor (in G minor). However, something unusual soon takes place. After the first measure of straightforward subject, the subject seems to dissolve into sixteenth notes. Then, in m. 26, beat 3 (soprano), the subject takes up again—beginning with its third note!—and continues normally to an ending in m. 30. This is what has happened: The entry in the tenor voice is a "false" entry, or "anticipation." The actual subject begins in the soprano in m. 26. Its first two notes are present, but are embedded in the flow of sixteenth notes. Ex. 2-7 illustrates the false and proper entries.

Where does the next episode begin, and into what key does it **modulate** *for the next exposition?* The episode beginning in m. 30 (beat 3) leads to a cadence in B-flat major (m. 33), where the next exposition begins (alto). Hear how well Bach's subject sounds in the relative major key. Mm. 33–45 is a kind of central section in this fugue. In it, Bach presents two expositions separated by an episode that stays close to B-flat major.

OTHER EPISODES. *Examine the episode beginning in m. 37 (beat three).* It develops a

Bach's G Minor Organ Fugue: A Closer Look

Please refer to the score of the Fugue in G Minor, beginning on page 1 of the Score Anthology

soprano Highest vocal range for a woman's or child's voice.

bass (1) The lowest men's voice range; (2) the lowest range in a family of instruments; (3) in a musical texture, the lowest-sounding part.

line A particular melody in a particular musical context. Sometimes synonymous with melody.

modulate To make a transition from one key to another. N.: modulation.

THREE BAROQUE FORMS

Ex. 2-7 Mm. 25–27, showing a false entry in the tenor (m. 25) and the actual entry in the soprano (m. 26).

figure, figuration In music of the 17th and 18th centuries, a short, stereotyped melodic pattern used repeatedly, especially in keyboard accompaniment textures. Adj.: *figural.*

figure taken from the subject. At the end of the subject, shown in Ex. 2-8a, this sixteenth-note figure is bracketed and marked "x." *In the score, find figure "x" in the m. 37 episode and draw brackets over all occurrences of it. Check your work against Ex. 2-8b.* Notice that in m. 37, Bach has constructed a motive by preceding figure "x" with another figure of four sixteenth notes. Ex. 2-8b shows this with a dotted arc. The motive repeats sequentially by downward steps. In m. 39, the motive then shifts from the soprano voice to the alto, where it continues sequentially downward until the next exposition. *In your score, draw a dotted arc over every occurrence of the motive, beginning in m. 37 (beat three).*

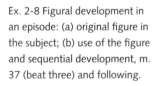

Ex. 2-8 Figural development in an episode: (a) original figure in the subject; (b) use of the figure and sequential development, m. 37 (beat three) and following.

Find the episode beginning in m. 45. Into what key does this episode modulate to prepare for the next exposition, and in what measure does that exposition begin? The accidentals, A-flat and B-natural, suggest C minor, and that is exactly where the music arrives in a dramatic cadence (mm. 50–51) on the first three notes of the subject (soprano). The fugue is now in the key of the subdominant (C minor), beginning to drive back to the home key of G minor.

How long is the final episode, and where does the final exposition begin? Bach's masterful sense of proportion and psychological preparation comes out in the big eight and one-half measure episode that leads to the last exposition (bass) in m. 63 (beat 3). Choosing the bass voice for the final subject entry contributes to the grandeur of the fugue's ending, capped by a conclusive **chord** containing the **Picardy third**. Ex. 2-9 shows a technical diagram of the entire fugue.

chord Three or more tones sounded simultaneously, usually a consonance.

Picardy third In the final chord of a movement or piece in a minor key, raising the third a half step to form a major chord.

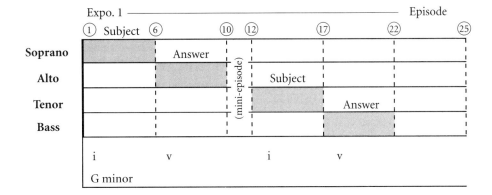

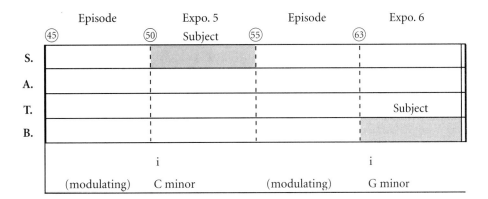

Ex. 2-9 Diagram of Bach's Organ Fugue in G Minor, showing expositions, episodes, and key changes.

recitative In an opera, oratorio, or cantata, a section of dialogue or monologue. Recitatives imitate the rhythms and rise-fall patterns of heightened, dramatic speech. Thus they are not usually very melodic, in contrast with more lyrical "set pieces" (e.g, arias).

aria, air Literally, song. In opera, a set piece for solo voice where action stops so that a character can lyrically reflect or emote. An aria can be through-composed but more often follows an established form. Arias also appear in other vocal genres such as cantatas (chamber or sacred) and oratorios.

HENRY PURCELL

Portrait in black chalk highlighted in white, attributed to Godfrey Kneller (1646–1723). Believed to be the only extant portrait of Purcell made during his lifetime. By courtesy of the National Portrait Gallery, London.

song Music for one solo voice, usually accompanied by a single instrument. The text may be secular or sacred (but nonliturgical). For this study, music for two or more voices is not considered song but vocal ensemble literature (considered in Chapter 9). Songs accompanied by more than one instrument belong in the literature of either vocal chamber music or orchestral song.

RECITATIVE AND ARIA: PURCELL'S "DIDO'S LAMENT" FROM *DIDO AND AENEAS*

Recitatives (narrative, speechlike musical interludes) and **arias** (full-scale song) are two of the key elements of traditional opera. In England, both developed through earlier musical forms, such as the English masque, which incorporated recitative, spoken recitation, **song**, and dance. The first great English operatic composer was Henry Purcell, whose *Dido and Aeneas* was an important early example of the genre. Perhaps the most famous part of this work is "Dido's Lament." This aria has something special about it, something that concerns the illustration of emotion. In a period when other composers were content with superficiality, Purcell dove right to the heart, plumbing to depths only hinted at in the text. His full potential as an opera composer is revealed in these 64 measures. Opera historian Donald Jay Grout pithily wrote that "Dido's Lament" is "one of the most affecting expressions of tragic grief in all opera."

Dido and Aeneas: Background

HISTORY Most English musical theater during Purcell's time was Restoration semi-opera, a combination of spoken play and music (similar in many ways to 20th-century Broadway musicals). Londoners, however, were also exposed to occasional French and Italian productions, which were entirely sung. Purcell's *Dido and Aeneas* of 1689 was not the first all-sung Restoration opera, but it was the first *full-length*, all-sung English opera. Purcell's three-act work was intended for a private performance rather than the public stage. Josiah Priest's Boarding School for Young Ladies and Gentlewomen commissioned Purcell to write the opera. The premiere performance was in 1689. Material in the opera's Prologue suggests a commem-

Henry Purcell was born in 1659, probably in London. He came from a musical family, but his exact parentage is a matter of dispute. Two men, another Henry Purcell and a Thomas Purcell, were both Gentlemen of the Chapel Royal of England, so either could have been young Henry's father. Purcell had three brothers, one of whom, Daniel, was also a composer. As a boy, Henry Purcell was a chorister in the all-male Chapel Royal. A catch (round) published in 1667 shows that, a prodigy, he began composing at a very early age. Pelham Humfrey (1647–1674) was probably his teacher, or at least exerted great influence on Purcell's later music. Humfrey had spent some years in France and possibly also Italy. In 1672, he was appointed Master of the Children of the Chapel Royal.

When Purcell's voice broke in 1673, he began apprenticing with the keeper of the king's instruments, and during 1674–1678 his job was to tune the organ at Westminster Abbey. In 1677, Purcell succeeded Matthew Locke (1621–1677) as the king's "composer-in-ordinary for the violins," and in 1679 he succeeded John Blow (1649–1708) as organist of Westminster Abbey.

The year 1680 was an important one in Purcell's life. He composed the first of his Welcome Songs for Charles II. He also published the fruits of his labor as composer for the king's "violins": his incomparable anthology of Fantasias for strings. Purcell's first music for the Restoration stage also came from that year. In 1680 or 1681 he married Frances (maiden name uncertain), and their first child arrived in 1682. The next year saw the publication of Purcell's chamber music, *Sonatas of III Parts*, and his appointment as royal organ maker and keeper of the king's instruments.

Purcell's music enhanced the coronation of Charles II in 1685. The Westminster Choir sang "I Was Glad When They Said Unto Me" at the entrance of the king and queen and "My Heart Is Inditing of a Good Matter" as the climax—both verse **anthems**. For the coronation of William III in April 1689, we have no record of the music performed, but Purcell was surely involved as organist of Westminster Abbey. The crown reconfirmed his court appointments by July. Purcell composed his famous three-act opera, *Dido and Aeneas*, in 1689.

Little is known of the last five years of Purcell's life; however, his activity as a theater composer intensified. Of the forty-three productions to which he contributed music in his lifetime, all but six were mounted in 1690–1695. Among his scores are five semi-operas with spoken dialogue and extensive music, including *Dioclesian* (1690), *King Arthur* (1691), *The Fairy Queen* (after Shakespeare's *A Midsummer Night's Dream*, 1692), *The Indian Queen* (1695), and *The Tempest* (c. 1695).

Purcell's sacred music is extensive, and some of it has remained part of the modern repertoire. Among the most famous titles are the *Te Deum* and *Jubilate* in D (1694). The anthem "Thou Know'st, Lord, the Secrets of Our Hearts," which the composer wrote for Queen Mary's funeral in 1695, was also performed at his own funeral the same year. Purcell died on November 21, 1695, in London. He was buried in his beloved Westminster Abbey, a rare honor for a musician. His epitaph expresses the high esteem in which his contemporaries held him: "Here lyes Henry Purcell, Esq.: who left this life, and is gone to that blessed place where only his harmony can be exceeded."

chamber music Music composed for a small group of instruments (fewer than ten), one instrument to a part.

anthem An English sacred choral composition, either accompanied or unaccompanied. Verse anthems include sections for vocal soloists.

oration of William and Mary's coronation, which took place in April of that year. The **libretto** was by Nahum Tate (1652–1715), who wrote for the theater and became England's poet laureate three years after completing *Dido*. Although the premiere of *Dido and Aeneas* was mostly undocumented, it must have required, besides the boarding-school cast, a few experienced soloists for lead roles and a few males for the **chorus**.

Purcell wrote no true operas after *Dido and Aeneas*. Had he lived longer, he might have created a national opera tradition in England. However, for that he needed better librettos than Restoration theater provided, and the English public's taste needed to mature further. Unfortunately, he did not live to see either. Claude Palisca summarizes, "Under the circumstances, the English Restoration stage got better music than it deserved in the work of Purcell. A born opera composer in search of an opera house, he might have found one had he not died so young."

DRAMA. In the opera's final scene, Dido (Queen of Carthage) and Aeneas, her lover, have a confrontation. He claims he must follow the gods' decree to sail to Troy. She calls him a hypocrite (since he had promised to defy Fate for her love), and orders him to leave. He implores her to take him back, but she threatens suicide if he stays. He leaves, but she knows she must now die because he has dishonored her. The magnificent ending of the opera begins with a short recitative ("Thy hand, Belinda") followed by "Dido's Lament." Cupids having appeared in clouds over Dido's tomb, and a brief mourning chorus rounds out the musical tragedy.

Exploring "Dido's Lament"

THE RECITATIVE. Part of Purcell's greatness lies in his ability to synthesize elements from the Italian and French musical cultures into English music, for example, his style of recitative.

libretto The script or "book" of an opera (or oratorio). A libretto includes dialogue, stage directions, and texts of the "set pieces" such as arias and ensembles. A librettist is a poet who writes librettos.

chorus (1) A movement for a large ensemble of voices; (2) a large ensemble of voices (usually mixed: soprano, alto, tenor, and bass) performing theatrical or concert music. See also **choir**.

coloratura A passage of rapid notes (often on a single syllable) designed to express emotion, show off the voice, or both.

arioso A style of writing for the voice less tuneful than an aria but more melodic than a recitative. Ariosos, like recitatives, are through composed.

harmony The aspect of music resulting from a progression of chords, either sounded or implied. Adj.: harmonic. Verb: harmonize.

ostinato A continually repeating melodic/rhythmic phrase, motive, or other pattern.

ground bass A continually repeating ostinato in the bass part that supports varying music above it, usually throughout a movement.

vocal chamber music A song or group of songs accompanied by a small group of instruments, one instrument to a part.

"Dido's Lament":
A Closer Look
Please refer to the score of "Dido's Lament," beginning on page 6 of the Score Anthology.

chromaticism In melody or harmony, the organic use of the chromatic scale containing 12 pitches per octave. Adj.: chromatic.

transposition The rewriting or performance of music in a key other than its original. Verb: transpose.

Ex. 2-10 Descending ground bass patterns in laments: (a) Monteverdi's "Il lamento della ninfa" (1638); (b) lament aria in Cavalli's *Egisto* (1643); (c) Purcell's "Dido's Lament" derived from (b).

"Thy hand, Belinda," the recitative that introduces "Dido's Lament," has both flow and dramatic impact. The **coloratura** with which Purcell infuses this recitative is not for decoration but for emotional emphasis. Purcell's recitatives also show a deep sensitivity to his native language, following the rhythms of heightened (dramatic) speech as well as its natural rise and fall.

Using a free **arioso** melodic style, the composer creates four musical phrases, which masterfully set up the following aria. *Listen to this recitative and note how the melody and* **harmony** *bring each textual phrase to a momentary point of rest, as follows:*

> Thy hand, Belinda; darkness *shades* me,
> On thy bosom let me *rest*;
> More I would, but Death in-*vades* me;
> Death is now a welcome *guest*.

THE ARIA. As the recitative ends, the music changes character. We now hear the orchestral bass line, shown in Ex. 2-10c, which introduces the aria. *Listen to the aria and notice that this bass line consists of a phrase repeated incessantly until the last note.* We call this repetitive procedure an **ostinato**. In Baroque music, when an ostinato in the bass part is the foundation for music above it, we call that ostinato a **ground bass**. Thus, "Dido's Lament," built on a ground bass, is termed a *ground-bass aria*. Italian operas and chamber cantatas of the time were generously peppered with arias built on short ground basses. French operas borrowed the ground bass approach, taking it a step further by using it to bring a scene to a climax. That is the function of "Dido's Lament," which also is the climax of the entire opera.

LAMENTS AND CHROMATICISM. Laments were a traditional variety of arias in 17th-century operas and **vocal chamber music**. Purcell followed another tradition by building his lament over a ground bass. In the Baroque period, such a ground bass would invariably be a descending line, for example, Ex. 2-10a by Monteverdi. Further, a **chromatically** descending line was consistently associated with the idea of sadness, grieving, or lamenting, such as Cavalli's ground bass in Ex. 2-10b. *In Ex. 2-10, examine the melodic direction and chromatic intervals in Purcell's ground bass (c), comparing it with Cavalli's (b). Do they begin with the same shape? For how many measures does (c) run compared with (b)?* Purcell has adapted Cavalli's ground bass (b) by **transposing** it and extending it from four to five measures. *Now find the beginning of Purcell's ground bass in the score, m. 9 (third beat). Trace the ground bass through a few repetitions.*

Examine the aria's postlude, beginning in m. 54. Has Purcell derived any of the upper string parts from the ground bass melody? How does he carry out the idea of descending chromatic melody? Starting on the note D, a line descends chromatically to A. *However, examine the line that imitates it two measures later, beginning on the note G.* This melody continues downward through the chromatic scale for almost a complete octave (mm. 57–63).

OVERLAP PHRASING BETWEEN THE VOCAL LINE AND THE BASS LINE. One of the most fascinating technical features of "Dido's Lament" is that the vocal phrases are sometimes

congruent with the phrasing of the ground bass and sometimes not. *Trace the first vocal phrase, ending with "no trouble in thy breast," and compare it with repetitions of the ground bass under it.* The vocal line corresponds to exactly two occurrences of the ground bass, including the cadence. This music repeats (mm. 24–34). *Now notice that the brief repeated textual phrase "Remember me" begins to break away from the phrasing of the ground bass. Compare the musical setting of "But ah! forget my fate" (m. 37–40) with the position of the ground bass that goes with it. Where does the ground bass begin and end?* The bass repetition that began between the two vocal phrases, "Remember me," is finishing as "But ah! forget my fate" begins: an *overlap* between vocal and bass lines. *Make the same comparison in the following "Remember me, but ah! forget my fate" (mm. 40–44).* Purcell starts the vocal phrase a measure after the ground bass phrase, then enables the vocal line to catch up, cadencing with the bass on the downbeat of m. 44. (Chapter 8, Opera, will take up the further development of recitatives and arias.)

BINARY FORM (BAROQUE DANCE-SUITE MOVEMENT): HANDEL'S *WATER MUSIC* SUITE NO. 1 IN F MAJOR, "HORNPIPE" MOVEMENT

Instrumental music began to take an important position in the late Renaissance, and dance music was an area that came to the fore with the rise of instrumental music. The Baroque method of presenting dances was to order them into sets or suites. Within a suite, each movement was usually organized in two repeated sections. This two-part musical structure became known as **binary** form (*bi* = two). Binary form would become an important building block during the following Classical period. At this point, however, we will study the nature of the dance suite, where it was found, and see how Handel employed binary form in the "Hornpipe" movement of his *Water Music* Suite No. 1 in F Major.

Dance Music in France

In the 17th century, the French court was consumed with dance music. The focus of interest was the *ballet de cour* (court ballet), a spectacular form of theater that included sets of choruses and dances, ending with a *grand ballet* in which the King of France himself would dance. From the *ballets de cour*, dances could be extracted for listening enjoyment. At first, dances were arranged for the lute, a portable instrument that could be played on a moment's notice. Soon, however, lutenists connected to the French court were composing their own very stylized dances—too stylized to be actually danced. Original music was based on the most favored dance types found in ballets: the Allemande, the Courante, and the Sarabande. This three-dance group became the core of a form known as a *suite* or dance suite, unified by writing all of its movements in the same key. The Gigue soon also became a core movement, and "optional" dances appeared here and there.

Gradually, the harpsichord gained favor, and the lute's popularity faded. Keyboard suites found their way to the German-speaking world largely through Johann Jakob Froberger (1616–1667), who spent time in Paris around 1660. Froberger's suites influenced the keyboard suites of Bach and Handel.

Orchestral Dance Suites (Overture-Suites)

French orchestral dance suites were not concert music originally, but collections of dances and dance songs (*airs*) culled from ballets and French operas. The French **overture** (derived from the brief *entrées* in *ballets de cour* and from the **sinfonias** to middle-Baroque Italian operas) invariably introduced each stage work and headed each orchestral dance suite. The French over-

binary In two parts. A binary form consists of two sections, each of which is repeated.

overture (1) An orchestral movement that precedes a theatrical work, such as an opera, a ballet, or a play. (2) An independent orchestral concert piece, related to the symphonic poem.

sinfonia (1) An orchestral movement preceding an early Italian opera; (2) an instrumental prelude to an essentially vocal work; (3) the Italian term for symphony.

ture became a powerful form in the middle and late Baroque period, appearing at the beginning of operas outside France, such as Purcell's *Dido and Aeneas* and all of Handel's operas. It also introduced many sacred works, such as Handel's oratorio *Messiah* and some of Bach's cantatas.

Seventeenth-century French orchestral dance suites—about 170 of them—were created chiefly for Louis XIV's entertainment. Typically, each suite began with a French overture and continued with a series of dances and airs in no special order. Orchestral suites drawn from French ballets and operas became the precursors to *original* orchestral dance suites called *overture-suites*. These were first composed in Germany. In 1664, 1670, and 1682 the first sets appeared. By 1718, the prolific Georg Philipp Telemann (1681–1767) claimed 200 orchestral suites (we know of at least 131). Telemann revealed the background-music function of orchestral overture-suites by including three of them in his *Musique de table* (*Dinner Music*, 1733). He titled each suite merely *Ouverture*, an abbreviation adopted by J.S. Bach.

Bach's four *Ouvertures* (orchestral suites), composed in Cöthen and Leipzig, included **woodwinds** in Nos. 1 and 2, and both woodwinds and brass in Nos. 3 and 4. Ouverture No. 2 in B Minor is noteworthy for its use of a solo flute, especially prominent in the suite's final movement, a *Badinerie* (Banter, a "*galanterie*" or **character piece** rather than a dance).

Handel composed no overture-suites during his years in Germany and Italy. Only after he settled in England, two opportunities arose to compose orchestral suites. The first work was the *Water Music* (c. 1717, actually an overture-suite followed by two shorter suites). The second was the *Royal Fireworks Music* of 1749. Both works, like Bach's *Ouvertures*, contain woodwinds or brasses or both.

woodwind A family of instruments (all originally made from wood) that includes the recorder, saxophone, flute, oboe, clarinet, and bassoon.

character piece A composition intended to convey a programmatic idea or a mood.

GEORGE FRIDERIC HANDEL

Anonymous etching

clavichord A small keyboard instrument in early music, mostly for practice in the home. Pressing a key causes a metal tangent to strike one of its strings.

Born the son of a barber-surgeon at Halle, Germany, on February 14, 1685, George Frideric Handel showed an unusual aptitude for music at an early age. However, since his father intended him to study law and forbade him access to musical instruments, young George had to practice in secret on a small **clavichord** in the attic. On the urging of the Duke of Saxe-Wiessenfels, his father's employer, Handel received harpsichord and organ instruction under Friedrich Wilhelm Zachow (1663–1712) in Halle. There he began to compose both vocal and instrumental music for church use. In 1702, Handel entered the University of Halle, probably to study law (though his father had died in 1697), and was for a year the organist at the Calvinist cathedral.

Hamburg was the center of public opera (Italian and Italian-style) in Germany. Since Handel's ambition was to be a successful opera composer, he moved there in 1703. At first he played in the opera house orchestra's second violin section, but later he became a harpsichordist. Along with his new friend, singer-composer Johann Mattheson (1681–1764), Handel traveled to Lübeck to look into succeeding the town's aging organist, Dietrich Buxtehude (1637–1707). When it came out that the successor would have to marry Buxtehude's 30-year-old daughter, both young musicians declined. (Handel remained a bachelor all his life.) *Almira*, Handel's first opera, was premiered in Hamburg in 1705. That year, *Nero* also premiered, and Handel was commissioned to compose two more operas, but in 1706 he left for Italy instead.

Over the next four years, Handel spent time in several Italian centers, mastering the art of opera composition. First he composed *Rodrigo*, which premiered in Florence in 1707. *Agrippina* was such a success in Venice in 1709 that it then received 27 performances in Rome, a long run at that time. There he had completed his first sacred oratorio, *La Resurrezione*, in 1708. Handel also spent time in Naples, where he encountered the opera composer Alessandro Scarlatti (1660–1725) and his son Domenico (1685–1757), the famous harpsichordist.

By the time Handel was 25, his reputation was so widespread that it preceded him in Germany and England. Through contacts he made in Italy, he was appointed *Capellmeister* to the Elector of Saxony (later, King George I of England) in 1710. Handel made it a condition of his appointment, however, that he obtain an immediate 12-month leave of absence to visit London. He spent about eight months there on his first visit, having been received graciously by Queen Anne and her court. *Rinaldo*, Handel's first opera written for England, premiered in February 1711 and was a great success, receiving 14 more performances up to June, when the composer returned to Hanover. For the next 15 months, Handel composed chiefly instrumental music, there being no opera in Hanover. In the fall of 1712, he again requested a leave to return to London, and it was granted on condition that he return "within a reasonable time."

Handel was now in England to stay, however. Within the first year he had composed three more Italian operas for London. His introduction to English church and ceremonial music came in 1713, the result of commissions from the queen. In quick succession, he composed the *Ode for Queen Anne's Birthday* and, to celebrate the Peace of Utrecht, he wrote a *Te Deum* and *Jubilate* (all modeled on Purcell). That year Handel obtained a permanent release from Hanover, and the queen bestowed on him an annual pension of £200. When Queen Anne died in 1714, Georg Ludwig of Hanover was crowned King George I of England. Handel's royal patronage continued, and the king even doubled his pension (raised to £600 later by Queen Caroline). A significant musical event during King George's first years was the performance of Handel's music for a royal barge excursion in 1717, resulting in part or all of the *Water Music*. Handel's court duties included giving keyboard instruction to the daughters of the Prince of Wales. For that purpose, he composed his first suites, published in 1720. With such light responsibilities, in 1717 Handel was able to become resident composer for a time to the Duke of Chandos, for whom he composed the eleven *Chandos Anthems* (1717–1718).

London, at the time, had no resident Italian opera company. In 1718–1719, under the leadership of the king, prominent members of the nobility formed a syndicate to sponsor a company that would offer continuing productions at the King's Theatre. Handel was installed as the company's "Master of Musick" and was authorized to obtain the finest singers possible from elsewhere in Europe. To that end, he made a whirlwind journey in mid-1719, briefly visiting Halle (where J.S. Bach, traveling from Cöthen, barely missed meeting him), and eventually finding the singers he needed in Dresden. The Royal Academy of Music, as they named the venture, opened in April 1720. Handel's *Radamisto* was its second production. Of the dozen operas Handel wrote for the Royal Academy between 1721 and 1728, the most famous is *Giulio Cesare* (1724). During the 1727–1728 season, the Academy fell into heavy financial difficulties and was further plagued by intense rivalries among its singers. The company's *coup de grâce* came in January 1728, when *The Beggar's Opera* premiered in London. It was in English, it was funny, and Londoners were ready for a change from dreary productions of Italian opera. *The Beggar's Opera* ran 62 performances, and the financiers of the Academy dissolved it on the first of June.

Handel now became manager of the King's Theatre. Early in 1729 he went on a scouting expedition for singers in Italy and rebuilt his company with mostly new talent. Handel's new company opened in December with his *Lotario*, which was unsuccessful. In fact, only one out of his next five operas was a success. Then, in 1732, a momentous event took place. Handel

(continued)

GEORGE FRIDERIC HANDEL *(continued)*

revised and enlarged *Esther*, an oratorio he had written for private performance before the Duke of Chandos in 1718. Now presented before the public, *Esther* was successful enough to garner repeat performances. Two new oratorios, *Deborah* and *Athalia*, were performed the following year. His opera company was not going so well, however. A rival company had sprung up, and London could barely support one company, let alone two. Both failed in 1734, but Handel tried one last time to produce operas, this time at Covent Garden. The venture struggled along with revivals, pastiches, and a few new operas, but one fact was growing increasingly obvious: The London public favored Handel's oratorios much more than his operas. The opera company closed, financially ruined, in June 1737.

Beginning in 1736, Handel had begun a tradition of playing his own new organ concertos during oratorio intermissions, an additional attraction for audiences. The public also now expected a regular "season" of his oratorios. Gradually, the timing for these performances gravitated to Lent, though Handel also presented his newer oratorios at other times. For example, *Saul* had six well-received performances in January 1739. During some 1741 performances in Dublin, Handel conducted the premiere of his *Messiah*.

Oratorio composition occupied Handel for most of the next 15 years. Most of his subjects were biblical, for example, *Belshazzar* (1745), *Judas Maccabaeus* (1747), and *Jephtha* (1752). His oratorios also included a generous sprinkling of mythological or allegorical subject matter, for instance, *Hercules* (1745) and his last oratorio, *The Triumph of Time and Truth* (1757). Handel's health declined during this period, reducing his productivity and his ability to rehearse and conduct.

In 1749, celebrating the Treaty of Aix-la-Chapelle, the king commissioned Handel to compose music to accompany a display of fireworks in Green Park. A public rehearsal of the *Music for the Royal Fireworks* in Vauxhall Gardens drew an audience of 12,000 and stopped traffic for three hours. The event followed six days later (April 27). The fireworks were a fiasco, but the music was splendid. Handel repeated the *Royal Fireworks* suite at a Foundling Hospital charity concert a month later, which also included two of his anthems.

Handel's last appearance in public was at a performance of *Messiah* on April 6, 1759. He died on April 14, the day before Easter. The composer's place in the hearts of the English had already been publicly acknowledged while he was alive: A statue of him had stood in Vauxhall Gardens since 1738. Now they accorded him the highest honor: burial in Westminster Abbey under an appropriate monument. As with Purcell, this was an extraordinary wonder for a composer, but for a composer not born in England, it was a superbly unique tribute. (Handel had, however, become a naturalized British subject in 1727.) The memorial bears no epitaph, but Handel's statue shows him holding an aria from *Messiah*, "I Know That My Redeemer Liveth."

Handel's Water Music Suites

HISTORY. Occasionally one can still read the apocryphal legend of the *Water Music*'s origin, started by Handel's contemporary, John Mainwaring. The legend goes that after Handel's former employer, Georg Ludwig, Elector of Hanover, became King George I of England in 1714, the composer was in disfavor and was afraid to appear at court. (Handel had never returned to Hanover, as he had promised.) When the king and his entourage took an excursion on the Thames in 1717, Baron von Kielmansegge, a friend of Handel, diplomatically arranged for a second barge to follow, full of musicians playing Handel's music under his direction. The music so delighted the king that he reconciled with the composer.

Some facts of this story are correct but the thrust of it is not. When Handel remained in London instead of returning to Hanover, Queen Anne was in poor health, and he knew it was merely a matter of time before she died and his Hanoverian patron became King of England. In 1713, Handel obtained official release from service from Hanover, but he continued to be useful. We know that the future King supported Handel's music.

As for the water excursion, several events actually took place. Some occurred in July and August 1715 but were not well documented. On the other hand, a newspaper reported the barge trip of July 17, 1717. Baron von Kielmansegge was the *host* of that occasion. At the king's request, it fell to him to arrange for the music and musicians. Two days after the event, London's *Daily Courant* reported:

> On Wednesday Evening, at about 8, the King took Water at Whitehall in an open Barge … and went up the River towards Chelsea. Many other Barges with Persons of Quality attended … a City Company's Barge was employ'd for the Musick, wherein were 50 Instruments of all sorts, who play'd all the Way from Lambeth … the finest Symphonies, compos'd express for this Occasion, by Mr. Hendel [sic]; which his Majesty liked so well, that he caus'd it to be plaid over three times in going and returning.

(Note: The term "symphony" was often used generically to mean instrumental ensemble music.)

Very likely, Handel composed music for similar occasions. In fact, Handel's salary payment from Hanover, coming in October 1715, suggests that he supplied music for the water excursions of that year. A royal barge trip much later, in 1736, may also have included music by Handel.

THE THREE SUITES. These circumstances help to explain the diversity of 18th-century sources and publications of *Water Music* movements. Copyists and publishers freely ordered movements in various keys and with various instrumentations. Arrangements for other instruments were also common. Only one movement of one suite has come down to us in Handel's manuscript. Modern editors have had to reconstruct the three suites according to principles that were prevalent in orchestral suites of the late Baroque period. Thus, three distinct suites have emerged:

Suite No. 1 in F Major	Suite No. 2 in D Major	Suite No. 3 in G Major
(2 horns, 2 oboes and bassoon, strings, and basso continuo)	(2 trumpets, 2 horns, 2 oboes and bassoon, strings, and basso continuo)	(flute, recorder, 2 oboes and bassoon, strings, and basso continuo)
1. Ouverture	1. [undesignated]	1. [undesignated]
2. Adagio e staccato	2. Alla Hornpipe	2. Rigaudon
3. [undesignated]	3. Minuet	3. [undesignated]
4. Andante	4. Lentement	4. Minuet
5. [undesignated]	5. Bourrée	5. [undesignated]
6. Air		6. [undesignated]
7. Minuet		7. [undesignated]
8. Bourrée		
9. Hornpipe		
10. [undesignated]		

tempo The speed at which the
music is performed.

horn Brass instrument, circular
shaped with a flared bell. The
modern instrument is called a
French horn.

THE SUITE IN F MAJOR. The spirit of French and German overture-suites is still alive in Handel's F Major Suite. Beginning with a French overture, nine more movements follow—a few of them dances, one designated as an air, and the other three (Nos. 3, 5, and 10) airs with no title or **tempo** designation.

Two prominent features in this suite are: (1) Handel's use of **horns** and of double reeds (oboes with bassoon); and (2) his methods of repeating movements to extend the music. At certain times, he uses the two horns or the three double reeds to great advantage. For example, the Minuet's bold first section is a fanfare scored entirely for horns (Ex. 2-11a). Handel first introduces the oboes right after the overture in a unison melody accompanied by the strings. Later, he entrusts the oboes and bassoon with the unaccompanied opening of the Andante (No. 4) and of the final movement (Ex. 2-11b).

Ex. 2-11 *Water Music*, Suite No. 1, effective use of wind instruments: (a) Minuet: horn fanfare; (b) final movement: oboes and bassoon in trio.

reprise (1) The return of a
theme or section of music after
intervening material. (2) Repetition. (3) To bring back or recollect.

We can imagine Handel's task in 1717 of providing several hours of music using a limited complement of players. The solution was to repeat parts of the score in different ways. One method was the literal repetition of a movement. Handel marks movements 5, 6, and 7 simply "3 times." Another method was to **reprise** a movement after playing the following movement. (Thus, Handel's instructions for movements 3 and 4 result in an A-B-A pattern.) A third method was to repeat a movement immediately but change its instrumentation, providing both unity and variety. For movements 8 and 9 ("Bourrée" and "Hornpipe"), Handel designates the following plan for the four parts of the texture:

FIRST TIME	SECOND TIME	THIRD TIME
Violin I	Oboe I	Violin I, Oboe I
Violin II	Oboe II	Violin II, Oboe II
Viola		Viola
Cello	Bassoon	Cello
Contrabass		Contrabass
Harpsichord		Harpsichord

In both the "Bourrée" and the "Hornpipe," Handel has composed the inner viola part to be dispensable when the reeds play, thus lightening the texture of the second statement. Then, the third time, the music carries climactic power by doubling the reeds and strings. Handel succeeded in using a small amount of music to fill a long space and, at the same time, gave it **orchestrational** shape instead of merely repeating the music literally.

Exploring the "Hornpipe"

Originally, beginning in the Middle Ages, the hornpipe was a reed instrument, and the oldest country-dance types bearing the title "Hornpipe" may have been performed on it. Danced in Scotland, Wales, and Ireland, hornpipes began to appear in print in England in the mid-17th century. Simple hornpipes were notated in 2/4 or 4/4 time (the type associated with English sailors), whereas the more complex, **syncopated** hornpipes appeared in 3/2 time. The latter is the type Handel composed for his *Water Music*.

ACCENTUATION. In music, we usually feel a subtle, natural accentuation on the first beat of each measure; a secondary accent may also be felt in 4/4 or 12/8 (on beat 3), and in 6/8 (on beat 2). This is called *metrical accentuation*. Musical accentuation can also occur in any of three other ways:

- *Dynamic accentuation*—One moment in the music is simply louder than the music before and after it, usually symbolized by markings such as >, *sf*, or *sfz*.
- *Tonic (melodic) accentuation*—High points in a melody may be felt as accents, especially if preceded or followed by a leap. A melodic low point approached by downward leap may also be felt as a tonic accent.
- *Agogic (rhythmic) accentuation*—A note longer than the notes before or after it may be felt as an accent.

In the "Hornpipe," Handel does not apply any **dynamic** accents (in fact, dynamic markings are completely missing). However, by cleverly coordinating tonic and agogic accents, he achieves fascinating patterns that play against the "natural" metrical accents. *Listen to the "Hornpipe" once, noticing high points in the melody and how irregularly they occur. These are the tonic accents. Listen again, this time noting agogic accentuation in the rhythm.* Ex. 2-12 shows the melody. Above it, each "T" indicates a tonic accent, and below it, each "A" shows an agogic accent.

How do the tonic and agogic accents align with metrical downbeats? All three types align on four different downbeats in the first eight measures (mm. 1, 3, 4, and 5) and only three in the second eight (mm. 9, 13, and 15). Other accents are less predictable. The "jerky" melody of the "Hornpipe," full of leaps in the second half, generates many tonic accents, sometimes coming in quick succession (e.g., mm. 13–15). The most prominent agogic accents in the

orchestration The art of combining instruments in an orchestral composition or arrangement. Adj: orchestrational.

syncopation A shifting of rhythmic accentuation that causes a momentary contradiction of natural metric accentuation.

Sforzando, sforzato A strong dynamic accent on a single note or chord.

dynamics, dynamic markings Gradations of loudness in music. The most common markings are *pp* (*pianissimo*, very softly), *p* (*piano*, softly), *mf* (*mezzo-forte*, medium-loud), *f* (*forte*, loud), *ff* (*fortissimo*, very loud), *crescendo* (becoming louder), and *diminuendo* or *decrescendo* (becoming softer).

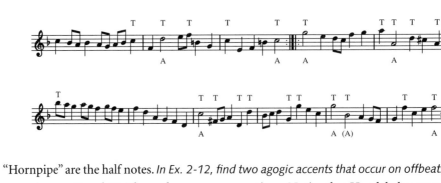

Ex. 2-12 "Hornpipe" melody, showing tonic accents ("T") and agogic accents ("A").

"Hornpipe" are the half notes. *In Ex. 2-12, find two agogic accents that occur on offbeats.* These occur in mm. 7 and 10. These places are syncopations. Notice that Handel also creates tonic accents at just those moments, which underline the agogic accentuation. Finally, see in mm. 8 and 16 that Handel ends each section not on a downbeat but on the last beat, adding both tonic and agogic accents for culminating emphasis.

HEARING BINARY FORM. Now that you have some acquaintance with its melody, listen to the "Hornpipe" again (once through). If you wish, follow the melody in Ex. 2-12. As you listen, notice that halfway through, the music comes to a point of rest where all motion ceases. That section then repeats. Listen as the music continues with the second section and its repetition. You can hear that the "Hornpipe" is in two sections, each of which repeats. The form of this movement is called *binary form.* "Binary" means "in two sections." Each section of a binary form was often just one continuous phrase, spun out until reaching its point of rest at a cadence.

Handel used binary form for this dance (and most others in the *Water Music*) because it had been established in dances heard in the old French *ballet de cour* and in French operas. Binary form was also employed in all the dances in suites for keyboard or other instruments. Thus, binary form had become *traditional* by Handel and Bach's time. We will learn in Chapter 3 how binary form developed much further, finally becoming the basis of *sonata form.*

In the Baroque period, binary form did not contain distinguishable themes. However, a composer might weave a motive into the melody to be used recurrently through the movement. In the "Hornpipe," Handel employs a motive in this way. Occurrences are shown by brackets in Ex. 2-13.

The "Hornpipe":
A Closer Look

Please refer to the score of the "Hornpipe," beginning on page 9 of the Score Anthology.

Ex. 2-13 "Hornpipe" melody. Brackets show where Handel weaves in a recurring motive.

The "Hornpipe" begins, of course, in the key of F major (the key of the suite). *Examine m. 8 for a cadence. In what key is the cadence?* We see a full cadence in the key of C major. This key is closely *related* to F major, since it is built on the dominant of F. We would say that in F major, C major is *the key of the dominant*. In binary form, it is crucial that the first section end with either: (1) a half-cadence in the original key; or (2) a full cadence in a closely related key. If the original key is a major key (as here), this related key will invariably be the key of the dominant.

Now examine the second section (mm. 9–16). In what key does it begin, and in what key does it end? Clearly, the first chord is I in C major, but the music does not remain in C major for long. B-flats in m. 9, and the C-sharp in mm. 10–12 suggest that the music is moving around D minor. Later (m. 13), some F-sharps draw the music toward G minor. However, since the G minor triad is in F major, the music easily slips back into F major for the final cadence in that home key.

We have just explored the *harmonic form* within the binary structure of the "Hornpipe." To be a true binary form, a movement must satisfy both the structural and harmonic binary requirements outlined in Ex. 2-14. The "Hornpipe" is an excellent example. (In Chapter 3, Keyboard Music, we will see how binary form evolved further, eventually becoming sonata form.)

Structural form: ‖: { one motive, recurrently } :‖ ‖: { one motive, recurrently } :‖

Harmonic form: T ⟶ R   R ⟶ T

(T=tonic key; R=related key)

Ex. 2-14 Binary form: structure and harmony, exemplified in Handel's "Hornpipe."

𝄢 C H A P T E R   T H R E E

Keyboard Music

Keyboard literature stretches back to the 14th century and extends to our day. Various literatures and playing traditions have arisen during that time and have been applied to the chief keyboard instruments: the organ and the string keyboard instruments— clavichord, harpsichord, and piano. The organ has a distinct literature of its own. Stringed keyboard instruments have an evolutionary history and therefore a unified literature. This chapter will concentrate on the music of stringed keyboard instruments, tracing its chronological and stylistic development through the works of three major composers: Scarlatti, Mozart, and Chopin.

Beethoven, *Hammerklavier Sonata* (1817–1818) –
Beethoven, "Waldstein" Sonata (1803–1804) –
Sonata pathétique (1799) •
C. P. E. Bach, *Versuch* (1743–1762) •— —•
J. S. Bach, *6 Partitas* (1726–1731) —
Invention of the piano (c. 1700) •
Froberger's suites published (1697) •
• *Fitzwilliam Virginal Book* (c. 1620)
• *Parthenia* (1611)
• Cabezón, *Obras de música. . .* (1578)

Ex. 3-1 Time line of Keyboard Music History: Renaissance through Beethoven; the 19th century (p. 47); the 20th century (p. 48).

1500	1600	1700	1800

─ ─└──────────────┴──────────────┴──────────────┘─ ─

──────── Antonio Cabezón (1510–1566)
──────────── William Byrd (1543–1623)
──────────── Jakob Froberger (1616–1667)
──────────── Jean-Henri d'Anglebert (1628–169
François Couperin (1668–1733) ────────
J. S. Bach (1685–1750) ────────
Domenico Scarlatti (1685–1757) ────────
G. F. Handel (1685–1759) ────────
C. P. E. Bach (1714–1788) ────────
Joseph Haydn (1732–1809) ────────
Wolfgang Amadeus Mozart (1756–1791) ────────
Ludwig van Beethoven (1770–1827) ──── ─ ─

Brahms, *Eight Piano Pieces,* Op. 78 (1878) •
Mussorgsky, *Pictures at an Exhibition* (1874) •
Brahms, *Handel* and *Paganini Variations* (1861–1863) —
Liszt, First *Mephisto Waltz* (c. 1860) •
Liszt, Sonata in B Minor (1852–1853) —
Liszt, *Years of Pilgrimage* (1848–1877) •— — — — — — — •

• Mendelssohn, V*ariations sérieuses* (1841)
                    — Chopin, Polonaise in F-sharp Minor, Op. 44
                      (1840–1841)
                    • Liszt, *Transcendental Etudes,* I (1839)
                    • Chopin, Sonata No. 2 in B-flat Minor (1839)
                    — Chopin, 24 Preludes, Op. 28 (1838–1839)
                    • Chopin, Scherzo in B-flat Minor, Op. 35 (1837)
                 ___ Schumann, *Symphonic Etudes* (1834–1837)
                  __ Schumann, *Carnaval* (1833–1835)
                ___ Chopin, First Ballade, Op. 23 (1831–1835)
        • — — — — • Mendelssohn, Songs Without Words
                      (1829–1845)
               ___ Chopin, 12 Etudes, Op. 10 (1829–1833)
                 • Schubert, *Valses sentimentales* (1825)
              • Schubert, *Wanderer Fantasy* (1822)

```
   1800        1825        1850        1875        1900
_ _ |_____|_____|_____|_____|_ _
```

_ _ _____ Ludwig van Beethoven (1770–1827)
_____ Franz Schubert (1797–1828)
        _____ Felix Mendelssohn (1809–1847)
         _____ Robert Schumann (1810–1856)
        _____ Frédéric Chopin (1810–1849)
          _____ Franz Liszt
                                        (1811–1886)
Johannes Brahms (1833–1897) _____

SCARLATTI, SONATA IN E MAJOR (KK. 380)

The Harpsichord, Scarlatti's Main Instrument

The harpsichord came into use in the early 16th century and continued to be the predominant keyboard instrument until after 1750. Equipped with metal strings, the harpsichord sounded when pressing a key caused a *plectrum* (pick) to pluck the string, much as a guitar pick plucks a guitar string (see Ill. 3-1). Harpsichords were constructed in a variety of shapes: oblong, wing-shape, and upright. Until the early Baroque period, all harpsichords had just one *manual* (keyboard) and one string per key. Then larger Flemish harpsichords appeared containing two or three sets of strings, playable separately or in combination. Two of the string sets were tuned

Crumb, *Gnomic Variations;* Martino, *Fantasies and Impromptus* (1981) ·

Rzewski, *The People United . . .* (1975) ·

Takemitsu, *For Away* (1973) ·

Davidowsky, *Synchronisms No. 6* (1970) ·

Shchedrin, *24 Preludes and Fugues* (1963–1964) —

Copland, *Piano Fantasy* (1957) ·

Stockhausen, *Piano Piece XI* (1956) ·

Messiaen, *Catalog of Birds* (1955–1958) ——

Cage, *Music for Piano* (1952) · Dallapiccola, *Musical Notebook* (1952)

· Hindemith, *Ludus Tonalis* (1942)

· Copland, Piano Variations (1930)

· Bartók, *Out of Doors* (1926)

· Stravinsky, Piano Sonata (1924)

· Rachmaninoff, *Études-tableaux,* Op. 33 (1911)

——— Ives, "Concord" Sonata (1910–1915)

——— Debussy, *Préludes,* Books I & II (1909–1913)

· Schoenberg, Three Piano Pieces, Op. 11 (1909)

· Ravel, *Gaspard de la Nuit;* Bartók, *14 Bagatelles* (1908)

```
      1900         1925         1950         1975         2000
  _ _ |_____|_____|_____|_____| _ _
```

_ _ ——————— Claude Debussy (1862–1918)

_ _ ————— Alexander Scriabin (1872–1915)

_ _ ——————————————— Sergei Rachmaninoff (1873–1943)

_ _ ——————————————— Maurice Ravel (1875–1945)

_ _ ————————————— Béla Bartók (1881–1945)

_ _ ———————————————————— Igor Stravinsky (1882–1971)

——————————————————————— Aaron Copland (1900–1990)

——————————————————————— Oliver Messiaen (1908–1992)

————————————————————— John Cage (1912–1992)

Karlheinz Stockhausen (1928–) ——————————————————— _ _

George Crumb (1928–) ——————————————————— _ _

Toru Takemitsu (1930–1996) ———————————————

Donald Martino (1931–) ——————————————————— _ _

Rodion Shchedrin (1932–) ——————————————————— _ _

Mario Davidowsky (1934–) ——————————————————— _ _

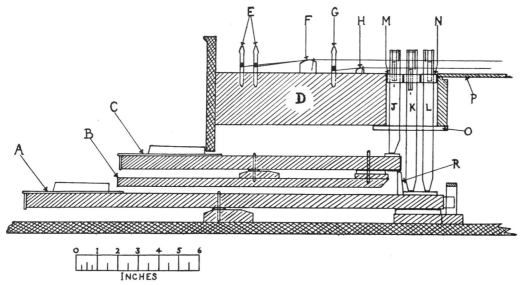

Figure 1. FRENCH HARPSICHORD, BY BLANCHET. SECTION AT c¹.

A. Lower keyboard.
B. Upper keyframe.
C. Upper keyboard.
D. Wrestplank.
E. Eight foot wrestpins.
F. Eight foot nut.
G. Four foot wrestpins.
H. Four foot nut.

J. Eight foot jack, upper manual.
K. Four foot jack, lower manual.
L. Eight foot jack, lower manual.
M. Eight foot slide, upper manual.
N. Eight foot slide, lower manual.
O. Jack guide.
P. Soundboard.

R. Coupler, by means of which the lower manual keys depress those of the upper keyboard. If the upper keyboard and keyframe (B) are drawn towards the player—a movement of only ⅜″—the uprights (R) will no longer engage the upper manual keys when the keys of the lower manual are depressed.

in unison (called "8-foot," a remnant of organ-pipe terminology), and the third set was tuned a octave higher (called "4-foot"). One 8-foot set also had a set of felt pads called a *buff stop* that could be moved into contact with the strings to imitate a lute or other string instrument playing *pizzicato*. Finally, instrument builders added a second manual (8-foot strings), typifying the full-size Baroque harpsichord, shown in Ill. 3-1. From that point, players could make heavy-light dynamic contrasts in their music by switching manuals or playing on one with each hand.

Keyboard Ornamentation

An important feature of Baroque and Classical keyboard music was **ornamentation**. Derived from the lute, but developed chiefly by French keyboardists of the 17th century, melodic ornamentation became part of the harpsichord idiom throughout Europe. One reason for using ornamentation was the harpsichord's inability to sustain long notes. Another was the Baroque period's love of decoration and artifice. Melodic ornamentation on the keyboard was important enough to Johann Sebastian Bach (1685–1750) that he wrote out a table of ornaments for his son Wilhelm Friedemann (shown in Ill. 3-2; transcribed in Ex. 3-2).

We frequently find ornamentation in the keyboard music of Scarlatti, and Classical composers like Wolfgang Amadeus Mozart (1756–1791) and Ludwig van Beethoven (1770–1827) continued to employ some of the earlier ornaments. As late as Frédéric Chopin (1810–1849), a few Baroque ornaments (e.g., trill and turn) appear, and use of the trill persisted into the 20th century.

Side notes:

49

SCARLATTI, SONATA IN E MAJOR (KK. 380)

Ill. 3-1 Cutaway diagram of a two-manual Flemish harpsichord from the 18th century. Raymond Russell, *The Harpsichord and Clavichord: An Introductory Study*, 2nd ed. (London: Faber and Faber, 1973), p. 56.

pizzicato The technique of plucking a string instrument that is normally bowed.

ornamentation Embellishments added usually to melody (sometimes to rhythm), most frequently employed in the 17th–18th century.

Ill. 3-2 J.S. Bach's "Explication," or table of ornaments, from the *Clavierbüchlein* for Wilhelm Friedemann Bach. Yale University Music Library. Used by permission.

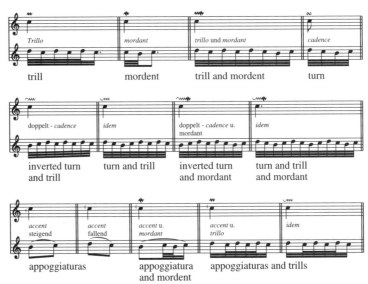

Ex. 3-2 Transcription of J.S. Bach's table of ornaments in the *Clavierbüchlein* for Wilhelm Friedemann Bach.

DOMENICO SCARLATTI

Lithograph by Alfred Lemoine, 1867. Based on an 18th-century portrait. Yale University Music Library. Used by permission.

conservatory A high school or college of music; originally (Baroque period), an orphanage where music was usually taught vocationally.

Domenico Scarlatti was born in Naples, Italy, on October 26, 1685 (the same year in which Bach and Handel were born). He was the son of Alessandro and Antonia (née Anzalone) Scarlatti, the sixth of ten children. Unfortunately, only sparse information exists about Domenico's life.

His musical training is a matter of conjecture. Domenico's father, the famous Neapolitan Baroque opera composer, would surely have made a knowledgeable teacher, but so would a half dozen other Neapolitan composers. Also, Naples had four budding **conservatories**. However, we have no records of Domenico at a conservatory or working under any composer of the time. Shortly before Domenico's 16th birthday in 1701, he was appointed organist of the viceroyal chapel in Naples, where his father was *maestro di cappella* (music director). However, their future there was uncertain. So father and son went looking for employment with the Medici court in Florence. Domenico soon returned to Naples, where he had some success as an opera composer. Alessandro, having moved to Rome in 1703, continued to seek better employment for his son.

We know nothing certain about Domenico Scarlatti's four years alone in Naples. However, according to an eyewitness account from English keyboardist Thomas Roseingrave, he had a well-earned reputation there as a harpsichord **virtuoso**. In 1709, Scarlatti moved to Rome, where he became composer to the exiled Polish queen. Although he specialized in opera, Scarlatti never renounced the keyboard. The evidence of this is a famous anecdote told by John Mainwaring of a playing contest in Rome between Scarlatti and Handel involving both the harpsichord and the organ. Scarlatti won on the harpsichord, but Handel prevailed at the organ. Obtaining his information from Handel, Mainwaring reported, "The characteristic excellence of Scarlatti seems to have consisted in a certain elegance and delicacy of expression. Handel had an uncommon brilliancy and command of finger. …"

Scarlatti next found employment at the Basilica Giulia (The Vatican), where he became *maestro di cappella* in 1714. Early that year he also received an appointment from the Portuguese ambassador to the Vatican to become his *maestro di cappella*. This appointment undoubtedly led to the most momentous event of Scarlatti's life: his move to Lisbon, Portugal, in 1719. There he was appointed to the court of the King of Portugal, whose colonial income maintained one of the most lavish courts in Europe.

At the court of Lisbon, Scarlatti's chief job was to provide music for the zealously Catholic royal chapel. He also composed occasional chamber cantatas. In addition, Scarlatti was expected to give keyboard training to the king's brother and to his musically talented daughter. For the rest of the composer's life, he would be loyally attached to the princess's entourage. Scarlatti returned to Italy only twice again in his life. The first time was in 1724, when he went to Rome and then to Naples to pay his final respects to his father, who died the following year. The second was in the spring of 1728, this time to marry Maria Caterina Gentili; Scarlatti was 42 years old, and Maria was 16. She would bear his first five children.

The royal courts of Spain and Portugal arranged the marriage of the Portuguese princess, Maria Barbara, to Spain's crown prince, Fernando. After the wedding in 1729, Scarlatti followed the princess to Spain as part of her retinue. This was another turning point in the composer's life, after which he would concentrate most of his musical efforts on composing keyboard **sonatas**.

The court was based in Seville for the next few years, then in Madrid, and Scarlatti became the keyboard instructor of both the prince and princess. The royal family made frequent excursions to various parts of the Iberian peninsula, and Scarlatti probably went along. One can imagine the variety and richness of his musical experiences, hearing the folk songs and dances of Spain's different provinces.

The late 1730s brought important events to Scarlatti's life. In 1737, Farinelli (Carlo Broschi, 1705–1782), the famous singer and countryman of Scarlatti, came to the Spanish court. He became a sensation among the royal family, remaining with them until 1759. In 1738, Scarlatti became a Knight of the Order of Santiago, an honor sponsored by Portugal's king. Shortly after that event, Scarlatti's first publication was issued in London, the *Essercizi per Gravicembalo*, which he dedicated to the Portuguese monarch. In 1739, Scarlatti's first wife died, but

(continued)

virtuoso A musical performer possessing highly developed technical abilities. Adj.: virtuosic.

sonata (1) A plan of three or four movements applied to works for piano, chamber music ensembles, or orchestra (the symphony); (2) a form usually employed for the first movement in a sonata plan; it consists of three sections (exposition, development, recapitulation) within a binary type of structure.

DOMENICO SCARLATTI (*continued*)

by 1742 he had married Anastasia Ximenes, who bore him four more children. (None of the surviving children from either marriage became musicians.)

Prince Fernando ascended the throne of Spain in 1746. Despite Farinelli's popularity, Queen Maria Barbara never wavered in her loyalty to Scarlatti. Under her patronage, he became *maestro de càmera* (master of chamber music), and his flow of royal keyboard sonatas continued, eventually exceeding 550. Undoubtedly the volumes of manuscript copies of these, which are our only sources for most sonatas, were written under her sponsorship.

In Spain Scarlatti's example prompted a small "school" of keyboard composers. Several younger Spanish keyboardists of the mid-1700s composed sonatas in the same binary form and general style as his. Notable among these was the cleric Padre Antonio Soler (1729–1783), who was probably Scarlatti's student from 1752 to 1756. Following Scarlatti's death in Madrid on July 23, 1757, however, little was known of his music outside a small circle in Spain. Sporadic publications and manuscript copies later circulated in Europe, but these must have been from the early *Essercizi*. The resurrection of Scarlatti's keyboard sonatas and other music had to wait until the 20th century, when his historical and artistic importance became fully recognized.

Scarlatti's Keyboard Sonatas

In the Baroque period, the dance suite was predominant (see Chapter 2), and keyboard sonatas were rare. It remained for the rise of Classical style to develop an idiomatic type of keyboard sonata. During the early decades of the 18th century, certain composers struck out on a new path that focused on developing the sonata. Scarlatti was among the first of these. He composed about 555 pieces for the keyboard, mostly from about 1723 to his death in 1757. Although the term "sonata" would later come to mean a multimovement work, Scarlatti used the term to mean a single piece in an expanded binary (pre-sonata) form. Scarlatti's period of sonata composition corresponded to the lengthy term of service on the Iberian peninsula, when he was keyboard instructor to Maria Barbara.

Scarlatti left no autograph manuscripts of his sonatas. The main sources of these works are two collections of manuscripts in libraries at Venice and Parma, Italy. The music in the manuscripts had been copied in Spain as one big collection over the years 1742–1757. Then the sonatas found their way to Italy two years after Scarlatti's death through his compatriot, Farinelli, who evidently inherited all the volumes of music and took them with him when he returned to Italy in 1759.

Altogether, the sonatas in the two manuscript collections number 555. A few have been identified as not being keyboard sonatas but pieces for a **treble** instrument and *basso continuo*. In recent years, a few previously unknown Scarlatti sonatas have been discovered in Spain. Since some of these (and a few of the sonatas in the main sources) may be the work of Scarlatti's Spanish students, notably Soler, the exact number of authentic keyboard sonatas by Scarlatti cannot be determined. The number remains around 555, however.

There were only 12 publications of Scarlatti's sonatas during his lifetime, and many sonatas were printed repeatedly in them. Thus, few sonatas became known outside the Portuguese and Spanish courts. Four of the 12 collections came out in England. The first publica-

treble The highest range among voices or families of instruments. In vocal music, synonymous with soprano.

Ill. 3-3 Title page to Scarlatti's *Essercizi per gravicembalo*, London, 1738/1739. "Cavaliero di S. Giacomo" was the knighthood given Scarlatti by the Portuguese king. By permission of The British Library (shelfmark K.5.c.8).

tion is noteworthy. Under the title *Essercizi per gravicembalo* (*Exercises for the Harpsichord*), this group of 30 sonatas appeared in London in 1738 or 1739 (see Ill. 3-3). Probably the word *essercizi* was a close approximation of the term "lessons," which the English applied at the time generically to most harpsichord music, including the keyboard suites of Handel. Each of the 30 pieces in the Scarlatti collection, however, is titled "sonata."

The 20th-century Scarlatti revival started with Alessandro Longo (1864–1945), a Neapolitan pianist-teacher-composer, who compiled a "Complete Works for Harpsichord" in 1906–1908. Working from the Venice manuscripts, Longo's 11 volumes encompassed 545 sonatas. Although Longo's ordering of the sonatas was completely arbitrary, the Longo numbers ("L.") were used for more than 50 years to identify specific sonatas. In 1953, American harpsichordist-**musicologist** Ralph Kirkpatrick (1911–1984) published a new catalogue of the sonatas, placing them in approximately chronological order. The Kirkpatrick catalogue numbers ("Kk.") are currently the standard. Thus, the Sonata in E Major, Kk. 380, is not necessarily the 380th sonata Scarlatti composed; it is the 380th in an order that uses the chronology of the *sources*: Kirkpatrick's catalogue tells us that the prime source of Kk. 380 was copied in 1754. Thus, the sonata was probably a late work, but not later than 1754.

musicology The scholarly study of music. By itself, the term often means "historical musicology." Someone who studies musicology is called a musicologist.

Ill. 3-4 First page of Scarlatti's Sonata in E Major (Kk. 380), as it appears in the Venice manuscript, Vol. VIII, No. 23. Sezione musicale della Biblioteca Palatina, Parma. MS Ψ.I.48/I-XV.

Features of Scarlatti's Sonatas

The sonatas of Scarlatti are usually considered harpsichord music, and that was probably the principal instrument he had in mind for most of them. However, Scarlatti's patron, Maria Barbara, also kept pianos in each of her residences. Possibly Scarlatti intended several sonatas for the piano, and, at the very least, the piano is a historically legitimate instrument for modern Scarlatti performances.

register A segment of the total pitch-range of a voice or an instrument.

KEYBOARD TECHNIQUES. Scarlatti's sonatas brought Italian keyboard music of the 18th century to a point of perfection. They also developed a true keyboard idiom, foreshadowing the piano music of the following century. In establishing that idiom, Scarlatti emancipated keyboard music from polyphonic textures derived from earlier lute, harpsichord, and organ music. Scarlatti replaced these most often with a simple, two-element texture—usually placing one element in each hand.

Crossing hands is among the most prevalent features in Scarlatti's earlier, more flamboyant sonatas, although its frequency decreases in later ones. With most late Baroque keyboard composers this technique is rare; it happens only a few times in the music of J.S. Bach. Scarlatti used the technique to express widely separated **registers** of the keyboard and to display virtuosic technique. The most frequent hand crossings occur in the D Minor Sonata (Kk. 120). (See Ex. 3-3.)

Ex. 3-3 Hand crossing in Scarlatti's Sonata in D Minor (Kk. 120): (a) m. 13, where the left hand crosses over right-hand figuration; (b) m. 19, where the roles are reversed, as the left hand plays steady chords, and the right hand crosses over.

Related to the idea of crossed hands are the wide leaps within one hand often encountered in Scarlatti's sonatas, for example in his D Major Sonata (Kk. 299), mm. 27–31:

Scarlatti also used contrasting registers to explore the sound of musical ideas in his sonatas. For example, the opening of the E Major Sonata (Kk. 380) in the right hand:

is echoed in the left an octave lower in m. 5:

Runs and extended scales (ascending or descending) are also common in the sonatas. The E Major Sonata employs a series of these in mm. 9–11, alternating between right and left hands:

In other sonatas, runs may combine hands in parallel thirds or sixths. Extended broken chords are also common, as in the opening of the C Minor Sonata (Kk. 84):

ROCOCO FEATURES. Don Michael Randel's *Harvard Concise Dictionary of Music* (1978) defines *rococo* as "an 18th-century style in which light, ornate decoration … and emphasis on elegance and refinement replace the massive structures of the baroque." In reaction against the Baroque period's heavy, contrapuntal, grandiose, and sometimes pretentious musical practices, many composers of Scarlatti's time sought a simpler, more "natural" style—a style that might produce music more accessible to listeners. *Rococo* (from French words for "rockwork" or "shellwork") was a trend in music rather than a new style period. Its composers emphasized clear, open textures (usually **homophonic** melody and accompaniment), simply constructed phrases that were **periodic**, repetitive motives, and simple harmony; yet their highly ornamented melodies carried on the French and Italian Baroque traditions.

Scarlatti was a *rococo* composer straddling the dying Baroque and the newborn Classical periods. The most general *rococo* feature of his music is its open, two-element texture, an elegant trait. With *rococo* simplicity, Scarlatti built his musical structures as a series of short musical ideas, most often repeated immediately. In the first four measures of the E Major Sonata, the composer presents a two-measure motive, which he immediately repeats:

homophony Music in which one melody leads or predominates, while supported by the rest of the texture, which is of secondary importance. In some homophony, the supporting parts move in the same rhythm as the melody. Adj.: homophonic.

periodic (1) A natural division of a melody into regular, equal lengths; (2) the grouping of even-length phrases or subphrases.

At times, Scarlatti continued to repeat a short melodic idea literally in one hand, while the harmony progressively changes in the other. That is the essence of mm. 12–15 of the E Major Sonata, which keeps repeating a one-measure motive:

Finally, we can observe the *rococo*'s characteristic "light, ornate decoration" in the judiciously placed trills with which Scarlatti has ornamented this sonata. Commonly, these occur at cadence points (e.g., mm. 18, 25, and 39), but he also decorates his opening motive with trills (shown above).

PAIRING OF SONATAS. Scarlatti's sonatas are self-contained compositions. Yet he may have composed many of them in pairs, probably intending to perform them that way. Repeatedly, in the Venice and Parma sources, two sonatas in the same key appear side by side. Or a sonata in the minor mode precedes another in the parallel major. Sometimes the two sonatas are in contrasting tempos, as with the E Major pair, Kk. 380 and 381. The first sonata (Ex. 3-4a, under study here) shows a tempo marking of *andante commodo* (i.e., *comodo*, comfortable). The second (Ex. 3-4b) is marked *allegro*. Ex. 3-4 shows the opening measures of both sonatas.

Ex. 3-4 Openings of a pair of Scarlatti sonatas in E Major: (a) *Andante commodo* (Kk. 380) and its companion, (b) *Allegro* (Kk. 381).

LOCAL COLOR. In Lisbon and Spain, Scarlatti composed his keyboard sonatas in an atmosphere rich with indigenous musical sounds. Many of these either crept unconsciously into his sonatas or were placed there purposely for effect. Two different varieties of music are easily recognizable:

- Military music featuring brass and drums
- Gypsy music featuring plucked instruments (chiefly the guitar) and castanets.

In the E Major Sonata, we can hear both varieties. The fanfare style of the opening eight measures is in a brassy idiom, as if high trumpets were echoed by more mellow horns (Ex. 3-5a). Scarlatti continues with a passage reminiscent of horns and drums (Ex. 3-5b). Kirkpatrick describes this music as "processional." In 18th-century Spain, where religious or military processions were frequent, it is not surprising that Scarlatti adapted this flavor into his keyboard music.

Ex. 3-5 Fanfare or processional-style passages in Scarlatti's Sonata in E Major (Kk. 381): (a) mm. 1–8; (b) mm. 19–21.

Passages in Scarlatti involving patterns of repeated notes can be attributed to the influence of the Spanish guitar. In the E Major Sonata, two different patterns occur, emphasizing repeated notes. The first (Ex. 3-6a) is basically an ascending scale in which each note is repeated. The second (Ex. 3-6b) focuses on a figure involving three repeated notes. Its clicking rhythm may suggest castanets as well as guitar.

Ex. 3-6 Guitarlike passages in Scarlatti's Sonata in E Major (Kk. 381): (a) mm. 22–23; (b) mm. 36–37.

Exploring the Sonata in E Major

Listen to the entire E Major Sonata. What is the overall structure of sections and repeats? The sonata is cast in two main sections, each of which is repeated. *Does this structure bear a resemblance to that of Handel's "Hornpipe"?* The "Hornpipe" is also in two sections, each repeated.

The structural form of both pieces is *binary*, but each section of the Scarlatti is longer than the Handel.

   MOTIVES. In the sonata's first section, Scarlatti introduces most of the motives and other musical ideas he will employ in the piece. *Listen to the first section only. On a piece of paper, take notes identifying each motive or musical idea you hear. Compare your notes with Ex. 3-7.*

Ex. 3-7 Motives and other musical ideas exposed in the first section of Scarlatti's E Major Sonata.

   Notice that the composer achieves unity in the first section by (1) repeating ideas or whole passages and (2) letting two ideas share the same melodic/rhythmic characteristics. Regarding the second method, notice, in Ex. 3-7, that the first beat of (a) and of (c) have identical rhythm and share the same melodic shape. The rhythm of (d) and (d') is identical, and the general melodic idea of (e) and (e') is the same.

   Let's see what Scarlatti does to develop a few of these ideas in the second section of the sonata. In your score, look over mm. 41–56. Try to find the derivation of these rhythms and whole ideas. Compare your findings with lettered ideas in Ex. 3-7 (a–g). M. 41 uses only the *rhythm* and repeated-note idea of (d), combining it with a new melody:

The Sonata in E Major: A Closer Look

Please refer to the score of Scarlatti's Sonata in E Major, beginning on page 10 of the Score Anthology.

Mm. 42 and 43 each begin with the repeated-note rhythm of (d), but they continue with the syncopated rhythm from (c):

The fusion of the two motives is a sophisticated technique of *development*. M. 44 follows the rhythm of (d) except for the syncopated downbeat:

The full echo pairing in (d) returns in mm. 46–47, but now is developed by using minor chords in place of the original major ones:

In mm. 50–51, Scarlatti again joins (d) and (c), but now we hear a full measure of the (d) rhythm (with its melody varied at the end) and a full measure of syncopation derived from (c):

Scarlatti completes his development of motives and musical ideas in mm. 52–56 with a transitional passage of new melodic interest based on the rhythm of (d)'s first beat:

STRUCTURAL FORM AND HARMONIC FORM. Through listening, you have already established that the sonata is in an extended binary form. *Now confirm this with your eyes by looking over the score.* You can see each of the two sections with its repeats, and you can visually compare the structure of this score with that of Handel's "Hornpipe" on p. 9 of the Score Anthology. From our present study, we have also established that the Scarlatti sonata introduces several motives and musical ideas, some of which have similarities with others, and some of which he develops in the second section. Now that we have looked at several details of this piece, let's stand back to gain a bigger picture: a view of the structural and harmonic form, both within each section and between sections. We will call the first section (mm. 1–40) section A, and the second section (mm. 41–79) section B.

Examine section A from m. 1 through m. 18 for harmony. The composer firmly establishes the key of the tonic (E major) from the beginning through m. 12 with lots of I and V chords. Now, however, A-sharps begin to creep in (mm. 13, 15), suggesting V/V and a new emphasis on the area of the dominant (V). *Analyze the root progression in the cadence at mm. 17–18.* You can analyze it two ways:

E major: I–vi–V–V/ii | V/V

or

B major: IV–ii–V/V | V

depending on whether you feel the music is still in E major or has modulated to B major, the key of the dominant.

In either case, Scarlatti now (m. 19 ff.) firmly establishes the new key of the dominant. He repeatedly drives home that point by stressing V in that key. *Find the two V–I cadences toward the end of section A.* These occur at mm. 33–34 and 39–40.

This entire portion in the key of the dominant (mm. 19–40) is extremely important to this sonata as a representative of advanced, enlarged binary form. Recall the harmonic form of section A of a Baroque binary form, such as Handel's "Hornpipe." The Scarlatti sonata establishes the related key much earlier. (See Ex. 3-8.) Moreover, in the Scarlatti, the portion in the dominant has its own *distinctly new musical material.*

In section A, both (1) the earlier establishment of a related key and (2) new musical material in that key contributed to the development of the full *sonata form,* discussed in the Mozart piano sonata, below. Kirkpatrick has called this portion of Scarlatti's form the "crux," and with good reason. *Examine section B of the sonata, beginning in m. 57. How do mm. 57–79 (in section B) compare with mm. 19–40 (in section A)?* With a couple of minor deviations, every note

(a) Binary, Section A (Handel):

(b) Extended Binary, Section A (Scarlatti):

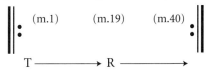

Ex. 3-8 Comparison between Section A of a binary and extended binary form: (a) Handel's "Hornpipe"; (b) Scarlatti's Sonata in E Major.

of the section A passage in the key of the dominant is now literally *recapitulated* (or reprised) in section B, but in the key of the *tonic*. This achieves balance between the two sections. The technique of *recapitulation* in the tonic is another precursor to full-blown sonata form. In summary, Ex. 3-9 is a diagram of the three parameters (structural, motivic, and harmonic) of the expanded binary form found Scarlatti's Sonata in E Major.

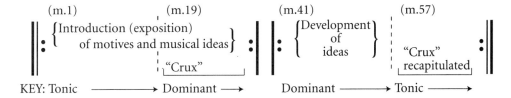

Ex. 3-9 Expanded binary form (structural, motivic, and harmonic) in Scarlatti's Sonata in E Major (Kk. 380).

MOZART, PIANO SONATA IN C MAJOR, K. 309 (284B), FIRST MOVEMENT

Wolfgang Amadeus Mozart was born in Salzburg, Austria, on January 27, 1756. He was the second surviving child of Leopold and Anna Maria (née Pertl) Mozart. Leopold was a violinist and author of the famous *Violinschule* (Violin Method), published the year Wolfgang was born. He made his living as a musician in the Archepiscopal court orchestra of Salzburg. Wolfgang's father was his first teacher, as little as he needed one. His musical gifts and ability to absorb musical knowledge and practice were in evidence from an extremely early age. By four, he had learned some pieces at the keyboard, and at the age of five he composed his first original music, an *Andante*, K. – (1a) and an *allegro*, K. – (1b). Mozart's sister, Maria Anna ("Nannerl"), four and one-half years his senior, was also musically talented as a keyboardist. Leopold soon recognized the commercial value of his child prodigies, especially Wolfgang, and decided to show them off in front of the wealthy and powerful. In January 1762 he took them to Munich, where they performed before the Elector of Bavaria, and in September they played in Vienna for the Emperor and Empress of Austria.

These appearances were so successful that Leopold resolved to take his children on a grand tour of Europe. Departing Salzburg in June 1763, the tour took in Frankfurt, Paris, London,

(continued)

WOLFGANG AMADEUS MOZART

K. Abbreviation for "Köchel" (Ludwig Köchel, 1800–1877), meaning Köchel's chronological catalogue of the works of Mozart, first edition, 1862. The catalogue number follows "K." In the third edition, Alfred Einstein (1880–1952) adjusted the chronological position of many works, resulting in new numbering for them. Whenever a work is so affected, the adjusted number appears in parentheses following the original number.

symphony A composition for orchestra, usually in four movements.

serenade A multi-movement work, usually instrumental, originating in the 18th century, performed outdoors in the evening for the benefit of a specific individual.

divertimento A multi-movement chamber-music work of the Classical period, usually intended as background music at parties, banquets, etc.

WOLFGANG AMADEUS MOZART *(continued)*

and the Netherlands, with shorter stops along the way. The trio arrived home at the end of November 1766. In Paris, where they played for Louis XV, Wolfgang received his first musical publications: four sonatas for keyboard and violin, K. 6–9. During their London stay in 1764–1765, the Mozarts performed for George III and became acquainted with Johann Christian Bach, who made a significant impression on Wolfgang's music. In London, the nine-year-old genius composed his first two **symphonies**, K. 16 and K. 19.

The family was together again in Salzburg for no more than nine months when Leopold moved everyone to Vienna for 15 months. His plans were foiled by a smallpox epidemic in the city, however. His hopes were partially fulfilled when Wolfgang composed his first full opera, *La finta semplice*, in mid-1768 and conducted his Mass in C Minor, K. 139 (47a), before the royal family that autumn. Returning to Salzburg, Wolfgang was appointed concertmaster of the court orchestra, but without pay.

However, the job did not last. Leopold, still determined to exploit Wolfgang's talent and also broaden the 13-year-old's artistic contacts, set out on the first of three journeys to Italy. The first, taking place between December 1769 and March 1771, included stops in Verona, Bologna, Rome, Naples, and Milan. Wolfgang gave private and public concerts during most stops. In Rome, Wolfgang transcribed Allegri's eight-part *Miserere* from memory, and he received the Order of the Golden Spur from the Pope. He wrote his first serious Italian opera, *Mitridate*, in Milan at the end of 1770. The other two Italian journeys were confined to Milan. The second sojourn, from August 1771 to December 1771, resulted in the premiere of the serenata *Ascanio in Alba*, and the third (October 1772 to March 1773) saw the premiere of the opera *Lucio Silla*.

Between the second and third Italian journeys, the old archbishop of Salzburg died. He had been a music lover and supporter of the Mozarts' efforts. The new archbishop was just the opposite. Despite the indifference of the archbishop, Mozart spent his longest Salzburg interval, 1773–1781, under his patronage, interrupted for any appreciable time only by the last tour. Mozart composed most of his Masses for the archbishop's services. During this period, he also developed as an instrumental composer, producing remarkable symphonies like those in G minor, K. 183 (173dB) and A major, K. 201 (186a), both products of 1773–1774. Most of his **serenades** and **divertimentos**, written for parties and special occasions, also stemmed from this period, as did his earliest piano sonatas and concertos, and the five violin concertos. Short stays in Vienna (1773) and Munich (1774–1775) advanced Mozart's reputation in instrumental music and opera.

Mozart embarked on his last tour in September 1777. This time his mother accompanied him as a kind of personal manager. Leopold, who had gone into debt to sponsor the tour, stayed in Salzburg and tried to direct matters by mail. In Munich, Mozart offered his services to the elector and was politely refused. After visiting Augsburg, where Mozart was greatly impressed with piano maker Andreas Stein's instruments, they moved on to Mannheim, then one of Europe's musical crossroads. Mozart had frequent successes there, garnering some commissions for new music, and they stayed from the end of October until the following March. However, it was not music but infatuation that caused Mozart to tarry in Mannheim. The object of his affection was Aloysia Weber, a soprano aged 16. Unfortunately, she did not share his feelings, as he discovered much later. Frustrated at Wolfgang's frivolity and limited accomplishment in Mannheim, Leopold ordered, "Off with you to Paris!" Without his father there to help with business, Paris was more than Mozart could handle comfortably. The intrigues in Parisian musical politics were complicated. Although he received several successful performances, notably the "Paris" Symphony in D Major, K. 297 (300a), he was cheated out of money and was otherwise mistreated. Mozart's mother became ill with fever in June 1778 and died on July 3. Despondent and disappointed, he started the homeward journey in September, arriving the following January.

A new, better appointment awaited him in Salzburg: court organist. Otherwise, life was much the same as before. In 1780, however, Mozart received a long-awaited commission to compose an opera for Munich. This would be *Idomeneo*, his best serious Italian opera and arguably the best of his century. In January 1781, the opera received three successful performances. The archbishop, who was in Vienna for the accession of Emperor Joseph II, summoned Mozart there in March. At that point began a professional crisis that would change the course of his whole life.

Mozart wanted better treatment (such as improved lodgings in Vienna), and he resented the archbishop's forbidding him to make additional money while there. The archbishop did not care about Mozart's true value and treated him like a lackey, demanding complete subservience while in Vienna. In early May, the archbishop abused Mozart verbally. The composer then asked for his release from service, which was refused. A month later, however, the archbishop's chief steward summoned Mozart and fired him, in Mozart's words, "with a kick in the rear … by order of our worthy Prince Archbishop."

Thus began Mozart's final creative period, his decade living in Vienna. Throughout that time, teaching the piano was the mainstay of his income. Mozart first moved in with the Webers, formerly of Mannheim. Aloysia had married in 1780, but he now became attracted to her younger sister, Constanze. However, to silence any possible gossip, he found other quarters.

The following year initiated a period of great success for Mozart in Vienna. He began participating in public and private concerts, playing the piano and presenting other works. In July, his German comic opera *Die Entführung aus dem Serail* (*The Abduction from the Harem*) premiered. On August 4, 1782, Wolfgang and Constanze were married. They did not visit Leopold and "Nannerl" until summer of the following year. In 1784, Mozart's concertizing in Vienna intensified, reflecting his popularity. He also began to keep a catalogue of his works, starting (significantly) with a piano concerto, that in E-flat Major, K. 449.

In 1785, Leopold visited Vienna. During that time, Mozart completed his six string quartets dedicated to Franz Joseph Haydn, and they were played at a party in April where Haydn and the Mozarts, father and son, were present. That occasion prompted Haydn's famous words to Leopold, "Before God and as an honest man, I tell you that your son is the greatest composer known to me in person or by name. He has taste, and, what is more, the profound knowledge of composition." Later that year, Mozart began to compose his great Italian comic opera, *Le nozze di Figaro* (*The Marriage of Figaro*), which premiered on May 1, 1786. The opera's librettist was court poet Lorenzo da Ponte, and the collaboration proved to be one of the best in the history of opera. Following a moderate success in Vienna, *Figaro* was produced in Prague, where people loved it. Mozart visited Prague toward the end of the year, and received a commission to write another opera with da Ponte, this time for a Prague premiere. Through most of the next year, Mozart worked on the new opera, *Don Giovanni* (*Don Juan*). His father died at the end of May 1787. Before completing *Don Giovanni*, Mozart composed a pair of famous instrumental works, *Ein musikalischer Spass* (*A Musical Joke*) and *Eine kleine Nachtmusik* (*A Little Night Music*). The occasions for their composition are unknown.

Don Giovanni was a huge success in its Prague run, beginning in October 1787. Back in Vienna, Mozart received the only Imperial court appointment he would ever have: "*Kapellmeis-*

(continued)

ter" with a small annual salary attached. His only responsibility was to write a little dance music for the occasional court ball, so it was almost an honorary position. *Don Giovanni* came before the Viennese public in May 1788, receiving 14 performances but not much enthusiasm from audiences. Mozart had now reached the first of many financial crises and began to borrow money from his friend Michael Puchberg, making blue-sky promises of repayment when his music started earning money again. At the same time, he composed diligently. In the remarkably short period of about six weeks between June and August, Mozart wrote his "final great trilogy" of symphonies: No. 39 in E-flat Major, K. 543; No. 40 in G Minor, K. 550; and No. 41 in C Major, K. 551. We are unsure as to the composer's intent for these incomparable works.

Mozart now found it extremely difficult to obtain commissions or performances, resulting in a continuous financial disaster for him and his family (Constanze and their first surviving son). Early in 1789, in hopes of earning money, Mozart accepted an invitation from Prince Karl Lichnowsky to accompany him on a trip to Berlin. There, King Friedrich Wilhelm II was an amateur cellist and his daughter an able pianist. Apparently the monarch commissioned some string quartets (the "Prussian" Quartets) and piano sonatas from Mozart, which he only partially completed later. Mozart's creative productivity grew slower about this time. However, he and da Ponte completed another opera that year, *Così fan tutte* (*So Do All Women*), which was accepted warmly at its premiere the following January. In December 1790, Mozart saw Haydn off as he left for London, the last time they would meet.

The works of 1791 were few, but some of them rank among Mozart's greatest music. He performed his last piano concerto, in B-flat Major, K. 595, when making a guest appearance at a clarinetist's concert. That year, Mozart received two commissions for operas. For a Prague coronation festival, he composed *La Clemenza di Tito* (*The Clemency of Titus*), a project he detested; and for a small comedy theater outside Vienna he wrote *Die Zauberflöte* (*The Magic Flute*), a project he loved. The libretto for *Die Zauberflöte* was by Mozart's Masonic brother Emanuel Schikaneder, who also sang a leading role in the premiere in early September.

While at work on *Die Zauberflöte* during the summer, Mozart received a commission to write a **Requiem** Mass (Mass for the Dead) secretly for a local nobleman, who wished to pass it off as his own work the following January. In poor health and nearly destitute, Mozart accepted the 50 percent advance payment and promised the music, though he had a premonition that it would be his *own* Requiem. He had difficulties completing the *Requiem*, due mainly to professional commitments, even after *Die Zauberflöte* had opened. He was also growing weak. The spirited Clarinet Concerto, K. 622, written in October, hides the sad state of Mozart's health at the time. At the end of November, he became suddenly ill and was confined to bed. Knowing that the *Requiem* (K. 626) would bring Constanze and their two sons a little money after his death, he worked as hard to complete it as his condition would allow.

Years later, Constanze's younger sister described the scene on December 4, the day before Mozart died:

> There was Süssmayr [Mozart's student and friend] by Mozart's bed, the well-known Requiem lay on the coverlet, and Mozart was explaining to him how in his opinion he should complete it after his death.

She also gave a poignant description of a reading that afternoon of the completed portions of the *Requiem*:

When they got to the first bars of the Lacrimosa, Mozart began to weep violently, and laid the score aside. Eleven hours later, at one in the morning, he passed on.

The cause of Mozart's death was for two centuries a matter of dispute, not aided by all sorts of false assumptions and the fantasy story projected in the play and film *Amadeus*. A full, scientific explanation was finally put forth by Peter J. Davies, M.D., who studied Mozart's lifelong history of illnesses. Briefly, Mozart suffered from recurring streptococcal infections. The last infection in 1791 was complicated by Schönlein-Henoch Syndrome, resulting in kidney failure, which was the immediate cause of Mozart's death. As early as fall 1791, Mozart knew his end was coming soon, and it saddened him that he would not be able to develop further as a composer. Da Ponte later reported that in September Mozart had written him, saying:

> I have nothing more to fear. I know well, from what I am experiencing, that my hour is near, that I am on the point of death: I shall die without having known any of the delights my talent would have brought me. And yet life is so full of beauty, and in the beginning my career showed auspicious prospects!

Mozart and the Early Classical Piano Sonata

Two trends dealing with keyboard music help us define the onset of the Classical period:

- The sudden flowering of keyboard sonata composition around 1740
- The transition of popularity from harpsichord to piano, which occurred during the 1760s

Both deeply affected the music of Classical composer Wolfgang Amadeus Mozart. The publications that he might have seen as a youngster came from a variety of musical centers, notably Naples, London, Nürnberg, and Amsterdam. The keyboard sonatas of Italian composers such as Domenico Alberti (1710–c. 1740), Baldassare Galuppi (1706–1785), and Giovanni Rutini (1723–1797) were widely distributed, helping to set standards of structure and keyboard style. Among German composers, the expressive keyboard sonatas of Carl Phillip Emanuel Bach (1714–1788), son of J.S. Bach, were especially well known. C.P.E. Bach composed nearly 180 sonatas besides other keyboard works. His *Versuch über die wahre Art das Clavier zu spielen* (*Essay on the True Art of Playing the Keyboard*, 1743–1762) was a unique guide—then and now—to the authentic taste and method of playing 18th-century keyboard literature. Mozart met C.P.E. Bach's younger brother, Johann Christian Bach (1735–1782), during his stay in London (1764–1765) and probably knew J.C. Bach's six sonatas published in Paris in 1763. Mozart might also have known the six Haydn sonatas published in 1777 as Op. 13. We also know that many minor composers influenced Mozart, because he mentioned them in his letters.

The piano came into permanent vogue in the 1760s; however, for many years, harpsichords were still played, chiefly in homes and at some courts. Therefore, publishers who wished to address the widest possible market for their music continued to design title pages stating that the music inside was suitable for either instrument.

Invention of the Piano, Mozart's Instrument

The inventor of the harpsichord is not known, but we do know who developed the first working "fortepiano" (*fort' e piano*, pianoforte, or, later, simply "piano") and about when. Laboring in Florence, Italy, Bartolomeo Cristofori (1655–1731) had completed at least one piano by

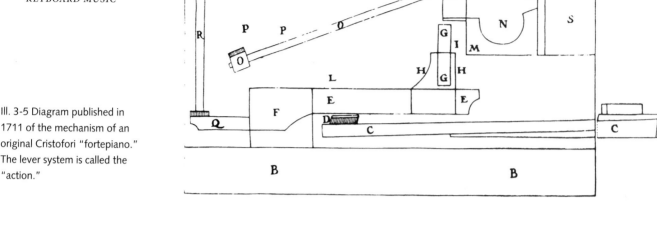

Ill. 3-5 Diagram published in 1711 of the mechanism of an original Cristofori "fortepiano." The lever system is called the "action."

action Part of a piano's mechanism consisting of a system of levers that throws the hammer against the string(s).

escapement Part of a piano's mechanism allowing a hammer to fall back to an intermediate position after striking the string(s), preventing it from striking a second time.

crescendo Becoming louder.

diminuendo Becoming softer (quieter).

1700. Soon Cristofori was making many improvements, notably in the **action**. About 1720, both of the essentials of a piano mechanism, the action and the **escapement**, were in place.

The piano was an instrument for its time, and news of the work of Cristofori and other experiments spread quickly. In 1713, the famous harpsichordist-composer, François Couperin (1668–1733), wrote:

> The harpsichord is perfect as to its compass and is brilliant in itself, but as one can neither swell nor diminish its sounds, I will be forever grateful to those who, with infinite pains guided by taste, succeed in rendering this instrument capable of expression.

As Couperin indicated, dynamic expression was the crux of the matter. On the harpsichord, a player could only approximate the *effect* of loud and soft by registering the two manuals differently and then switching back and forth between them. Neither *crescendo* nor *diminuendo* was possible. On the piano, however, a player could obtain loud and soft (*forte e piano*) dynamics merely by adjusting the energy used in pressing the keys. The speed with which the hammers struck the strings would do the rest. All sorts of dynamic gradations were also possible, including *crescendo* and *diminuendo*.

The pianos played by Mozart had a mechanism different from the Cristofori/Silbermann type. By the 1760s, piano makers in Bavaria (southern Germany) had developed the so-called "German action," which placed the action for each key on top of the moving key lever (see Ill. 3-6). An Augsburg builder, Andreas Stein (1728–1792), perfected this mechanism by adding a workable escapement. Mozart did not discover Stein's pianos until 1777, when he visited Augsburg at the beginning of his last tour. He was so enthusiastic that he immediately wrote to his father:

> When I play vigorously, whether I leave the finger down or lift it up, the tone is finished the moment I sound it. I can attack the keys any way I want, the tone will be even, it will not block, will not come out too loud or too soft or perhaps even fail to sound; in one word, everything is even. … His instruments have this distinguishing feature: They are made with an escapement. Not a man in a hundred bothers with this; but without an escapement it is impossible for a pianoforte not to block or leave an aftersound. When you strike the keys, his hammers fall back again the instant they jump against the strings, whether you leave the keys down or up. …

[Arthur Loesser, *Men, Women and Pianos: A Social History* (New York: Simon and Schuster, 1954), pp. 100–101.]

Ill. 3-6 Model of the mechanism of a "German action" Stein piano. The action is mounted on the moving key lever while the escapement (f) remains stable. Photo courtesy of Division of Cultural History, National Museum of American History, Smithsonian Institution.

Mozart's Piano Sonatas

We do not know whether Mozart had in mind the harpsichord or the piano for the six keyboard sonatas he composed in 1766, because they are lost. However, beginning with the next six, written eight and nine years later, dynamic markings show that he definitely intended these and the rest of his keyboard works for the piano. The earliest surviving Mozart piano sonata is that in C Major, K. 279 (189d), composed in Salzburg in 1774, as were his next sonatas.

A series of tours between 1775 and 1778 inspired Mozart to compose more sonatas, undoubtedly for his own performance, including the sonata in C Major, K. 309 (284b), composed in Mannheim early in 1778, and the subject of our close study in this chapter. Sometime during the months in Paris (March–July 1778), Mozart composed his Sonata in A Minor, K. 310 (300d). Some writers have tried to connect this, the composer's first piano sonata in a minor key, with his grief over his mother's death that summer. Certainly the turbulence and poignant **dissonance** of the first movement and the **Storm-and-Stress** finale are like nothing Mozart had previously written for the piano. The drama of the A Minor Sonata made it an emphatic conclusion to Mozart's piano sonatas up to that point, and he would not turn his attention to creating new ones for another five years.

Mozart returned to the piano sonata in 1783, composing a trilogy of them for a fall visit to Salzburg that are among his most ingratiating music. The first, the C Major Sonata, K. 330 (300h), is "one of the most lovable works Mozart ever wrote," in the words of musicologist Alfred Einstein. The Sonata in A Major, K. 331 (300i), is famous for two of its movements: the unusual opening **variation** set on an infectious *andante grazioso* theme, and the famed final **Rondo** "*alla Turca*" with its brash imitation of percussion instruments. The Sonata in F Major, K. 332 (300k) completes the set. On the journey back to Vienna, Mozart composed the B-flat Major Sonata, K. 333 (315c), and it differed from the previous group in its more virtuoso style, including a **cadenza** in the last movement.

For the rest of his life, Mozart composed piano sonatas individually and sporadically. From 1784 we have his Sonata in C Minor, K. 457, the last in a minor key. Much has been written about this work's darkness, pathos, emotion, and "grim seriousness" (Einstein). The sonata also foreshadows Beethoven in its passion, composed in a key that Beethoven reserved for pathos, tragedy, and concentrated seriousness. In places Mozart's style of writing for the piano is heavier than usual, employing octaves or sixths at moments needing power. This ran against his usual approach to the instrument (see Ex. 3-10).

dissonance In Western music before the 20th century, a combination of tones not in repose, requiring resolution. Adj.: dissonant. Ant.: consonance.

Storm and Stress A tendency in some music by Haydn and, to a lesser degree, Mozart during the early 1770s. Its main characteristics were turbulent fast movements in minor keys and poignant slow movements.

variation, variations, theme and variations Variation technique modifies or transforms a musical idea in a way that retains some essential features of that idea. Theme and variation form uses a stated theme, which is then modified/transformed differently in each succeeding variation.

rondo A form, often the final movement in a sonata plan, consisting of a main theme (A) alternating with digressive sections (B, C, …). Typical rondo forms are A–B–A–C–A and A–B–A–C–A–B–A.

cadenza — In a solo concerto, a virtuosic passage for unaccompanied soloist in free tempo. Occasionally, such displays occur in sonatas and chamber music.

Ex. 3-10 Passages in octaves and sixths from Mozart, Piano Sonata in C Minor, K. 457: (a) mm. 1–8; (b) mm. 117–122.

Mozart composed the F Major Sonata, K. 533, in 1788, the same year as his last symphonies, and it shows the same high degree of maturity. As in the "Jupiter" Symphony (No. 41), Mozart was fascinated with counterpoint in this F Major Sonata for interesting textures and developing ideas. By contrast, the very popular C Major Sonata, K. 545, was a work that the composer designated in his personal catalogue as a "little piano sonata for beginners."

The last two piano sonatas belong to the year 1789. Composed in the technically easy style of K. 545, the B-flat Major Sonata, K. 570, is nonetheless rich in imaginative themes and luxuriant harmonies. The central *adagio* is particularly advanced in style, verging on the Romantic. Mozart's final piano sonata, that in D Major, K. 576, ostensibly was to have been part of a set of "easy" sonatas for Princess Frederike of Prussia. Oddly, it is instead one of the most demanding of his sonatas in both technique and interpretation. From the hunting-horn opening theme through the flowing thirty-second notes of the *adagio* to the dizzying triplets of the final *allegretto*, this is the ideal work to crown Mozart's exquisite body of 17 piano sonatas.

The C Major Sonata, K. 309 (284b): The Mystery Behind the Music

During the Classical period, piano sonatas were not the mainstays of public concerts, but they could be advantageous vehicles for a young pianist who wanted to make an impression before a select group of nobles and gentry. It took a Mozart to put across a piano sonata in a large concert gathering. The origin of the C Major may have occurred *ex tempore* during a lengthy concert Mozart gave on tour in Augsburg in late October 1777. Describing the climax of the event, he wrote his father:

> Then I gave a solo, my last sonata in D [K. 284 (205b)], written for Baron Dürnitz, and after my concerto in B-flat. I then played another solo, quite in the style of the organ, a fugue in C minor, and then all of a sudden a magnificent sonata in C major, out of my head, and a Rondo to finish up with. There was a regular din of applause.
>
> [Emily Anderson, *The Letters of Mozart and His Family* 3rd ed. (New York: W.W. Norton, 1985), p. 340.]

For years, this C Major Sonata was thought to be K. 330 (300h), but recent research has assigned that sonata to the later Salzburg group of 1783. So, did Mozart ever write down the improvised "magnificent sonata in C major"?

We can try to solve this mystery. Mozart's correspondence to his father on November 4, 1777, from Mannheim mentioned a sonata he was finishing for Rosa, the 15-year-old daughter of Mannheim conductor Christian Cannabich (1731–1798),

> … who plays the piano quite nicely; and in order to make a real friend of him, I am now working at a sonata for her, which is almost finished save for the Rondo. When I had composed the opening Allegro and the Andante, I took them to their house and played both to them. Papa cannot imagine the applause which this sonata won.

[Anderson, *The Letters of Mozart and His Family*, p. 355.]

The next day, Mozart also mentioned a sonata in a letter to his cousin Maria Anna Thekla in Augsburg, which he had promised to her friend, Josepha Freysinger. Presumably this was a different work, or Mozart may have intended to copy Rosa's sonata and send it to Josepha. Could either sonata be the one he improvised at the concert, and could Rosa's sonata be K. 309 (284b)? Historically that is possible. Although Mozart never mentioned the key of Rosa's sonata, the three movements of the C Major are *Allegro con spirito*, *Andante un poco adagio*, and *Rondo: Allegretto grazioso*—as Mozart's letter outlined. We know that he finished the rondo to that sonata four days later. However, he also composed another sonata about the same time—that in D Major, K. 311 (284c). It has a similar movement tempo plan: *Allegro con spirito*, *Andante con espressione*, and *Rondeau: Allegro*. Was this, then, Rosa's sonata? Was it Josepha's?

Historians now theorize that the Sonata in C Major was that given to Rosa Cannabich, and that the following D Major Sonata was intended for Josepha Freysinger. That way works out neatly from a *historical* standpoint but is not entirely satisfactory from a *musical* one. If we look at the impressive first movement of the C Major Sonata, we see that it may actually have been the one improvised brilliantly during the Augsburg concert. Yet, could this also have become the beginning of a work crafted for a young lady "who plays the piano quite nicely"? The opening, shown in Ex. 3-11a, is powerful, and the sonata that unfolds from it is brilliant and often technically demanding. The opening of the D Major Sonata, shown in Ex. 3-11b, is music that emphasizes gentility rather than power. And, as a whole, the D Major Sonata is not as difficult as the preceding one. The D Major Sonata is challenging for a talented player at home, while the C Major Sonata is showy enough to impress one of Mozart's audiences.

Ex. 3-11 Comparison of the opening measures of two Mozart piano sonatas composed in late 1777: (a) C Major, K. 309 (284b), mm. 1–14; (b) D Major, K. 311 (284c), mm. 1–10.

(continued)

(b)

One last piece of evidence strongly suggests that the D Major Sonata, not the C Major, was Rosa's. On November 14, 1777, Mozart wrote to his father regarding her sonata:

> I began to teach it to Mlle Rosa three days ago. We finished the opening Allegro today. The Andante will give us most trouble, for it is full of expression and must be played accurately and with the exact shades of forte and piano, precisely as they are marked.

Key words here are "it is full of *expression*." The slow movement of the D Major Sonata (not the C Major) contains the word "expression" in its tempo marking: *Andante con espressione*. The C Major Sonata's slow movement is marked *Andante un poco adagio*.

Thus, judging by the music itself and Mozart's remark about "expression" in the *Andante*, a new theory about the two sonatas is plausible:

- Mozart first improvised, then wrote out, the C Major Sonata for his own professional use.
- Moreover, he composed the charming D Major work for Rosa Cannabich, intending to copy it for Josepha Freysinger. (Incidentally, probably neither young lady was of romantic interest to the 21-year-old Mozart, since he had become enamored of Aloysia Weber at the time.)

Sonata Plan and Sonata Form

Before investigating Mozart's sonata movement, we must explore the term "sonata" more thoroughly as it applies to music in the Classical period. The most important thing is to distinguish between two ideas: *sonata plan* and *sonata form*. Sonata plan was the pattern or *plan of movements* that composers applied equally to orchestral, chamber, and keyboard genres in the Classical period. The earliest sonata plan included three movements:

Fast movement	(Home key)
Slow movement	(Related key, often subdominant)
Fast movement	(Home key)

This was applied to early symphonies, much chamber music, and most sonatas for keyboard (or violin and keyboard) from Haydn through Beethoven.

After about 1760, another movement, the minuet (later the **scherzo**), was inserted into the sonata plan in some cases. This expanded sonata plan usually ran:

Fast movement	(Home key)
Slow movement	(Related key, often subdominant)
Minuet/Scherzo	(Home key)
Fast movement	(Home key)

Composers applied the four-movement sonata plan to symphonies, **string quartets**, and some other chamber music. The three-movement sonata plan, however, remained in effect for any musical work titled "sonata," for much chamber music, and for all concertos.

As you read about music, you may see the term "sonata form" applied indiscriminately to mean either sonata *plan* or the *form* of a single movement. More correctly, "sonata form" (or "sonata-allegro form," or "first movement sonata form") refers only to a *single movement*— usually part of a sonata plan. (Independent sonata-form works are also possible.) The first movement of a sonata plan is usually cast in sonata form, such as in the Mozart movement studied below. The slow movement and the final fast movement can also contain that form.

Exploring the First Movement of Mozart's Sonata in C Major

Listen to the entire movement. Mozart composed this movement in *sonata form. Listen to the beginning of the movement again, and notice that the first big section is repeated literally. Stop listening at the end of the repetition.* The large section that was repeated is called the *exposition*, since in it, the movement's important themes and motives are first exposed.

Now listen to the rest of the movement. In the first section you encounter, do you hear themes and motives from the exposition? Are they organized differently from the exposition? Does Mozart move freely from key to key, including some time spent in the minor mode? This part of the form is called the *development*. The idea of *developing* themes and motives is to use them in new ways, sometimes breaking up a theme and using only certain of its motives. A composer rarely develops all the themes from the exposition, but here Mozart works on several. In a development section, the composer is free to modulate from key to key. Mozart does this masterfully, sometimes landing in a minor key to try out a theme or some motives in minor-mode "clothing."

After Mozart has been developing for a while, does the exposition seem to begin again? After some seemingly false starts outlining minor or diminished broken triads, the opening theme of the exposition returns in the home key of C major. You hear, however, that Mozart does not simply rehash the whole exposition; several features are different. *After sounding the first theme in C major, what happens?* Mozart presents a new version of the theme in C minor. (He is still developing!) You might hear other differences along the way, too. For example, when you think the music is starting to move to a new key, it merely circles back to the home tonality of C.

NOTE ON THE EDITION IN THE MUSIC ANTHOLOGY. The score of this Mozart sonata movement is reproduced from Nathan Broder's authoritative edition of *Mozart's Sonatas and*

scherzo A quick movement in triple meter in a form derived from the minuet. In a sonata plan, it is usually positioned immediately before the final movement.

string quartet (1) A chamber music ensemble consisting of two violins, one viola, and one cello; (2) a composition intended for a string quartet ensemble, usually consisting of four movements.

The C Major Sonata, First Movement: A Closer Look
Please refer to the score of Mozart, Piano Sonata in C Major, beginning on page 13 of the Score Anthology

Fantasies (Bryn Mawr, PA: Theodore Presser, 1956 and 1960). In editing this sonata, Broder used the earliest sources: (a) the first edition published by M. Heina, Paris, c. 1782; and (b) the first Breitkopf & Härtel edition of 1799. The two early prints have been combined here to form a single modern edition, with parentheses in the music specifying a marking found only in (b).

SURVEYING THE FORM. Look through the score and notice its overall structure. Like the Baroque binary form (Handel) and the extended binary form (Scarlatti), Mozart's movement in sonata form is written in two portions, each defined by repeat marks. (In modern performances, the second pair of repeat marks is usually ignored.)

What are the relative sizes of the two portions? From the beginning to the repeat are 58 measures. This is the *exposition*. From that point to the end (mm. 59–155) are 97 measures, a little less than *twice* the size of the first portion. Compared to the historically earlier binary movements we have studied, the second portion of a sonata form is much larger. That is because it now contains two major sections instead of one: the *development* and the *recapitulation*. Briefly, the three sections of Mozart's sonata-form movement look like this:

‖: Exposition :‖[:] Development | Recapitulation [:]‖

Now let us examine each of these sections.

EXPOSITION. The structure of a Classical exposition comprises four elements, analytically labeled this way:

P   Principal theme or theme *group*, presented at the outset of the movement. If P is a group of themes, each theme is designated with a subscript: P_1, P_2, etc.

T   Transition. Its purpose is to modulate from the key of the tonic to a related key, where the secondary theme/theme group will be heard. Therefore, T is usually not a complete theme but a group of motives that may be repeated, often in sequences. Each motive is labeled separately, however (T_1, T_2, etc), since the composer may use it later by itself.

S   Secondary theme or theme group. It is presented after the transition has arrived at the related key (key of the dominant in this case). If S is a group of themes, each theme is designated with a subscript: S_1, S_2, etc.

K   Concluding theme or theme group. "K" is used to avoid confusion with the subsequent label "C" for "codetta." The function of the concluding theme/theme group is to reinforce the new, related key. Thus, it may contain one or more cadences in that key. Similar to P, T, or S, members of a concluding theme group are represented as K_1, K_2, etc.

C   Codetta. Meaning "little tail," this short segment briefly rounds out the exposition, offering one last cadence in the new key to terminate the exposition.

With these labels, we can now identify the important themes Mozart presents in his exposition. *First, listen to the exposition, mm. 1–58, following the score. Now, as we go along, mark all the labels in your score. Examine mm. 1–2.* This two-measure fanfarelike motive is so important to the movement that we must give it an independent label:

Now look at mm. 3–8. Here is the first real *theme*, a whole phrase of music:

Notice that the downbeat of m. 8 is both the ending of P_2 and the beginning of another P_1. We call this type of overlap an *elision*. (It is common among Classical and Romantic composers.) *What happens in mm. 8–14?* Mozart repeats P_1 and P_2, except that he *varies* P_2 a little and gives it a new ending that will lead to P_3:

P_3 is immediately repeated with a bit of decoration, leading to a full cadence in C major at m. 21. Again Mozart creates an elision, for this beat also initiates the transition. The music changes rapidly now, as the transition presents no fewer than four motives in the space of 11 measures:

In mm. 21–32, find all of these and mark them in your score, including all repetitions and sequences.

Mozart's transition has successfully modulated to the key of G major, the closely related dominant of the home tonality. Measure 32 outlines a V chord in the new key. Then, after two introductory measures, the secondary theme begins:

S =

Here, in two 4-measure phrases, Mozart presents his one, full-blown secondary theme. To balance the multiplicity of the principal theme group, however, he treats us to several concluding (K) ideas. *Find K₁.* It looks like this:

K1 =

After a purely cadential measure (m. 45), K_1 repeats, followed by a flurry of two-measure motives we could call K_2, K_3, and K_4—the idea of which is to drive to an exciting cadence at mm. 53–54:

Find and mark the whole K theme group in your score. Again, an elision occurs, tying the concluding theme group to the codetta, which spans mm. 54–58. Two motives dominate the codetta:

C1 =
C1 =

In summary, Ex. 3-12 shows how all the themes in the exposition are placed (the thematic form) along with a summary of the main harmonic areas (harmonic form):

| Measure : | 1 | 3 | 15 | 21 | 32 | 35 | 43 | 48 | 54 | 58 |

Themes & Motives : ‖: P_1 P_2 P_3 ┊ T_1 T_2 T_3 T_4 │ …S ┊ K_1 $K_{2,3,4}$ C_1 C_2 :‖

Harmony : C : I   I ~~~~~~➤ G : V   I   V   I   VI

Ex. 3-12 Diagram of the exposition, summarizing basic thematic and harmonic form.

DEVELOPMENT. Now that Mozart has shown us what he is working with, we can appreciate what he does with his material in the development section. *Listen to mm. 59–93, following the score. Now, examine mm. 59–62. From what theme does Mozart derive this material?* Obviously he has brought back the very first idea, P_1, but he states it dramatically in G minor, parallel minor to the key he just drove home at the end of the exposition. Also, he has extended P_1 with two measures of *echo*, a striking effect:

Do the next four measures (63–66) relate to any theme from the exposition? No, but composers often insert new material into the development, especially when modulating (here, between G minor and D minor). We may call mm. 63–66 theme "X". *After Mozart states P_1 in D minor (mm. 67–68), what happens?* Theme X returns, a bit enhanced melodically, to get the development from D minor to A minor. *How would you describe mm. 73–78?*

You would, of course, relate it to P_1, stated twice, with a left-hand accompaniment and a new extension based on its second measure. *What happens in mm. 79–82 (first beat)?* This is new material, but of a generic, spun-out sort; we do not need to label it. *Now, in your score, compare the next passage in the development, mm. 82–85, with mm. 54–57 (back in the codetta).* What was originally in G major is now being tested in an A minor guise. *What is going on in mm. 86–93?* Mozart closes his development much the way he opened it (mm. 59–62). The two iterations of the *echo* version of P1 start on the notes A and B, respectively. Cleverly, they lead up to the *genuine* P1, starting on the note C in m. 94, which signals the start of the recapitulation. Ex. 3-13 shows the development section's thematic and harmonic activity.

Ex. 3-13 Diagram of the development section, summarizing thematic usage and harmonic motion.

Measure :	59	63	67	69	73	79	82	86	90	94	(recap.)
Themes & motives (developed) :	P$_1$ ("echo")	"X"	P$_1$	"X"	P$_1$	"generic" (accompanied)	C$_1$ C$_2$	P$_1$ ("echo")	P$_1$ ("echo")	P$_1$	
Harmony :	g:i		d:i	i	i ～～～→ a:i		V i....V	(a:)→(b:)→C:I			

RECAPITULATION. *Now, with your score in hand, listen from m. 94 to the end of the movement. In examining the recapitulation, we wish to note differences between it and the exposition. What is the first deviation you notice?* It is the shift to C minor (m. 101) for the repetition of P$_2$. We noted this when we were "exploring" without a score. *Now, looking at the score, compare mm. 101–107 with mm. 9–14 from the exposition.* Mozart works his way back to C major to present P$_3$ in the home key. P$_3$ and the beginning of the transition remain close to those in the exposition. *What does Mozart leave out of the transition?* T$_2$, originally found in mm. 27–28, is now missing, but Mozart compensates by providing an extra measure of T$_3$ (m. 124). *Notice that by the end of the transition in m. 126, the harmony has worked its way back to the dominant of C major, our original key:*

Now we have arrived at the secondary theme (S). *Other than the key, how does S at m. 129 differ from S back at m. 35?* As a charming surprise, Mozart reprises the first phrase of his graceful S theme in the left hand, accompanying it with the right. Then he switches back to the original position for the second phrase. Discounting details, the music of the recapitulation from this point to the codetta is a tonic-key reflection of the dominant-key exposition. *What happens at m. 152?* Brilliantly rounding out the movement, Mozart brings back P$_1$ again, now with a cadential extension, expanding the codetta to complete the movement.

Ex. 3-14 illustrates themes and harmonic motion in the recapitulation.

Measure :	94		101	110	116		126	129		137	142		148	152	

Ex. 3-14 Diagram of the recapitulation, summarizing thematic and harmonic form.

MOZART'S KEYBOARD ORNAMENTS. Many ornaments that Bach and Scarlatti used in the first half of the 18th century continued in use in the second half of the century and beyond. In this movement, however, Mozart employs only two main types of ornament: the trill and the **appoggiatura**. Trills were to be executed much as shown in Bach's "Explication" (Ex. 3-2). If the note was long and at a cadential point, a mordent at the end might be improvised:

appoggiatura A Baroque ornament; a relatively accented non-chord (non-consonant) tone.

Appoggiaturas were different from **grace notes**, despite their appearance as very small symbols. Performers played appoggiaturas *on* the beat, where the main note normally would have fallen, not before the beat. Under most circumstances, the appoggiatura would "borrow" *half* the value of the main note, delaying the main note. Thus, in m. 27:

grace note An ornamental note printed smaller than its context. Its value is quick but indefinite, usually taking time from an adjacent note.

If the main note was short and in a fast tempo, such as m. 23:

the appoggiatura might be shorter but still played *on* the rhythmic position of the main note and not before.

Summary Comparison: Binary, Extended Binary, and Sonata Forms

In this textbook, we have explored the historical development of sonata form by examining a movement from each stage of its development:

- Binary form (Handel, "Hornpipe"—Chapter 2)
- Extended binary form (Scarlatti, sonata—this chapter)
- Sonata form (Mozart, sonata movement—this chapter)

This development was evolutionary in structure, themes, and harmony, as shown in the following table.

	STRUCTURE	THEMES	HARMONY
Binary Form	In two parts, each repeated.	No distinct themes; in two continuous phrases, containing perhaps one motive used here and there.	First section establishes home key; arrives at a related key by the end of that section. Second section works its way back to the home key.
Extended Binary Form	Basically the same as binary, but the movement is longer.	Several motives, some of which are developed in the second section.	Arrives at related key about halfway through the first section. In Scarlatti, entire "crux" remains in the related key to the end of the section. Second section works its way back to the home key; entire "crux" recurs literally in that key to finish the movement.
Sonata Form	Similar to extended binary, but movement is longer. Second part (development and recapitulation) show repeat sign but might not be repeated in performance.	Full themes and several motives, some of which are used in the development section.	Exposition arrives at the related key just before the secondary theme, continuing there for the concluding and codetta might not be repeated in per-formance.material. Development modulates, preparing for the reca-pitulation, which remains close to the tonic, analogous to the "crux" in extended binary form.

To graphically illustrate the evolution described above, Ex. 3-15 shows structural, the-matic, and harmonic form in the three movements studied. One of the glorious features of sonata form, observable in Ex. 3-15, is that it comprises *three sections*; exposition–develop-ment–recapitulation, contained within a *two-part* (highly evolved binary) structure.

Handel:

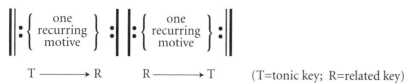

$$T \longrightarrow R \qquad R \longrightarrow T \qquad (\text{T=tonic key; R=related key})$$

Scarlatti:

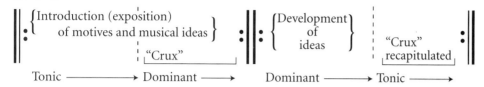

Ex. 3-15 Summary of the evolution of sonata form: a comparison of movements by Handel, Scarlatti, and Mozart.

Mozart:

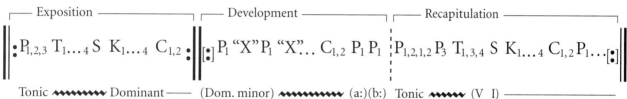

CHOPIN, THREE SHORT PIANO PIECES

Frédéric (Fryderyk) Chopin was born in Zelazowa Wola, near Warsaw, on March 1, 1810, the second of four children. His father was Nicolas Chopin, a Frenchman who had come to Poland to seek his fortune; his mother was named Tekla-Justyna (née Skarbeck). Eight months after Frédéric was born, the family moved to Warsaw, where Nicolas taught French language and literature at a new high school. Frédéric was educated there. His precociousness at the piano was evident from about the age of six. Although he had a teacher from 1816 to 1822, he taught himself mostly, intuitively finding his technique. Frédéric first performed in public at the age of eight, playing a piano concerto by Adalbert Gyrowetz. He also improvised and composed from a young age. An early polonaise was published in 1817. Besides his high-school education, young Chopin began formal studies in music theory under Jósef Elsner, director of the Warsaw Conservatory. An early result of his work under Elsner was the Rondo in C Minor, published as **Opus 1.**

On graduation in 1826, Chopin continued giving concerts in Warsaw and other cities in Poland. He also entered the Conservatory to study further with Elsner. We know that Elsner's three-year curriculum was formal and thorough: harmony, theory, and counterpoint for two years; composition only in the last year. We do not know, however, whether Chopin took full advantage of the instruction. Whenever he composed according to the "rules," the result was nondescript, as in his First Piano Sonata (Op. 4). When he was allowed free rein, the result was

(continued)

FRÉDÉRIC CHOPIN

Photograph by Louis Auguste Bisson, c. 1846, now lost.

opus Literally "work," used to indicate the chronological position of a composition within a composer's *published* output. Thus, an opus number is part of a publisher's cataloguing system, rather than an entry in the log of a composer's output. Abbr., Op., (pl.) Opp.

improvisation Spontaneous music making, often based on an existing theme or harmonic pattern.

salon The drawing room of an aristocratic or wealthy person's home. In Paris or Vienna during the 19th century, it was often the gathering place for intellectuals, poets, artists, and musicians. The "appointments" of a salon usually included a piano.

FRÉDÉRIC CHOPIN *(continued)*

astonishing, as in his Variations on Mozart's "La ci darem" (Op. 2), about which Robert Schumann wrote, "Hats off, gentlemen! A genius!"

Wishing to broaden his horizons and begin building a career as a pianist-composer, Chopin traveled to Vienna in 1829. There he gave a successful concert with orchestra, including his Variations, Op. 2, his *Krakowiak* Rondo, Op. 14, and a solo **improvisation** on a Polish folk song. The favorable Viennese reception convinced Chopin that his place was in western Europe, where he fascinated the public with both the Polish character of his music and his special piano style. However, he first returned to Warsaw, where he premiered both of his piano concertos (Opp. 21 and 11, published in reverse chronological order). The Polish uprising against Russia in 1830, coupled with his first "crush" on a young lady, delayed his departure until late that year. By late November, he was back in Vienna to begin an extended concert tour that would take him to Linz, Salzburg, Dresden, and Stuttgart, en route to his final destination, Paris.

Paris was a haven for Polish emigrants, and it was one of Europe's great cultural centers. Chopin arrived there in September 1831. Quickly he gained many friends in musical and literary circles, notably Franz Liszt (1811–1886). After he gave his first Paris concert in February 1832, he became the darling of fashionable **salons** and was even patronized by the wealthy Rothschilds. Chopin earned the main part of his living by teaching piano for high fees to members of high society, chiefly young women. His personality was far more suited to the intimate salon gathering than the large public concert hall, and so his concertizing gradually decreased after 1832. Amazingly, his fabled celebrity as a performer continued to grow, although he gave only about 30 public performances during his career.

With Paris as his base, Chopin traveled a few times during the 1830s. In 1834 he accompanied Ferdinand Hiller to Germany, where he met Robert and Clara Schumann (who played some of Chopin's music) and Felix Mendelssohn. In 1837 he went to London for two weeks with his publisher, Camille Pleyel, on a pleasure trip.

By that time, Chopin had met the woman who would play a crucial role in his life over the next few years, Aurore Dudevant. An early feminist, writing under the pen name of George Sand, she completed about 80 popular novels in her life and usually appeared in public wearing men's clothing. Fresh from an 1836 divorce from her aristocratic husband, she supported herself and her children on her earnings as a socially conscious author. Sand's liaison with Chopin would not be her only affair, and she flaunted them all openly before the public.

Chopin, recovering from an unhappy love affair, was gradually drawn into a continuing relationship with Sand in 1837. By the summer of 1838, they were "lovers." However, documentation of the relationship shows it to be less of a torrid love affair than a mother-son type of attachment. Sand took care of every need for the already sickly composer, and he amazed her artistically, becoming her greatest source of pride. Sand fascinated Chopin, and her passion for life stimulated his muse over the next nine years as nothing else could. The time they spent in Majorca during the fall and winter of 1838–1839 was typical. Supposedly a holiday from the swirl of Parisian life, it became a time of intense creative production for Chopin, during which he composed most of the *24 Preludes*, Op. 28. Chopin, Sand, and Sand's two children then traveled in spring 1839, finally summering at her villa in Nohant (near Châteauroux). Chopin's tuberculosis was now irreversible, but Sand's affection and care enabled the composer to carry on and achieve new artistic triumphs.

Life in the 1840s was not very eventful for Chopin. He kept apart from most of the musical world and composed only during summers at Nohant. Because of this, his worsening health, and the departure for America of Julius Fontana (his lifelong friend and music copyist), Chopin's output slowed considerably over this time. In 1844, for example, he composed only one work, the B Minor Sonata, Op. 58. Also, his relationship with George Sand cooled during the mid-1840s. Sand and her children involved Chopin as a pawn in their intrigues, leading finally to her "dismissing" him in 1847.

Chopin's last years were sad ones. After the break with George Sand, he composed very little. The year 1848 saw his last concert in Paris followed by a period in England. In London, he was taken up immediately by fashionable society as he had been in Paris. His performances took place in the homes and palaces of the wealthy. During a short period that was intended to aid his failing health and improve his finances, he left London and gave public performances in Manchester, Glasgow, and Edinburgh. He made his final public appearance as a performer in London at the beginning of November.

Returning to France, Chopin suffered from acute tuberculosis. After a summer in Chaillot, the composer settled into his last home in Paris in autumn. His sister and several Polish friends were with him when he died on October 17, 1849. Mozart's *Requiem* was sung at his funeral, which was attended by nearly 3,000 people.

Frédéric Chopin, Master Miniaturist

Every work that Frédéric Chopin composed included the piano. The piano was his life. Aside from his shorter piano pieces, he made several contributions to Romantic music in larger genres. His two piano concertos from around 1830 proved that he could think in larger forms and ably execute them, as do his four additional one-movement works for piano and orchestra. Yet, able as he was at handling forms of any size and complexity, he "thought" for the piano, not for the orchestra. In each of these works, the spotlight rarely leaves the piano soloist, reducing the orchestra to an accompaniment function nearly always. Chopin dabbled in chamber music occasionally from his student days to three years before his death, and he produced four works. The most extensive of these are his Piano Trio (violin, cello, and piano, 1828–1829) and his Cello Sonata (1845–1846). Both of these tasteful multimovement works reflect the highest standards of chamber music and are still in the repertoire. Similarly, the 18 **art songs** he composed are high-quality music but are neglected, probably due to the remoteness of their Polish texts.

art song A song of serious artistic intent as distinct from a folk-song or popular song.

In the field of solo piano music, Chopin composed three sonatas, the last two of which are most substantial. However, Chopin did not incline strongly toward composing within the sonata plan or any other Classical-period form (with the occasional exception of theme and variations). Rather, the *microcosm* of an individual piece, or a set of such pieces, was what intrigued him. Among the most famous of these were stylized *mazurkas* and *polonaises*, folk dances from his native Poland. Chopin was, to a degree, the first **nationalist** composer, because he drew on these traditional dances. He was interested also in the European waltz, and his waltz compositions set standards for many piano composers and others. Whereas John Field was the first to compose *nocturnes*, Chopin seized on the idea and perfected it with the ideal salon idiom of the character piece. The *preludes* and *impromptus* were also character types. Individual technical-artistic pieces were a particular specialty of his, and his etudes reflect his work in the concert hall, the teaching studio, and the fashionable salon.

nationalism A trend in music in which the folk songs, dances, and lore of a particular country provide the basis for works of art music that express national feeling or personality. Adj.: nationalistic, nationalist.

IMPROVISATIONAL STYLE. The many reports on Chopin's playing show that he improvised at the piano throughout his life, and from those improvisations came a large amount of his written music. Undoubtedly, Chopin's improvisations generated his most characteristic textures and playing style. The so-called "nocturne texture" was most prevalent. Shown in Ex. 3-16, this consisted of a single melody in the right hand accompanied harmonically in the left. The accompaniment could draw from a vast variety of figural patterns. Coupled with this and related textures, Chopin developed a personal style of interpretation in slow or moderate tempos, which gives this music an additional improvised sound.

Ex. 3-16 "Nocturne" texture observed in Chopin's Nocturne in E-flat Major, Op. 9, No. 2.

rubato A style of interpretation in which the tempo is slowed expressively at times and may be slightly rushed at others.

A part of the general Romantic trend toward expressiveness, Chopin would play in a *rubato* style, slowing the music slightly at one point and speeding it up slightly at another. Sometimes he indicated these places in the score, but more often not. The development of a phrase might require some hesitations here and there, or the use of ornamentation in the melody might *require* slowing down. (We will learn more about this in the section on the "Raindrop" Prelude.) One of Chopin's students, Wilhelm von Lenz, later quoted him as giving these instructions for playing *rubato*:

> The left hand is the conductor. It must not relent or bend; it is a clock. [However,] do with the right hand what you wish and are able to do. A piece lasts for, say, five minutes, only in that it occupies this time for its total performance. Internal details are another matter. And there you have rubato.

damper In a piano mechanism, a felt pad that prevents the string(s) of a key from sounding. It is released when the key is pressed. The piano's damper pedal releases all the dampers at once.

A careful use of the piano's **damper** (sustaining) pedal was a corollary to the *rubato-*improvisational style. Although Chopin admired clarity in the music of Bach and Mozart, his own textures require more pedaling, much of it shown in the score. At times, even a slight amount of blurring is desirable.

HARMONY. Chopin was among the greatest of intuitive composers; his ear was infallible, and through it he developed an individual style of harmony. He maintained a highly personal approach to chromaticism, employing a *finger logic* derived from improvisation rather than an intellectual logic derived from the study of harmony. His music often took full advantage of the **equal-tempered** keyboard, moving between chords and between keys by **enharmonic** means.

equal temperament A method of tuning keyboards in which the interval between every semitone is exactly equal. Adj.: equal-tempered.

enharmonic In an equal-tempered scale, the equivalency of two notes of different names or spellings, such as C-sharp = D-flat.

INFLUENCE. In his harmony, Chopin influenced other "chromatic composers" of his generation, notably Liszt and Richard Wagner (1813–1883). However, his chromaticism can be felt as late as César Franck (1822–1890) and in the early piano music of Arnold Schoenberg

(1874–1951). Chopin's general piano style made a deep impression on the French. The piano music of Gabriel Fauré (1845–1924), Franck, Camille Saint-Saëns (1835–1921), Claude Debussy (1862–1918), and Maurice Ravel (1875–1937) all owes much to Chopin's approach to the instrument and his interest in the short, individual piano piece.

Character Pieces

The most numerous among Romantic short piano pieces, favored by composers from Ludwig van Beethoven (1770–1829) to Johannes Brahms (1833–1897), was the character piece. This very general type had a basic purpose of projecting one or more moods. Some character pieces carried **programmatic** titles, while others received generic names, and a few were untitled. Some of the earliest were Beethoven's bagatelles, a generic name implying music easy to play. His best known was *Für Elise* (**WoO** 59) composed about 1808.

Two types of generically named character pieces appear among Chopin's works: the *nocturne* and the *prelude*. Expanding on the nocturne idea devised by pianist-composer John Field (1782–1837), Chopin composed nocturnes (night pieces) over the entire period of his creative life. As the title implies, most of these pieces carry a nocturnal atmosphere, often one of dreaminess, reverie, or peacefulness. Chopin's preludes usually convey mood also. Some of them are very brief, consisting perhaps of only a pair of phrases. The more fully developed preludes in the set usually provide a contrast between two moods cast in A–B–A or A–B–A–B–A form.

The "Raindrop" Prelude: A Character Piece

Bach and Mozart were Chopin's most revered composers. It is said that on the piano in his Paris studio, he always kept Bach's *The Well-Tempered Clavier* and Mozart's collected piano sonatas. It is not surprising, then, that Bach's great double cycle of preludes and fugues in all 24 keys was the inspiration for Chopin's 24 Preludes, Op. 28. Fugues were not part of Chopin's own musical expressions. However, he was fascinated with the imaginative variety Bach had applied to preludes, as well as the tactile and audible differences among all the different major and minor keys. Bach had organized the order of keys in *The Well-Tempered Clavier* in a simple way: A major key followed by its parallel minor, then up a half-step to the next pair.

This logical upward chromatic progression was fine for Bach's mind but not for Chopin's. In Chopin's music (as generally in Romantic music) the key relationships between movements are crucial, and that idea often also carried over into organizing groups of loosely related pieces like the Chopin preludes. (We can observe this also in Schumann's music.) Two basic relationships dominate the organization of Chopin's cycle of preludes: (1) the **circle of fifths**, going from sharps to flats, and (2) relative minor keys. Like Bach, Chopin applied a preordered key plan to his anthology of alternating major and minor keys, but the pattern was purely his own:

PRELUDE NO.:	1	2	3	4	5	6 …	15	16 …	23	24
MAJOR:	C		G		D		D-flat		F	
RELATIVE MINOR:		a		e		b		b-flat		d

Thus, the position of the Prelude in D-flat Major, for example, is No. 15, because that is where it falls in the pattern: circle of fifths and alternating major and relative minor keys.

THE PROJECT.   Chopin may have begun composing the 24 Preludes as early as 1836, although the project did not take shape until late 1838. In October of that year, Chopin, George Sand, and her children traveled to the island of Majorca to spend the late fall and winter. Camille Pleyel, piano manufacturer and Chopin's Paris publisher, was to have sent a piano to

program music Instrumental music inspired by or based on something nonmusical, e.g., a piece of literature, a painting, or a legend. Adj.: programmatic. Ant.: absolute music.

WoO In Beethoven's catalog, an abbreviation for *Werke ohne Opuszahl* (work without Opus number).

circle of fifths — An arrangement of the 12 tonalities starting with C major, in order by ascending fifths, symbolized as clockwise points along a circle. Moving through the sharp signatures, the keys turn to flat signatures at (F-sharp = G-flat), returning to C.

their villa. The composer's dependence on composing at the piano came out vividly when the instrument did not arrive. In November, Chopin rented an inferior instrument just so he could work; the Pleyel piano did not arrive until mid-January. Up to then he could only sketch the preludes, but with the better instrument he could polish and test his music more to his satisfaction. That month Chopin sent his finished manuscript to his copyist in Paris to prepare it for the publishers.

COMPOSING THE "RAINDROP" PRELUDE. Besides the lack of a good instrument, conditions on Majorca were miserable for Chopin. The natives showed resentment toward the vacationing Parisians. The weather was also unfriendly. Sickly and consumptive, Chopin benefited at first from the autumn sun, but he experienced the Majorca damp rainy season with great discomfort. That rain may have inspired one or more of the preludes, however. The incessant dripping of the rain off the roof of the former monastery where the party was staying could have made its way into the repeated notes and repetitive figures in four of the preludes: A Minor, E Minor, B Minor, and D-flat Major. However, the Prelude in D-flat Major, nicknamed the "Raindrop" Prelude, is generally thought to be most directly inspired by rain, chiefly because it has been associated with an anecdote George Sand wrote in her autobiography:

It was there [Majorca] he composed these most beautiful of short pages which he modestly entitled the Preludes. … There is one that came to him through an evening of dismal rain—it casts the soul into a terrible dejection. Maurice [her son] and I had left him in good health one morning to go shopping in Palma. … The rain came in overflowing torrents. … We hurried, knowing how our sick one would worry. Indeed he had, but now was as though congealed in a kind of quiet desperation, and, weeping, he was playing his wonderful Prelude. …

His genius was filled with the mysterious sounds of nature, but transformed into sublime equivalents in musical thought, and not through slavish imitation of the actual external

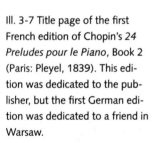

Ill. 3-7 Title page of the first French edition of Chopin's *24 Preludes pour le Piano*, Book 2 (Paris: Pleyel, 1839). This edition was dedicated to the publisher, but the first German edition was dedicated to a friend in Warsaw.

sounds. His composition of that night was surely filled with raindrops, resounding clearly on the tiles of the Charterhouse, but it had been transformed in his imagination and in his song into tears falling upon his heart from the sky. …

[Trans. Thomas Higgins in *Chopin, Preludes, Op. 28*, ed. by Thomas Higgins (New York: W.W. Norton, 1973), pp. 94–95.]

Exploring the "Raindrop" Prelude

Listen to the entire Prelude in D-flat Major. How many sections constitute the structural form of this piece? We hear three distinct sections in this piece. The third section closely resembles the first section but is shorter. We could call this form: A–B–A'. Another general term for a three-section form is "ternary" (binary = two sections; ternary = three sections).

Listen again from the beginning, through section A and into section B. What big differences does Chopin make in the music to set off section B? The most general change is one of *mood*. Specifically, the composer changes from the major mode in section A to the minor mode in section B. Another feature is the register. Chopin moves into a darker register of the piano for section B. *What musical factor remains constant during the change between sections A and B?* The repeated notes continue at the same pitch. As Ex. 3-17 shows, the repeated A-flats that begin and dominate section A are translated enharmonically to G-sharps (in the same octave) at the beginning of section B. Later in section B, they are sometimes doubled at the octave. *Subjective question: If section A symbolized light raindrops, does section B sound more like a storm?*

(a)

(b)

Ex. 3-17 Chopin, Prelude in D-flat Major, initial measures of sections A and B, showing the same repeated pitch (enharmonically): (a) m. 1; (b) m. 28.

Listen again to section A only. Notice that the pianist slows down and speeds up in the midst of phrases. What is this rhythmic liberty called? The term for this is *rubato* ("robbed"), because, figuratively, the performer "robs" time from a steady tempo. Often that time is "paid back" immediately or later by speeding up slightly.

Look at the first section of the "Raindrop" Prelude. What is this melody-and-accompaniment texture called? The general term is "homophony," but we call Chopin's particular song-like texture "nocturne texture," because his nocturnes all employ it.

Several 18th-century keyboard ornaments continued to be used in the Romantic era, especially by Chopin. (Recall his esteem for Bach and Mozart.) *In section A, find three written-out Baroque turn ornaments and identify the measures where they occur. (Hint: see Ex. 3-2 for the shape of a turn.)* The turns are found in m. 11, m. 15, and m. 17. Unlike Bach's turns, these are to be played *before* the beat. Another ornamental formation in Chopin is the *gruppetto*.

The "Raindrop" Prelude:
A Closer Look
Please refer to the score of Chopin's "Raindrop" prelude, beginning on page 19 of the Score Anthology.

gruppetto An ornamental group of notes.

This is an extraordinary number of melodic notes played within a single beat. In section A, the first gruppetto appears in m. 4 (last beat). *Find another gruppetto in section A and identify it by measure number. Do the same in section A' (mm. 76–89).* Gruppettos occur in m. 23 and m. 79, the latter shown here:

Looking further into the prelude, in what measure does section B begin, and into what key does the music move at that point? The change of key signature at m. 28 is one clue that section B begins there. The change from five flats to four sharps looks more radical than it is. Chopin has moved from D-flat major to C-sharp minor. Since D-flat equals C-sharp enharmonically, the change of mode is simply to the *parallel* minor key. Notice that besides the minor mode, the mood change is aided by the lower (darker) piano register and several details in the texture. *Identify a few of these textural details.* First is the low placement of melody in section B's opening measures:

Another feature is the replacement of repeated single notes and sometimes also the bass line with octaves:

Later in the section, Chopin employs thick-sounding chords:

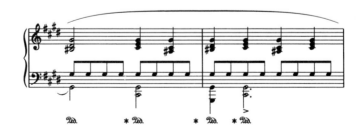

At the end of section B, the composer brings back a short version of section A to round out the form. *Compare section A' (beginning in m. 76) with the original section A.* With small **variants**, Chopin reprises the whole first phrase of A, and he begins the second phrase. However, at m. 81, that melody is broken off, and a two-measure transition (mm. 82–83) leads to a **coda** at m. 84, which completes the piece.

Stylized Dances

In the early Romantic period, Franz Schubert (1797–1828) contributed liberally to pianistic dance music. His minuets, *Ländler* or *Deutscher* (forerunners to the waltz), waltzes, *ecossaises*, and *galops* represent the social ballroom/parlor types of his day. Their musical value certainly warranted concert performances also, which is where we continue to hear these pieces today. By the next generation, the older types of dance had faded from popularity. Dancing in the home was still common, but many ballroom and folk dances written for the piano had become

variant A varied presentation of previously exposed musical material. See also **variation**.

coda A section at the end of a movement that brings the music to a conclusion.

Ill. 3-8 The first page from the first German edition of the Mazurka in A Minor, Op. 59, No. 1. The light double bar shows the beginning of the piece's second section, where a characteristic chromatic harmony shift occurs between the second and third measures.

stylized. These were purposely in undanceable tempos or contained virtuosic display inappropriate to supporting the dance. In brief, a wholly artistic dimension to dance music for the piano now appeared.

It was for Chopin to define the stylized dance, a type that comprises most of his solo piano pieces. He concentrated on three dances: the *waltz*, the *polonaise*, and the *mazurka*. Chopin's 17 waltzes often expanded the dance's usual size by adding introductions, codas, and more digressions from the main theme than usual in the ballroom. Some Chopin waltzes can actually be danced, but most cannot. This is usually due to their fast tempo, as in the famous "Minute" Waltz, Op. 34, No. 2. Polonaises and mazurkas were national dances from Chopin's homeland, Poland. Like the waltz, both of these were in 3/4 time. Chopin's greatest polonaises have a grandiose air, and he makes some of them into extended, virtuosic pieces, for example, the *Polonaise-Fantaisie*, Op. 61. The mazurka, on the other hand, was known to Europeans before Chopin as a parlor dance. He, however, used it to convey expressiveness, mood, and unusual rhythmic subtleties.

The Mazurka in G Minor, Op. 67, No. 2: A Stylized Dance

Chopin's Poland was the birthplace of the Mazurka, a folk dance for couples from the region of Mazovia near Warsaw. Peasants of that area were called *mazurs*, thus the name of the dance, mazurka. In Poland, the mazurka became popular in "polite" society in the 17th century. It spread to Germany in the early 18th century, and then to the rest of western Europe. In the early 19th century, the mazurka became a fashionable drawing-room dance in Paris. Thus it was well established by the time Chopin settled there.

TEMPO AND RHYTHM. Several musical characteristics are important in the mazurka. Tempos among mazurkas can vary widely, because originally three different types of mazurkas existed in Mazovia, differentiated partly by tempo. Rhythmically, mazurkas are interestingly varied. The dance is always in triple meter, but at various unpredictable points, an accent may fall on the second or third beat (normally unaccented parts of a measure). The dance itself had improvised moments, which could have produced similar surprises in the music. For that reason also, some of Chopin's mazurkas contain passages that sound spontaneous, or that slow down considerably, or are to be played very rubato. The G Minor Mazurka contains an eight-measure section for the right hand alone that might reflect an improvisational part of the dance.

FORM AND HARMONY. The mazurka's form was simple. It usually contained two or four sections, any of which could be repeated. Harmonically, the mazurkas could be fascinating. Often Chopin would temporarily put aside the major-minor harmonic system in favor of a modal scale. The most commonly used mode was the Lydian, a major scale with a raised fourth scale degree. Modes with a lowered seventh scale degree appeared occasionally. The modes were native to the *mazurs* but added an exotic flavor for Western listeners. Some native mazurkas freely altered normal scale tones, and that may have inspired Chopin to write some of his most chromatic melody and harmony in his mazurkas.

SCOPE. Chopin composed more mazurkas—58 in all—than any other type of piece. Also, he composed them throughout his career as a composer-pianist, the earliest dating from 1825 and the latest from his last months of life in 1849. Chopin preferred to publish his mazurkas in groups, usually three or four to a set. No established patterns of keys or tempos were employed. During his lifetime, the first 56 mazurkas came into print. **Posthumously**, eight more became known; three were early works (before 1830), two were from the year 1835, one from 1846, and two from his final year, 1849. In 1855, a Berlin publisher grouped them into two sets of four (not chronologically, however) and published them as Opp. 67 and 68. The Mazurka in G Minor became Op. 67, No. 2. However, it was the next-to-last mazurka Chopin composed.

NATIONALISM. The mazurkas and polonaises of Poland were already well known in western Europe by the time Chopin arrived there. No one, however, surpassed him in these types, which drew considerable attention both to Chopin and to Polish culture. His great body of mazurkas show a lifelong love for his homeland, and, although he was not a political activist, he did what he could to draw attention to Poland and its political condition during the 1830s.

The part of Poland where Chopin's Warsaw was located was ruled "in personal union with the czar of Russia." A Polish national revival led to a general insurrection there in 1830, the "November Uprising." It looked at first as if Poland would win independence. However, in 1831, Russian troops soundly defeated the Polish forces, reentered Warsaw, and made Poland virtually part of the Russian Empire. One can imagine how Chopin felt. Music became his means to heighten Europe's awareness of Poland as a unique cultural entity, not just an extension of Russia. His students and friends perceived this nationalistic aura about Chopin and his work, especially the mazurkas. His pupil Lenz conveyed his impression of Chopin's nationalistic feelings:

> Chopin's Mazurkas are the diary of his soul's journey through the socio-political territories of his Sarmatian dream-world! There, his playing was truly at home; *in them resided* Chopin's originality as a pianist. He represented Poland, *the land of his dreams*, in the Parisian salons … which *his* point of view allowed him to use as a political platform. Chopin was the *only political* pianist. He *incarnated* Poland, he *set* Poland *to music*!

Exploring Chopin's G Minor Mazurka

Listen to the entire mazurka and note its overall form. How many sections are there, and what is the pattern? This mazurka has four sections. After the first (A), the second (B) is formally repeated. Then C is a short section for one hand only. Finally Chopin brings back a reprise of the entire section A. Thus, the form of this mazurka could be represented:

A ‖: B B :‖ C A

Listen to section B again and count the beats of each measure to yourself, "1-2-3." Do the agogic (rhythmic) accents in the melody consistently fall on beat number one? (If necessary, see Chapter 2 to review agogic accents.) In some measures, a melodic long note comes on the downbeat. However, in many others a melodic *triplet* rhythm falls on several downbeats in the phrase, offsetting the agogic accent to the *second* beat of the measure:

Let's look at the issue of offset accents a little further. *In the first section, look at mm. 6–8. Does the score show us Chopin's intentions for accentuation?* In each of these measures, Chopin

posthumous Literally, after death, usually referring to music published or discovered after the composer's death. Adv.: posthumously.

The G Minor Mazurka:
A Closer Look

Please refer to the score of the Mazurka in G Minor, beginning on page 22 of the Score Anthology.

has added a dynamic accent (*sf*) on the *third* beat. The dynamics try to trick our ear into believing that the downbeat has actually shifted: 3-1-2, 3-1-2. At the same moment, the harmonic progression reinforces the imaginary downbeats. In reality, Chopin's harmony simply alternates between iv and i in the home key. The accented beat, however, falls on iv, and the *un*accented beat on i, a rather backward situation. It is as if the composer is inviting us to hear the progression another way in mm. 6–8:

The progression suggests a *modal* alternation between an "i" chord (on C) and its modal "v" chord (on G).

Other harmony in the G Minor Mazurka is very "Chopinesque." For example, the harmonic progression in mm. 21–25 is a chain of "secondary" dominant sevenths (root position) that soon wander out of the B-flat major orbit. *In mm. 21–25, trace the order of bass notes, writing the note name of each of them below the music.* You should have something like this:

G, C, F, B-flat, E-flat, A-flat, D-flat, G-flat

pitch class Any one of the 12 tones of the chromatic scale without regard to octave position.

What is this pattern of pitch classes called? The term is "circle of fifths." Carried to this extreme, it is a type of chromatic harmony. You can also find chromatic melody in this piece. *Examine m. 38. What melodic shape do you find?* The melody is built on a descending chromatic scale.

Finally, let's visually explore the structural form of this piece. *Find the beginning of each section of the mazurka. Mark it in your score, and also indicate the key in which it begins and how that key relates functionally to the home key of G minor.* Here is how the piece lays out:

MEASURE:	1	17	33	41
SECTION:	A	B (with repeat)	C	A
KEY:	g	B-flat	g	g
FUNCTION:	Tonic	Relative Major	Tonic	Tonic

The Concert Etude

Beginning with Beethoven's sonatas, piano technique became more demanding than ever. Special attention was required to address the development of specific figural techniques as well as more general ones like velocity. Piano pedagogues, such as Carl Czerny (1791–1857), addressed the development of technique by composing short *etudes*, that is, studies, each of which would concentrate on one or two individual techniques. However, these were usually dry-sounding, suitable for the practice studio but not for audiences. It remained for the next generation to write etudes that both developed technique and were pieces of art.

Chopin was the consummate composer of concert etudes. In these pieces he presented a complete picture of what the Romantic piano virtuoso ought to be, technically and artistically. Each of his etudes usually addresses just one technical problem—or one problem in each hand. However, each is also imbued with high artistic value—high enough that such an etude could be played successfully on a concert program. Chopin himself performed many of them in public.

The Etude in A Minor, Op. 25, No. 11: A Concert Etude

Chopin composed 27 etudes in all, the most famous being the two sets of 12 he published as Op. 10 (1833) and Op. 25 (1837). Although he did not organize the order of keys as systematically as he did in the Preludes, Op. 28, he did juxtapose some etudes in relative major-minor keys, particularly in Op. 10. There, for example, we have:

NO.	KEY	NO.	KEY
1	C Major	2	A Minor
3	E Major	4	C-sharp Minor
5	G-flat Major	6	E-flat Minor
9	F Minor	10	A-flat Major
11	E-flat Major	12	C Minor

Many etudes have received nicknames, though none from Chopin himself. The more common nicknames reveal the technical problem exercised in the etude, for example:

Op. 10, No. 5	"Black keys"
Op. 25, No. 6	"Double thirds"
Op. 25, No. 8	"Double sixths"
Op. 25, No. 10	"Octaves"

Chopin addressed more general problems of technique and interpretation in other etudes (without nicknames), for example:

Op. 10, No. 1	Wide-ranging right-hand **arpeggios**
Op. 10, No. 9	Extended left-hand figuration
Op. 10, No. 11	Widely spaced, rolled chords
Op. 25, No. 4	Wide left-hand skips

arpeggio Broken chord.

Certain of the etudes have become known by programmatic nicknames that suggest the effect or mood of the piece rather than its technical problem:

Op. 10, No. 12, "Revolutionary"	Turbulent in spirit.
Op. 25, No. 1, "Aeolian Harp"	Intricate arpeggios in both hands simultaneously.
Op. 25, No. 9, "Butterfly"	Light, fluttering figuration.
Op. 25, No. 11, "Winter Wind"	Forceful melody in one hand and an effect suggesting a sweeping wind in the other.
Op. 25, No. 12, "Ocean"	Rapid parallel motion in wave-shape melodic patterns.

Three of the etudes are slow, making sensitive interpretive demands on the player. The improvisational, **rhapsodic** left-hand part in Op. 25, No. 7, plays against a countermelody in the right, with a steady accompaniment in the middle:

rhapsody Free fantasy, often employing virtuosic techniques. Adj.: rhapsodic.

Op. 10, Nos. 3 and 6, test the player's ability to bring out a treble melody while playing a full-bodied accompaniment below. The E Major Etude (Op. 10, No. 3) contains one of Chopin's most beautiful and famous melodies:

Important as the etudes are to developing pianistic techniques, their high quality *as music* has assured them a treasured place in music literature. In his text on keyboard literature, Stewart Gordon summarizes this point well for listeners and performers:

> The quality that has made these etudes so important in the literature, however, is their unsurpassed musical interest and refinement, often combined with a wonderful sense of dramatic excitement…. Thus, meeting and conquering the technical difficulties of these etudes is rewarded with a finished product that is both musically valuable and pleasing to audiences.

[Stewart Gordon, *A History of Keyboard Literature* (New York: Schirmer Books, 1996), p. 286.]

Listen to the etude. Subjective question: For you, does this piece live up to its nickname, "Winter Wind"? The slow introduction's solo melody has been likened to the tolling of bells. *Another subjective question: Does it sound like that to you?*

Objective question: Does the slow introduction serve a musical function? Both the solo melody and the following harmonized phrase introduce the chief motive of the melody heard next. *Listen to about 30 seconds of the main, fast part of the etude. What type of technique would you say is being tested in the right hand? In the left?* The right hand executes a constant rapid figuration that sweeps down and back up the keyboard. The left hand employs the important technique of playing both a bass line and a strong melody. *Listen to the rest of the piece. Does the composer ever reverse these two roles (placing melody above and figuration below)? Are there any times when both hands play rapid figuration simultaneously?* Yes, to both questions. You will find these places in the score during the next section of study.

Beginning in m. 4, look closely at the right-hand figuration. You can easily see that it rapidly rocks back and forth between upper and lower notes. *Now, examine just the upper notes in mm. 4–8 (third beat). How would you describe this shape?* Although the varying intervals between the upper and lower notes disguise it, all the upper notes form a long descending chromatic scale, running nearly three octaves:

You have already heard the hands reverse the roles in figuration and melody. Now find the one place in the score where this occurs. It happens for a brief, four-measure passage in mm. 41–44. *In the score, find two places where both hands execute figuration (with no melody).* The first occurrence begins in m. 61 and lasts until m. 68. Again, as Chopin brings the piece toward its climactic ending, the music for both hands is figural: from m. 85 through m. 92.

The A Minor Etude:
A Closer Look
Please refer to the score of the Etude in A Minor, beginning on page 24 of the Score Anthology.

𝄢 C H A P T E R   F O U R

Song

The literature of song and vocal chamber music heard in today's concert and recital halls is of relatively recent vintage. Similar to many instrumental repertoires, most of the current vocal repertoire runs from the 18th century to the present with a heavy emphasis on 19th-century music. In this chapter, we will trace this later growth through three important works by Schubert, Fauré, and Ives.

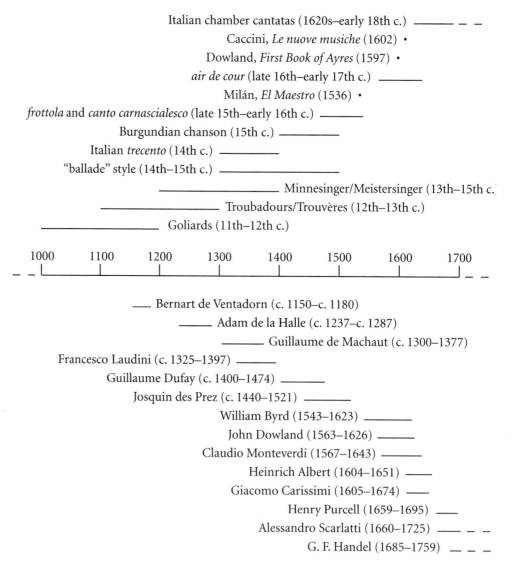

Ex. 4-1 Time line of Song and Vocal Chamber Music History: Middle Ages through Baroque period: 18th–19th centuries (p. 95); 20th century (p. 96).

Italian chamber cantatas (1620s–early 18th c.) ——— _ _

Caccini, *Le nuove musiche* (1602) •

Dowland, *First Book of Ayres* (1597) •

air de cour (late 16th–early 17th c.) ———

Milán, *El Maestro* (1536) •

frottola and *canto carnascialesco* (late 15th–early 16th c.) ———

Burgundian chanson (15th c.) ———

Italian *trecento* (14th c.) ———

"ballade" style (14th–15th c.) ———

——— Minnesinger/Meistersinger (13th–15th c.)

——— Troubadours/Trouvères (12th–13th c.)

——— Goliards (11th–12th c.)

| 1000 | 1100 | 1200 | 1300 | 1400 | 1500 | 1600 | 1700 |

—— Bernart de Ventadorn (c. 1150–c. 1180)

——— Adam de la Halle (c. 1237–c. 1287)

——— Guillaume de Machaut (c. 1300–1377)

Francesco Laudini (c. 1325–1397) ———

Guillaume Dufay (c. 1400–1474) ———

Josquin des Prez (c. 1440–1521) ———

William Byrd (1543–1623) ———

John Dowland (1563–1626) ———

Claudio Monteverdi (1567–1643) ———

Heinrich Albert (1604–1651) ——

Giacomo Carissimi (1605–1674) ——

Henry Purcell (1659–1695) ——

Alessandro Scarlatti (1660–1725) —— _ _

G. F. Handel (1685–1759) _ _ _

Although the modern body of literature comes from recent centuries, the foundations for it are very old. The antecedents of modern song go back to Middle-Ages sacred and secular song. The Renaissance favored vocal ensemble music over song. Overshadowed by opera in the Baroque period, song reemerged in the late 18th century along with new Classical aesthetics. Because of differences in language and culture, song literature has divided naturally. Art song composers such as Schubert set standards for the Romantic German *Lied*, then song literature in the French and English languages followed with their own variants.

Lied A solo art song in German with keyboard accompaniment. Plural: Lieder.

SCHUBERT, "ERLKÖNIG"

German Art Song before Schubert

Opera cast a long shadow in the early 18th century, obscuring the growth of the independent art song. The greatest vocal composers of the late Baroque were Handel and J.S. Bach. Bach poured his loftiest vocal chamber music into movements of his choral works such as sacred cantatas, and Handel's chief vocal outlets were the arias in his Italian operas and later his opera-influenced oratorios. Bach's touchingly intimate *basso continuo* song, "Bist du bei mir" from Anna Magdalena Bach's *Clavierbüchlein*, is even more precious because of its uniqueness in his music.

Bach's son Carl Philipp Emanuel (C.P.E.), on the other hand, was a song composer among other significant accomplishments. C.P.E. Bach was the first among the "Berlin School."

Debussy, *chansons de bilitis* (1899) ·
Fauré, *La bonne chanson* (1894) ·
Wolf, *Spanische Liederbuch* (1891) ·
Brahms, *Vergebliches Ständchen* (c. 1881) ·
Duparc, *L'Invitation du voyage* (1870) ·
Schumann, *Dichterliebe* (1840) ·
· Schubert, *Winterreise* (1827)
· Beethoven, *An die ferne Geliebte* (1816)
· Schubert, *Erlkönig* (1815)
· Mozart, *Das Veilchen* (1785)

1700	1800	1900

C. P. E. Bach (1714–1788)
Wolfgang Amadeus Mozart (1756–1791)
Carl Zelter (1758–1832)
Ludwig van Beethoven (1770–1827)
Franz Schubert (1797–1828)
Robert Schumann (1810–1856)
Charles Gounod (1818–1897)
Johannes Brahms (1833–1897)
Gabriel Fauré (1845–1924)
Hugo Wolf (1860-1903)
Claude Debussy (1862–1918)

Crumb, *Ancient Voices of Children* (1970) •

Davies, *8 Songs for a Mad King* (1969) •

Rorem, *Poems of Love and the Rain* (1963) •

Boulez, *Le Marteau sans maître*, rev. version (1957) •

Stravinsky, *3 Songs from Wm Shakespeare* (1953) •

Copland, *12 Poems of Emily Dickinson* (1950) •

• Britten, *Serenade* (1943)

• Messiaen, *Poemes pour Mi* (1937)

• Barber, *Dover Beach* (1933)

• Ravel, *Chansons de medécasses* (1926)

— Hindemith, *Das Marienleben*, 1st version (1922–1923)

• Warlock, *The Curfew* (1922)

• Ives, *114 Songs* published (1922)

• Poulenc, *Le Bestiaire* (1919)

• Schoenberg, *Pierrot Lunaire* (1912)

• Vaughan Williams, *On Wenlock Edge* (1909)

1900	1925	1950	1975	2000

Ralph Vaughn Williams (1872–1958)

Charles E. Ives (1874–1954)

Arnold Schoenberg (1874–1951)

Igor Stravinsky (1882–1971)

Peter Warlock (1894–1930)

Francis Poulenc (1899–1963)

Samuel Barber (1910–1981)

Benjamin Britten (1913–1976)

Ned Rorem (1923–)

Pierre Boulez (1925–)

George Crumb (1929–)

ballad An early Romantic type of German *Lied* based loosely on popular ballads of England and Scotland. Besides Schubert, Johann Zumsteeg (1760–1802) and Carl Loewe (1796–1869) excelled at ballad composition.

Toward the end of the 18th century, Johann Schulz (1747–1800) and Johann Friedrich Reichardt (1752–1814) also became prominent Berlin song composers. This group favored simple, natural melodies—some in folk-song style—and an unobtrusive keyboard accompaniment, often consisting of mere block chords. Another important Berlin composer of the time was Carl Zelter (1758–1832), whose *Lieder* on poetry by Johann Wolfgang von Goethe (1749–1832) that poet preferred. Songs in a more advanced style, such as Zelter's "Am Mitternacht" (text by Goethe), employed an independent piano accompaniment and expressive harmonies that looked forward to the *Lieder* of Schubert. Johann Zumsteeg (1760–1802) was another influence on Schubert, especially regarding the **ballad**.

Franz Peter Schubert was born into a middle-class Vienna family on January 31, 1797. His father was master of a school he ran out of his home. Franz learned the violin from his father and the piano from his brother, Ignaz. He soon outstripped them both as his prodigious talent began to develop. From a parish organist, the boy received organ and voice lessons and probably also counterpoint instruction when he was nine or ten.

In 1808, young Schubert became a soprano choirboy in the Imperial Court Chapel, and with his duties came a formal education. He also played violin in the student orchestra, where he met Josef von Spaun, eight years his senior. Their close friendship lasted the composer's entire lifetime. Schubert's vast musical gifts caused the school's chief music teacher to exclaim, "This one has learned from God!" Those gifts also attracted the attention of Antonio Salieri (the villain of the fictional play and film *Amadeus*, but actually a kind man), with whom Schubert began to study composition in 1811. Some of Schubert's earliest works stem from 1810–1813. He composed piano music, chamber music, and his first songs. His earliest string quartets of 1811–1814 were intended for the family quartet.

When Schubert's voice broke in 1813, he continued his schooling for awhile, but at the same time he began training to become an elementary teacher in his father's school. By autumn 1814, he was an assistant to his father, a job he held for four years, detesting it the whole time. Meanwhile, Schubert composed—with that lightning speed he always had—his first five symphonies, his first attempts at opera, and a plethora of songs. (In 1815 alone, he wrote more than 140 songs, including the famous "Erlkönig.") He composed because of an inner drive to do so, not because a patron or publisher wanted his music. The first time he earned money for a composition was in 1816 for his cantata *Prometheus*. The fee was about $50.

While Schubert was still a schoolteacher, he began developing the circle of friends and supporters with whom he would socialize (and usually live) throughout the rest of his life. Von Spaun's lodgings were the hub of activities surrounding the composer, the place where, on a given evening, a *Schubertiad* might take place. That was a sociable, private concert devoted to the music of Schubert, the composer being at the center of the music making. Another musician often seen and heard at Schubertiads was Johann Michael Vogl, a prominent baritone, who become Schubert's chief song interpreter and a close friend. Schubert's circle of friends promoted his music and even tried to get it published.

The year 1818 saw two important events in Schubert's life. One was his public debut as a composer, when one of his "Italian" Overtures was performed in a restaurant concert hall in March (then repeated in May). The second event was his break with schoolteaching to become a full-time composer. For obscure Schubert, that meant living a "**bohemian**" life: seldom having money, living with friends, and spending much time in cafés. The life agreed with Schubert, however, and he brought joy to those around him; a member of the circle commented: "We were the happiest people in Germany—no, in the world!" Schubert and Vogl's walking tour of Steyr (northeast Austria) the summer of 1819 was a high point. There he began his famous "Trout" Quintet for piano and strings based on his song "Die Forelle" ("The Trout"), which had become popular since its creation in 1817.

(continued)

FRANZ SCHUBERT

Copperplate engraving by J. H. Passini from Rieder's Aquarell, on sale in Vienna, December 1825. Historisches Museum der Stadt Wien.

bohemian An old slang term for alternate lifestyles, often associated with the avant-garde in the arts. "Bohemia" in this context, therefore, did not mean the central European country but any bohemian neighborhood, such as Greenwich Village in the first half of the 20th century.

lyric, lyrical Melodious or song-like.

Singspiel An opera in German from the 18th or early 19th century. Singspielen were usually comic and used spoken dialogue between musical numbers.

song cycle A group of songs unified by a literary theme or story line. A song cycle is, therefore, distinct from a collection or anthology of songs.

FRANZ SCHUBERT *(continued)*

Employment opportunities were rare for Schubert, but an important one came from the Esterházy family (former patrons of Haydn) to serve as music tutor to the Count's children. The composer repeated this service in 1824.

Schubert always wanted to "break into" opera, as attested by his 16 settings of opera librettos. With his immense **lyrical** gifts, opera might have been a wonderful outlet for him. However, two things were against him. The first was the craze for Rossini, which first gripped Vienna in 1816 and never let up. Schubert wrote German opera—in style and language—not Italian. Thus, it was impossible for him to compete. The second problem was that Schubert could never find even a *good* libretto to work with, never mind a great one. So his operatic works were doomed to failure. In 1820, Schubert's one-act **Singspiel**, *Die Zwillingsbrüder*, was produced—nearly the only performances of his operatic music during his lifetime. On the positive side, the production gave Schubert visibility and enlarged his following in Vienna.

The greatest mystery of Schubert's life is his extraordinarily beautiful torso of a Symphony No. 8, "The Unfinished." Why he completed only two movements and a sketch for the third in 1822 has never been satisfactorily explained. The final movement may have been lost or Schubert may never have written it. The best evidence favors the latter theory, because Schubert left several projects around this time. On top of that, 1822 was the year Schubert contracted syphilis, and the resulting illness produced psychological and financial chaos. Depressed and hospitalized part of the time, he nonetheless continued to compose, overcoming his problems to create his first **song cycle**, *Die schöne Müllerin* (*The Pretty Mill-Maid*), in 1823.

Gradually Schubert recovered, beginning to gain recognition through publications and turning his hand again to chamber music. One notable result was the 1824 String Quartet in D Minor with second-movement variations based on the piano part to his 1817 song "Der Tod und das Mädchen" ("Death and the Maiden"). The years 1825–1826 were even more productive for Schubert, and his reputation continued to flower proportionately. Piano music flowed from his pen, and it appears that 1825 also saw the first sketches of his Ninth Symphony (the "Great" in C Major). He began to receive more public performances of his music, especially songs.

Schubert started his second (and last) song cycle, *Winterreise* (*Winter Journey*), in February 1827. The following month he visited Beethoven on his deathbed. Living his life in Beethoven's shadow, the timid Schubert had never before ventured to meet the master. This occasion may have resulted from Beethoven looking over some of his songs, though there is no proof that Beethoven ever experienced any of Schubert's music.

Beethoven died two weeks after the meeting, and about that time Schubert's own health began to fail. The completion of *Winterreise* in the spring marks the beginning of Schubert's last creative phase. The flood of masterpieces he produced, especially during 1828—and the promise of what he might later have written—make his early death even more tragic. Completion of the "Great" C Major Symphony topped the list. Two piano trios, the String Quintet in C Major, and his last three piano sonatas crowned Schubert's achievements in chamber music and keyboard composition. The Mass in E-flat Major and several remarkable songs rounded out his vocal production. The only public concert devoted exclusively to Schubert's works was given on March 26, 1828, under the sponsorship of his friends. It went unreviewed.

Schubert died on November 19, 1828. The cause of death has been variously attributed to typhus or syphilis; however, what we have of incomplete medical records seems to rule out either. It was only after death that Schubert began to gain recognition. In 1829 a publisher released a collection of his last songs as *Schwanengesang (Swan Song)*—a title Schubert never gave to them). A decade after Schubert's passing, Robert Schumann discovered the score to the "Great" C Major Symphony among some manuscripts owned by Schubert's brother. The world premiere of that masterpiece took place in 1839, but the "Unfinished" Symphony and String Quintet had to wait until the 1860s to be heard. Already long established as the premier *Lied* composer, Schubert now took his place also among the masters of instrumental music. Schubert was an early Romantic composer whose genius was recognized only in time to influence late Romantic composers such as Brahms, Dvořák, and Mahler.

Schubert as a Song Composer

Franz Schubert composed in every musical genre except the concerto. However, masterful as he was in such areas as symphony, chamber music, church music, and even opera, his genius manifested itself most fully in the German *Lied.* The intimacy and immediacy of these art songs not only complimented his particular gifts for melody and harmony, they also reflected his congenial lifestyle, where performance opportunities occurred at intimate gatherings of friends rather than public concerts. Thus, Schubert's fame rests chiefly on the more than 600 songs he composed in his short lifetime. He invented neither the *Lied* nor the song cycle, but his individual songs and cycles became the leading examples of these genres for nearly a century of German art-song composers.

At the heart of Schubert's talent was his gift for melody. Always lyrical, always singable, the Schubertian melody captures the full emotional and poetic content of the text. Many of Schubert's melodies are "catchy," either in the folk-song manner of "Heidenröslein" ("Little Hedge-

Ill. 4-1 Schubert Evening at Joseph von Spaun's (sepia drawing by Moritz von Schwind). Schubert is at the piano, Johann Michael Vogl is on his right, and von Spaun is on his left. Historisches Museum der Stadt Wien.

Rose," text by Wolfgang Goethe) or in the classic manner of his famous "Ave Maria" (Ellen's third song from *Lady of the Lake*, a novel by Sir Walter Scott.).

Piano accompaniments to Schubert's songs are what most clearly separate them from earlier German *Lieder*. Schubert used the power of music both to paint a picture and to evoke emotion. Through accompaniment patterns and harmonic color, he expressed both the outer (graphic) and inner (emotional) interpretation of the poetry. For example, the accompaniment to "Gretchen am Spinnrade" ("Gretchen at the Spinning Wheel," text by Wolfgang Goethe) portrays the continuous whirring of the spinning wheel (Ex. 4-2), yet it also expresses Gretchen's turbulent thoughts.

Ex. 4-2 Opening measures of "Gretchen am Spinnrade."

The German *Lied* at the time of Schubert was closely related to traditions of the German folk song. Much of the contemporary poetry consciously emulated (or imitated) folk **lyrics** both in content and form. The procedure most favored in folk lyrics is stanzaic: a series of strophes of equal length and meter. Schubert did not outgrow or discard **strophic** form; it is in his "An Silvia" ("Who is Silvia?," text by Shakespeare in German adaptation) composed in the last year of his life. Schubert did not limit himself to that form, however, but explored wider territory determined by what a poem might suggest to him. In each of his songs, Schubert followed one of the following formal procedures:

Strophic: Schubert applied only minor variants to the melody to accommodate different word accentuations in different strophes. In keeping with the folk tradition, many strophic Schubert songs have simple, chordal accompaniments, often in imitation of a guitar (then considered a quasi-folk instrument). An example is "Heidenröslein" ("Little Hedge-Rose," text by Goethe) (see Ex. 4-3).

lyrics Words, usually poetic, set to music.

strophic The form of song composition where each verse (or strophe) of text is set to the same music.

Ex. 4-3 Opening measures of "Heidenröslein."

Modified Strophic: Schubert sometimes retained elements of cyclic strophic design, while varying others. In "Gretchen am Spinnrade," the composer kept the size and shape of each strophe the same while altering features in the melody and the accompaniment's harmony. In "Die Forelle" ("The Trout," text by Christian Friedrich Schubart), he composed the first two strophes identically, then digressed into a more dramatic style for a time, but finally returned to a reminiscence of the opening strophe.

Through-composed: In this procedure, melodic patterns may change and recur at will.

Although melodic regularity is avoided, the accompaniment achieves unification by remaining similar throughout. Schubert's most notable example is "Erlkönig" ("Elf King," text by Goethe).

Dramatic scena: As in a scene of opera, the tempos, melodies, accompaniments, and moods in this type of song can change often. Usually containing dialogue, a *scena* commonly employs recitatives. A famous example is "Der Tod und das Mädchen" ("Death and the Maiden," text by Matthias Claudius).

Schubert was born at a time when German-speaking peoples were experiencing a rebirth of culture. The German language was elevated to higher standards than ever, and in the late 18th century there was an explosion of literature and poetry. Writers such as Wolfgang Goethe and Friedrich Schiller were the founders of the movement. Many minor poets, including friends of Schubert, followed them. Schubert set to music poetry by many different German poets and by Shakespeare, then being published in German for the first time. Much of the poetry Schubert used was not of a high quality, but his music made it sound better than it actually was. This is the case with his two song cycles, *Die schöne Müllerin* and *Winterreise*, both based on poetic cycles by Wilhelm Müller. Scholars have criticized Schubert for his wide range of taste in poetry. However, he chose his texts not for their literary value as much as for two other attributes: immediate aural comprehension and musical possibilities.

"Erlkönig": Background

Goethe occupies a position in German literature roughly parallel to that of Shakespeare in English letters. As a novelist, poet, dramatist, and scientist, Goethe influenced German art and thought for more than a century. His most famous work, *Faust* (a philosophical dramatic poem), fired the imaginations of many Romantic composers and artists, and it remains among the greatest monuments of literature in Western civilization.

Goethe's lifetime saw the birth of pride in folklore among the German-speaking peoples. Through publications such as *Grimm's Fairy Tales*, Brentano and von Arnim's *Des Knaben Wunderhorn* (*The Youth's Magic Horn*), and Johann Herder's translations of foreign folk songs, the simple, straightforward style and messages of folk poetry also became an inspiration to early modern German poets. Goethe and many others were moved to write their own "folk" poetry characterized by the uncomplicated manner and moral messages of the originals. The ballad was a story-telling poetic genre drawn from folklore that held Goethe's attention. Made famous through song settings by Reichardt, Löwe, and Schubert, "Erlkönig" ("Elf King") became Goethe's most outstanding ballad. Originally written for the first act of a 1782 Singspiel, the text of "Erlkönig" runs:

Wer reitet so spät durch Nacht und Wind?	Who rides there so late through the night dark and drear?
Es ist der Vater mit seinem Kind;	The father it is, with his infant so dear;
Er hat den Knaben wohl in dem Arm,	He holdeth the boy tightly clasped in his arm,
Er fasst ihn sicher, er hält ihn warm.	He holdeth him safely, he keepeth him warm.
"Mein Sohn, was birgst du so bang dein Gesicht?"	"My son, wherefore seek'st thou thy face thus to hide?"
"Siehst, Vater, du den Erlkönig nicht?	"Look, father, the Elf King is close by our side!

102

SONG

Den Erlenkönig mit Kron und Schweif?"	Dost see not the Elf King, with crown and with train?"
"Mein Sohn, es ist ein Nebelstreif."	"My son, 'tis the mist rising over the plain."
"Du liebes Kind, komm, geh mit mir!	"Oh come, thou dear infant! oh come thou with me!
Gar schöne Spiele spiel ich mit dir;	Full many a game I will play there with thee;
Manch bunte Blumen sind an dem , Strand	On my strand, lovely flowers their blossoms unfold,
Meine Mutter had manch gülden Gewand."	My mother shall grace thee with garments of gold."
"Mein Vater, mein Vater, und hörest du nicht,	"My father, my father, and doest thou not hear
Was Erlenkönig mir leise verspricht?"	The words that the Elf King now breathes in mine ear?"
"Sei ruhig, bleibe ruhig, mein Kind:	"Be calm, dearest child, 'tis thy fancy deceives;
In dürren Blättern säuselt der Wind."	'Tis the sad wind that sighs through the withering leaves."
"Willst, feiner Knabe, du mit mir gehn?	"Wilt go, then, dear infant, wilt go with me there?
Meine Töchter sollen dich warten schön;	My daughters shall tend thee with sisterly care;
Meine Töchter führen den nächtlichen Reihn	My daughters by night their glad festival keep,
Und wiegen und tanzen und singen dich ein."	They'll dance thee, and rock thee, and sing thee to sleep."
"Mein Vater, mein Vater, und siehst du nicht dort	"My father, my father, and dost thou not see,
Erlkönigs Töchter am düstern Ort?"	How the Elf King his daughters has brought here for me?"
"Mein Soh, mein Sohn, ich seh es genau:	"My darling, my darling, I see it aright,
Es scheinen die alten Weiden so grau."	'Tis the aged gray willows deceiving thy sight."
"Ich liebe dich, mich reizt deine schöne Gestalt;	"I love thee, I'm charmed by thy beauty, dear boy!
Und bist du nicht willig, so brauch ich Gewalt."	And if thou'rt unwilling, then force I'll employ."
"Mein Vater, mein Vater, jetzt fasst er mich an!	"My father, my father, he seizes me fast,

Erlkönig hat mir ein Leids getan!"	Full sorely the Elf King has hurt me at last."
Dem Vater grausets, er reitet geschwind,	The father now gallops, with terror half wild,
Er hält in Armen das ächzende Kind,	He grasps in his arms the poor shuddering child:
Erreicht den Hof mit Mühe und Not:	He reaches his courtyard with toil and with dread,—
In seinen Armen das Kind war tot.	The child in his arms finds he motionless, dead.

[Metrical, rhymed translation by E.A. Bowring, published 1882; edited slightly by Michael Fink.]

The origin of the "Erlkönig" tale is Danish rather than German. In the folk ballad "Sir Olaf," a knight on the way to his wedding encounters the Elf King's daughter in a wood. She entrances him with wonderful promises, then kills him. Goethe no doubt knew the German translation of this poem by his friend Herder. One evening Goethe witnessed a man riding by his gate at full gallop. He later learned that the man was a farmer rushing his sick child to the doctor. The great poet then synthesized "Sir Olaf" and the real-life incident into his own ballad, "Erlkönig."

Schubert set 59 of Goethe's poems to music, some several times. In 1815 alone, Schubert composed "Erlkönig" and 25 other songs to texts by Goethe. Schubert's friend Josef von Spaun later described how the 18-year-old composer wrote "Erlkönig" in his father's home in October 1815:

> … We found Schubert all aglow, reading the "Erlkönig" aloud from the book. He paced up and down several times with the book, suddenly he sat down and in no time at all (just quickly as one can write) there was the glorious Ballad finished on paper. We ran with it to the seminary, for there was no pianoforte at Schubert's, and there, on the very same evening, "Erlkönig" was sung and enthusiastically received.

[Otto Erich Deutsch, ed., *Schubert: Memoirs by his Friends* (London: A. & C. Black, 1958) p. 131.]

Ill. 4-2 Woodcut, c. 1840, inspired by "Erlkönig." A streak of mist appears behind the father, and the willows on the right resemble human forms.

The following year, von Spaun tried to obtain an endorsement for Schubert by sending Goethe a group of songs Schubert had composed on his poetry. Goethe never replied. The version of "Erlkönig" in this group had a simplified piano accompaniment, and Goethe must have heard it, for he wrote following a performance in 1830, "I have heard this composition once before, when it did not appeal to me at all. However, sung this way, the whole shapes itself into a visible picture."

"Erlkönig" was among the first songs Schubert attempted to publish. In 1817 he sent it to Breitkopf & Härtel in Leipzig. They were not the least interested and mistakenly returned the packet to another Franz Schubert in Dresden, who was insulted at someone else using his name. However, interest in the song generated by prestigious and successful performances in 1820 and 1821 led to its publication. Some of Schubert's friends pooled their money to pay the Viennese publisher Diabelli to print "Erlkönig" as Schubert's Opus 1. Within 18 months, 300 copies were sold, and Diabelli was already publishing more of Schubert's songs. Suddenly Schubert became a recognized and popular *Lied* composer. The fame of "Erlkönig" grew during the 19th century, making it one of Schubert's most celebrated songs.

Exploring "Erlkönig"

VISUAL AND PSYCHOLOGICAL SCENE SETTING. Much has been written about the galloping sound of the repeated notes in the piano accompaniment, suggesting a picture of the father riding as fast as possible, clutching his son. That is the *external* picture we get from the opening of the song. However, this music also portrays an *internal*, psychological picture. The father's emotional anxiety and anguish over his child's condition is the most obvious idea. *Listen to the song's piano introduction.* The repeated notes also give the piano part a "daemonic drive," according to Schubert authority John Reed. We could further make a case for the higher repeated notes representing the galloping horse and the lower melody signifying the father's feelings (see Ex. 4-4).

Ex. 4-4 "Erlkönig," mm. 1–3.

DRAMATIC ELEMENTS. The poem is a dramatic scene including a narrator (who presents a prologue and an epilogue to the scene) and three characters: the father, the child, and the Elf King. *Listen to the entire song and notice the vocal differences between the four personages.* Schubert differentiates the characters most clearly by differences in vocal **tessitura**. The narrator has the widest tessitura. The father's tessitura is low during his first two statements, when he is trying to calm and reassure the child. During his third statement, the tessitura extends upward, possibly showing his growing worry. The child's voice has a medium-high tessitura at first, but it moves higher with each outcry. The first two statements by the Elf King are in a medium tessitura. When he loses patience in the third statement ("I love you, your fair form allures me,/And if you don't come willingly, I'll use force."), the tessitura extends upward slightly. This is a very challenging song to perform, since it requires the singer's voice to express four different persons. The narrator's part must sound dramatic yet objective. The father's voice must be dark in relation to the other characters'. The high child's voice might be sung

tessitura The portion of a pitch range used most consistently in a passage or a work, as opposed to the total range.

with a "straight" tone, lacking **vibrato**. The Elf King's voice is mostly light and as full of charm as possible in his first two statements, but his sinister intent must be revealed in the third. He takes three different approaches: At first, he tries to woo the child with fantastic promises of games and beautiful sights. Next he tries seduction, offering his daughters to do the child's bidding. Finally his real nature comes out as he threatens (and then uses) force.

KEY RELATIONSHIPS.   The choice and order of keys in a Schubert song (or instrumental movement) is significant and usually colorful. This song begins in G minor. *See mm. 50–54, where the harmony is V–I in the closely related key of B-flat.* The father is reassuring the child for the first time here. The second time the father speaks *(see m. 81 with* **upbeat***)*, Schubert establishes the distant key of B minor, but then moves to C major as the Elf King speaks for the second time *(see m. 87 with upbeat)*. Thus far, the music has reflected the child's terror in passages of unstable harmony (mm. 73–79 and 98–104). *Notice how, in m. 106, Schubert shows the father's growing agitation through modulating harmony (beginning in the very distant key of C-sharp minor).* At the end of the father's statement, the music starts returning to the home key by reaching the key of D minor. *(see m. 112)*. The home key of G minor is not reached, however, until the child's last syllable (m. 131), which also initiates the music to the narrator's epilogue.

VARIANTS IN THE PIANO ACCOMPANIMENT: THE ELF KING. *Find the Elf King's entrances on the upbeats to mm. 58, 87, and 117.* Under the first of these speeches, the piano changes texture subtly by alternating bass notes on the beats in the left hand with offbeat chords in the right. *See m. 87, where again there is a change, as the piano plays broken chords in the right hand against bass notes on each beat in the left.* These variants in the accompaniment underline the charm the Elf King wishes to project. When he makes his final appearance *(see upbeat to m. 117)*, however, his violent intent shows in the continually hammering chords in the right hand—no more charm now!

EMOTION IN "MEIN VATER, MEIN VATER." We hear "Mein Vater, mein Vater" in mm. 73, 97, and 124 (with upbeats). See Ex. 4-5 a, b, and c.

"Erlkönig":
A Closer Look
Please refer to the score of "Erlkönig," beginning on page 31 of the Score Anthology.

vibrato Slight, rapid fluctuations of pitch and/or intensity applied to sustained notes.

upbeat One or more notes that come before the first full measure of a phrase. More technically termed an "anacrusis;" sometimes called a "pickup."

(a)

Mein Va - ter, mein Va - ter,

(b)

Mein Va - ter, mein Va - ter,

(c)

Mein Va - ter, mein Va - ter,

Ex. 4-5 "Erlkönig," (a) m. 73, (b) m. 97, (c) m. 124 (with upbeats).

Find these places in the score. Each time, a minor-second dissonance occurs between the voice and the piano's right-hand notes. *What is the voice's starting note at each occurrence?* Starting notes are D, E, and F, respectively. The rising pitch shows the child's rising terror, an effect that also invites increased tension in vocal quality each time it moves higher.

QUASI OPERA AT THE END. Just before the last line of the poem, the relentless rhythm of the piano part stops suddenly on a chord. The final measures *(see mm. 146–148)* are marked "*Recit.*" This designation is short for "Recitative" (or in Italian, *Recitativo*), and it derives from operatic recitation (see Chapter 2). Using this technique at the song's conclusion gives a stark yet dramatic interpretation of the poem's shocking climax, when the child is dead.

German Art Song after Schubert

Schubert was a deep influence on German *Lied* composers throughout the Romantic period. Robert Schumann (1810–1856), beyond his vast lyrical gifts, took *Lied* textures a step further than Schubert by making the piano more of an equal partner with the voice. In many of Schumann's *Lieder*, the voice ends on an inconclusive chord, leaving the completion of the song to the piano. Schumann's protégé, Johannes Brahms (1833–1897), inherited his mentor's love of song, but Brahms's *Lieder* are closer to those of Schubert in some respects. Many Brahms *Lieder* are like folk songs, and he favored a technically challenging piano part that is always subordinate to the voice. One of Brahms's lighter songs is his setting of the folk poem "Vergebliches Ständchen" ("Useless Serenade").

Hugo Wolf (1860–1903) was the undisputed master of late Romantic German *Lieder*. The depiction of poetic emotion and concentration of inmost feeling in Wolf's 300 songs is unparalleled. His model was outside the *Lied* tradition. While maintaining strong melodic lines, he

Ill. 4-3 Page 1 of Brahms's manuscript of his song "Vergebliches Ständchen" (1882). Photo: Stock Montage, Inc.

adapted Richard Wagner's declamatory vocal syntax to the *Lied*. Similarly Wagnerian are Wolf's piano parts, which sometimes employ **tremolo** and other quasi-orchestral effects. In many of Wolf's songs, the accompaniment is a polyphonic web in the manner of the orchestral parts of a Wagnerian opera (e.g., *Tristan und Isolde*). Most of his *Lieder* are through-composed. Wolf usually concentrated on a group of German poets or one poet at a time, such as Goethe, Eichendorff, or Mörike. In addition, he set two extended anthologies of folk poetry from Spain and Italy in German translation: the *Spanisches Liederbuch* (44 songs) and the *Italienisches Liederbuch* (46 songs).

FAURÉ, "APRÈS UN RÊVE"

The French Mélodie before Fauré

French song in the Romantic age grew from two predecessors. One was the *romance*, a type of short, strophic love song originating in the 18th-century French *opéra comique*. The other source was the body of *Lieder* by Schubert published in France as a genre called the *mélodie*. Early composers associated with the *mélodie* included Hector Berlioz (1803–1869) and Giacomo Meyerbeer (1791–1864), who employed strophic design in most of their songs. Like German *Lied*, most French *mélodies* were for voice and piano.

Charles Gounod (1818–1893) made a significant contribution to the *mélodie* by establishing ideal **prosody**, the patterns of syllabic accents so subtle and idiomatic to the French language. Gounod was a model for young Romantic composers. Jules Massenet (1842–1912) followed Gounod's example and refined the *mélodie* even further. Like Schumann's, his songs divide musical interest between voice and piano. Massenet also established song cycles as part of the *mélodie* tradition

Although César Franck achieved greatness in instrumental music and Camille Saint-Saëns

tremolo On a string instrument, the rapid and continuous repetition of a single note. On a piano, the rapid and continuous alternation of notes in a chord, meant to resemble several string instruments playing the chord using tremolo technique.

opéra comique French comic opera originating in the 18th century, employing spoken dialogue. A serious/tragic operatic type developed from it, also called *opéra comique*.

prosody The pattern of natural stresses (accents) in a text when spoken or sung; versification.

Ill. 4-4 Informal song performance in a European salon of about 1830. (Lithograph by Achille Devéria.) Germanisches Nationalmuseum, Nürnberg.

mastered the operatic stage, their *mélodies* are not noteworthy. However, France reached the pinnacle of song composition in the works of Gabriel Fauré, Henri Duparc (1848–1933), and Claude Debussy. Fauré brought to the *mélodie* a unique grace and elegance, separating the genre completely from the *Lied*. His balanced melodic lines were a perfect foil for the piano's subtle harmonic colorings.

GABRIEL FAURÉ

Pencil drawing by John Singer Sargent, 1896. Courtesy of the Fogg Art Museums. Bequest of Grenville L. Winthrop. © President and Fellows, Harvard College, Harvard University Art Museums.

avant-garde Literally, "advance guard": Relating to new or experimental trends in the arts and people associated with those trends.

Gabriel Urbain Fauré was born in Pamiers, Ariège, France, on May 12, 1845, the youngest of six children. Coming from a family of minor aristocrats and educators, Fauré was raised in an atmosphere conducive to his natural artistic directions. Some of his earliest recollections were of playing the harmonium in the chapel that adjoined the École Normale at Montgauzy, where his father was director. Young Fauré's musical gifts developed, and in 1854 his father enrolled him—not in the Paris Conservatoire—in the newly established École Niedermeyer (Paris), where he remained for 11 years. Trained there for a future as an organist-choirmaster, Fauré also had the benefit of studying piano with Saint-Saëns, whose classes also branched into composition. Saint-Saëns introduced his students to music by Liszt and Wagner, then considered *avant-garde* in the conservative music circles of Paris. Fauré was École Niedermeyer's shining student, winning first prizes in every subject and a special prize in 1862. His earliest compositions came from his student days.

Fauré began his career in 1866 as a provincial organist. He enlisted for service in the Franco-Prussian war in 1870, saw action, and was discharged less than a year later. In the early 1870s, Fauré was teaching composition at the École Niedermeyer and helping to form the Société Nationale de Musique together with Vincent d'Indy (1851–1931), Édouard Lalo (1823–1892), Henri Duparc, and Emmanuel Chabrier (1841–1894). A series of organist jobs in Paris culminated in an appointment as choirmaster at the Church of the Madeleine in 1877. In July of that year, Fauré became engaged to Marianne Viardot, whom he had loved for five years. However, she broke off the engagement in October, plunging Fauré into depression. Six years later, he married Marie Fremiet, and they had two sons, but the marriage was never happy.

Around 1880, Fauré became fascinated with the music of Richard Wagner, but he remained the only composer of his generation free of Wagner's influence. During the 1870s, Fauré had composed many art songs, some piano pieces, and his first masterpieces in chamber music. However, in the 1880s, he concentrated mostly on songs and piano music. During 1887–1888, Fauré completed the first version of his famous *Requiem*, Op. 48 (five movements only, for a small orchestra). He produced a second version (seven movements and a slightly larger orchestra) between 1887 and 1900, but he did not complete the orchestration of the third version (for full orchestra) until 1900. The chief reason for these delays—and perhaps also for Fauré writing so much in shorter forms (e.g., piano solos and songs)—was that he could find time to compose only during summer holidays, which he usually spent in Switzerland.

During the 1890s, Fauré's music began to be recognized outside France, and his career at home reached a turning point. He became an inspector of government conservatories in 1892, and in 1896 he was appointed organist at the Madeleine and professor of composition at the Paris Conservatoire (over the objections of colleagues who thought him too revolutionary). Among his students were Maurice Ravel, Charles Koechlin (1867–1950), George Enescu

(1881–1955), Émile Vuillermoz (1878–1960), and Nadia Boulanger (1887–1979). Fauré also found fresh directions in his music during this decade, expressed through works like his song cycle *La bonne chanson* (*The Fine Song*), Op. 61 (1892–1894, text by Verlaine), the four-hand piano suite *Dolly*, Op. 56 (1894–1897), and his one orchestral masterpiece, the *Pelléas et Mélisande Suite*, Op. 80.

Beginning in 1905, Fauré was finally recognized fully. In that year, he became director of the Paris Conservatoire. He had a keen ability in this job, and the reforms he instituted earned him the nickname "Robespierre" because of all the resignations that followed. Fauré remained director until his retirement in 1920. He also accepted the presidency of the Société Musicale Indépendante, started by renegades from the former Société that he had helped form earlier. In 1909, Fauré was accorded the highest honor in his lifetime: election to the Institut de France.

This busy period left him little time to compose, and tragically, he also began to lose his hearing. Fauré's growing deafness was accompanied by distortions of pitch: very high notes sounded flat and very low notes sounded sharp, while the middle range remained correct. Heroically, he overcame this difficulty, producing *Pénélope* (1907–1913, his second work for the lyric stage), some of his most masterful piano pieces (*Nocturnes* Nos. 9–11, *Barcarolles* Nos. 7–11), and songs such as the cycle *La chanson d'Eve* (*Eve's Song*), Op. 95 (1906–1910, texts by Charles van Lerberghe).

From the outset of World War I (1914) until his death ten years later, Fauré maintained a steady flow of creativity. His fervor for piano music and songs now abated in favor of chamber music. In his final years, Fauré composed his most masterly chamber works: sonatas for violin and for cello, his Second Piano Trio and Piano Quintet, and his only string quartet (one of his last works). He continued to be honored. In 1920 the French government awarded him the Grand Croix of the Légion d'honneur. A national tribute took place at the Sorbonne in 1922. Young composers, especially Arthur Honegger (1892–1955), admired him and sought him out.

Gabriel Fauré died in Paris on November 4, 1924. Historians consider him the greatest French composer between Berlioz and Debussy and one of the greatest song composers in history. His innovations, especially in harmony, influenced following generations of French composers. Yet, perhaps because he composed chiefly for intimate genres—producing only two operas but neither a symphony nor a concerto—Fauré has been underrated. His genius has been celebrated chiefly in France and among a small group of foreign admirers. Writer-critic Harold Schonberg summarizes Fauré's music as containing "everything Gallic—form, grace, wit, logic, individuality, urbanity," and concludes that "those who love the music of Fauré love it as a private, cherished gift from one of the gentlest and most subtle of composers."

[Harold Schonberg, *Lives of the Great Composers*, 3rd ed. (New York: W.W. Norton, 1997), p. 412.]

Fauré's Mélodies and His "Après un rêve"

Many historians of French music regard Gabriel Fauré as the leading composer of the *mélodie*. He wrote 97 songs, most of them published in collections or as cycles. At the core of his work are the three collections, 20 *mélodies* each, published in 1879, 1897, and 1908. In the last 20 years of his life, most of Fauré's *mélodies* were concentrated into four song cycles.

The earliest Fauré *mélodies* show the influences of Gounod and Fauré's teacher, Saint-Saëns, with a predilection toward Romantic poets such as Victor Hugo. After Charles Baudelaire's introduction of elements of **Symbolist** poetry and with that movement's growing circu-

Symbolism A movement in French poetry during the second half of the 19th century. It employed free verse and conveyed impressions by suggestion rather than by direct statement. Counterparts in the visual arts and in music were called Impressionism.

declamation In text setting, the technique of making textual accent patterns coincide with musical accent patterns at the levels of syllable, word, phrase, and sentence.

mediant In harmony, a triad whose root lies a third above the tonic. The term can be generalized to mean the relationship of any two chords lying a major or minor third apart.

lation, Fauré's poetic taste changed, and so did the compositional style of his *mélodies*. Still occasionally passionate, his work now showed more coolness, more detachment from the subject. The *mélodies* in his first collection, including "Après un rêve" ("After a Dream") illustrate the transition. The second collection solidifies the connection, notably in Fauré's setting of Paul Verlaine's famous "Clair de lune" ("Moonlight"). Verlaine was also the author of *La bonne chanson* from which Fauré selected, organized, and composed (1892–1894) a work many consider the pinnacle of his song writing. This cycle, which describes a man's great happiness upon his betrothal, is unified not only by its story but also by six recurring musical themes. Its adventurous harmony also set new standards in Fauré's music.

La chanson d'Eve was the sequel to *La bonne chanson*. In it, Fauré also used recurring themes, but concentrated on only two, focused the vocal style closely, and gave polyphonic richness to the piano accompaniment. *La chanson d'Eve* is the Genesis story retold with Eve as the central character. Fauré returned to the poetry of Lerberghe for his next song cycle, *Le jardin clos* (*The Secret Garden*, 1914). Here the composer achieved a restraint and subtlety previously unknown in his style. In this cycle and the last two—*Mirages* (1919, text by the Baronne de Brimont) and *L'horizon chimérique* (*The Imagined Horizon*, 1921, text by Jean de la Ville de Mirmont)—unity is not achieved by a central literary theme but by musical atmosphere.

French *mélodie* authorities Rita Benton and Frits Noske have written of the homogeneity of Fauré's style. They list its characteristics as:

• A balanced melodic line

• Correct though not pedantic **declamation**

• A preference for the middle voices (mezzo-soprano and baritone)

• Moderate harmonic tension involving **mediant** relationships

• Flexible structure

As in the work of most great song composers, the *mélodies* of Fauré unite poetry and music so closely as to give the impression that they were created simultaneously. In Fauré, not only the content but the atmosphere of the poem—what the French sometimes call the *parfum* (perfume)—is brought out superlatively in the music. Vuillermoz, Fauré's biographer and one of his pupils, described this quality:

> Fauré has a means of dissolving his poem in the music which internalizes it so that it makes the poet as much a composer as the composer himself. In working out this fusion, Fauré gives us, really, something beyond the words of the poet's idea which is more intimate, more secret and, consequently, more profoundly convincing.

[Émile Vuillermoz, *Gabriel Fauré*, tr. Kenneth Schapin (Philadelphia: Chilton Book Company, 1969), p. 50.]

The crowning work of Fauré's first published *mélodie* collection (1879) is "Après un rêve," one of his most famous songs. It was one of his "Italianate" songs, of which two appeared in the first collection, the other being "Sérénade toscane." The original texts to "Après un rêve" and "Sérénade toscane" were anonymous Italian poems. Romain Bussine (1830–1899), a singer and voice teacher at the Paris Conservatoire, made very free French adaptations of both texts for Fauré, which the composer set to music, probably in 1878. Fauré first met Bussine through Saint-Saëns, and they became close friends during the 1870s.

In the printed collection, "Après un rêve" was dedicated to Marguerite Baugnies, whose salon in the 1870s hosted the most progressive composers of the day. In publication, both the

French and Italian texts appeared. Following are the Italian, French, and English versions of "Après un rêve."

ITALIAN ORIGINAL (ANONYMOUS)	FRENCH ADAPTATION BY BUSSINE	ENGLISH TRANSLATION FROM THE FRENCH
Levati sol che la luna' elevata	Dans un sommeil que charmait ton image	In a slumber that your image charmed
Levadagli occi miei tanto dormire,	Je rêvais le bonheur, ardent mirage,	I dreamed of happiness, glowing mirage,
Il traditor del sonno m'ha ingannata,	Tes yeux étaient plus doux, ta voix pure et sonore.	Your eyes were gentler, your voice pure and resonant.
Il bello amante m'ha fatto sparire,	Tu rayonnais comme un ciel éclairé par l'aurore;	You shone like a sky illumined by sunrise;
Se lo ritrovo quell'amo giocondo	Tu m'appelais, et je quittais la terre	You called to me, and I left the earth
Io mai più mi faró tradir del sonno,	Pour m'enfuir avec toi vers la lumière,	To escape with you toward the light,
Se lo ritrovo quell' amor gentile,	Les cieux pour nous entr' ouvraient leurs nues,	The skies opened their clouds for us a little, unknown
mai più dal sonno, mi faró tradire...	splendeurs inconnues, lueurs divines entrevues,	splendors, divine glimmerings, Alas! Alas, sad awakening
	Hélas! Hélas, triste réveil des songes,	from dreams,
	Je t'appelle, ô nuit, rends- moi tes mensonges,	I call to you, o night, give back to me your illusions,
	Reviens, reviens radieuse,	Return, return radiant one,
	Reviens, ô nuit mystérieuse!	Return, o mysterious night!

[transl. Michael Fink]

Exploring "Après un rêve"

BALANCE. *Listen to the song, noticing the simplicity of the piano part.* The exquisitely florid vocal part stands out from the piano's chordal accompaniment. Such an austere piano part is rare in Fauré and has been compared to Schumann's "Ich grolle nicht" ("I Bear No Grudge," from *Dichterliebe*). One critic even wrote that "the voice steals all the song's interest and reduces the accompaniment to impoverished chord repetitions that serve at most to harmonize or furnish bass support." *Subjective question: Do you agree?* Song literature in every language and period contains songs where the piano merely provides harmonic support.

FORM. The first two-thirds of this song uses strophic procedure. *From the beginning, listen for the recurrence of the opening melody.* This signals the start of the second strophe, where the text motivates Fauré to connect it to the opening. The second strophe begins: "Tu m'appelais, et

"Après un rêve":
A Closer Look

Please refer to the score of
"Après un rêve," beginning on
page 37 of the Score Anthology.

dolce Sweet, sweetly.

je quittais la terre." ("You were calling me, and I left the earth."). *Does Fauré bring back the opening again?* Continuing to respond to the demands of the text, Fauré does not bring the opening melody back a third time, but moves on to new melodic material. That makes the song a modified strophic form comparable to Schubert's "Die Forelle," mentioned above.

STROPHIC MODIFICATION. *Find the strophic repetition beginning in m. 17. Does the melodic content begin to digress in m. 26?* Fauré makes dynamic differences between the two strophes. The opening is marked "*dolce*" in the vocal part (*pp* in the piano part). The second strophe begins apparently softly (see m. 17) but builds immediately to a *f* in the voice (*mf* in the piano). Dynamics do not make a *diminuendo* then until m. 22.

DYNAMIC/MELODIC HIGH POINT. The only other *f* occurs at m. 31 on the word "Hélas!" (Alas!). *Find that place now.* The note is a high G, the only time the song's high point is reached:

HARMONIC RICHNESS. Though simple, the piano accompaniment contains rich varieties of harmony. *See, for example, m. 2,* where a passing chord on the third beat leads to a colorful dominant ninth chord on the downbeat of m. 3:

An augmented triad comes in m. 6:

Fauré was noted for mediant relationships in his harmony: root progressions of a third. *Follow the piano part at the end of the song (mm. 44–48).* The root progression III–V is a good example of a mediant relationship:

MEASURE		44	45	46	47	48
HARMONY:	(D minor)	III	V———		I———	

IVES, "THE CAGE"

In the United States, popular songs have always overshadowed art songs. With roots in the sentimental and minstrel songs of Stephen Foster, along with the birth of the Broadway stage, most American song culture at the end of the 19th century was dominated by commercial motives. Surely there were art-song composers at the time such as Edward MacDowell (1861–1908), George Chadwick (1854–1931), and John Alden Carpenter (1876–1951), but all were under strong Germanic influences, reflected in a derivative song style. The arrival of radio entertainment and sound movies in the 1920s prolonged the dominance of popular music in the United States. Thus, as lovely and refined as are the songs of George Gershwin (1898–1937), Jerome Kern (1885–1945), Cole Porter (1891–1964), Richard Rodgers (1902–1979), and Leonard Bernstein (1918–1990), for example, theirs is not a tradition of the art song running parallel to those of England and Europe. A few U.S. composers have, however, composed significant art songs and vocal chamber music, finding their own original idioms. The earliest of these was Charles Ives.

Charles Edward Ives was born in Danbury, Connecticut, on October 20, 1874. Charles's father, George, had been a prominent Civil War bandmaster, and, after the war, he led the town band and made music at home. Although George was not a composer, he had a keen interest in musical experimentation and was probably the single most important influence on Charles's becoming a composer. From his father, Ives received conventional musical training in theory, performance (piano and horn), and music of the masters (notably Bach). However, George also directed experiments in **microtonal** tuning. In addition, the family often tried singing a hymn tune in one key accompanied on the piano in another: an early and unusual experiment in **bitonality**.

Ives's entire boyhood, including his relationship and experiences with his father, were a lifelong treasure to him—a resource on which he drew frequently for subject matter in his compositions. We could say that "the world through a boy's eyes" was a topic threaded through much of his music. At 12, Ives began composing (with the **polytonal** sketches for a "Song for Harvest Season" and some "fugues in four keys") and playing in the town band. At 14 he became the youngest professional church organist in Connecticut. Besides music, the young Ives loved baseball and became a good high-school pitcher. The baseball/music duality became the first of many paradoxes that stamped his whole life.

During his four years at Yale University (1894–1898) in a general-studies curriculum, Ives studied composition with Horatio Parker, a German-trained music professor new to the department. In his lessons, Ives experienced inner conflict between the traditional, European-conservatory-style assignments he had to write for Parker and the avant-garde experiments to which he was drawn by nature. He later reflected, "I found I *could not* go on using the familiar chords only. I *heard* something else."

When Ives graduated, he knew that for two reasons he would have to compose "underground": (1) no audience for his music existed at the time; and (2) the exigencies of professional music would hamper him in writing what he *heard*. Thus, he entered a New York insurance firm to earn a living by day, while composing nights and weekends—a paradoxical double life. During 1898–1902, Ives was also a church organist in New York. He wrote his first large-scale works about this time, such as his First and Second Symphonies (1895–1898 and 1900–1902, respectively).

The year 1906 was significant in Ives's business and artistic lives. That year he established

(continued)

CHARLES E. IVES

Photograph by W. Eugene Smith, c. 1947. The Charles Ives Papers, Yale University Music Library. Used by permission.

microtone Any interval smaller than a semitone. Splitting semitones into quarter-tones is the most common microtonal application.

bitonality, polytonality The presence or impression of more than one key (tonality) in a single musical passage. Bitonality has two keys at once; polytonality contains more than two simultaneous keys.

spatial music Music in which performing forces are separated rather than grouped together traditionally. The most common spatial effects are splitting ensembles within the hall and the offstage instrument(s) or voice(s). In 20th-century music, spatial effects have been used to add "dimension" and special "imaging" to sound.

atonality Literally, "without tonality." In 20th-century music, the conscious avoidance of tonalities (keys) in a piece of music, usually accomplished by avoiding traditional harmony and traditional treatment of consonance and dissonance. Adj.: atonal.

polymeter The simultaneous use of more than one meter.

tone cluster A chord with notes spaced very close, usually produced on the piano by striking a group of keys with the hand, fist, or forearm. The effect is very dissonant.

serial music, serialism In the 20th century, music organized by a predetermined series. Most commonly, pitch is organized by serializing the 12 tones of the chromatic scale. Called "12-tone music," this system provides an organizational alternative to tonality, resulting in atonal music. A composer who writes serial music is called a serialist.

indeterminacy, aleatory, "chance" music A 20th-century compositional technique in which the composer purposely leaves certain features of the music incomplete for the performer(s) to determine at the moment of performance. The result is unpredictable, and usually no two presentations of an indeterminate work sound the same.

CHARLES E. IVES *(continued)*

an independent insurance agency in partnership with an old colleague, Julian Myrick—an agency that would make the name Charles E. Ives as famous in American insurance as it has become in American music. He also composed his most famous (and perhaps quintessential) piece, *The Unanswered Question* in 1906. Originally part of a two-movement work, *The Unanswered Question* for strings, trumpet, and woodwinds is **spatial music** employing **atonality** and **polymeter**. Typical of Ives's desire to express the totality of human experience, the music deals with the perennial question of the meaning of existence.

Two years later, Ives married Harmony Twitchell of Hartford, and they later adopted a daughter, Edith. Ives composed the bulk of his surviving music between 1906 and 1916. During that time (and before), he pioneered nearly every 20th-century development in acoustically made (nonelectronic) music. In addition to those already mentioned, some of these features were **tone clusters**, harmony built on fourths and fifths, **serial music**, complex rhythmic patterns (such as "4 in the space of 5"), jazz and ragtime elements, and **indeterminacy**. Interestingly, the subject matter of much of his music during this time dealt with the countryside and customs of New England: bucolic pictures, often recalling his own boyhood in musical quotations from his memories (e.g., hymns, patriotic songs, and popular tunes). We can hear this extraordinary paradox in orchestral works such as his Third Symphony: "Camp Meeting" (1904), *Three Places in New England* (1908–c. 1914), and *Holidays Symphony* (1909–1913); in several songs; and in Ives's paean to his beloved transcendental authors, The Second Piano Sonata: "Concord, Mass., 1840–60" (1910–1915). Critic-writer Harold Schonberg colorfully summarizes this paradox with the words:

> His music is a constant reflection of his New England youth: remembrances of life in a simpler age. He yearned for the virtues of an older, town-hall-meeting, village-band, transcendentalist, Emersonian America, and expressed those yearnings in the most advanced, unorthodox, ear-splitting, grating music composed by anybody anywhere up to that time.

[Harold Schonberg, *Lives of the Great Composers*, 3rd ed. (New York: W.W. Norton, 1997), pp. 555-556.]

In 1912, the Iveses bought a farm in Redding, Connecticut. When the United States entered World War I five years later, Charles became involved with the Red Cross and selling Liberty Bonds. From a life of literally "burning the candle at both ends," Ives had a severe heart attack in 1919, forcing him to become a semi-invalid for a year. He then began putting his musical affairs in order, a process that included assembling and privately publishing the *114 Songs* in 1922. About that time, Ives began to burn out as a composer, exhausted from his double life and resulting failed health. He realized in August 1926 that he would not begin another composition. By 1930, Ives's health had gotten even worse, forcing him to retire from business.

Ironically late, American and European interest in the music of Ives began to stir in the late 1920s and early 1930s. Henry Bellamann wrote of the emerging composer:

> Mr. Ives is no wild-eyed revolutionary inhabiting the regions of Bohemia. He is a normal citizen and has for more than a quarter of a century pursued his own way, going to business in the down-town New York district where many of his associates did not know of his interest in music, and all the time accumulating an imposing heap of scores, some of which anticipated the means and methods of the most advanced of the contemporary music—anticipating it by twenty years in some cases.

["Charles Ives: The Man and His Music," *The Musical Quarterly*, January 1933, p. 46.]

Important performances and favorable reviews inspired Ives to reassess, revise, and recopy some of his older music, which was now coming into demand. In 1932, he wrote and dictated his autobiographical *Memos*. John Kirkpatrick's much-lauded 1939 performance of Ives's "Concord" Sonata (which Kirkpatrick had spent ten years preparing) placed Ives in the respectable company of younger American composers of the time. Late recognition continued to grow when Ives won the 1947 Pulitzer Prize in Music for his Third Symphony, composed four decades earlier. Leonard Bernstein conducted the premiere of Ives's Second Symphony in 1951, about *five* decades after its composition. The excessively retiring, semiconfined composer had his wife attend the concert in his place while he listened at home on the radio, secretly delighting in the audience's overwhelmingly positive response.

Charles E. Ives died quietly in New York on May 19, 1954, a few months before his 80th birthday. Most of the musical publications, biographies, dissertations, and recordings were yet to come. Uncompromising in his aesthetic standards, Ives always believed that the whole of human experience (ranging from religious mysticism to lessons learned in the business world) could and should be expressed in music. Although he had been unrecognized in his earlier years, the Western world finally acknowledged Ives as the most striking innovator of the 20th century, one of its most original-sounding composers, and the first American composer whose music sounded truly American.

Ives and His 114 Songs

Charles Ives's earliest known composition was the song "Slow March" (c. 1887), and he continued to compose songs through the rest of his creative life, his last work being the song "Sunrise" (1926). Thus, more than any other Ives works, his entire corpus of about 150 songs encapsulates and shows the many facets of his personality and most of the musical innovations for which he has become famous. The composer was conscious of this, and, although he had an aversion to promoting his own music, in the early 1920s he felt compelled to place his lifetime of songs "out on the clothes line." In 1922, entirely at his own expense, Ives hired the engraving and printing services of the noted music publishing house, G. Schirmer, to prepare 500 copies of his lyrical compendium, *114 Songs*. Ostensibly, this collection was to be sent to "friends," although at the time Ives had no close musical friends. He made the mistake, however, of sending a review copy to the New York *Sun*, which printed a wry notice titled "Here's a Chance to Get a Nice Song Book for Free" on the assumption that such music would have to be free. Ives was deluged with requests from people who had no idea what they were asking for. Although it angered him, he honored all orders, necessitating a second printing of 1,000 copies.

114 Songs included footnotes (some self-deprecatory) to several songs and a "Postface," a rambling, Ivesian collection of paragraphs. Feeling that some songs were inferior, and apparently realizing that the collection was too broad and scattered to show his talent at its best, Ives set about editing a new, more concise collection. He culled 50 of the *114 Songs*, eliminated the Postface, and published the new edition in 1923. Ives sent out 500 copies but still did not become generally known in the American musical world. The first recognition of *114 Songs* came in 1932. Composer Henry Cowell's Cos Cob Press published seven of the songs, which Hubert Linscott and Aaron Copland performed at the Yaddo Festival that May. The following year, Henry Bellamann wrote his article on Ives and his music for *The Musical Quarterly*, using the *114 Songs* to illustrate some of the composer's innovations (see quotation above). Copland reviewed the *114 Songs* for the journal *Modern Music* in 1934. Thus, a general awareness of Ives came initially through his *114 Songs*.

Ill. 4-5 Program of the May 1, 1932, Yaddo concert including seven songs by Ives. The Charles Ives Papers, Yale University Music Library. Used by permission.

THIRD CONCERT

SUNDAY AFTERNOON   MAY FIRST

At two-fifteen

SONATA FOR FLUTE AND PIANO   *Walter Piston*
   1. Allegro moderato e grazioso   2. Adagio
         3. Allegro vivace
        MR. LAURENT and MR. SANROMA

* SEVEN SONGS   *Charles Ives*
   1. The Indians (Charles Sprague)
   2. Walking (Ives)
   3. Serenity (Whittier)
   4. Maple Leaves (Thomas B. Aldrich)
   5. The See'r (Ives)
   6. Evening (Milton)
   7. Charlie Rutlage (Cowboy Ballads)
        MR. LINSCOTT and MR. COPLAND

* SUITE FOR FLUTE AND PIANO   *Henry Brant*
   1. Madrigal 2. Minuet 3. Saraband 4. Toccata
        MR. LAURENT and MR. SANROMA

INTERMISSION

PIANO VARIATIONS (1930)   *Aaron Copland*
        THE COMPOSER

SUITE FOR FLUTE SOLO   *Wallingford Riegger*
   1. Moderato 2. Vivace 3. Molto con sentimento
       4. Allegro ironico
        MR. LAURENT

† SECOND STRING QUARTET   *Silvestre Revueltas*
Allegro giocoso—Lento—Molto vivace—Allegro molto sostenuto
        HANS LANGE QUARTET

First Festival

of

Contemporary American Music

Yaddo

Saratoga Springs
New York

April thirtieth and May first
nineteen hundred thirty-two

ASSISTING ARTISTS

ADA MAC LEISH, Soprano   HUBERT LINSCOTT, Baritone
JESUS MARIA SANROMA, Pianist   JOHN KIRKPATRICK, Pianist
    GEORGES LAURENT, Flutist

HANS LANGE QUARTET

J. LANGE, First Violin   Z. KURTHY, Viola
A. SCHULLER, Second Violin   P. SUCH, Cello

LEAGUE OF COMPOSERS QUARTET

N. BEREZOWSKY, First Violin   M. STILLMAN, Viola
M. MUSCANTO, Second Violin   D. FREED, Cello

COMPOSER-PIANISTS

GEORGE ANTHEIL   AARON COPLAND
VIVIAN FINE   OSCAR LEVANT

Ives applied only a haphazard organization to his varied collection of *114 Songs*. They are not ordered chronologically, although in his table of contents, Ives groups *some* of his songs together topically (e.g., "4 Songs Based on Hymntune Themes"). We can better understand the variety of Ives's songs by dividing them into four large categories:

- *Songs in the Euro-American art-song tradition* were written to well-known *Lied* or *mélodie* texts, many composed during his college years.

- *Sentimental "household" songs* were in the style of Stephen Foster and other 19th-century popular composers.

- *Songs in vernacular idioms* adapted or parodied the popular music, marches, early ragtime, and hymn tunes that Ives knew from his youth—plus a few musical styles of which he knew little, like cowboy songs of the Southwest.

- *Songs with radical musical organization* introduced new compositional techniques. For example, the first song in the collection, "Majority" (1921, text by Ives), liberally used tone clusters, which Ives was one of the first to bring to the piano. "Walking" (No. 67, 1902, text by Ives) employed daringly novel harmonies to imitate the sound of bells. "Rough Wind" (No. 69, 1902, text by Shelley) is heavily chromatic, changes keys rapidly, and finishes in bitonality. The three songs "From Early Italian Poets" ("August," "September," and "December"—Nos. 35–37) had no time signatures and were barred irregularly. "The Cage" (No. 64, 1906, text by Ives), discussed below, omitted most barlines and had atonal qualities.

Another innovative hallmark found in many of Ives's songs and most of his other music is quotation from other music. His sources are as varied as his experiences: folk songs, church hymns, "classical" music, patriotic songs, popular tunes, bugle calls, etc. Ives wove these quotations into his music at unexpected moments, often relating his own themes to them. The effect of Ives's quotation technique is sometimes humorous, sometimes impressively serious.

"He is there!" (No. 50, 1917, text by Ives) is especially rich in quotations of patriotic material. In a footnote, Ives identifies the quoted songs as "Tenting Tonight," "Battle Cry of Freedom," and "Marching Through Georgia."

Ives did not include all of his songs in the 1922 collection, however. In 1933, a collection of *34 Songs* appeared, and 1935 saw the publication of *19 Songs*. These contained several reprints or new versions of songs from the *114 Songs*, but some new songs also appeared, notably "Soliloquy" (1907, text by Ives) and the epic "General Booth Enters into Heaven" (1914, text by Vachel Lindsay), which many consider to be Ives's greatest song. Subsequent publications have printed later-discovered Ives songs.

Ives's "The Cage": Background

In a 1933 article on Charles Ives and his music in *The Musical Quarterly*, Henry Bellamann commented that "The Cage" (No. 64):

> … is a song taken from a Chamber-Orchestra Set; chords of fourths and fifths throw the melody and whole harmonic scheme into complete atonality; the rhythm changes in each measure; there are no measures consecutively of the same time duration.

The "Chamber-Orchestra Set" was Ives's *Set for Theater or Chamber Orchestra*, a suite of three movements written in 1906–1911. The first movement, titled "In the Cage," was composed in July 1906. Ives made an adaptation, "The Cage," for voice and piano, in the same year. In 1932, it was published in the influential quarterly *New Music*. The music to "In the Cage" and Ives's song text were the result of an observation, which Ives describes in his *Memos* (No. 17):

> The *Theater or Chamber Orchestra Set* is a combination of separate things. The first [movement] is the result of taking a walk one hot summer afternoon in Central Park with Bart Yung (one-half Oriental) and George Lewis (non Oriental). … Sitting on a bench near the menagerie, watching the leopard's cage and a little boy (who had apparently been a long time watching the leopard)—this aroused Bart's Oriental fatalism—hence the text in the score and in the song. Technically this piece is but a study of how chords of 4ths and 5ths may throw melodies away from a set tonality. … Technically the principal thing in this movement is to show that a song does not necessarily have to be in any one key to make musical sense. To make music in no particular key has a nice name nowadays—"atonality."

[Charles E. Ives, *Memos*, ed. John Kirkpatrick (New York: W.W. Norton, 1972), pp. 55–56. Text from Charles E. Ives' *Memos*. Copyright © 1972 by The American Academy of Arts and Letters. Reprinted by permission.]

Exploring "The Cage"

MEANING OF THE TEXT. Ives's text for "The Cage" runs:

A leopard went around his cage from one side back to the other side;
he stopped only when the keeper came around with meat;
A boy who had been there three hours began to wonder,
"Is life anything like that?"

Could this be a fatalistic view of life: pacing here and there, never achieving anything of importance that would give life meaning? In this rather negative view, humans are on a kind of treadmill of monotonous, dead-end work, punctuated only when our supervisor (or professor) throws us some "meat"—our paycheck (or grades). Ives may have felt at times that his intense double life as insurance man/composer was like the leopard's. However, he viewed the two aspects of his life as feeding each other, and he felt stimulated and rewarded by all he turned his hand to (spiritually by music, materially by business). Note, too, that it is a boy with his life ahead of him who asks the "life" question, not some disillusioned person looking back on his or her life and finding it meaningless.

MELODIC SHAPE. Listen to the song, and notice how the melody goes straight in one direction for a short while, then turns and goes in the other direction for a short while. Is this some type of symbol? The weaving shape may be intended to illustrate the leopard's pacing "around his cage from one side back to the other side." The voice's rhythm is mostly even note values, which could emphasize the monotony of the leopard's existence:

RHYTHM AND ACCENTUATION IN THE PIANO. Listen to the song and follow this rendering of the text. (Italics show a syllable where a chord falls within a word, and "|" shows the position of a chord between words.)

| A leopard went *a*-round *his* cage *from* one side *back* to the o-ther *side*;

he stopped | *on*-ly *when* the keep-*er* came *a*-round with meat;

| A boy who *had* been there *three hours* | be-*gan* to *won*-der,

| "Is life an-*y*-thing *like* that?

The placement of chords is anything but regular, denying any feeling of rhythmic organization. Although chords appear on punctuation marks and on some syllables where natural accentuation occurs, Ives upsets the natural prosody of the text by placing some chords on syllables or words that would not be normally accented.

ABSENCE OF SIGNATURES AND BAR LINES. Look at the beginning of the score. What are the irregularities? The song has no time signature because it is in no single meter (free pulse). It lacks a key signature because it is in no one key or tonality (that is, atonal). *Find the two places where bar lines occur.* There are only two places: (1) around the repeated piano introduction and (2) just before the word "wonder."

PIANO INTRODUCTION: RHYTHMIC PATTERN. The rhythm of the chords in the introduction runs:

What is the rhythmic pattern here? Between the first and last chords, the duration of each chord is slightly shorter than the previous one. This is called a "composed *accelerando*."

WHOLE-TONE MELODIES. Study the vocal melody in Ives's setting of the words "A leopard went around his cage" and "only when the keeper came around with meat." Ives is using a **whole-tone scale**:

"The Cage": A Closer Look
Please refer to the score of "The Cage," beginning on page 41 of the Score Anthology.

accelerando Accelerating the tempo of the music.

whole-tone scale A scale consisting of whole tones only (no half tones), six tones to the octave. Only two such scales are possible.

The whole-tone scale lacks a definite, single tonality because of the run-on equality of whole-tone intervals (no half-tones) and there being only six tones per octave. Thus, the scale contributes to the unstable, atonal qualities of the song.

PIANO CHORDS. Another factor contributing to the absence of key-feeling is that Ives builds most of the chords of "The Cage" chords on the interval of the perfect fourth. *Notice, however, that a few chords emphasize the perfect fifth (e.g., on "three hours").* The chord on the word "wonder" comes at a position of emphasis. *Find this chord and notice three features that make it distinctive.* Three things that make it different from other chords are: (1) it contains several intervals of a third, (2) it contains more notes than any other chord in this song, and (3) it contains the piano's highest and lowest pitches in this song.

American Art Song after Ives

Between the 1920s and the 1940s, most prominent American composers ignored the solo vocal media in favor of orchestral or choral-orchestral music. A notable exception was Virgil Thomson (1896–1989). Thomson's experiences in France fostered his willingness to mix banal and original musical elements with leanings toward the surrealistic poetry of Gertrude Stein. Many of his songs, however—*Five Songs from William Blake* (1951), for example—carry an entirely serious tone.

Aaron Copland (1900–1990) was not an avid song composer, but his *Twelve Poems of Emily Dickinson* (1950) is an important contribution to American song literature. By contrast, two later composers were drawn strongly to song: David Diamond (1915–) and Samuel Barber (1910–1981). Diamond composed more than 100 individual songs and seven song cycles. Barber was an extraordinary song composer. A neo-Romantic singer-pianist-composer, he employed an unusually emotional and sensitive style. Song composition spanned his entire career, topped by such masterworks as *Hermit Songs* (1953, Irish texts from the 8th to 13th centuries).

Ned Rorem (1923–) is a prolific song composer with a natural feeling for vocal line and textual accentuation. His songs are atmospheric, sometimes to the point of being macabre. Rorem has concentrated on song cycles, experimenting with their form. For example, in his *Poems of Love and the Rain* (1963, texts by various poets), the second half of the cycle consists of contrasting settings of the poems from the first half in reverse order. Rorem is regarded as one of the 20th century's leading U.S. song composers.

Outside the mainstream of American song composition, Milton Babbitt (1916–) has maintained an interest in solo vocal music. Babbitt has composed **12-tone** songs with piano accompaniment such as the cycle *Du* (1951, text by August Stramm). As part of the American avant-garde of modernism, Babbitt is also an electronic composer who has combined voice and taped sounds in works like *Philomel* (1964, text by J. Hollander). A representative of postmodernism, George Crumb (1929–) has contributed two works in the voice-and-piano art-song tradition: *Apparition* (1979, texts by Walt Whitman); and *The Sleeper* (1984, text by Edgar Allan Poe).

12-tone, dodecaphonic A method of composition in which all 12 tones of the chromatic scale are preordered serially and treated equally without regard to any key or to consonance and dissonance.

₿ CHAPTER FIVE

Chamber Music

**HAYDN, STRING QUARTET IN C MAJOR, OP. 76,
NO. 3 ("EMPEROR"), SECOND MOVEMENT**

18th-Century Chamber Music before Haydn

In the Baroque period, nearly all ensemble music was composed on an accompaniment foundation called a *basso continuo*. Above the *basso continuo*, one or more solo instruments would play, and usually these would be in a treble range. The violin was by far the most usual instrument for the solo part, but the **recorder** and later the transverse flute and oboe became popular. Thus, the typical Baroque chamber ensemble had a "polar" treble-bass sound with light harmonies etched in between the higher and lower lines. Italian composers were the first leaders in this field, and they called their chamber compositions "sonatas." The solo keyboard sonata had not yet emerged, but ensemble sonatas gravitated toward two main types: the *duo* sonata for one treble instrument and *basso continuo;* and the *trio* sonata for two treble instruments and *basso continuo*.

recorder An end-blown (mouthpiece) flute in use from the Middle Ages through the Baroque period.

Ill. 5-1 Arcangelo Corelli, shown holding a piece of music. Engraving by John Smith c. 1715, taken from a portrait by Hugh Howard.

Schubert, String Quintet in C Major (1828) •

Schubert, "Trout" Quintet (1819) •

Beethoven, "Archduke" Piano Trio (1810–1811) ‒

Beethoven, "Razumovsky" Quartets (1805–1806) ‒

Haydn, "Emperor" Quartet published (1799) •

Mozart, "Haydn" Quartets published (1785) •

Haydn, String Quartets, Op. 33, published (1782) •

• Handel, Trio Sonatas, Op. 2 (c. 1732)

• Couperin, *Les Nations* (trio sonatas) published (1726)

‒ Bach, Violin Sonatas; Flute Sonatas (c. 1717–1723)

• Purcell Trio Sonatas published (1683)

⎯⎯⎯ Corelli Trio Sonatas published (1681–1694)

1650	1675	1700	1725	1750	1775	1800	1825

⎯⎯⎯⎯⎯⎯⎯ Archangelo Corelli (1653–1713)

⎯⎯⎯⎯⎯ Henry Purcell (1659–1695)

⎯⎯⎯⎯⎯⎯⎯⎯ J. S. Bach (1685–1750)

⎯⎯⎯⎯⎯⎯⎯⎯ G. F. Handel (1685–1759)

Joseph Haydn (1732–1809) ⎯⎯⎯⎯⎯⎯⎯

W. A. Mozart (1756–1791) ⎯⎯⎯⎯

Ludwig van Beethoven (1770–1827) ⎯⎯⎯⎯⎯⎯

Franz Schubert (1797–1828) ⎯⎯⎯⎯

Ex. 5-1 Time line of Chamber Music History: Corelli to the death of Schubert; Hensel to the present (p. 122).

CORELLI, HANDEL, AND BACH. The peak of this trend in Italy was reached in the music of violinist-composer Arcangelo Corelli (1653–1713), who wrote both duo and trio sonatas. Among these, the most influential genre was the *sonata da chiesa* (church sonata) in four movements: slow—fast—slow—fast. Soon the "church" sonata lost its sacred association, and Corelli's *sonata da chiesa* plan and procedures became the standard for the late Baroque duo and trio sonata. George Frideric Handel (1685–1759) and J.S. Bach (1685–1750) adopted the Corelli model in their chamber music. Handel's Op. 1 comprised 12 sonatas for one treble instrument (flute, recorder, violin, or oboe) and *basso continuo;* later he also published trio sonatas. The *sonata da chiesa* pattern was Bach's model for nearly every work he titled "sonata": six for violin and harpsichord, three for viola da gamba and harpsichord, and two for flute and harpsichord. In all of these works, the harpsichordist's right hand often provided a second treble part to approximate a trio-sonata texture. Two flute sonatas with *basso continuo* and two conventional trio sonatas have also been authenticated.

PRE-CLASSICAL CHAMBER MUSIC AND STANDARD INSTRUMENTATION. By the time Bach and Handel were gone, a younger generation of composers had already replaced the Corelli *sonata da chiesa* movement plan with the newer Classical sonata plan of fast–slow–fast movements. Also, the *basso continuo* eventually disappeared from chamber music; keyboard parts (when present) were now written out. In some chamber music, notably string quartets, a *basso continuo* was no longer necessary and was eliminated. Early examples of string quartets (two violins, viola, and cello) were the *Sonate a quattro* by Alessandro Scarlatti

Glass, *Music in 12 Parts* (1974) •
Crumb, *Black Angels* (1970) •
Riley, *In C* (1964) •
Davidowsky, *Synchronisms* (1963–1974) ____
Shostakovich, String Quartet No. 8 (1960) •
Carter, String Quartet No. 2 (1959) •
Barber, *Summer Music* (1953–1955) _
Stockhausen, *Kontra-Punkte* (1952–1953) _
Carter, *Four Etudes and a Fantasy* (1952) •
Bartók, *Contrasts* (1942) •
Messiaen, *Quartet for the End of Time* (1940–1941)
Schoenberg, String Quartet No. 4 (1936) •

• Bartók, String Quartet No. 4 (1929)
_ Berg, Lyric Suite (1925–1926)
• Stravinsky, Octet for Winds (1923)
• Hindemith, *Kleine Kammermusik,* Op. 24, No. 2 (1927)
_ Ravel, String Quartet (1902–1903)
_ Brahms, Violin Sonata No. 3, Op. 108 (1886–1888)
• Franck, Violin Sonata (1886)

• Hensel, Piano Trio, Op. 11 (1846)
• Schumann's "chamber music year" (1842)
• Mendelssohn, Octet for strings, Op. 20 (1825)

| 1800 | 1825 | 1850 | 1875 | 1900 | 1925 | 1950 | 1975 | 2000 |

_____ Fanny Hensel (1805–1847)
_____ Felix Mendelssohn (1809–1847)
_____ Robert Schumann (1810–1856)
_____ Johannes Brahms (1833–1897)
Arnold Schoenberg (1874–1951) _____
Béla Bartók (1881–1945) _____
Igor Stravinsky (1882–1971) _____
Paul Hindemith (1895–1963) _____
Dmitri Shostakovich (1906–1975) _____
Elliott Carter (1908–) _____ _ _
George Crumb (1929–) _____ _ _
Terry Riley (1935–) _____ _ _

(1660–1725—father of Domenico) written between 1715 and 1725. However, the earliest continuing trend in string quartet composition occurred in Vienna around 1745, notably in the six quartets by Georg Matthias Monn (1717–1750). Parisian composer Johann Schobert (c. 1735–1767) wrote progressive sonatas for keyboard and strings: violin solo, violin and cello, or two violins and cello.

This pre-Classical music greatly influenced the full development of Classical chamber music in the hands of Joseph Haydn (1732–1809) and Mozart. During the third quarter of the 18th century, the Classical string and keyboard-string chamber combinations became standardized. The most common combinations were:

	VIOLIN(S)	VIOLA(S)	CELLO(S)	PIANO
String Trio	1	1	1	
String Quartet	2	1	1	
String Quintet	2	2	1	
or	2	1	2	
Violin Sonata	1			1
Piano Trio	1		1	1
Piano Quartet	1	1	1	1

(Franz) Joseph Haydn was born in Rohrau, Lower Austria, on March 31, 1732. The son of a wheelwright, he was the second of 12 children. Although Haydn's father loved music, his decision to allow the boy to pursue a musical education arose from his desire for his son to become a clergyman. This education started in Hainburg at the age of six. In 1740 Haydn auditioned for St. Stephen's Cathedral in Vienna and was accepted as a choirboy, where he remained for the next nine years. When his voice broke he was excused, probably in late 1749 or early 1750. At the **choir** school he learned to play the keyboard and the violin but received no instruction in composition or music theory. Nonetheless, his earliest extant composition, a Missa Brevis (Short Mass), came from about 1749.

Despite his parents' continued desire for him to enter the church, Haydn was now determined to make a musical career for himself. To do that, he had to struggle for the next several years. Living in an attic room, he gave a few music lessons, played professionally on occasion, and studied composition—chiefly on his own. Opera librettist Pietro Metastasio lived in the same building, and through him Haydn met Nicola Porpora (1686–1768), a composer and singing teacher, who would make a great difference in the young composer's life. Haydn worked for Porpora as an accompanist and learned much from him about composition and the voice. Porpora was well connected, and he introduced Haydn to influential noble persons.

Haydn gained his first permanent appointment, probably in 1759, as music director for Count Carl von Morzin. He composed his first symphonies for the count's small orchestra and some divertimentos for wind instruments. This appointment did not last long, however. By 1760, the count had squandered his entire fortune and had to disband the orchestra. That year was an eventful one, because Haydn married Maria Keller and found a new employer, Prince Anton Esterházy, who had been impressed by one of his few early symphonies. In May 1761, Haydn signed a contract to become the Prince's *Vice-Kapellmeister* (Assistant Music Director), but his duties included full charge over the orchestra. Haydn's association with the Esterházy

JOSEPH HAYDN

Anonymous sillhouette, c. 1798.
Collections of the Gesellschaft
der Musikfreunde in Wien.

choir In church music, a large ensemble of voices (usually mixed: soprano, alto, tenor, and bass).

Theme & Variations

T. violin

V₁

V₂

V₃

V₄

(continued)

family would eventually last nearly 30 years in fulltime service and beyond that in occasional work, providing the composer patronage for the bulk of his life's vast creative output.

The Esterházys were among the wealthiest of the Hungarian aristocracy, and when Prince Anton died in 1762, he was succeeded by his brother Nikolaus, who spared no expense for entertainment as part of a lavish lifestyle. Immediately, he had the family's hunting lodge rebuilt as a huge palace he named "Esterháza," intending it to rival Versailles. The building included opera and marionette theaters besides two extravagant music rooms. In time, Esterháza became one of the musical crossroads of Europe, through which Haydn's reputation easily spread to other important musical centers such as Paris and London. (The prince also allowed Haydn to have his music published after it was premiered at Esterháza.)

Nikolaus was a great music lover. Under the prince's patronage, Haydn expanded the court orchestra from 12 players to about double that size. With these musicians, he could immediately hear everything he wrote; the court musical establishment became his laboratory for experimentation and developing his craft. Yet the prince's demands for new music were great. He required chamber-music performances almost daily, and two operas per week were given (mostly works not by Haydn). Also, two weekly concerts were presented, and Haydn had to write some of this music and also much *Tafelmusik* (dinner music) for the prince. Nikolaus was an amateur musician himself. He played a peculiar string instrument called a *baryton*, which was equipped with two sets of strings: one bowed, the other plucked. Haydn's chamber music includes 126 trios for baryton, viola, and cello besides other music for the instrument.

In 1766, the Court *Kapellmeister* died, and Haydn inherited full responsibility for all court music, sacred and secular. By that time he had composed at least 11 symphonies for the Esterházy orchestra and about the first dozen of his string quartets, which he called "divertimentos." Haydn's life over the next 14 years was very industrious but also very routine. Apart from brief yearly vacations, he remained at court composing, performing, and conducting. Rarely meeting outside musicians during all that time, Haydn amazingly became the leading composer in Europe. He once stated:

> My prince was pleased with all my work, I was commended, and as a conductor of an orchestra
> I could make experiments, observe what strengthened and what weakened an effect, and there-
> upon improve, substitute, omit, and try new things. I was cut off from the world; there was no
> one around to mislead and harass me, and so I was forced to become original.

That originality is the stamp of many of the 92 symphonies Haydn composed for the Esterházy court orchestra before 1790.

Occasionally, Haydn would visit Vienna, and in 1785 during one of those stays, Mozart's famous string quartet party occurred (see Mozart's biography in Chapter 3). The report of another party tells of Mozart and Haydn playing together along with two other popular composers of the day, Karl von Dittersdorf (1739–1799) and Jan Vanhal (1739–1813). Haydn's music was also performed publicly in Vienna. One event was the production of his opera *Lo speziale* in March 1770 in a private court theater. In 1779, Haydn began publishing his music through the Artaria firm, which was pioneering music publication in Vienna. One of Artaria's most important offerings was Haydn's group of six string quartets brought out in 1781 as Op. 33.

Haydn's marriage was unhappy, and when an Italian singing couple was engaged to perform court music in 1779, he became attached to the wife, Luigia Polzelli. This love affair lasted until 1791, when her husband died and she moved to Italy. Haydn continued to support her and her two sons financially for many years.

In September 1790, Prince Nikolaus Esterházy died. His son and successor, Prince Anton, was not a music lover and disbanded most of the court's musical organization. Haydn retained the title of Music Director and full salary but without any regular duties. Thus, he now retired, living in Vienna as a private citizen. His retirement was not long, however. In early December, Johann Peter Salomon, a German-born musician working in London as a concert promoter-violinist, arrived on Haydn's doorstep and reportedly declared, "I am Salomon from London, and I have come to fetch you. Tomorrow we will conclude an agreement." Haydn and Salomon departed from Vienna that month, and Mozart saw them off with the words, "I fear, father, that this will be our last farewell." (Mozart was thinking of Haydn's advanced age of nearly 60, but his prophesy turned out otherwise, for he himself died less than a year later.)

Haydn arrived in London on New Year's Day for the first of two tours, lasting until July 1792. The second ran from February 1794 to August 1795. He composed six symphonies for each journey, collectively called the "London" Symphonies, plus generous amounts of chamber music. Salomon's concerts and many others were very successful, and Haydn received more offers of commissions and publications than he could possibly fulfill. He was honored while in England, notably obtaining his 1791 honorary Doctor of Music degree from Oxford University. Also, he was received at the royal court. Much English music impressed him, especially Handel's oratorios. These would soon affect his own music.

Yet another Esterházy (Prince Nikolaus II) had ascended before Haydn returned from England for the second time, and the composer went back to limited service late in 1795. Chiefly Haydn wrote Masses for the name days of family members; thus most of his Masses came from that period. With time for his own projects, Haydn now composed some string quartets, notably those published as Opp. 76 and 77. However, a much bigger project loomed: *Die Schöpfung* (*The Creation*).

The innovative Haydn wished to compose a German-language counterpart to Handel's English oratorios, and he had brought back from England a libretto originally intended for Handel himself. For the German translation of this libretto, he turned to Baron Gottfried van Swieten (1733–1803), himself a devotee of Handel. Haydn worked on *Die Schöpfung* during 1796–1798, and the result was monumental. Van Swieten organized the premiere performances given on April 29 and 30, 1798. Only the select nobility and "the flower of the literary and musical society of Vienna" were in the invited audiences. Outside the building, large crowds gathered, and mounted guards had to maintain order. It was an awesome occasion and one of deep emotion. Even the 64-year-old Haydn, who conducted, later reported, "One moment I was cold as ice, the next I seemed on fire. More than once I was afraid I should have a stroke."

Haydn lived out his last years in Vienna as a "grand old man" of music, the recipient of many honors and awards. He also held extensive conversations with Georg Griesinger, who compiled the earliest Haydn biography. A performance of *Die Schöpfung* conducted by Antonio Salieri in March 1808 was Haydn's last appearance in public. When Napoleon occupied Vienna in mid-May 1809, he ordered an honor guard placed at Haydn's door, and on May 31, the 77-year-old Haydn died quietly.

Joseph Haydn: Father of the String Quartet

Haydn's string quartets are, of all his works, the most faithful mirror of his human and artistic personality and the most complete chronicle of his growth as a composer, since they span the entire half-century of his creative life.

[Rosemary Hughes, *Haydn String Quartets* (Seattle: University of Washington Press, 1969), p. 5.]

Haydn was among the earliest pioneers of the Classical string quartet at a time when it was emerging from the Baroque trio sonata as the chamber-music medium of choice. Concerning the genesis of Haydn's quartets, his early biographer, Georg Griesinger, relates the following episode dealing with Baron Karl von Fürnberg, whom violinist Haydn had met through Porpora:

[Fürnberg] invited from time to time his pastor, his steward, Haydn, and Albrechtsberger (a brother of the celebrated contrapuntist, who played the cello) for small musical gatherings. Fürnberg requested Haydn to compose something that could be performed by these four amateurs. Haydn, then 18 years old, took up this proposal, and so originated his first quartet, which, immediately it seemed, was so acclaimed that Haydn was encouraged to work further in this form.

Griesinger is probably mistaken about Haydn's age, because he did not meet Fürnberg until a few years later. More likely, these gatherings took place about 1757 and led to Haydn's appointment with Count von Morzin two or three years later.

DIVERTIMENTOS. Haydn's first ten quartets (later published as Opp. 1 and 2) were early Classical works. Although their instrumentation made a harpsichord unnecessary, the viola part here did not usually fill in the harmony, and it most often doubles the cello (at the unison or an octave higher). This reminds us of the trio-sonata texture left over from the Baroque era: two treble lines (violins I and II) and a bass line (cello, now doubled by viola).

Yet progressive features also abound within each work and in its overall plan. That plan was an enlarged sonata plan including two minuets, placed both before and after the slow movement:

Fast—Minuet—Slow—Minuet—Fast

This symmetry is remarkable. Because Haydn titled each of these works "Divertimento," we could call the movement pattern "divertimento plan." Although a Classical divertimento or serenade did not have a prescribed number of movements, this symmetrical divertimento plan was attractive enough that Mozart also cast many of his own serenades and divertimentos in it.

Haydn continued composing string quartets during his early years with the Esterházy family. In the six divertimentos of Op. 9, he gravitated to the four-movement sonata plan, placing a single minuet either before or after the slow movement. By Op. 17, composed in 1771, the viola had achieved a completely independent part, and Haydn was exploring the contrapuntal possibilities of the ensemble. The six divertimentos of Op. 20, composed the following year, were landmarks in Haydn's quartet evolution. In them, his sonata forms became more sophisticated, and the string-quartet texture was fully realized. Nos. 3 and 5 of this set are in minor keys and explore Haydn's more emotional side. Three of the works are noteworthy for their fugal **finales**, "learned" Baroque throwbacks combining two, three, or four subjects.

OPUS 33. Nine years passed before Haydn published another set of string quartets, Op. 33, which made chamber music history. In the dedication, Haydn stated that he wrote them "in an entirely new, special way," and for the first time he gave each work the title of "String Quar-

finale (1) The final movement of a multimovement instrumental work, usually fast and climactic. (2) The last piece in an operatic act, usually long and elaborate.

tet" instead of "Divertimento." On the whole, these works are more cheerful than previous quartets—all the minuet-type movements are faster and labeled *scherzo* (joke) or *scherzando*. (This was the origin of Beethoven's scherzo-type movement.) By contrast, the slow movements are more personal and expressive than before; they explore the intimate possibilities of the quartet medium. The originality and charm of Op. 33 inspired Mozart to compose his six "Haydn" Quartets in 1782–1785.

OPP. 42–64. Between 1785 and 1790, Haydn published 19 more string quartets: the single work of Op. 42, six Quartets in Opp. 50, three each in Opp. 54 and 55, and six in Op. 64. We know the Op. 50 Quartets as the "Prussian" Quartets, because Haydn composed them for the King of Prussia, an avid amateur cellist. Some of these Quartets (especially Nos. 1 and 3) are noteworthy for containing *monothematic* sonata forms. In these, instead of presenting a distinctly different secondary theme in the exposition, Haydn restates the primary theme in the new key.

Haydn dedicated the remaining 18 quartets to Johann Tost, a fine violinist hired for the Esterházy orchestra in 1783. In 1789, Tost left for Paris, where he got Haydn's quartets published as Opp. 54, 55, and 64. Because of Tost's violinistic ability, the Violin I parts of these works are quite demanding. More unexpected are the subtle influences of Mozart here and there and the tinges of Romantic emotion that color many of these works. Perhaps the most original and most beautiful is the String Quartet in D Major, Op. 64, No. 5, nicknamed "The Lark." This may be the most often-played string quartet by Haydn. It takes its nickname from the high register of the opening theme. This beautiful tune is played against a **staccato** accompaniment, which becomes one of the main motives of the movement (see Ex. 5-2).

staccato Articulation that shortens notes or detaches them from each other.

Ex. 5-2 Opening measures of Haydn's "Lark" Quartet in D Major, Op. 64, No. 5.

LATE QUARTETS. Soon after returning from his first journey to England in 1792, Haydn began making preparations for a second English tour. Having now achieved international fame as the "Father of the String Quartet," Haydn introduced six new works. Owing to the whims of later publishers, these first appeared in print divided into two groups of three works under the opus numbers 71 and 74. Intended for London's concert halls, Haydn's Op. 71/74 quartets display a certain extroversion rarely found in his earlier chamber music.

The years during which Haydn worked on *Die Schöpfung* were also filled with string-quartet composition. In 1797, Haydn wrote the six Quartets published in 1799 as Op. 76. The set bears a dedication to Count Joseph Erdödy, a Hungarian noble Haydn had come to know during his years in the Esterházy household. These works are considered a high point in Haydn's development of the string quartet. They also contain certain individual movements that are among the most famous in all of Haydn's works. The first movement of No. 2 in D Minor, with its countless interlocking pairs of fifths, gives the quartet its nickname, "Quinten" ("fifths" in German). The second movement of No. 3 in C Major ("Emperor") is a set of variations on the "Emperor's Hymn," which Haydn himself had composed. No. 4 in B-flat Major, takes its nickname, "L'Aurore" ("Sunrise"), from the ascending flow of the violin melody at its opening. For many critics, Haydn reached the pinnacle of string-quartet composition in the pair of Quartets published in 1802 as Op. 77. Of these, scholar Rosemary Hughes remarks, "Nowhere in the great procession of his quartets is the quartet writing, as such, more balanced, varied, and rich in scoring."

Haydn had worked hard for 40 years, producing a phenomenal amount of music. Now, in 1803, he had grown tired. In that year, he began what was to be his last composition, a String Quartet in D Minor. However, his powers were failing him, and after three years he had completed only the middle two movements. Haydn had Griesinger write to the publisher Breitkopf & Härtel: "Haydn sends you his characteristic visiting card as an apology that the quartet is not complete." Griesinger went on to suggest that the card be printed instead of a final rondo movement. Its message was a brief melodic setting of words by C.F. Gellert:

Ill. 5-2 Silhouette of a string quartet at the court of Prince Krafft Ernst Oettingen-Wallerstein in 1791. Notice that the cellist holds the instrument between his knees and the other musicians stand to play. Fotohaus Hirsch, D-86720, Nördlingen.

Gone forever is my strength;
old and weak am I.

Griesinger concluded that "Always, where this quartet is heard, one will immediately come to know why it is not complete, from the few words [of the card], and will be moved by them. ..."

The "Emperor's Hymn" and the "Emperor" Quartet

There are two different stories about the origin of the "Emperor's Hymn." In one, circulated by musicians, Haydn—influenced by the British national anthem, "God Save the King"—wished to compose something similar to honor Austria's ruler, Emperor Franz. He took this matter to his friend and patron Baron van Swieten, who consulted with Count Franz von Saurau (president of Lower Austria). Von Saurau then commissioned a text from Lorenz Leopold Haschka, which Haydn used. In the other version, von Saurau took credit for the idea. He claimed to have approached Haydn with Haschka's text, because "I felt, [Haydn] was the only man capable of creating something that could be placed by the English 'God Save the King.'"

Whoever had the idea first, it was a grand one. In 1796, Napoleon was sweeping through Europe, and his opponents—Austria, Prussia, and England—were losing the fight. A year earlier, France had adopted the "Marseillaise" as its national anthem, so the new Austrian hymn was meant to counteract that melody as well as be on an equal footing with that of England. Also, Von Saurau needed to raise an army of Austrian troops to fight Napoleon, and a new patriotic "hit" song was just the propaganda tool he needed for enthusiasm among potential recruits. The text was completed in October 1796, and Haydn finished a piano-vocal version of the music the following January.

Von Saurau not only commissioned the poetry and music to the national hymn, he organized a national event in which to introduce it. February 12, 1797, was the birthday of Emperor Franz. On that date people were to gather in every theater in Austria to sing the "Emperor's Hymn." Von Saurau and Haydn had the music published, and before February 1, copies had been distributed to music directors in all cities within the Austrian domain (see Ex. 5-3 for that score). Ostensibly, each music director was to arrange the music for whatever instrumental forces were available. Haydn himself arranged it for an orchestra of one flute, two oboes, two bassoons, two horns, two trumpets, timpani, and strings. The vocal part was a unison melody.

Here is the first stanza (of four) in the original German and an 18th-century English translation by Charles Burney (1726–1814). (Note that Burney took the liberty of adding a pair of lines in the middle, a place where the music repeats.)

Gott! erhalte Franz den Kaiser,	God preserve the Emp'ror Francis
Unsern guten Kaiser Franz!	Sov'reign ever good and great;
Lange lebe Franz der Kaiser	Save, o save him from mischances
In des Glückes hellstem Glanz!	In Prosperity and State!
Ihm erblühen Lorbeer-Reiser	May his Laurels ever blooming
Wo er geht, zum Ehren-Kranz!	Be by Patriot Virtue fed;
Gott! erhalte Franz den Kaiser,	May his worth the world illumine
Unsern guten Kaiser Franz!	And bring back the Sheep misled!
	God preserve the Emp'ror Francis!

43. Gott, erhalte den Kaiser!

L. L. Haschka

(1797)

Ex. 5-3 Modern edition of Haydn's piano-vocal score to the Emperor's Hymn, "Gott erhalte den Kaiser" ("God Preserve the Emperor"). The melody is in the topmost part, and the totality of the composer's arrangement includes elegant voice-leading and harmonization. (Joseph Haydn *Werke*, Reihe XXIX, Serie 20, Band 1, p. 89. Munich: G. Henle Verlag, 1960.)

Von Saurau's plan was a huge success. The emperor was present to hear Haydn's music in the Burgtheater as the climax of what we might call a "gala" concert. The new hymn was an instant "hit" and one that would endure for centuries to come. After Kaiser Franz died, many poets tried to replace the text. In 1841, the children's song composer, Hoffmann von Fallersleben, wrote "Deutschland, Deutschland, über alles" to Haydn's melody, and that became the national anthem for both Germany and Austria until after World War II. The tune continues today as Germany's national hymn. The solemn ceremoniousness of Haydn's music has spawned religious adaptations as well. Starting in the 19th century, several English-language Protestant hymnals have carried a hymn using Haydn's melody under the title "Glorious Things of Thee Are Spoken."

Haydn's hymn became his best-known work. He was extremely proud of it and of the reception it had received before the sovereign and the people. In his last years, he would play it on the piano for visitors. Also, such a fertile creative mind as Haydn's naturally sought a highly artistic adaption of this finely chiseled piece. The answer lay in working it into one of the six String Quartets he was then composing for Count Erdödy. Haydn made a place for it in the third Quartet of the series (Op. 76, No. 3), in C Major. As the second movement, Haydn presented an arrangement of his hymn as a theme, following that with a set of four variations. This movement is the high point of the entire Quartet (if not of all six Quartets).

The String Quartets of Op. 76 were published in both Vienna and London beginning in

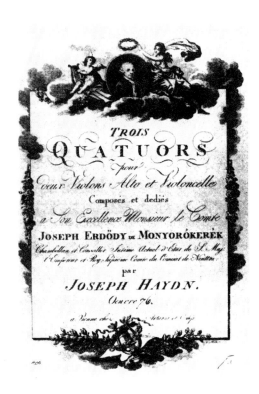

Ill. 5-3 Title page to one of the two books of Haydn's String Quartets, Op. 76, from the Artaria edition (Vienna). The composer is pictured at the top being crowned with a laurel wreath. The name of the dedicatee, Count Erdödy, appears above that of the composer and in lettering almost as large.

1799. They came out in two books of three quartets each (see Ill. 5-3). Charles Burney heard the first three the year they appeared and wrote to Haydn from England, mentioning the "Emperor's Hymn":

> I had the great pleasure of hearing your new *quartetti* (opera 76) well performed before I went out of town, and never received more pleasure from instrumental music: they are full of invention, fire, good taste, and new effects, and seem the production, not of a sublime genius who has written so much and so well already, but of one of highly-cultivated talents, who had expended none of his fire before. The Divine Hymne, written for your imperial master, in imitation of our loyal song, "God save great George our King," and set so admirably to music by yourself, I have translated and adapted to your melody, which is simple, grave, applicating, and pleasing.

What was amazing to Burney is still amazing to us: that this composer, who was already one of the most prolific in history, still had new ideas to express, and that those ideas were "full of invention, fire, good taste, and new effects."

Exploring the "Emperor" String Quartet, second movement

THEME AND VARIATIONS. Over the past five centuries, composers have been attracted to a method of elaborating, developing, commenting, and illuminating a musical idea or short piece of music—a theme—using a technique called *variation*. The choice of themes is purely personal. Composers have sometimes chosen traditional themes, such as Renaissance dance types (e.g., the Folia) or themes by other composers (often as a type of homage). Equally or more often, their themes have been original, as with Haydn's "Emperor's Hymn," which he used as a theme with four variations to produce the second movement of his "Emperor" String Quartet. The dimensions of a theme may differ in the extreme, ranging from a brief ostinato or a 12-tone series up to a succession of phrases cast in a small musical form. In presentation, a theme can range from a single melody or bass line to a full musical texture.

alla breve A duple meter equivalent to 2/2 time, with a time signature of ¢.

The melodic structure of Haydn's theme is in several phrases. Listen to the theme. (If you wish, follow along in the piano-vocal score to the original hymn, given in Ex. 5-3 above.) On a piece of paper or on Ex. 5-3, identify each melodic phrase of the theme.

You should have something like this:

	a	a	b	c	c
MEASURE:	0–4	4–8	8–12	12–16	16–20

(Measure "0" consists of the first two beats before the first full measure. Throughout this movement, each measure is felt in four beats, despite the *alla breve* time signature.) Notice the "classic" symmetry of the melody, using phrase "b" as the central point.

How would you describe the texture in the presentation of the theme? Haydn presents the melody with a full harmonization in the lower parts.

In a theme-and-variations movement, such as Haydn's, the theme is followed by a chain of variations (the number of them being purely at the composer's discretion), analogous to the verses of a song in strophic form:

|| Theme | Var. I | Var. II | Var. III | …

But what *is* a variation? American composer-musicologist Halsey Stevens (1908–1989) once stated, "The principle of variation is that some things change while others remain the same." This terse, general guideline describes music in variation form extending from its beginnings in the Renaissance through the 20th century. When we listen to or examine a variation, we compare it to the theme, noting which elements have been changed and which have been kept constant. As a method helpful to us in considering specific variations, scholars have categorized the most common types of variation. In *The New Harvard Dictionary of Music* (ed. Don Michael Randel), Elaine Sisman's article, "Variation," offers seven variation types. Briefly, they are:

1. Ground bass variation — The theme is a bass line (often short), which the composer repeats unchanged, while the music above it is constantly altered. (Chiefly Baroque, but Modern and Postmodern forms generated from ostinatos derive from this type. We explored a vocal form of this procedure in Purcell's "Dido's Lament," Chapter 2.)

2. Constant melody variation — The melody of the theme is heard intact, while other elements (texture, harmony, etc.) are varied. (Renaissance through Modern periods)

3. Constant harmony variation — The general harmonic form associated with the theme remains fixed, while the melody and other elements may change. (Baroque through Romantic periods)

4. Melodic outline variation — The theme's melody is retained only in a skeletal outline, which may be varied by ornamentation, rhythmic alteration, or melodic simplification. (Classical through Romantic periods)

5. Formal outline variation — The theme's phrase structure is recognizable,

although phrase lengths may be changed, and other aspects of variation may go far afield. (Beethoven through Modern period)

6. Fantasy variation

Freely developmental, only the loosest connection with the theme is present. (Chiefly Romantic period)

7. Serial variation

(1) A variation on a 12-tone theme in which accompaniments, countermelodies, etc. are derived from the 12-tone series. (2) The 12-tone series is considered the "theme," and a variation is a musical structure that explores some possibility implicit in the series. (Modern period, chiefly Schoenberg [1] and Webern [2])

With this information in mind, listen to the entire movement. Which type of variation does Haydn employ? In each variation the melody is present in its original form while other elements of the theme have been varied. Therefore, Haydn is using the constant melody type of variation in every variation. We might point out an interesting connection with English music here, because Haydn's hymn emulated the English *God Save the King*, and this string quartet was written for publication in both London and Vienna: English composers have favored the constant melody variation from the time of the 16th/17th-century virginalists to the 20th century (e.g. Ralph Vaughan Williams, *Five Variants of Dives and Lazarus*, 1939). Consciously or unconsciously, Haydn chose a variation type close to British tradition.

HEARING THE INSTRUMENTATION. You now know that the melody of the theme appears in each variation. You are also acquainted with the instrumentation of a string quartet: two *violins* as the highest instruments; the *viola* as the middle part; and the *cello* as the lowest part. The viola and cello can also play eloquently in their higher ranges. *Listen again to the movement and try to identify which instrument is playing the theme melody in each successive variation. To distinguish between instruments, listen closely for subtle differences in the brightness or darkness between the instruments.*

Here are the answers:

Theme: Violin (I)

Variation I: Violin (II)

Variation II: Cello—middle-high range

Variation III: Viola—middle-high range

Variation IV: Violin (I)

THE VIOLA CLEF. At the opening measure of the score, observe that the violin parts are notated in the treble clef, and the cello part is in the bass clef. Both clefs are very familiar to us. The viola part, however, because of its usual range, uses one of the C clefs: the one known as the alto or viola clef. Notice that viola clef's shape encloses the middle line of the staff. That line represents middle C:

 ← Middle C

The lowest note on the viola is one octave below middle C:

♪

The "Emperor" String Quartet, second movement: A Closer Look

Please refer to the score of the "Emperor" String Quartet beginning on page 42 of the Score Anthology.

Now examine the viola part playing the theme melody in Variation III. How does the viola's pitch level (m. 60) compare with the violin's pitch level in the original theme's presentation (m. 0)? Both play the theme at the same pitch level, though the notation looks different:

Reading music in the viola is not difficult with a little practice. If you wish to become more proficient, transcribe portions of the viola part to another clef, for example, all of Variation II to the bass clef or all of Variation III to the treble clef.

HAYDN'S HYMN "ARRANGEMENT." Originally Haydn cast the "Emperor's Hymn" for voice(s) and piano (see. Ex. 5-3). In adapting that score to the string-quartet theme, he made a few adjustments, some out of necessity, others for pure enhancement.

Compare Ex. 5-3 with the String Quartet score in the Anthology and identify a few differences in the first phrase only (mm. 0–4).

In the string quartet score:

1. Voicing in the chord on the first beat has been reduced to four parts.

2. In m. 1, the "tenor" melody notes A and B are missing entirely, and the C on the next downbeat (m. 2) is played by Violin II, where the "alto" D is missing. Here the voice leading in the viola part is entirely original.

3. The rest of the phrase runs closer to the piano version except, again, the viola part near the end of the phrase.

4. A *turn* ornament decorates the violin melody near the end of the phrase. (See Ex. 3-2 for interpretation.)

THE VARIATIONS. Now let us examine each of the four variations to discover a few of Haydn's compositional techniques. In Variation I, the melody appears in Violin II, while Violin I plays a contrapuntal duet part against it. We could also call this line a countermelody. Note, however, that its nature is not very lyrical compared with the theme melody. Instead, much of it consists of broken chords.

Taking phrase c, analyze the functional harmonies outlined in the Violin I part. Beginning in m. 28 (beat 3) and ending on the downbeat of m. 32, write out the harmonic progression outlined only in Violin I, either in the score or on a separate piece of paper. In this exercise, do not be concerned with the inversion of each chord.

You should have something like this:

MEASURE:	28 29	30	31	32
G:	V I $\vert$ V	I $\vert$ V	IV $\vert$ vi	V_7/V $\vert$ V

In Variation II, how many instruments are playing at any given time? Three or four: this variation alternates between a trio and the full quartet. *Which instrument keeps dropping out?* The viola has frequent rests. *How would you describe the "job" of each of the other instruments?* The cello plays the theme melody throughout. With the cello, Violin II harmonizes closely, often in parallel thirds above the melody. Violin I constantly plays an elaborate **countermelody**.

    Examine Variation III. The prevailing texture is polyphonic, but in how many parts? Beginning in two parts (Violin I, viola), it becomes a trio at m. 2 (Violins I and II, viola). For phrase "c" the trio texture shifts to Violin II, viola, and cello, and we hear the full quartet during the final phrases (mm. 73–80). ***Countermelodies** are important in this variation. Examine that of Violin I, mm. 60–64. Now compare this with the Violin II countermelody of mm. 64 (beat 3) to 66 (downbeat). Describe points of similarity between those two lines.* Violin II begins like Violin I but one octave lower. The music of both parts is identical from m. 2 (beat 3) and m. 66 (beat 3) to the end of each phrase.

    The texture of Variation IV is simpler and more homophonic, like that of the theme itself, but richer with moving parts. Also, the melody returns to Violin I. *Comparing variation IV to the theme, identify some differences in the melody.*

In Variation IV:

1. The melody moves up an octave from the second "a" phrase to the end.

2. The fermata at the end of the second "a" phrase has been removed.

3. In mm. 95–96, a scalar run elaborates the theme's simple octave leap.

Now identify two differences in the harmony.

1. In the opening phrase of Variation IV, some emphasis is placed on the V/vi–vi progression instead of V–I:

2. Chromatic details can be heard in the supporting string parts in the second "c" phrase:

countermelody A contrapuntal part designed to accompany another part to which the countermelody is only slightly subordinate.

Haydn concludes Variation IV and the entire grand movement with a quiet, dignified coda, mm. 100–105, which adds some sweetly chromatic touches:

This table represents the entire theme and variations movement, summarizing the characteristics we have discussed:

SECTION	THEME MELODY	CHARACTERISTICS
Theme	Violin I	Hymnlike lower parts.
Var. I	Violin II	Violin I plays contrapuntal duet part (broken chords).
Var. II	Cello	Textures alternate between trio and quartet.
Var. III	Viola	Polyphonic; countermelodies are important.
Var. IV	Violin I	Texture resembles original theme presentation; melody and harmony enriched with variants of theme.
Coda	——	Touches of chromatic harmony.

HENSEL, PIANO TRIO IN D MINOR, OP. 11, SECOND AND THIRD MOVEMENTS

Piano Chamber Music from W.A. Mozart to Fanny Mendelssohn Hensel

Since the piano was Mozart's instrument, it is not surprising that he excelled in piano chamber music. His seven piano trios written during the Vienna years defined that medium for other composers, and he composed an incomparable pair of piano quartets in G Minor and E-flat Major. The majority of Haydn's 31 piano trios were composed for his London journeys, years after Mozart's works.

From one end of his creative life to the other, Beethoven maintained an abiding interest in chamber music. Among his earliest works are three Piano Quartets (WoO 36), which, along with Mozart's two works, helped to define that medium. In Vienna, his Opus 1 (1795) was a set of three piano trios. Masterful violin sonatas came at regular intervals in his middle period, and his work with the piano trio culminated in the famous, lengthy "Archduke" Trio. Beethoven contributed significantly to the evolution of piano chamber music. During his time, professional string players needed repertoire, and Beethoven, a former string player himself, was happy to give it to them.

Ill. 5-4 Keyboard trio, an engraving from the cover of Joseph Haydn's Op. 80, published by Artaria (Vienna) in 1798.

The long shadow of Beethoven always hung over Franz Schubert (1797–1827), particularly his chamber music, although he struggled to find his own voice. As an adult composer, Schubert's chief musical outlets were private gatherings, where his chamber music was frequently featured. One exceptional work, composed for a village ensemble, was the "Trout" Quintet in A Major for piano, violin, viola, cello, and contrabass. Schubert's Piano Trios in B-flat Major and E-flat Major (**D.** 898 and 929) were composed in his final year (1828) and are among his finest chamber music.

D. Abbreviation for "Deutsch," meaning Deutsch's catalog of works by Schubert.

Fanny Cäcilie Mendelssohn was born in Hamburg, Germany, on November 14, 1805, four years earlier than her famous brother, Felix Mendelssohn (1809–1847). Two more siblings followed. They were grandchildren of the famous Jewish philosopher Moses Mendelssohn and the children of Abraham and Lea (née Salomon) Mendelssohn. Abraham, a well-to-do businessman, saw his Hamburg-based business wither because of Napoleon's blockade of the city, so in 1811 he moved his family to Berlin. There the Mendelssohns established a cultured household, where they could nurture the children's talent and intelligence.

Fanny's mother probably first taught her the piano. During 1816, the family spent some months in Paris, where Fanny and Felix began their musical education formally with piano lessons under Mme. Marie Bigot, famous for interpreting both Haydn and Beethoven. On their return to Berlin, the children continued piano lessons with Ludwig Berger. That year, following the lead of Lea's brother Jakob, Abraham and Lea had their four children baptized in the Lutheran Church, because of the widespread prejudice against Jews. For those and business reasons, Abraham himself converted six years later, adding the more gentile-sounding name Bartholdy to their family name (also as Jakob had done). Fanny was confirmed in 1819.

Fanny was a prodigy. With what her mother called "Bach-fugue fingers," she played *The Well-Tempered Clavier*, Book I, in its entirety from memory at the age of 13. That year, 1818, Fanny and Felix began composition studies at the Berlin Singakademie with its director, Carl

FANNY MENDELSSOHN HENSEL

Drawing by Wilhelm Hensel.
Photo: Stock Montage, Inc.

(continued)

FANNY MENDELSSOHN HENSEL *(continued)*

Friedrich Zelter (1758–1832), the noted *Lied* composer. Soon Fanny composed her first song for her father's birthday in 1819. Between 1820 and 1822, the family and the Singakademie began to spur on Felix and to rein in Fanny. Zelter took Felix to Weimar in 1821 to meet the renowned Goethe, who became acquainted with a song of Fanny's through her brother. The following year, returning with her family from a vacation in Switzerland, Fanny met Goethe personally. In 1825, he wrote to Felix, "Give my regards to your equally talented sister."

The subject of Fanny playing in public (and, by extension, composing music for her performances) was long debated between her and her father, with Felix taking their father's side. We must understand that Abraham Mendelssohn's upper-middle-class position (now as a banker) in European society demanded much decorum. At that level, only a *man* (i.e., Felix) might travel as a concert pianist or conductor and publish his music. Abraham's admonition, "Only that which is feminine befits a woman," says it all, and Fanny's natural aspirations for a life as a concert artist and composer were suppressed from that time. She seems to have taken all this in good spirit, however. Devoted to her brother, she did not mind living in his shadow. In 1822, she became his "biographer," directly through her diary and indirectly through their correspondence when he was away. (If Fanny had received the support, encouragement, and advantages that Felix did, she probably would have developed into as celebrated a composer as he.)

The chief outlet for Fanny's musical talent was the series of private Sunday recitals in the Mendelssohn home, which Lea directed. Fanny also channeled much energy into promoting Felix's career, and he now reciprocated by encouraging her to compose. She wrote songs and piano pieces mainly, which could be presented at the Sunday recitals. Fanny's first music to be published was a group of six songs attributed to her brother as part of his Op. 8 (1828) and Op. 9 (1830). As a composer also of piano and chamber music, Fanny was developing during the early 1820s. She completed a piano sonata in 1821, and the following year she wrote a piano quartet.

Clearly it was Fanny's destiny to marry, and she was extremely fortunate to find someone with a kindred artistic spirit who supported her development as a composer: Wilhelm Hensel (1794–1861), a painter of portraits and historical scenes, whom she had met in 1821. The wedding took place in October 1829, and the Hensels moved into a wing of the large Mendelssohn home. Fanny had some misgivings, as she expressed to her brother, "Once I have produced a good piece after I am married, I will feel relieved and believe I can make progress in the future." Dependent on the Mendelssohn fortune, Wilhelm Hensel reinforced Abraham's dictum against Fanny performing in public, but he wholeheartedly supported her composing and private music-making. He even illustrated some of her manuscripts with miniature drawings, and he preferred to paint while she played or composed in the next room. "My husband makes a point of having me sit down at the piano every morning, immediately after breakfast," she wrote to her brother early in her marriage. "This morning he came, and without saying anything, put a piece of paper on the piano. Five minutes later I called him back and sang him the music, which was set down on paper in another quarter of an hour."

The Hensels' only child arrived in 1830, and Fanny named him Sebastian Ludwig Felix after her father's favorite composers: Bach, Beethoven, and her brother. (In 1879, Sebastian Hensel wrote *Die Familie Mendelssohn, 1729–1847*, based mainly on his mother's diaries and correspondence.) Marriage and family did not slow Fanny Hensel at all. Following her son's birth, she reinstituted her mother's Sunday concerts, which had been discontinued earlier. Central to this project was the formation of a chorus to sing her cantatas and those by Felix. She had composed four of them in 1831 alone. By December of that year, Hensel had conducted her first concert, involving a small chorus and orchestra. The Sunday concerts continued brilliantly and were some of the best music making in Berlin. For one concert in 1833, for example, Hensel's diary tells us the program:

> String Quartet by Mozart
>
> G Major Piano Concerto by Beethoven
>
> Second Duet from *Fidelio* by Beethoven
>
> Keyboard Concerto in D Minor by Bach

She also seized opportunities when traveling artists would visit, for example, when Felix brought home the piano virtuoso Ignaz Moscheles in 1835. Her own String Quartet in C Minor, written in 1834, may have been intended for this concert series.

After her father died in 1836, Fanny Hensel considered publishing some of her music under her *own* name. Felix opposed the idea at first, but her husband encouraged it. Early in 1837, she made a tentative publishing debut with one song, "Die Schiffende" ("Sailing By"), in an anthology of various composers. Felix was enthusiastic after the publication, writing to his sister, "Are you a real composer now, and are you enjoying it?" The only time Hensel performed in public was for a benefit concert given by "amateurs" in February 1838. She played her brother's Piano Concerto No. 1 in G Minor, Op. 25.

For years Fanny Hensel had wished to visit Italy, so in autumn 1839 she, Wilhelm, and Sebastian spent a one-year vacation there. First visiting Milan, Venice, and Florence, they arrived in Rome toward the end of November. Wilhelm was professionally well connected there, and Felix had left many enthusiastic friends from his visit nine years earlier. The Hensels also made new friends, especially the three Prix-de-Rome students from Paris: composer Charles Gounod, conductor Georges Bousquet, and painter Charles Dugasseau. They loved Hensel's music and encouraged her to compose. Years later, Gounod remembered her in his memoirs as "an incomparable musician, a remarkable pianist, a woman of superior intelligence, small and slender. ... She had rare gifts as a composer."

On their return, Hensel resumed her Sunday concerts, now presenting the best performances by Berlin musicians. Felix was a frequent guest, and it was here that his cantata *Die erste Walpurgisnacht* (*The First Walpurgis Night [Witches' Sabbath]*) premiered in its final form in 1843. Hensel had now become such a celebrity locally that Franz Liszt paid her a visit while in Berlin for a recital of his own. The death of Hensel's mother in December 1842 probably increased her resolve to carry on the tradition her mother had initiated. During these years she continued to be creative, producing chiefly piano works: character pieces and her *Sonata in G Minor*.

In 1846, Hensel began publishing her music seriously. Now, with her brother's blessing, she brought out her Opus 1, a selection of six *Lieder* followed by another half dozen songs (Op. 2). Opp. 3–7 followed in 1847–1848: six songs for a vocal ensemble (Op. 3), six piano pieces (Opp. 4–5), four *Songs Without Words* for piano (Op. 6), and six more *Lieder* (Op. 7). A review of Op. 2 shows the male chauvinism so common in the musical scene at the time. In the January 11, 1847, issue of the *Neue Zeitschrift für Musik* (*New Musical Periodical*), a reviewer wrote about music "whose outward appearance does not at all betray a woman's hand but suggests an artistic study of masculine seriousness. ..." Four months later, Hensel's *Gartenlieder* (*Garden Songs*, Op. 3) received slightly better treatment in a review that admitted that they "stand out from

(continued)

FANNY MENDELSSOHN HENSEL *(continued)*

many others of the same kind. … The harmonic language is highly select, and one cannot fail to recognize an artistic hand."

No one could know that Fanny's days were numbered. Like her parents and siblings, she had a delicate constitution. In previous years, she had suffered slight temporary paralysis in her hands—no doubt mild strokes, the result of high blood pressure. Now, in early May 1847, she suffered a series of violent nosebleeds, which she could control. However, on Friday, May 14, she drove herself particularly hard rehearsing *Die erste Walpurgisnacht*, which she was to conduct that Sunday. Suddenly, her hands were stricken with paralysis, which soon became general. The last thing she uttered was, "It's a stroke, like Mother had." Then she lost consciousness and died at eleven o'clock that night.

The Mendelssohn family, always extremely close, was overwhelmed. Felix, especially, was devastated; his life had been so intertwined with Fanny's, musically and personally. In late October, Felix also had a series of strokes, leading to his death on November 4, less than six months after Fanny's passing. He was buried in Berlin next to her.

In 1848 and 1850, Fanny Hensel's family released several more compositions for publication. One of these was her Piano Trio in D Minor, the final Hensel publication until her rediscovery in the 20th century.

Hensel's Piano Trio in D Minor: An Overview

Fanny Hensel's chamber works are not numerous. Following the Piano Quartet and *Adagio* for violin and piano from her student years, she composed two works for cello and piano, a *capriccio* movement and a whole sonata in the later 1820s. After her String Quartet in C Minor, written in 1834, she apparently composed no more chamber music until 1846, when she wrote the Piano Trio in D Minor (Op. 11), now considered her masterpiece. We do not know the exact date Hensel completed her Piano Trio, but it was before December 1, when a letter from Hensel to her brother speaks of an upcoming premiere. That event was probably the performance on April 11, 1847, when she opened the new season of Sunday musicales in her home; it was the date of her sister Rebecka's birthday, the occasion for which she composed the Piano Trio. The work received "universal applause," according to the composer's son.

Ill. 5-5 Title page to Fanny Mendelssohn Hensel's Piano Trio in D Minor, Op. 11, published by Breitkopf & Härtel in 1850 as "No. 4 of the legacy of works."

Hensel cast her work in a four-movement sonata plan. The first movement is in sonata form, an essay of sweeping passion evident in the opening measures. Ex. 5-4 shows how she plunges immediately into the broad, emotional principal theme.

Ex. 5-4 Opening measures of Hensel's Piano Trio in D Minor, Op. 11. The stormy piano part supports a passionate first theme in the strings.

Simulating an orchestral string section with **tremolo** technique in the piano part, the cello sings out the lyrical secondary theme (m. 58):

tremolo On a string instrument, the rapid and continuous repetition of a single note. On a piano, the rapid and continuous alternation of notes in a chord, meant to resemble several string instruments playing the chord using tremolo techniques.

After a full, well-organized development section, Hensel begins the recapitulation pre-dictably with the principal theme. However, unpredictably, she assigns the melody in broad chords to the piano and the stormy accompaniment to the strings (m. 253):

The middle two movements are an *Andante espressivo* and an *Allegretto*. We discuss these below; however, we can mention two features here. First, the movements are joined without a break (see pp. 52–53 of the Score Anthology). This makes them function somewhat as a unit, especially since their tempos are not too dissimilar (*Andante* and *Allegretto*). Thus, the Piano Trio's overall plan carries a certain Romantic ambiguity: Is the work in four movements or three?

The second feature relates to the third movement only. Instead of the expected whirlwind scherzo, Hensel presents an *Allegretto* movement titled "*Lied*." By this she does not mean liter-ally a vocal art song, but an instrumental movement in the spirit of a *Lied*. It is a *Lied ohne Worte* (Song Without Words), a designation that both Fanny and her brother Felix used for solo-piano character pieces, here transferred to the chamber-music idiom. Perhaps also she is deferring to her brother, who was a master of the scherzo. As biographer Françoise Tillard points out, "Why would she need scherzos, when Felix wrote such good ones!"

The entire work places the piano in the foreground much of the time. However, the finale, marked *Allegro moderato,* focuses on it even more intensely, casting it in a virtuoso role. Ex. 5-5 shows the first page of the movement, an extended, rhapsodic piano solo.

FINALE.

HENSEL, PIANO TRIO IN
D MINOR, OP. 11, SECOND
AND THIRD MOVEMENTS

Ex. 5-5 The opening of the finale to Hensel's Piano Trio in D Minor, Op. 11, a rhapsodic piano solo unusual in chamber music.

The first movement's passion and tempestuousness return in the finale, now with additional tension due to more complex rhythms, for example, two against three at the opening of the coda (m. 193):

This excerpt also illustrates the shift between D minor and D major, which characterizes the movement and brings it to a triumphant finish in the major mode.

Exploring the Piano Trio's Middle Movements

Listen to the two movements, and notice that they are joined without a break. Identify the point in the music where the Andante espressivo ends and the Allegretto "Lied" begins. The rhythmic and harmonic motion slow radically in the last two measures of the *Andante*, and the composer introduces an entirely new musical idea at the beginning of the *"Lied"*:

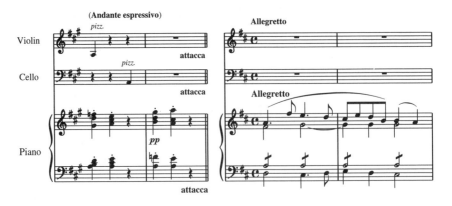

Now listen to only the Andante espressivo. Its form is in how many sections? How would you symbolize the form in letters, using "A" for the first section, "B" for the second, etc.?

After the second section, the first returns in a modified form, so the symbols would be:

A–B–A or A–B–A'

How can you tell when section B begins? Two things happen: (1) A different melody is introduced (piano); and (2) the stringed instruments begin to play a *staccato* accompaniment not heard before.

How can you tell when section A returns? The piano plays the music that opened the movement.

Listen now to the "Lied" movement. Is it based nearly entirely on the piano's music at the beginning?

Yes, the piano plays a phrase made up of three motives:

Hensel then builds the rest of the movement almost exclusively on restatements of those motives in various harmonic contexts.

Where do the violin and the cello first play one these motives? We hear the violin first with motive b and a variant of motive c:

Much later, toward the end of the movement, the cello plays the whole phrase, including all three motives:

As we learned above, the Andante is an A–B–A' form. In the score, find the beginning of section B and of the A' section. Section B begins with the upbeat to m. 38, and section A' begins in m. 69.

CANON. *Examine the cello part in mm. 18 (with upbeat) to the downbeat of m. 20. Now compare this with the melody the violin begins to play one measure later. What is the relation-*

The Andante espressivo and "Lied": A Closer Look
Please refer to the score of Hensel's Piano Trio in D Minor, beginning on page 47 of the Score Anthology.

ship? For about two measures, the violin plays an octave higher *exactly* what the cello has played. This is a contrapuntal technique called *canon.* This particular passage is a canon at the octave, because the following part answers an octave away from the leading part.

Now, in section B, find a passage that comes close to being a strict canon at the octave between violin and cello. Measure 54 (with upbeat) begins such a passage. After the first three notes, however, the cello's melodic intervals differ from the violin's. This makes the passage merely imitative instead of canonic. If you look, you can find other imitative passages in the A' section.

MELODIC UNITY. Examine and listen to the theme of section A (mm. 1 ff.). Do the same with the theme of section B, but wait until the violin plays the melody at the upbeat to m. 46. Can you identify some ways Hensel has made these two melodies relate to each other? See Ex. 5-6.

Ex. 5-6 Hensel, Piano Trio, comparison of the two themes of the *andante espressivo:* (a) section A; (b) section B.

(a)

(b)

The most important correspondence is the dotted rhythm figure at the beginning of both themes:

Another similarity is an arch shape in each melody:

THE "LIED": FREE MATERIAL. We have noted above that in the *"Lied"* most of the movement is based on one of the three motives present at the beginning. *Now, listening with score in hand, find one passage where none of the instruments play a motive or a variant of it.* Measures 17–22 are a transitional passage. In its first two measures (piano), the *shape* of a figure from motive c appears, but then the music dissolves into free material until m. 23. *Regarding harmony and key relationships, what is the function of this transitional passage?* The cadence in mm. 16–17 is V–i in F-sharp minor, the mediant of the home key of D major. The transition takes the music back to the tonic key (m. 23, beat 2).

Does the coda (mm. 44–47) contain thematic material in the piano, or is it entirely free? The melody has only the general *shape* of a figure from motive a. Otherwise, it is free.

BRAHMS, VIOLIN SONATA NO. 3 IN D MINOR, OP. 108, FIRST MOVEMENT

The "golden age" of chamber music came to an end with Beethoven and Schubert. Composers in the next generations had different agendas. The purity and objectivity of Classical chamber music ran counter to the emotional, subjective spirit of the age. Thus, many of the leading romanticists were uninterested in its possibilities as music for music's sake. For example, Hector Berlioz (1803–1869) wrote only a few miscellaneous pieces for violin and piano, and Franz Liszt (1811–1886) composed fewer than ten chamber pieces, mostly with programmatic titles attached. Most of the noteworthy Romantic chamber music came from composers who revered the music of the Classical period and carried forth its standards. We have explored the music of one of these composers, Fanny Mendelssohn Hensel. Her brother had similar ideals and produced important string quartets and a famous piano trio. Robert Schumann (1810–1856), a close friend of Mendelssohn, also had a reverence for Classical chamber music, and even innovated in that field by inventing the piano quintet (piano plus string quartet). However Schumann's protégé Johannes Brahms, was the composer who brought Romantic chamber music to its culmination.

Johannes Brahms was born in Hamburg, Germany, on May 7, 1833, the middle of three children born to Jakob and Johanna Brahms. Jakob played the contrabass in the Hamburg city orchestra and was probably Johannes's first music teacher. The boy began studying piano formally at the age of seven and appeared in his first public concert at the age of ten. His eagerness to compose was rewarded with lessons in music theory from Eduard Marxsen beginning in 1846. Brahms developed along parallel tracks as a pianist and composer. He gave solo recitals in 1848 and 1849. About that time, at Marxsen's suggestion, Brahms sent a packet of his compositions to Robert Schumann for criticism; it came back unopened.

An important influence on Brahms's music then was the Hungarian Gypsy style, which became the rage in Hamburg. (A stream of Hungarian insurgents passed through the German city, fleeing their failed 1848 rebellion.) Irregular rhythms and *moto-perpetuo* triplet figures made a particular impression on Brahms's style, and he also learned Gypsy dances and *rubato*-style interpretation. Particularly influential was the violinist Eduard Reményi, who took Brahms on a tour of Europe in 1850. In Göttingen, Brahms met another violinist, Joseph Joachim, who became a lifelong friend. Franz Liszt received Brahms and Reményi in Weimar. On Joachim's recommendation, Brahms visited Robert and Clara Schumann in Düsseldorf in September 1853. They took the 20-year-old fledgling composer-pianist to their hearts. Robert went as far as publishing a laudatory article on Brahms's music, titled "New Paths," calling him

> … the one who would be chosen to express the most exalted spirit of the times in an ideal manner, one who would not bring us mastery in gradual development stages but who, like Minerva, would spring fully armed from the head of Jove. And he has arrived … his name is Johannes Brahms.

Schumann's words were, in fact, prophetic, for Brahms's compositional style was nearly mature at that early date, and it changed little over the years.

Returning to Hamburg, Brahms learned the next year of Robert Schumann's commitment to an asylum, and he rushed back to Düsseldorf to help the family. Clara Schumann (1819–1896), 14 years older than Brahms, became the object of an extended "puppy" love. Apparently, he confessed his love to her in 1855 (the year before Robert Schumann's death), but we have no record of her response. When Clara took her family to Berlin in 1857, Johannes returned to Hamburg. They were together in Berlin in spring 1858, but that summer Brahms

(continued)

moto perpetuo Perpetual motion, a type of composition in which constant rhythmic motion persists, usually based on a single note value throughout.

JOHANNES BRAHMS (*continued*)

fell in love with Agathe von Siebold in Göttingen. They did not marry, but Brahms later immortalized letters from her name in a theme of his G Major String Sextet (composed in 1864–1865).

During the years 1857–1858, Brahms spent the fall months at the princely court of Detmold, where he conducted a chorus, performed at the piano, and gave piano lessons. Those were also the years of Brahms's earliest orchestral music, the two Serenades, Opp. 11 and 16. He completed his Piano Concerto No. 1 in D Minor (Op. 15) in 1858. The following year he founded a women's chorus in Hamburg, which he conducted for three years. For this ensemble he arranged folk songs and composed some original music. The year 1859 also saw the earliest performances of his First Piano Concerto (with the composer as soloist); it was successful in Hanover and Hamburg but a failure in Leipzig. This may have been partly due to a growing ideological and political rift between two schools of Romantic music: the New German School led by Liszt and Richard Wagner on one side; and the conservative opposition led by Brahms and Joachim on the other. In 1860 Brahms, Joachim, and two other prominent musicians publicly dissociated themselves from the principles of Liszt and his circle. At this time Brahms occupied himself with writing chamber music and major variation sets for piano, also continuing work on *Ein deutsches Requiem* (*A German Requiem*), which he had begun in 1857.

Brahms's hopes of becoming the conductor of the Hamburg orchestra were crushed in May 1863, but that month he was offered the directorship of the Singakademie of Vienna (where he had moved the previous year). During the next two years, Brahms made his music known in Vienna through concerts, and he acquired valuable contacts, notably the conductor Hermann Levi, who became one of his most effective promoters. In 1865, Brahms's mother died, prompting further work on his *German Requiem*. Toward the end of the 1860s, Brahms again had friction with the New German School, because Wagner wrote a scathing polemic against his conducting in 1869. Wagner may have wished to intimidate Brahms, fearing that he would become a rival in the field of opera (the only musical medium Brahms never attempted). Brahms resisted returning the antagonism.

The *German Requiem*'s premiere at the cathedral in Bremen in 1868 brought Brahms international recognition as a composer. It was the longest work he had written, and its profundity moved the audience and critics alike. As a conductor, his career took another leap forward when he was offered the post of the Vienna Concert Society's orchestral conductor in 1870. At first he declined but accepted in 1872 for a time, on condition that he conduct the chorus as well. The following year, Brahms completed one of his most significant compositions, *Variations on a Theme of Haydn*, Op. 56, in two versions: for two pianos and for orchestra. The orchestral premiere was a triumph. Now Brahms was completely established as a composer and secure financially from concerts and publishers' royalties.

His next orchestral work, the First Symphony, had to wait another three years for completion. Brahms finished it in 1876 at the age of 43. Harshly self-critical and always concerned about being compared with Beethoven, he waited until he felt he had fully mastered the orchestral medium before introducing a work titled "Symphony." As it turned out, the comparisons came about anyway, and Brahms's Symphony No. 1 in C Minor (Op. 68) was often called "Beethoven's Tenth." He composed his symphonies and overtures in pairs. The Second Symphony followed close to the First in 1877. His Third and Fourth Symphonies were the products of 1883–1885. The *Academic Festival Overture* and *Tragic Overture*, like a pair of drama masks ("One of them weeps, the other laughs," he wrote), were both composed in 1880.

Brahms's honorary doctorate from the University of Breslau was the occasion of the *Academic Festival Overture*. By that time, the composer had also added to his orchestral *oeuvre* his Violin Concerto, Op. 77. His interest in piano works and chamber music continued, and 1878–1879 saw the creation of his Violin Sonata No. 1 in G Major (Op. 78). Brahms, since the age of 20, had been an avid composer of German *Lieder*. Now, in this period, one of his most productive, his interest intensified, and he completed seven collections of original songs between 1877 and 1879. He also enjoyed arranging folk songs for voice and piano, generating three big collections that totaled 91 arrangements. Beginning in these years, he usually spent winters giving concerts, doing most of his composing during summer months.

Brahms was by nature a kindly person, and on occasion he could be very generous toward members of his profession. One recipient of his generosity was Antonín Dvořák (1841–1904), who at the age of 33 applied for a government subsidy for composition. Brahms, a member of the awards committee, was impressed with his music and convinced the panel to give him a substantial grant. Brahms also befriended Dvořák and persuaded his own publisher, Simrock, to publish some of Dvořák's music.

The year 1881 involved Brahms with an old friend and a new friend. Joachim was the old friend with whom Brahms unwittingly became involved in a court matter concerning the violinist's wife. The rift in their friendship lasted until 1887, when Brahms composed the "Double" Concerto for Joachim and the famous cellist Robert Hausmann. (This was to be Brahms's last orchestral composition.) The new friend was Hans von Bülow, a brilliant pianist, who conducted his Meiningen court orchestra in a concert of Brahms's music in November 1881. By now, Hermann Levi had defected to the Wagner camp, so von Bülow became Brahms's beloved champion. Brahms could now use the Meiningen orchestra as a sort of "laboratory." However, between 1886 and 1888, he concentrated instead on chamber music, producing the last two violin sonatas (Opp. 100 and 108), his Second Cello Sonata in F Major (Op. 99), and the Piano Trio No. 3 in C Minor (Op. 101), among other works.

By the late 1880s, Brahms had become a musical celebrity, and he began amassing important honors. Two Austrian emperors bestowed honorary knighthoods on him, and his own native Hamburg belatedly made him a "freeman" of the city. In 1890, Brahms purposely began bringing his very fruitful compositional career to its "finale." However, he was far from retiring completely. Inspired by the Meiningen clarinetist Richard Mühlfeld, he rapidly composed the Clarinet Trio in A Minor and the Clarinet Quintet in B Minor (Opp. 114 and 115), following these in 1894 with two clarinet sonatas (Op. 120). He also turned his efforts to short piano pieces, producing four collections (Opp. 116, 117, 118, and 119) in 1892. Brahms completed his creative life with the *Vier ernste Gesänge* (*Four Serious Songs*, Op. 121) and *Eleven Chorale Preludes* for organ (Op. 122), both written in 1896.

That year Clara Schumann died. Brahms had grown extremely close to her over the years, and they had spent time together whenever opportunities arose. Their correspondence was substantial. Brahms would send her movements as he completed them, and she (a former composer in her own right) would give her reactions, often subjective but always valuable to him. He attended her funeral in Bonn in May 1896, but he soon became ill himself with cancer of the liver. By the following March his condition had advanced and he was bedridden. He died on the morning of April 3. Crowds attended his funeral in Vienna three days later, and the ships in Hamburg's harbor flew their flags at half-mast.

oeuvre In French, "work," normally used to mean an individual composer's entire body of works (collectively).

symphonic poem A one-movement orchestral composition; the epitome of program music.

neo-Classicism An anti-Romantic movement in 20th century music that revived many of the practices and aesthetics of the 18th century. Adj.: neo-Classical.

tone color Also called "timbre," the quality, nature, or type of sound produced by one instrument as distinct from that of another.

Brahms as a Chamber Music Composer

Throughout his life, Johannes Brahms took the self-effacing view that he was a student, not a master. He viewed himself as studying at the feet of Mozart, Haydn, Beethoven, and Schubert, and never considered himself their equal. At the same time, he knew that he was the torchbearer of the Classical ideals of those composers, a torch he received, figuratively, from the hands of Robert Schumann. In his own time, therefore, Brahms was something of an anachronism. The mainstream of music was following the New German School of Romanticism—Liszt and Wagner mainly—where music heavy in emotion and programmatic content was the norm. Brahms represented a beacon of propriety and emotional restraint. Instead of operas, **symphonic poems**, and programmatic piano pieces, Brahms quietly developed his craft as a composer of relatively abstract music: chamber music, **neo-Classical** symphonies, and self-contained piano music.

Among the top ranks of Romantic composers, Brahms surely composed more chamber music than any. Following an early scherzo for violin and piano, Brahms published 24 full-size chamber works. Some of his chamber music is for strings without piano; however, because he was a pianist, he had a greater interest in works that included his instrument.

String chamber music did not come easily to Brahms at first. About it he wrote, "It is not difficult to compose, but what is enormously hard is to leave the superfluous notes under the table." Brahms confided to his friends that before completing the two string quartets of Op. 51 he had made at least 20 attempts at string quartet writing. So he tried something different and produced the Sextet in B-flat, Op. 18, his first publishable music in the string medium. As with his symphonies, Brahms was always concerned that any string quartet by him would be compared to Beethoven's. Published as Op. 51, his first two string quartets required eight years for Brahms to complete to his own satisfaction.

After the early failure of the string quintet (with two cellos) version of Op. 34, Brahms waited until the spring of 1882 to write again for five strings. This time he employed the two-viola configuration for his Quintet in F Major, Op. 88, a work in three concise movements. The String Quintet in G Major, Op. 111 was one of his last compositions, but it is among his most youthful-sounding works.

Brahms involved wind instruments in some chamber music. The earliest work of this type was the Horn Trio, Op. 40. In it he required not the valve horn, which we are used to hearing, but the old "natural" valveless horn (*Waldhorn* in German), possibly a nostalgic throwback to the days of Haydn and Mozart. Brahms's choice resulted in a work in which the horn is not always featured as much as it might be but is often present as a shadow of **tone color** added to the piano and violin. Another old-fashioned feature of the Horn Trio is its movement plan: slow–fast–slow–fast, derived from the Baroque *sonata da chiesa* employed by Corelli, Handel, and Bach.

Brahms gave far more attention to the clarinet than the horn, producing a series of four late chamber works. All were the result of his enchantment with "Fräulein Klarinette," as he jokingly called Meiningen clarinetist Richard Mühlfeld because of his sweet tone. First he wrote the Trio for Clarinet, Cello, and Piano, Op. 114, but soon declared, in his typical self-deprecating style, that this was "twin to a much bigger piece of foolishness." The "twin" was the Clarinet Quintet, composed in emulation of Mozart's. Brahms's very last chamber works were a pair of sonatas for clarinet and piano completed two years before his death.

Brahms's Chamber Sonatas

The clarinet sonatas also capped Brahms's long line of chamber music with piano. Like Robert Schumann, he had composed a single piano quintet. Brahms's was the Piano Quintet in F Minor, Op. 34, the result of revising his unsuccessful string quintet on the advice of Clara

Ill. 5-6 The Joachim Quartet, founded in 1869. From left to right: Joseph Joachim (first violin), Robert Hausmann (cello), Emanuel Wirth (viola), and Carl Halir (second violin). Joachim and Hausmann were Brahms's close friends for whom he composed the "Double" Concerto in A Minor, Op. 102.

Schumann. Following his Classical bent, Brahms also created three piano quartets and three piano trios, ranging through the core of his career from 1853 to 1886. His interest in composing sonatas for the cello was sparked only twice, first in 1862 and then in 1886. The E Minor Cello Sonata, Op. 38, is a study in contrasting styles. From a romantically impassioned, lyrical first movement, the composer moved to a delicate, classical *Ländler* (forerunner to the waltz), and then on to a dynamic, Baroque-inspired fugal finale completed in 1865. More than 20 years later, he wrote his Cello Sonata No. 2 in F Major, Op. 99. Now he exploited a higher range and a greater scope of expression, because he had in mind the virtuoso Robert Hausmann, cellist with the Joachim String Quartet.

Brahms had destroyed three early violin sonatas, and the three surviving ones are all late music, created between 1878 and 1888. In composing the first in G Major, Op. 78, Brahms had Joachim in mind. Clara Schumann wrote to him in 1880, the year of the sonata's publication:

> Joachim was here … and for two days we had a lot of music. We played the *Regenlied* Sonata again, and I was deeply moved by it. I wish that the last movement could accompany me in my journey from here to the next world.

The nickname "*Regenlied*" ("Rain Song") comes from two Brahms settings of a poem by that title (by Klaus Groth). In quoting a song within a chamber work, Brahms was harking back to Schubert's "Trout" Quintet and "Death and the Maiden" Quartet. From his earlier song settings, Brahms derived an entire theme in the final movement.

Lake Thun (Switzerland) was the idyllic setting where the 53-year-old composer wrote the graceful and lyrical A Major Sonata, Op. 100, during the summer of 1886. Brahms alluded to several songs that "go with the sonata" as he had done in the First Violin Sonata. In the first movement, for example, the second theme is an adaptation of Brahms's *Lied* "Wie Melodien zieht es mir" ("Like Melodies, It Draws Me"), which later became Op. 105, No. 1. Analysts have recognized other *Lieder* in the first and third movements. This is the shortest of the three violin sonatas.

The Violin Sonata in D Minor, Op. 108: An Overview

The summer Brahms completed his Second Violin Sonata he began to compose his third. He made substantial sketches of the D Minor Sonata but put them aside to work on the Double Concerto. Two years later he finished the sonata. Biographer Karl Geiringer writes that this work "is more broadly planned, more brilliant, and also more vehement than the two preced-

Ill. 5-7 Brahms at the piano in the 1890s. Tempera painting by Willy von Beckerath after a sketch.

intermezzo (1) A two-scene Italian light musical theater piece of the early 18th century, forerunner to the full-length *opera buffa* (comic opera); (2) a lightweight instrumental movement or character piece sometimes placed between more serious movements.

ing violin sonatas. No delicate dreamer, but rather an untamed and fiery spirit speaks to us here." Several of Brahms's earlier works from the mid-1850s had the same "Storm and Stress" spirit. So, in a way, Brahms came full circle with the D Minor Sonata.

This work was "more broadly planned" by containing a four-movement sonata plan. The two middle movements are not lengthy, however, and the outer movements are as concise as possible. The opening *Allegro* (explored below), though restrained and often quiet, is charged with a dramatic tension. The *Adagio*, by contrast, is quiet and reflective, cast in an A–A' form. In place of a full scherzo, Brahms offers a tightly constructed A–B–A' *intermezzo*-style movement marked *Un poco presto e con sentimento*. The "more brilliant" aspect of the sonata lies chiefly in its final movement, *Presto agitato*. Brahms wastes no time introducing the movement's brilliance, beginning the movement with this rugged motive:

Critics agree that this sonata is the "apotheosis" of the three violin sonatas, and Geiringer goes further in concluding, "Perfect as each movement of the three Violin Sonatas is, they seem in this last movement, to have reached their culminating point."

Exploring the D Minor Sonata, first movement

Listen to the entire movement. You may have noticed that this is clearly a sonata form. Listen to the movement again; this time, identify the start of important structural and thematic points in the form. Stop and relisten as necessary. The exposition's primary theme (P) begins right away, and Brahms keeps its dynamics quiet, around a *piano. Identify the start of the start of the tran-*

sition (T). A sudden dynamic shift to *forte* announces the transition. The T section sounds at first like a development of P, but later takes on its own new motives. *Now identify the beginning of the secondary theme (S).* It is a lyrical melody in a major key played first by the piano alone:

The exposition contains no concluding theme, *per se*. The secondary theme group merely winds down to a quiet cadence, relaxing the rhythmic momentarily. *A change in texture signals the beginning of the development section. As you listen, identify this juncture in the music.* Here is the end of the exposition and the beginning of the development:

Begin listening again at the start of the development. Identify the beginning of the recapitulation. The recapitulation begins with a feeling of release and sounds much like the opening of the exposition, at least in the violin part (see Ex. 5-7).

Ex. 5-7 Brahms, Violin Sonata No. 3: comparison of (a) the exposition, m. 1, with (b) the recapitulation, m. 130.

In the recapitulation, listen for the main thematic features: P, T, and S (although Brahms enhances these in several ways).

At the end of the movement is a coda. Listen from the start of the recapitulation to the end of the movement, and identify the start of the coda. The coda is easy to hear because it begins like the development. Now, however, the music emphasizes the home key:

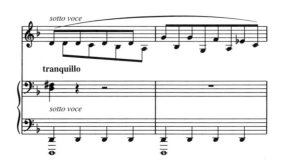

**The D Minor Sonata,
first movement:
A Closer Look**

Please refer to the score of the Brahms Violin Sonata in D Minor beginning on page 55 of the Score Anthology.

By studying the score, we can add to our knowledge of this masterful movement. Measure 1 begins the full P theme, which lasts about eight measures. However, Brahms also introduces some additional motives as part of the P group. After m. 8, identify one or two new motives. Here are two prominent motives:

Find the beginning of T at m. 24. As you have already heard, T begins with motives taken from P. Trace these motives as far as they go. Now identify where the music shifts to an idea not from the P theme. The new idea, with its wide leaps, is emotionally more intense:

pedal point A long note, usually in bass part, which is sustained while harmonies above it change.

Now we skip ahead to the development section, beginning in m. 84. This is an incredible *tour de force*. Here, Brahms supports the development's entire 46 measures with a continuous **pedal point** in the piano's left hand. *Look now at mm. 84–129, and notice the continually repeated note A in the bass.* This note is, of course, the dominant note of the home key, D minor. The continuous pedal point does more than anything to build tension in this movement. That is why we sense a release (or relief) when it finally resolves at m. 130, the Recapitulation.

The development concentrates closely on the P theme and other motives in that group. Although we can easily hear that the composer is developing, his techniques are subtle. For example, compare mm. 84–85 of the violin part with mm. 1–2, violin and piano. We find that the rocking violin figure contains the skeleton of the melody and accompaniment in the opening measures, as Ex. 5-8 shows.

Ex. 5-8 Brahms, Violin Sonata
No. 3: comparison of opening
measures of (a) the exposition,
violin and piano, and (b) the
development, violin only, showing closely related content.

Brahms, a master of counterpoint, sometimes weaves canons into his music, another subtle development technique. In mm. 100–103, find the canon between (1) the piano right hand, (2) the violin, and (3) the piano left hand. Brahms introduces a melody in the piano's right hand, beginning on middle C. The violin answers this in a strict canon on F after one measure. As this canon dissolves in m. 103, the composer brings in another canonic voice in the piano, beginning on note B-flat. The strictness of this line, however, is short-lived, and it continues by developing motives from the P theme.

In the score, find the beginning of the coda, and compare it with the beginning of the development section. The coda (m. 236) is an obvious reminiscence of the development section. However, the suspense of the dominant pedal point is now replaced by the relaxation of a tonic pedal point. (This is a good demonstration of Brahms's acute sense of balance and proportion.) The first two measures of each passage are shaped identically: the P theme and accompaniment rocking in the violin against the bass pedal point. From there, the coda deviates considerably. The only feature that continues to unify the two passages is a focus on the P theme. *Find a P-theme motive in the piano (mm. 240–241), then in the violin (mm. 242–243), in the piano again (mm. 244–247), and finally in the violin part (mm. 259–261).* Brahms ends this creative triumph with unity and economy.

𝄃𝄂 CHAPTER SIX

Orchestral Music

THE PRE-CLASSICAL AND CLASSICAL SYMPHONY

The origin of the symphony was in Italian opera. In the last 20 years of the 17th century, Alessandro Scarlatti devised a type of operatic overture—called a *sinfonia*—which employed three short contrasting sections. The tempos of the sections were:

Fast—Slow—Fast

The final section was usually dancelike in a triple meter (3/8 or 3/4).

By about 1700 this pattern had become universal for Italian operas. Because a *sinfonia* had no musical connection to other parts of its opera, it could easily be disconnected and performed separately in a concert or as dinner music. Publishing a *sinfonia* independently and without reference to its opera was also common. The three sections were now enlarged slightly and became independent movements. The *sinfonia*'s three-movement pattern thus gave birth to the original three-movement sonata plan (see Chapter 3).

Around 1730, Italian composers, notably Giovanni Battista Sammartini (1701–1775), began to compose independent works following the *sinfonia* model. Composers used an opera-theater-size orchestra: chiefly a small section of strings and *basso continuo*, sometimes augmented by a pair of woodwinds or horns (or both).

Pre-Classical Symphony in Germany and Austria

By mid-century, the *sinfonia* (symphony) as an independent instrumental genre had become established in various parts of Europe. In the court orchestra of Frederick the Great in Berlin, Carl Philipp Emanuel Bach was the leading symphony composer. He became well known especially for his slow movements, which were particularly expressive and emotional. The style of these movements later sparked the imagination of high Classical composers such as Haydn and Mozart.

The orchestra at the court of Mannheim (southwestern Germany) was ranked first in Europe at mid-century, chiefly due to the discipline and orchestral innovations credited to its director, Johann Stamitz (1717–1757). In his symphonies, Stamitz exploited a wide dynamic range and developed suspenseful *crescendo* techniques that thrilled audiences. By 1756, Stamitz had Europe's largest orchestra to work with:

STRINGS	WOODWINDS	BRASS & PERCUSSION
20 Violins	4 Flutes	4 Horns
4 Violas	2 Oboes	12(!) Trumpets
4 Cellos	2 Bassoons	Timpani (one pair)
2 Contrabasses		

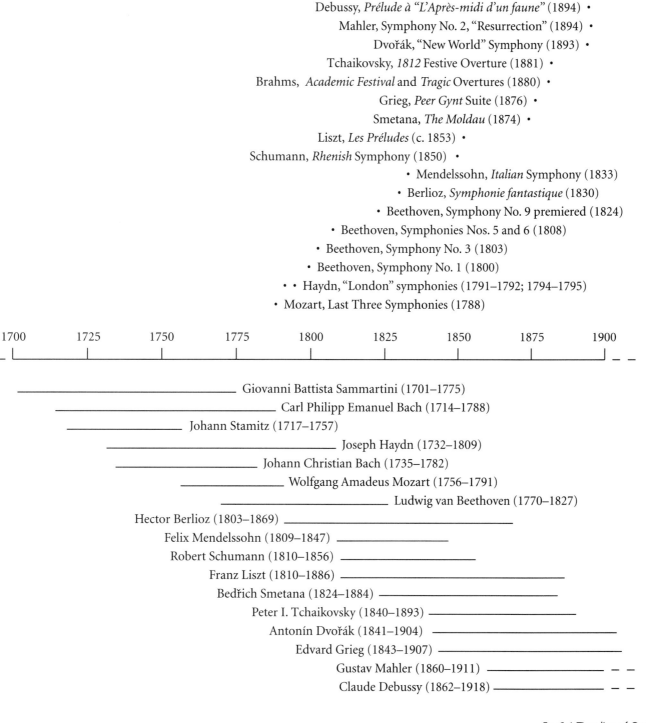

Debussy, *Prélude à "L'Après-midi d'un faune"* (1894) •
Mahler, Symphony No. 2, "Resurrection" (1894) •
Dvořák, "New World" Symphony (1893) •
Tchaikovsky, *1812* Festive Overture (1881) •
Brahms, *Academic Festival* and *Tragic* Overtures (1880) •
Grieg, *Peer Gynt* Suite (1876) •
Smetana, *The Moldau* (1874) •
Liszt, *Les Préludes* (c. 1853) •
Schumann, *Rhenish* Symphony (1850) •
• Mendelssohn, *Italian* Symphony (1833)
• Berlioz, *Symphonie fantastique* (1830)
• Beethoven, Symphony No. 9 premiered (1824)
• Beethoven, Symphonies Nos. 5 and 6 (1808)
• Beethoven, Symphony No. 3 (1803)
• Beethoven, Symphony No. 1 (1800)
• • Haydn, "London" symphonies (1791–1792; 1794–1795)
• Mozart, Last Three Symphonies (1788)

1700   1725   1750   1775   1800   1825   1850   1875   1900

Giovanni Battista Sammartini (1701–1775)
Carl Philipp Emanuel Bach (1714–1788)
Johann Stamitz (1717–1757)
Joseph Haydn (1732–1809)
Johann Christian Bach (1735–1782)
Wolfgang Amadeus Mozart (1756–1791)
Ludwig van Beethoven (1770–1827)
Hector Berlioz (1803–1869)
Felix Mendelssohn (1809–1847)
Robert Schumann (1810–1856)
Franz Liszt (1810–1886)
Bedřich Smetana (1824–1884)
Peter I. Tchaikovsky (1840–1893)
Antonín Dvořák (1841–1904)
Edvard Grieg (1843–1907)
Gustav Mahler (1860–1911)
Claude Debussy (1862–1918)

Ex. 6-1 Time line of Orchestral Music History: 1700 to 1895; 1896 to the present (p. 158).

Eighteenth-century Vienna (Austria) was the cultural crossroads of Europe. In music, it was open to influences from both the Italian and the German states. Symphonic influences flowed freely from both directions, and Viennese composers borrowed variously from Italian lyricism and from German emotion and dynamism. However, in their own lighthearted spirit, the Viennese also developed some unique style traits. Before Haydn, the most important symphony composers in Vienna were Georg C. Wagenseil (1715–1777) and Georg M. Monn

Daugherty, *Metropolis Symphony* (1993) •
Corigliano, Symphony No. 1 (1990) •
Zwilich, Symphony No. 1 (1982) •
• Panufnik, *Sinfonia Sacra* (1963)
• Messiaen, *Turangalîla Symphony* (1948)
• Stravinsky, *Symphony in Three Movements* (1945)
Prokofiev, Symphony No. 5 (1944) •
Copland, *Appalachian Spring* (1944) •
Bartók, *Concerto for Orchestra* (1943) •
• Shostakovich, Symphony No. 5 (1937)
• Chávez, *Sinfonia India* (1935)
• Hindemith, *Mathis der Maler* Symphony (1934)
• Still, *Afro-American Symphony* (1931)
• Nielsen, Symphony No. 5 (1922)
• Ravel, *La Valse* (1920)
• Sibelius, *Finlandia* (1899)
• Dukas, *L'apprenti-sorcier* (1987)
• Strauss, *Also sprach Zarathustra* (1896)

```
        1900          1925          1950          1975          2000
— —      |             |             |             |             |       — —

— — ———————————————————————————— Richard Strauss (1864–1949)
— — ——————————————————— Carl Nielsen (1865–1931)
— — ———————————————————————————— Jan Sibelius (1865–1957)
— — ——————————————————— Maurice Ravel (1875–1937)
— — ————————————————————— Béla Bartók (1881–1945)
— — ————————————————————————————— Igor Stravinsky (1882–1971)
— — ————————————————————— Sergei Prokofiev (1891–1953)
— — ————————————————————————— Paul Hindemith (1895–1963)
— — ———————————————————————————— Carlos Chávez (1899–1978)
— — ————————————————————————————————— Aaron Copland (1900–1990)
        ————————————————————————— Dmitri Shostakovich (1906–1975)
          ——————————————————————————————— Olivier Messiaen (1908–1992)
          ——————————————————————————————— Andrzej Panufnik (1914–1991)
John Corigliano (1938– ) ——————————————————— — —
Ellen Taaffe Zwilich (1939– ) ————————————— — —
Michael Daugherty (1954– ) ——————————— — —
```

(1717–1750). Wagenseil composed 82 symphonies, among which the late examples often use a quick 2/4-time rondo as a final movement, foreshadowing the symphonies of Haydn. In 1740, Monn composed the first four-movement symphony, using these movement designations:

Allegro—Aria—Menuetto—Allegro

Thus, the four-movement sonata plan was born.

The first symphonic music Joseph Haydn composed was for the court of Count von Morzin. The great bulk of Haydn's considerable output, however, was written for the Esterházy family during his nearly 30 years of service to them. Haydn cast many of his early symphonies in the three-movement sinfonia pattern. However, Symphonies No. 6, 7, and 8 (c. 1761) are all in four movements. In addition, these comprise a *cycle* of symphonies, representing three times of day: No. 6, *Le matin* (*Morning*); No. 7, *Le midi* (*Noon*); and No. 8, *Le soir* (*Afternoon*). The titles are probably by Haydn himself, although most other nicknames to his symphonies are not. One feature of Haydn's symphonies, established in his early symphonies and followed in nearly all his symphonic *oeuvre*, is a slow introduction to the main *allegro* of the first movement.

Haydn's symphonic style matured through experimentation. For example, several symphonies written between 1768 and 1774 are in the minor mode, a characteristic usually reserved for dramatic or highly emotional music in the Classical period. These works, called his *Sturm und Drang* (Storm and Stress) symphonies, have agitated, passionate fast movements, and warm, emotional slow movements. The famous "Farewell" Symphony, No. 45 (1772), is an excellent example of Haydn's Storm and Stress symphonies.

By contrast, most Haydn symphonies from the later 1770s and 1780s are far more cheerful. Fourth-movement finales are especially bubbly. Several symphonies from this time (for example, No. 77) contain a "sonata rondo" form in the last movement, one of Haydn's innovations in form that blended sonata form with rondo form. Haydn's orchestra at the Esterházy court seldom exceeded 23. Besides strings, its instrumentation when most lavish included pairs of flutes, oboes, horns, trumpets, and timpani.

Ill. 6-1 Title page to the first edition of Haydn's Symphonies Nos. 76, 77, and 78, published by Christoph Torricella in Vienna, 1784. Note at the top the coat of arms of the Esterházy family, Haydn's patrons. From the collections of the Music Division, Library of Congress. By permission of the Music Division, Library of Congress.

fortissimo Very loud, one dynamic level above *forte*.

The most famous symphonies by Haydn are his last 12, collectively called the "London" Symphonies. He composed six of these for each of his London journeys (1791–1792; 1794–1795), and some contain unique effects. For example, the "Surprise" Symphony (No. 94) astonished the audience with an unexpected *fortissimo* chord in the quiet slow movement. Instruments from the traditional Turkish band (triangle, cymbals, and bass drum) augment the instrumentation of the so-called "Military" Symphony (No. 100). In his last symphony, No. 104, Haydn allowed the timpani part to become independent of their usual coupling with trumpets during the Minuet movement, achieving a striking *crescendo* build to a dynamic climax. The London orchestras were similar to that at the Esterházy court except larger, especially the string section. Also, Haydn added a pair of clarinets in the last six symphonies. In all, Haydn composed 108 symphonies, although the order in their traditional numbering (reaching only 104) is not very exact.

Mozart

In 1765, at the age of nine, Mozart composed his first symphony in London: that in E-flat Major, K. 16. It is an incredibly professional work. This and other early Mozart symphonies show influences of London's early Classical composers, notably Johann Christian Bach (1735–1782, the youngest surviving son of J.S. Bach), whom the boy knew personally.

The popular system of numbering Mozart's symphonies (No. 1–No. 41) has come from the Breitkopf & Härtel editions in the early 19th century. However, several more symphonies were later discovered and authenticated, and a few thought to be by Mozart have turned out otherwise. Today the total is thought to be 52.

Mozart composed many of his youthful symphonies for various trips and tours. However,

Ill. 6-2 First page of eight-year-old Mozart's autographed manuscript to his Symphony No. 1 in E-flat Major, K. 16. The score layout differs slightly from the modern one, since the horn parts appear on the top line with oboes under them. Biblioteka Jagiello{n}ska Kraków.

the long, uninterrupted time at home in Salzburg, 1773–1777, gave him his finest opportunity to develop as a symphonist. Among the dozen Salzburg symphonies, two are still hailed today among his masterpieces. The first was the G Minor Symphony (No. 25), K. 183 (173d), composed in October 1773. It is sometimes called the "Little" G Minor to distinguish it from the "Great" G Minor (No. 40). The youthful work is outwardly passionate, especially the first movement. Mozart may have composed this symphony in emulation of Haydn's "Storm and Stress" symphonies from about that time. The Symphony in A Major (No. 29), K. 201 (186a), composed in April 1774, is also remarkable for its energy and flair. The distressed undertone of the first movement's opening is an amazingly mature expression for a composer only 18 years old.

Mozart wrote one symphony during his Paris sojourn in 1778: in D Major (No. 31), K. 297 (300a). As brilliant an essay as this is, it has been overshadowed by Mozart's final group of symphonies composed during the years 1782–1788. Like Haydn's "London" Symphonies, Mozart's Vienna symphonies are his most famous:

NO.	KEY	KÖCHEL NO.	YEAR	NICKNAME
35	D Major	385	1782	"Haffner"
36	C Major	425	1783	"Linz"
[37	G Major	444 (425a), Introduction only to a symphony by Michael Haydn]		
38	D Major	504	1786	"Prague"
39	E-flat Major	543	1788	
40	G Minor	550	1788	
41	C Major	551	1788	"Jupiter"

In 1782, nobility was conferred on Mozart's former schoolmate Sigmund Haffner. For the occasion Mozart was to compose a work, which became the "Haffner" Symphony. The "Linz" Symphony was written on the spur of the moment. In October 1783, Mozart and his wife were returning to Vienna after a three-month stay in Salzburg. Stopping in Linz to hear an opera, they were treated like royalty at the home of a certain Count Thun, who then prevailed on Mozart to give a concert. He wrote to his father, "… As I have not a single symphony with me, I am writing a new one at breakneck speed. …" He completed it in six days or less. Mozart wrote the "Prague" Symphony for concert given by popular request. Staying in Prague for the successful run of *The Marriage of Figaro* (1787), Mozart wrote this challenging three-movement work for an appreciative audience. He conducted this and one other (unidentified) symphony on the program. An eyewitness described these works as "true masterpieces of instrumental composition, full of unexpected transitions, and have élan and a fiery momentum, so that they immediately incline the soul to expect something sublime."

During the summer of 1788, Mozart completed his last three symphonies, sometimes referred to as his "final great trilogy": No. 39 in E-flat Major, K. 543; No. 40 in G Minor, K. 550; and No. 41 in C Major, K. 551 ("Jupiter"). Composed in the remarkable space of about three months, while Mozart was also occupied with other projects and with teaching, these works represent the pinnacle of Mozart's symphonic achievements. His reason for writing them has never been clearly discerned, although we have evidence that possibly all of them were performed during the composer's lifetime.

fugato A section of a movement composed in the manner of a fugue.

The E-flat Major Symphony, with the exception of its Haydnesque slow introduction, is a typically Mozartian creation. The Symphony in G Minor, more unusual, is most famous for its first movement, in which some writers have found a "tragic heroism." This is also one of the most perfect examples of sonata form. In the Symphony in C Major (nicknamed "Jupiter" after the turn of the 19th century), the final movement is the most famous. Here Mozart demonstrated the remarkable power of fugal techniques in symphonic composition. In the main body of the movement, he liberally employed fugal procedure to introduce most of the five themes. Toward the end of the movement comes a formal coda: a now famous grand *fugato* that combines all five themes at once. Each is heard in every register, a heady kaleidoscope of "quintuple counterpoint." This final passage is the crowning glory of the work and Mozart's culminating contribution to the history of the symphony.

BEETHOVEN, SYMPHONY NO. 5 IN C MINOR, OP. 67, THIRD AND FOURTH MOVEMENTS

LUDWIG VAN BEETHOVEN

Study in charcoal and chalk by August von Klöber, 1818, now lost.

Ludwig van Beethoven was born in Bonn, Germany, on December 17, 1770. His father, Johann, and his Dutch grandfather had been court musicians to the Elector of Cologne, resident in Bonn. Beethoven grew up with his father; his mother, Maria Magdalena; and two younger brothers, Carl and Johann. Beethoven's father was probably his earliest teacher at the piano, and he studied violin and viola with a relative. In 1779, Christian Neefe came to Bonn, becoming court organist in 1781. About that time Beethoven began studying under Neefe and was his assistant organist starting in 1782. Besides the keyboard, Neefe tutored Beethoven in the fundamentals of composition, and by the following year, the 12-year-old had published a set of variations (WoO 63) that earned him a glowing review in the *Magazin der Musik*: "This youthful genius is deserving of help to enable him to travel. He would surely become a second Wolfgang Amadeus Mozart if he were to continue as he has begun." That autumn his first piano sonatas (WoO 47) were also put into print.

Beethoven now composed avidly, played the organ in the Bonn court chapel at times, and studied the violin under another relative, Franz Ries. In spring 1787, Beethoven had the rare opportunity to spend time in Vienna, where very possibly he met (and took lessons from) Mozart. News of Beethoven's mother's impending death, however, cut the visit short, and he returned to Bonn to see her for the last time. By that time Beethoven's father had begun to drink heavily, which interfered with his job. In a bold step, Beethoven took charge of the family, petitioning the court for half his father's salary as a pension. It was awarded, and Johann was released from duty. To augment the small family income, Beethoven now began to play the viola in both the court and theater orchestras.

As a composer, Beethoven continued to develop, encouraged by the circle of aristocratic friends he had entered. The hub of this activity was the home of Frau von Breuning, where he came to know Count Ferdinand von Waldstein. Probably Waldstein was the person who engineered Beethoven's move to Vienna in 1792, convincing his close friend, the elector, to sponsor the journey and subsidize the composer for awhile there. Beethoven's father died that year, the same year in which his brothers turned 18 and 16, respectively, so there was no further need to remain in Bonn. The idea of Beethoven's studying with Haydn had probably been proposed two years earlier, when the old master had passed through Bonn on his way to England. In the fall of 1792, the idea was revived, and Beethoven set out for Vienna in October.

His career formally began in Vienna in 1792. Traditionally, we divide his career into three style periods, the first of which spans the decade of 1792–1802. It began with an apprenticeship under Haydn. Beethoven studied strict counterpoint and possibly free composition. The two men were temperamentally incompatible, though both masked their ill feelings toward each other. Beethoven's studies were cut short when Haydn made his second journey to England in 1794. Next Beethoven turned to Johann Albrechtsberger, a church musician and devotee of J.S. Bach's music. In the year Beethoven studied with him, he learned every contrapuntal technique, including fugue writing. He may also have sought some tutelage from Antonio Salieri, the Imperial music director, but no definite evidence of this exists.

While studying, Beethoven was also making an impressive reputation as a pianist, cultivating the best aristocratic circles as a protégé of Count Waldstein. In his first three years in Vienna, Beethoven could be found in the homes of such powerful names as Prince Lobkowitz, Prince von Lichnowsky, Prince Esterházy, Count Razumovsky, and Baron van Swieten (who also figured prominently in the careers of Haydn and Mozart). Beethoven performed in his first public concerts in 1793. On two of these occasions he performed one of his first two piano concertos; on another he played a piano concerto by Mozart. The year 1795 saw the publication of Beethoven's Opus 1, three piano trios. The Op. 2 piano sonatas dedicated to Haydn followed the next year. By 1800, Beethoven had composed several more works that helped to define his first style period: the six string quartets, Op. 18; the *Pathétique* Sonata for piano, Op. 13; and the Septet in E-flat Major, Op. 20. The occasion of Beethoven's first concert wholly for his own benefit in 1800 was the premiere of his Symphony No. 1 in C Major as well as the Septet. Besides performing one of his piano concertos on that program, he gave an exhibition of improvising.

By 1801, Beethoven had been experiencing a growing deafness for some time and had consulted several doctors, none of whom could help him. His situation depressed him terribly, not only because of his music. It also made him feel like a social pariah, and he avoided most social functions as a result. He suffered from otosclerosis, a complication of syphilis (a common disease in Vienna at the time), which he had contracted about 1796. Beethoven, who had been strong enough to take over the headship of his family at the age of 16, was not to be defeated by his tragic ailment. In letters from about 1801, he wrote heroic phrases like, "I will seize Fate by the throat! It will never crush me completely."

Beethoven became very productive in 1802, but his mood still vacillated widely between depression and exalted determination. He spent the summer and early fall in his favorite country village of Heiligenstadt, where he penned the famous "Heiligenstadt Testament," probably the single most important document the composer ever wrote. In it the reader can glimpse what Beethoven was going through as he faced his fate of worsening deafness. Also during this period, Beethoven fell in love for the first time. The object of his affections was the 17-year-old Countess Giulietta Guicciardi, of whom Beethoven wrote, "Unfortunately, she is not of my class."

Beethoven's second style period began in 1803, and the work that heralded it was his Symphony No. 3 in E-flat Major, the *Eroica* Symphony. This is among the most monumental of his symphonies. During this period, Beethoven also composed the Fourth through the Eighth Symphonies, including, notably, the Symphony No. 5 in C Minor, and the *Pastoral* Symphony

(continued)

(No. 6), both written in 1807–1808. During the middle style period, Beethoven's most productive, he composed most of the music for which he is best known. The "Waldstein," "Appassionata," and "Les Adieux" Piano Sonatas all stem from this time, as do the three revolutionary "Razumovsky" String Quartets, Op. 59 and Piano Concertos No. 4 and No. 5 (the "Emperor" Concerto). Beethoven's instrumental works became longer and more complex during the middle period, showing the enormity of his intellectual powers applied to music. His one opera, *Fidelio* (first named *Leonore*), also developed during these years, going through several revisions that yielded no fewer than four different overtures. Performers could not always master Beethoven's music, and listeners did not always understand it, but that did not deter him, for he had a vision of its worth for posterity. For example, musicians laughed aloud at the "Razumovsky" Quartets and laid them aside as unplayable. To one disgruntled player who thought him insane, Beethoven reportedly said of the Quartets, "Oh, they are not for you, but for a later age." Thus, Beethoven was the first great composer to think in terms of music for posterity.

In March 1809, he was able to secure a lifetime pension from a syndicate of three devoted patrons: the Princes Kinsky and Lobkowitz, and Archduke Rudolph, who was a piano pupil and beloved friend of Beethoven as well as the dedicatee of both the "Archduke" Piano Trio (Op. 97) and the "Emperor" Piano Concerto. Through 1811, Beethoven's creative energies had driven forward with great force. In 1812, however, a family squabble involving his brothers drained him emotionally. Coming on the heels of a marriage refusal the year before, it darkened Beethoven's mood considerably. He had had two torrid love affairs during this period, both ending disastrously for him. In 1804–1805, his relationship with Josephine von Brunsvik had ended because of the social-class barrier between them. Then, in 1811, he fell in love with and wished to marry Therese Malfatti, the niece of his doctor. Apparently, she or her family found him unsuitable. When Beethoven wrote the famous "Immortal Beloved" (or, more correctly, Eternally Beloved) letter in 1812, he was on the rebound from Therese. The exact identity of the "Immortal Beloved" to whom the composer wrote so passionately is uncertain. The most plausible guess (that of biographer Maynard Solomon) is Antoine Brentano, wife of a merchant from a family Beethoven had known in Vienna for two years. Apparently nothing came of the connection to his "Immortal Beloved," and all the emotional blows in 1811–1812 resulted in a radical slowing of Beethoven's creativity. In addition, his deafness now caused him to withdraw increasingly into himself. On the brighter side, Beethoven reached the high point of his fame in Vienna during 1813–1814, when his works were applauded by large audiences and he was accorded high honors from various royal dignitaries.

About 1815, Beethoven entered his third and final style period. Between that year and 1820, he composed only a few large works. The major reason was the diversion of his energies into litigation. In November 1815, his brother Carl died unexpectedly, leaving a wife, Johanna, and a nine-year-old son, Karl. The matter of the child's custody in Carl's will was questionable: Should it be Beethoven alone or Beethoven and Johanna as co-custodians? Beethoven, starved for family love, saw this as an opportunity to have a "son" of his own. Several rounds of court battles followed over the next four and one-half years, in which first Beethoven was victorious and then Johanna. Poor Karl was tossed back and forth between them and among tutors and schools. In July 1820, Beethoven succeeded in discrediting Johanna's moral character, and Karl was awarded to him exclusively. The composer now became intensely preoccupied with caring for Karl. He alternately smothered him with attention, intimidated him, and demanded his affection. That relationship culminated in Karl's attempted suicide in the summer of 1826.

Several general characteristics marked the music of Beethoven's final years:

- An introspective, meditative, mystical quality

- Remodeling Classical procedures, especially in sonata form

- Combining two or more tempos and forms within a single movement

- Increased use of counterpoint and concentration on fugal movements

- Increased use of variation form

- Extremes in the size of a work, either very long or very short

We can perceive these tendencies clearly in the last four piano sonatas—the *Hammerklavier* Sonata of 1817–1818 and the three sonatas of Opp. 109–111, composed 1820–1822—as well as in Beethoven's massive *33 Variations on a Waltz by Diabelli*, Op. 120 for piano.

In his final period, Beethoven composed two monumental choral-orchestral works: the *Missa solemnis* (*Solemn Mass*) in D Major and the Ninth Symphony in D Minor. The Mass, originally intended for Archduke Rudolph's installation as a cardinal, brought new symphonic aspects to the world of choral music and was a sacred testament for Beethoven. In the Ninth Symphony, Beethoven made history (again!) both by creating a symphonic work of unheard-of dimensions and by adding voices to the final movement. The poetry he chose was Johann von Schiller's *Ode to Joy*, which he had wished to set since at least 1792.

By 1826, in his 57th year, Beethoven had grown very ill. That would be the year of his final compositions, three of the six "last quartets." Spanning 1823–1826, these works are the most "mystical" of Beethoven's last period. They include five multimovement works (Opp. 127, 130, 131, 132, and 135) and the *Grosse fuge* (*Grand Fugue*), Op. 133, originally meant to be the finale to Op. 130. Some of this music is autobiographical, for example, a movement from Op. 132 he titled "*Heiliger Dankgesang eines Genesenen an die Gottheit*" (Sacred Song of Thanks from a Convalescent to the Godhead).

In December 1826, Beethoven's health failed; he was diagnosed with cirrhosis of the liver. Now confined, he received visitors daily. Leaving his entire estate to his nephew Karl, Beethoven died on March 26, 1827. His funeral three days later was a public event with an estimated 10,000 attending.

Beethoven's music was the culmination of the Classical period, yet he stood at the threshold of the Romantic period and opened its door through his music and by the example of his indomitable, independent spirit. His determination to overcome the seemingly impossible obstacle of his deafness is emblematic of that spirit. Although Beethoven had no known "motto" as such, he summed up his lifelong drive to persevere under all circumstances in the pithy words he placed as labels above two themes in his last complete work, the String Quartet in F Major, Op. 135:

Must it be?

It must be!

Beethoven as a Symphonist

Ludwig van Beethoven completed the circle of composers called the "Viennese School" or "First Viennese School," because their activities centered in or near Vienna. Joseph Haydn and Wolfgang Amadeus Mozart were the first two members of that school. Beethoven, born in 1770, was younger than either of them, yet his activity as a composer of symphonies followed the work of the older composers while it was still fresh. Mozart composed his last symphony in 1788; Haydn wrote his last in 1795. Beethoven began sketching themes for his First Symphony as early as 1796 and completed the work at the beginning of 1800.

As we have already learned, Haydn composed 106 symphonies and Mozart wrote 52. Why did Beethoven, who lived more than 20 years longer than Mozart, complete only *nine* symphonies? The answers are length and innovation/complexity. The average length of a symphony by Haydn or Mozart is about 20 minutes. Even Beethoven's First Symphony, running about 25 minutes, stretched the Classical standard slightly. His Symphony No. 3 ("Eroica," 1803) was the longest symphony ever heard at the time, running about 50 minutes. Symphony No. 5 (1808) was more concise, taking a little over half an hour to perform. However, the performing length of Beethoven's Ninth Symphony (premiered in 1824) ran well over an hour, with a final movement the length of an entire Haydn symphony!

Haydn's music was far more predictable than Beethoven's, enabling him to dash off pleasing music with speed and craftsmanship. Mozart's incredible genius for holding entire compositions in his mind made most composing a quick chore for him. Even his last symphony, with its fugal complexities, may have been penned in only 16 days. Beethoven, however, was a constant experimenter, and experimentation takes time. Just the plan of the Fifth or the Ninth Symphony was an astonishing intellectual feat, taking time to work out. Beethoven made many sketches of themes and passages, some of which he used; others he discarded—again, time-consuming experimentation.

Innovation and complexity went hand in hand. The complexity of a Beethoven work may be due to its innovative features. Conversely, some of the work's innovation may lie in some complex idea, for example, the unifying effect of the rhythmic "motto" in the Fifth Symphony. Another area of innovation was the personal significance Beethoven attached to some of his symphonies, especially the Third, Fifth, Sixth, and Ninth. Before Beethoven, composers usually remained detached from their music; Beethoven virtually reinvented the symphony as a vehicle for personal expression.

The question of whether Beethoven was the last significant composer of the Classical period or the first of the Romantic period may never be settled, but the duality of his art is apparent within the series of symphonies. *Very generally*, Beethoven's Symphonies Nos. 1, 2, 4, 7, and 8 are more Classical, while those numbered 3, 5, 6, and 9 have stronger Romantic tendencies. The following table gives an overview of Beethoven's symphonies and the unique achievement each represented.

Symphony No. 1 in C Major, Op. 21	With his First Symphony, Beethoven successfully capped the Haydn-Mozart symphonic tradition and simultaneously launched his own new era. In the first moment, Beethoven showed himself to be an unorthodox experimenter:

Beginning a symphony with a dissonance, a seventh—and not beginning it on a pure tonic chord—were unheard of in 1800. The main part of the movement is a sonata form so clear in its details that it is almost a "textbook" for opening movements. It has exactly four themes: principal, transition, secondary, and concluding.

The third movement, marked "Menuetto," is actually a fast, Beethoven-style scherzo. In the finale, Beethoven balances his first-movement *Adagio* introduction with a slow introduction here, which analyst Donald Tovey called "a Haydnesque joke, the violins letting out a scale as a cat from a bag."

**Symphony No. 2
in D Major, Op. 36.**

This bold, forceful work has some unique, lighthearted moments. Notably, the main theme of the boisterous final movement typifies Beethoven's unique sense of humor. Writer Edward Downes calls it "a startling orchestral somersault," but with its obvious joking manner it could as easily give the impression of a loud laugh or a sneeze.

**Symphony No. 3
in E-flat Major, Op. 55**

Published as *Sinfonia eroica* (*Heroic Symphony*), this symphony was astonishing in its day for its power and dimensions. It virtually redefined the symphony, carrying the genre to a new level of expressive possibilities. Originally it was to be the "Bonaparte" Symphony, dedicated to Napoleon and, implicitly, to the spirit of the French Revolution. However, after Napoleon declared himself Emperor, Beethoven renamed the work, with the additional comment, "composed to celebrate the memory of a great man."

The weighty second movement is a moving *Marcia funebre* (*Funeral March*) written in the tradition of commemorating the fallen heroes of the French Revolution. Beethoven expresses heroism especially clearly in the scherzo's trio section, which features *three* horns (an innovation, since two or four were the norm):

The finale is an extensive set of variations employing themes Beethoven borrowed from his only ballet, *The Creatures of Prometheus.*

Symphony No. 4 in B-flat Major, Op. 60

The Fourth Symphony, composed mostly during 1806, is a text-book example of Beethoven's Classical side. The first movement begins with a slow introduction, a hallmark of Haydn's symphonies. The woodwind-centered trio section of the *Menuetto* movement harks back to Classical wind chamber music. And the finale contains the effervescent fun of a Haydn finale. Hector Berlioz commented that this movement is "one animated swarm of sparkling notes, presenting a continual babble."

Symphony No. 5, in C Minor, Op. 67

(Discussed in detail below.) Completed at almost the same time as Symphony No. 6 in the summer of 1808, they were premiered together on December 22 of that year. As disparate in spirit as these two works appear on the surface, there are a few definite similarities. One is the use of trombones. Another is the continuity between the last two movements, played without pause.

Symphony No. 6 in F Major, Op. 68

This is Beethoven's only overtly programmatic symphony. In a notebook of 1807, he refers to it as his *Sinfonia pastorella* (*Pastoral Symphony*), and that name has endured. In the program for the first performance, the *Pastoral* Symphony was subtitled "Recollection of Country Life." Not only did Beethoven give the symphony a programmatic nickname, this is the only symphony for which the composer assigned programmatic titles to the movements:

I. Awakening of Cheerful Feelings on Arriving in the Country

II. Scene by the Brook

III. Merry Gathering of Country Folk

IV. Thunderstorm; Tempest

V. Shepherd's Song; Happy, Thankful Feelings After the Storm

Symphony No. 7 in A Major, Op. 92

Although it has its own unique personality, Beethoven carried over certain aspects of the Fifth and Sixth Symphonies into the first movement of the Seventh. From the Fifth came the motor impulse of a single driving rhythm. From the *Pastoral* Symphony, it inherited a spirit of the celebration of nature. This is particularly apparent in the peasant round-dance character of the first movement's main theme, introduced after a lengthy slow introduction.

The *Allegretto* second movement has a reputation of its own. At the symphony's premiere, the audience demanded that it be **encored**. The movement is a set of variations on one of Beethoven's famous hymnlike themes.

Symphony No. 8 in F Major, Op. 93

Beethoven began composing his Eighth Symphony in 1812, immediately upon completing the Seventh. At the time, he must have been reevaluating his own aesthetic in relation to the high

encore From the French for "again," (1) *n.* either an immediately repeated performance of a work, aria, or movement or a short piece added at the end of a program; (2) *v.* to repeat a work, aria, or movement.

Classical music of Haydn and Mozart, for both symphonies—
though progressive in many respects—owe much to the Classical
ideal.

As in the Seventh, the Eighth Symphony's high point is its
second movement. Like the Seventh, this is not a slow movement
at all. However, the Seventh's *Allegretto* is a study in tragedy, while
the Eighth's *Allegretto scherzando* is its most comic aspect. The wit
in this music is largely due to its constant, metronomic, ticking
accompaniment, a conscious effect. Johann Maelzel (1772–1838),
a good friend of Beethoven, had by 1812 invented a "musical
chronometer," the forerunner to the metronome he perfected in
1817. Composers in Vienna had become fascinated with the
novel invention, and when Beethoven composed his new *allegretto*, he was directly inspired—or at least influenced—by the
sound of the chronometer.

**Symphony No. 9
in D Minor, Op. 125**

The best-known part of Beethoven's Ninth is its fourth movement, involving vocal soloists and chorus in a setting of Johann
von Schiller's poem "Ode to Joy." This was the first time a composer had involved voices in a symphony—a genre previously
considered to be purely instrumental.

The general subject of the symphony is the brotherhood of
humankind as a source of joy, which is thoroughly worked out in
the choral finale. Writers have also sought related meaning in
other parts of the symphony, especially the first movement. For
example, its opening has often been identified with the Biblical
Creation, the quivering, sustained open fifth possibly suggesting
void and chaos. Similarly, annotator Edward Downes has sug-
gested that the movement's coda "with its ominous *ostinato* in
the depths of the orchestra, seems an apocalyptic vision." The
power and penetration of the Ninth does not depend on programmatic implications, however.

In the finale, Beethoven revolutionized the symphonic
medium by transcending its existing boundaries. By combining
the instrumental and vocal media, Beethoven redefined what a
symphony *could* be: a statement of deep feeling or philosophy
expressed both verbally and musically. Breaking down the distinction between instrumental and vocal forms of music was
essentially a Romantic thing to do, and the finale to the Ninth
Symphony is one of Western music's main bridges between Classicism and Romanticism. The heart of the movement is, of
course, the famous hymnlike melody:

which generates a breathtaking 25-minute movement involving variations, fugal sections, vocal solos and ensembles, and great orchestral development. The concluding section has the feeling of a summing up, beginning with the soloists and spreading to the chorus. The long *prestissimo* coda emphasizes Beethoven's personal "kiss for all the world" (taken from the text).

Beethoven's Fifth Symphony: Background

Beethoven's sketchbooks reveal that he conceived the *idea* of a *"sinfonia"* in C minor as early as 1799. However, he did not begin sketching his great C Minor Symphony until 1804. Between then and the end of 1808 was a period of unusual creative fertility for Beethoven. During that five-year period he produced many well-known masterpieces, including Piano Sonatas Nos. 21 ("Waldstein"), 22, and 23 ("Appassionata"); the three "Razumovsky" String Quartets; the Mass in C Major; the opera *Fidelio* (the first of two versions); and Symphonies Nos. 4, 5, and 6, among other outstanding works.

The first sketches for the Fifth Symphony come from a notebook dated 1804–1805. Other works took priority over the next few years, until at the beginning of 1807, Beethoven gave serious attention to his Fifth Symphony, although he could not ignore lucrative commissions demanded of him at the same time. Most of the work on the C Minor Symphony was done in 1807, possibly spurred by a new concert series inaugurated in Vienna that year. Three times between November 1807 and November 1808, Beethoven lent his music and his conducting services to charity concerts. Because of these charitable acts, Beethoven was given the use of the Theater-an-der-Wien for a concert to benefit himself. This was to be the occasion for the premieres of his Fifth and Sixth Symphonies on December 22, 1808.

The C Minor Symphony received its second performance in Leipzig about a month later.

Ill. 6-3 Beethoven's study c. 1827 (black and white lithograph by Gustav Leybold). Historisches Museum der Stadt Wien.

A review in the leading German music periodical, the *Allgemeine musikalische Zeitung* (*General Music News*), shows what a deep impression the famous first movement made:

> The first movement is a very serious, somewhat gloomy yet fiery allegro, noble both in feeling and in the working-out of idea, which is handled firmly and evenly, simply with a lot of originality, strength, and consistency—a worthy movement, which offers rich pleasure even to those who cling to the old way of composing a symphony.

[Trans. Elliott Forbes, *Ludwig van Beethoven, Symphony No. 5 in C Minor: An Authoritative Score; The Sketches; Historical Background; Analysis; Views and Comments* (New York: W.W. Norton, 1971), p. 13.]

Enthusiastic responses to the Symphony No. 5 became general during the Romantic period. Berlioz, in his "Critical Study of Beethoven's Symphonies" (part of his book, *A travers chants* [*On the Edge* or *Through Melody*, a play on words], 1862), emphasizes the personal aspect of the symphony in his introductory paragraph:

> It is his own intimate thought which is there developed; and his secret sorrows, his pent-up rage, his dreams so full of melancholy oppression, his nocturnal visions and his bursts of enthusiasm furnish its entire subject; while the melodic, harmonic, rhythmic, and orchestral forms are there delineated with an essential novelty and individuality, endowing them also with considerable power and nobility.

[Hector Berlioz, *A Critical Study of Beethoven's Nine Symphonies*, trans. Edwin Evans (London: William Reeves, 1958), p. 62.]

In the 20th century new perspectives on the Fifth Symphony have been expressed. Leonard Bernstein's 1954 telecast on symphonies presented a composer-conductor's view of the famous opening notes:

Ill. 6-4 Opening of Beethoven's Symphony No. 5 in C Minor, Op. 67, from a 19th-century edition.

Every time I look at this orchestra score I am amazed all over again at its simplicity, strength, and rightness. And how economical the music is! Why, almost every bar of this first movement is a direct development of these opening four notes [see Ill. 6-4]. And what are these notes that they should be so pregnant and meaningful that a whole symphonic movement can be born of them? Three G's and an E-flat. Nothing more. Anyone could have thought of them—maybe. ... The real meaning lies in all the notes that follow it, all the notes of the five-hundred measures of music that follow it in the first movement. And Beethoven, more than any other composer before or after him, I think, had the ability to find exactly the right notes that had to follow his themes.

[Leonard Bernstein, *The Joy of Music* (New York: Simon and Schuster, 1959), pp. 73–74.]

Exploring Beethoven's Fifth Symphony

Reportedly, Beethoven once pointed to the music shown in Ill. 6-4 and remarked, "Thus Fate knocks at the door." The big unison passage that opens the symphony contains two utterances of the so-called Fate motive. This four-note microcosm is Beethoven's source for generating much of the music in the symphony's first movement. Even when other material takes center stage, such as the secondary theme, the motive is present in the background:

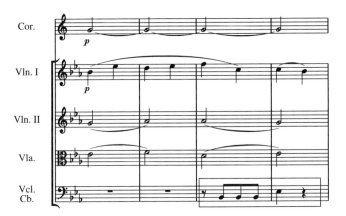

Notice that intervals between the notes of the motive can vary from occurrence to occurrence, but the *rhythm* always remains the same. Thus, the really important feature of the Fate motive is its *rhythm*. In this movement the rhythm is:

This rhythmic motive appears in some form in every movement of the Fifth Symphony, sometimes prominently, sometimes subtly. That was a great innovation in 1808, since Classical symphonists had always tried to make each movement of any sonata-plan work very different from the other movements. Now, in the Fifth Symphony, Beethoven wished to *unify* his work with a new device: *a recurring rhythmic motive*. The motive acts as a "motto," a term we will use here to identify it. Basically, the rhythm of the motto is: short–short–short–long, which we can show symbolically as:

In the symphony's second movement, *Andante con moto*, the motto is a building block of both melody and accompaniment, for example, the woodwind cadence in mm. 15–16:

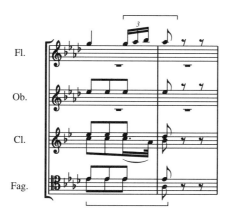

A few measures later, the clarinets and bassoons start a new phrase, which embeds the motto:

Many other examples of Beethoven's conscious use of the motto can be found in the movement.

EXPLORING THE SCHERZO MOVEMENT. In this study, we focus on the third and fourth movements of the symphony. *Listen to all of the third movement (the scherzo). This proceeds without pause to the fourth movement, so stop listening when you reach that point, shown in Ill. 6-5 (b).* The third movement as a whole, called the scherzo, is *not* in sonata form. Instead, it is in three main sections (the first and third also called the "scherzo" section) plus a bridge passage leading to the fourth movement:

Sections:	Scherzo	Trio	Scherzo (reprise)	bridge …
Structure:	A	B	A' ….	

Listen now to just the first scherzo section. (It ends when the bustling passage for cellos and contrabasses alone announce the opening of the trio section.) *Can you identify the part that first announces the motto?* The main theme group has two distinctly different themes: (1) a pair of introductory phrases in a "mysterious" mood; and (2) a "heroic" theme introduced by the horns. You can detect the motto four times in the heroic theme:

Notice, later in the first scherzo section, that both themes—mysterious and heroic—receive some type of development.

Listen now to the trio section, which begins with the bustling low strings and ends when the mysterious theme returns. At the beginning of the trio section, does Beethoven change key? The scherzo section was in C minor. For the trio section the music shifts to the parallel major (C major).

Again, listen to just the beginning of the trio section (which, when it was written, was considered extremely difficult for contrabass players). Keep listening as the same musical idea keeps entering higher and higher in the strings. Does this passage sound like a contrapuntal procedure you have already studied? It is very much like the opening exposition of a *fugue*:

Subject:	Cellos and contrabasses
Answer:	Violas and bassoons
Subject:	Second violins
Answer:	First violins

Then the music reaches a cadence and a literal repetition. The second portion of the trio section sounds somewhat like a fugal exposition also, but the music is more free.

Now listen to the scherzo reprise following the trio section. Stop listening when you reach the bridge passage. Does the music again change key? Yes, it now reverts to C minor. *Does Beethoven bring the first scherzo back literally the way you first heard it, or has he altered the mood/character of the heroic theme?* In this abbreviated reprise of music from the scherzo section, Beethoven maintains a "mysterious" mood, applying that mood also to the heroic theme. Thus, he changes its original character from heroic to mysterious, unifying the whole scherzo reprise, in preparation for the quiet, suspenseful bridge to the fourth movement.

Finally, listen to just the bridge passage. What is your impression of this music? This was part of the symphony that made musical history. No composer had yet joined two such different movements without a pause. The bridge passage was much misunderstood in its day and for years afterward. For example, as late as 1843 (25 years after the symphony's premiere), one writer offered the following criticism:

> I speak of the 50 measures of the *Scherzo* that precede the *Allegro*. There is a strange melody, which, combined with even a stranger harmony of a double pedal point in the bass on G and C, produces a sort of odious meowing and discords to shatter the least sensitive ear.
>
> [Trans. in Nicolaus Slonimsky, *Lexicon of Musical Invective: Critical Assaults on Composers Since Beethoven's Time*, 2nd ed. (Seattle, WA: University of Washington Press, 1984), p. 47.]

SCHERZO. *In your score, look at the instrumentation (lineup of instruments) shown at the opening of the third movement. How does it compare with the instrumentation shown in Ill. 6-4?* The instrumentation is identical; Beethoven has not changed it since the opening of the symphony. Now let's examine the instrumentation in the Score Anthology more closely. These are the main points:

- Woodwinds: Beethoven calls for woodwinds in pairs. "Clarinetti in B" means Clarinets in B-flat (a mixture of Italian and German terminology). "Fagotti" means bassoons.
- The two horns ("Corni") are pitched in "Es," German for E-flat, the relative major of the movement's key.
- "Trombe" are trumpets, here a pair. The valveless trumpet of Beethoven's time was similar to the horn; it could play only pitches of the natural **harmonic series** in one key at a time. Trumpeters and hornists changed keys by changing their instrument's tubular "crook."
- "Timpani in C and G": two timpani (kettledrums) tuned at these pitches for at least a movement:

- Cellos and contrabasses appear on the same staff. "Basso" means contrabass only, but "Bassi" means cellos and contrabasses together.

Examine the score at measure 18. In the horns ("Cor."), what theme appears here? This is the

The Scherzo and Finale: A Closer Look
Please refer to the score of Beethoven's Fifth Symphony, beginning on page 67 of the Score Anthology.

harmonic series A fundamental pitch together with a series of natural pitches above it (overtones) formed from multiples of the fundamental.

"heroic" theme, played in unison at first. When the horns divide into thirds (mm. 24–25) and a fifth (m. 26), we can see why Beethoven needed to pitch them in E-flat to obtain those notes.

Find the beginning of the trio section at m. 141 (with upbeat). Compare the instrumentation of mm. 141–145 with that of the opening of the scherzo section, mm. 1–4. Beethoven begins both sections with cellos and basses alone, unifying those places through instrumentation.

Find the beginning of the scherzo reprise section: change of key, m. 237. From that point until m. 325 (where the bridge passage starts), listen with score in hand and study the following:

• *Instrumentation*

• *Dynamics*

• *Staccato-style rhythmic detachment*

Notice how Beethoven uses all of these components together to produce the "mysterious" transformation of the scherzo material.

TERMS. Here are some new terms found in Beethoven's score.

TERM	DEFINITION	CONTEXT AND EXPLANATION
I	solo	(III, m. 60) In a part for a pair of woodwind or brass instruments, only one instrument plays the part at this point.
a2 (*a due*)	for two players	(III, m. 79) In a part for a pair of woodwind or brass instruments, both play the part in unison.
a Tempo	at proper tempo	(III: m. 8) Usually appears after a ritard or a break in the music.
arco	bow	(III: m. 128) Return to bowing after *pizzicato*.
dol. [dolce].	sweetly	(IV: m. 54, 263) Expression marking
Più	more	(III: m. 211) Usually seen with a dynamic marking (*più f*) or tempo indication (*più allegro*).
pizz. [*pizzicato*]	plucked	(III: m. 104) String instruments in a section pluck strings instead of bowing.
poco a poco	little by little	(IV: m. 324) Often seen with a dynamic marking (*cresc. poco a poco*).
poco ritard. [*poco ritardando*]	slow a little	(III: m. 117) Used often at an important phrase ending or for expression.
sempre	always, continuously	(III: 237) Usually seen with a dynamic marking (*sempre pp*).
sf [*sforzando* or *sforzato*]	literally, "forcing" or "forced"	(III: 38) Strong accent, possibly stronger than ">".
Tempo I [*Tempo primo*]	original (first) tempo	(IV: 155) Return to first tempo after change(s) in tempo.
//	break in the pulse	(III: m. 8) Used to make a momentary pause in the music.

Ill. 6-5 Beethoven's Fifth Symphony, comparison of instrumentation: (a) third movement; (b) fourth movement.

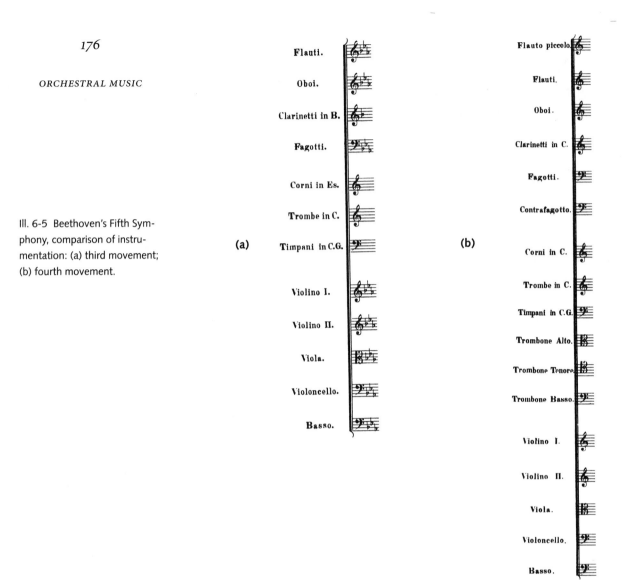

FINALE. Ill. 6-5 shows the instrumentation at the opening of the third (a) and fourth (b) movements of the symphony. *Make a comparison between the two movements. What instruments have been added at the opening of the fourth movement?* Beethoven made history by increasing the forces in the course of a symphony, something unheard of before this work. He has added instruments in two sections:

• *Woodwinds*: Piccolo and contrabassoon enlarge the section and increase its range: The piccolo sounds an octave higher than written, and the contrabassoon sounds an octave lower than written.

• *Brass*: Three trombones increase the orchestra's power. (This is the first appearance of trombones in a symphony. Previously they were found only in opera orchestras and in church music.)

Do the horns and trumpets remain in the same key between the third and fourth movements? Trumpets remain in C, but the horns have changed from E-flat to C. (Instructions appear in m. 271 of the scherzo in your score, where the horns have had a long rest.) Notice, too, that the clarinets have switched to instruments pitched in C. *Compare key signatures between (a) and (b) of III. 6-5. Does the music change key?* The music now changes from C minor to C major. Again, Beethoven made history by placing the last movement in the opposite mode from the first. However, as we will see, he had a plan.

Following the score, listen to the entire fourth movement, the symphony's finale. For a symphony that has already made several powerfully dramatic statements, Beethoven needed to create a finale that would bring the work to a *triumphant* conclusion, possibly symbolizing his own triumph over Fate. He accomplished this goal by several means:

- Momentum in the scherzo movement continues in the suspenseful bridge passage, which finally brings the explosion of the first measures of the finale.

- Instrumentation is bigger and more powerful.

- Mode changes from C minor to C major.

- Themes in the finale are noble, even a little military-sounding.

- Length of the movement is greater than any other in the symphony and includes a sizeable coda.

Now we will examine the symphony's fourth movement for a few of its important features. Beethoven composed this movement in sonata form. We will not do an in-depth analysis of it as we have done with other sonata forms. Finding the principal sections of the movement is still important, however.

First let's observe the exposition section to discover how Beethoven has used his rhythmic motto. *Look over the principal theme group of the fourth movement, mm. 1–25. Do you see any evidence of the motto in these measures?* Only near the end (mm. 22–25) is there the slightest suggestion of it, repeatedly marked off by dynamic accents:

Next comes the transition section, mm. 26–44. Do you find the motto in this section? In mm. 41–44, Beethoven briefly brings back something like it. *The secondary theme begins in m. 45 (with upbeat). Do you see how Beethoven has built this theme rhythmically on the motto?* The theme is a chain of rhythms constructed mainly on a pattern of three triplets plus a quarter note:

This is a miniaturization of the rhythmic motto he introduced in the first movement:

The concluding theme begins in m. 64, but it does not contain the motto. *In what measure does the first statement of the exposition section end? How can you tell?* M. 86 ends the first statement of the exposition. Here Beethoven places a formal repeat covering the entire exposition section—standard practice in Classical-period sonata forms.

.

The development section begins after this repeat. Notice how it is full of the triplet-quarter rhythmic motto. *The development section ends on the downbeat of m. 155. What normally comes at the end of a development section?* As you have learned, a development usually leads immediately to the recapitulation section. Here, however, Beethoven inserts something before the formal recapitulation.

What is happening in mm. 155–208? At this important structural and dramatic point in the fourth movement, the composer brings back a reminiscence of the scherzo movement. (Once more, Beethoven has made history—remodeling sonata form to suit his needs.) *Which is this passage more like, the first scherzo section or the scherzo reprise?* The string *pizzicato*, the quiet dynamic level, and detached articulation are characteristic of the "mysterious" treatment of the "heroic" theme found in the third movement's scherzo reprise section.

Beethoven's dramatic sense is masterfully acute here, for he sets up a quiet anticlimax that prepares for the psychological impact of the recapitulation. Essentially, he replays the effect he created before in the bridge passage to the opening of the fourth movement. *See m. 209 now for the explosive start of the recapitulation.*

In order to bring this movement and the entire symphony to an impressive conclusion, Beethoven adds a substantial coda at the end of the recapitulation. Because this coda is so lengthy and has its own faster tempo (*Presto*), it could be considered a separate major section in the movement's form. *Study the Violin I part at the opening of the coda, beginning in m. 364. Beethoven has derived this motive from one of the themes heard in the exposition and recapitulation. Which theme is it?* The source of the coda motive (mm. 364–365, Ex. 6-2b) is the concluding theme (mm. 64–65, Ex. 6-2a) in the woodwinds (see Ex. 6-2 for the comparison).

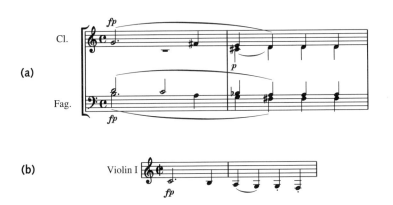

Ex. 6-2 Beethoven, Symphony No. 5, fourth movement: (a) part of concluding theme (mm. 64–65), from which Beethoven derives (b) coda motive (m. 364–365).

To obtain the full, sweeping power of the music, listen to the scherzo and finale, following the score.

WILLIAM GRANT STILL: *AFRO-AMERICAN SYMPHONY*, THIRD MOVEMENT

Ethnic and Nationalistic Expression in Orchestral Music

"I knew I wanted to write a symphony; I knew that it had to be an *American* work; and I wanted to demonstrate how the **blues**, so often considered a lowly expression, could be elevated to the highest musical level."

blues A song form based on a 12-measure harmonic pattern, originating among African Americans around 1900.

With these words, William Grant Still placed himself next to some of the greatest symphonists of the past, composers who wished to convey ethnic or nationalistic messages through their music. Beethoven, in his Sixth ("Pastoral") and Ninth ("Choral") Symphonies, had shown what a symphony could become when imbued with a composer's vision of scenic portrayal or philosophical expression. Some Romantic symphonists took the idea further. Felix Mendelssohn

(1809–1847) composed two symphonies that presented impressions from his travel experiences: the *Italian* (1833); and the *Scottish* (1842). Robert Schumann similarly painted a musical portrait of the Rhineland in his *Rhenish* Symphony (1850). At the end of the 19th century, Gustav Mahler (1860–1911) infused several of his nine symphonies with his personal philosophical/religious conceptions, and in the 20th century, Dmitri Shostakovich (1906–1975) built on Mahler's model. In several of his 15 symphonies, Shostakovich expressed personal growth (No. 5, 1937), or his experiences during World War II and the Stalinist regime (Nos. 7–10, 1941–1953), or Russian history (No. 11, "The Year 1905," 1957; and No. 12, "The Year 1917," 1961).

Even closer to the tradition from which Still drew were European and American nationalist composers. Like Still, these have often expressed themselves most vividly in their operas. However, orchestral music has been another important medium of expression. In Russia, Peter I. Tchaikovsky (1840–1893) often tinged his orchestral music with melodies and rhythms taken from his native folk music (e.g., Symphony No. 2, "Little Russian," 1880). Nicolai Rimsky-Korsakov (1844–1908) and Alexander Borodin (1833–1887) were even more intense about their nationalism. Rimsky-Korsakov's *Russian Easter* Overture (1888) and Borodin's *In the Steppes of Central Asia* (1880) are examples. In western Europe, two composers of Bohemia (now part of the Czech Republic) generated the most significant nationalistic music. These were Bedřich Smetana (1824–1884) and Antonín Dvořák. Smetana's cycle of symphonic poems *Má Vlast* (*My Fatherland*) contains the famous "Vltava" ("The Moldau," 1874). One of the first works to bring Dvořák to prominence was his first set of *Slavonic Dances* (1878). While Dvořák was in the United States, he became interested in Afro-American music and Native American music. However, his celebrated Symphony No. 9 ("From the New World," 1893) contains as much Czech flavor as it does American.

The 20th century has seen a latter-day nationalism arise in some European locations and in the Americas. The Hungarian music of Béla Bartók (1881–1945) has included adaptations of folk material as well as folk-influenced original works. In Mexico, Carlos Chávez (1899–1978) led what became known as the "Aztec Renaissance," a nationalistic movement built around Mexican Indian music. His *Sinfonia India* (1935) is the prime example. United States composer Aaron Copland (1900–1990) defined nationalism in this country chiefly through his trilogy of orchestral music for ballets: *Billy the Kid* (1938), *Rodeo* (1942), and *Appalachian Spring* (1944). These were the main pillars of his "American folk song period," which contained other instrumental works exhibiting an "American" feeling, such as *Fanfare for the Common Man* and *Lincoln Portrait* (both 1942) and the Symphony No. 3 (1946).

William Grant Still (Jr.) was born in Woodville, Mississippi, on May 11, 1895, to African-American parents, William Grant and Carrie Lena Still, who were both college graduates and teachers. When William Sr. died during the boy's infancy, the family moved to Little Rock, Arkansas. There Carrie taught high school English and married Charles Shepperson, a railway postal clerk. Still's mother and stepfather introduced him to classical music through violin lessons and attending **operettas**. Having skipped several grades, Still graduated high school as class valedictorian and enrolled in Wilberforce University, Ohio, in 1911. Starting in a science major, he soon gravitated to musical activities, teaching himself various instruments,

(continued)

WILLIAM GRANT STILL

Anonymous photograph from the 1930s. Photo courtesy of William Grant Still Music.

operetta A type of light opera that grew out of *opéra comique* in the 19th century, developing primarily in Vienna and London.

WILLIAM GRANT STILL *(continued)*

notably the oboe. While yet an undergraduate, he became the college's band director. On his own, Still studied opera scores and began to make arrangements for a campus string quartet. He became drawn to "serious" music and wrote his first compositions during his college years.

In 1914, Still left Wilberforce to become a professional musician based in Columbus, Ohio. He married a college sweetheart in 1915, Grace Bundy. Rather than share his precarious life, she lived with her parents in Danville, Kentucky. During their marriage, they had four children. Still's prospects improved when he joined the W.C. Handy band in Memphis, Tennessee, in 1916 as a player and arranger. He made the earliest arrangements of Handy's classic *Beale Street Blues* and *St. Louis Blues.* In 1917, Still came into an inheritance from his father, which he used to further his education at the Oberlin Conservatory of Music. Following a stint in the U.S. Navy in 1918 (at the end of World War I), he returned to Ohio, where he played professionally and took more courses at Oberlin. However, finding work was difficult, and Still decided to move to New York.

Grace joined William in 1919, as he began his first office job with W.C. Handy's publishing firm, Pace and Handy. Two years later, he became musical director of Pace's **phonograph** company. During his New York years, Still also arranged and played oboe in various theater orchestras, notably Eubie Blake's ensemble for the continuing, all-Black revue *Shuffle Along.* All the while, he found time to compose "serious" scores. In 1922, *Shuffle Along* played a run in Boston, and Still took the opportunity to study composition with George W. Chadwick at the New England Conservatory.

Returning to New York, Still went to work for the Black Swan **record** company, but soon received another opportunity for meaningful composition study. In 1923, he won a scholarship to study with *avant-garde* composer Edgard Varèse (1883–1965). Working with Varèse until 1925, Still learned to be freer and more daring in his music. He began to attract the attention of music critics and other composers. He also met important conductors—such as Leopold Stokowski, Eugene Goosens, and composer-conductor-educator Howard Hanson—who would perform Still's music in the coming years. Already Still was finding his voice as a spokesperson for Afro-American culture within the framework of the Euro-American musical style, in pieces like *From the Land of Dreams* (1925, a suite for three voices and orchestra in an *avant-garde* style); *Levee Land* (1926, a three-movement suite for voice and orchestra, blending jazz and European styles); *Sahdji* (1930, a ballet with narrator and chorus based on African proverbs); and *Africa* (1930, a symphonic trilogy).

During this period, Still made important discoveries about his natural musical style. His style was, by nature, not one of *avant-garde* experimentation but of fundamental Afro-American and Euro-American traditions. Years later, he reflected: "Melody, in my opinion, is the most important musical element. … I prefer music that suggests a program to either pure or program music in the strict sense." He immediately crystallized his style in a work that was to become his most famous, the *Afro-American Symphony.* Composed in 1930–1931, the symphony received its premiere the next season. This work, published in 1934, became Still's first published "serious" music.

All this time, Still was working as a successful radio arranger, but his heart was turned toward composing opera and concert music. In 1933, he applied for a Guggenheim Fellowship and was refused. Encouraged by composer-conductor Howard Hanson (1896–1981), he applied again the following year and received the award. He used the award money to move to Los Angeles and compose seriously.

phonograph Forerunner to the compact disc player. A stylus traced the wavy grooves in a disc (record), producing vibrations that were amplified into audible sound.

record A vinyl or shellac disc on which grooves have been scribed, which contain sound material playable on a phonograph.

Still's Guggenheim year (renewed twice later) was devoted to opera, first to *Blue Steel*, which he later scrapped, and then to *Troubled Island* (based on Haiti's first emperor, Jean Jacques Dessalines), not completed until 1941. He composed seven more operas between 1933 and 1962. The New York City Center opera company premiered *Troubled Island* in 1949. Part of the libretto for this opera and the complete librettos for the later ones were the work of Verna Arvey. A white pianist and talented writer, she first became Still's secretary when he settled on the West Coast, and in 1939 he married her, after obtaining a divorce from his first wife. William and Verna had two children.

National and international performances of movements from the *Afro-American Symphony* during the 1930s brought public visibility for Still. In Hollywood, he briefly worked as a film composer and orchestrator. Deems Taylor commissioned him to write a radio work in 1937. The result was *Lenox Avenue*, a suite of ten movements for orchestra, chorus, and narrator (text by Arvey). Each movement was an episode representing a scene the composer had witnessed during his life in Harlem. That year he also completed his Second Symphony, subtitled "Song of a New Race," which was premiered by the Philadelphia Orchestra, Leopold Stokowski conducting. In all, Still composed five symphonies. In 1938, he was commissioned to write the theme music for the 1939–1940 New York World's Fair.

Still continued to be a key musical voice of Black America during the 1940s, struggling at the same time with racism and the social problems of having a white wife. His massive 1940 work, *And They Lynched Him on a Tree*, was for a Negro chorus, a white chorus, narrator, contralto soloist, and orchestra. It received critical acclaim. His *In Memoriam: The Colored Soldiers Who Died for Democracy* (1943) was the most successful of the half-dozen patriotic works commissioned at that time by the League of Composers. Both Howard University and Oberlin awarded Still honorary doctorates during that decade (the first two of his six honorary degrees). Simultaneously, he faced discrimination and persecution in the musical world and the film business.

The Civil Rights movement of the 1950s and 1960s aided Still's situation in some respects. He finally won recognition in his home state, Mississippi, when the Jackson Symphony Orchestra premiered his children's piece, *The Little Song That Wanted to Be a Symphony*, in 1955. That year Still conducted the New Orleans Philharmonic-Symphony in a Baton Rouge concert—a landmark event in the Deep South. A new relationship with the University of Miami resulted in premieres of Still's symphonic poem *The Peaceful Land* in 1961 and his opera *Highway 1, U.S.A.* in 1963.

In 1970, the musical world celebrated Still's 75th birthday. By that time he had become firmly established as "Dean of African-American Composers." Honor upon honor was bestowed on him, from academic institutions and from associates in professional music. The following year, Still composed his last piece, *We Sang Our Songs*, dedicated to the Centennial of Fisk University and its Jubilee Singers. He could look back on a rich career as a composer and as a strong force in American music. Not all his music had focused on Afro-American culture; works like his *Festive Overture* (1944) contained a more general American flavor. He had also composed chamber music and piano pieces. As a "nationalist," he occasionally borrowed music or poetry from Latin America.

In 1975, Still suffered a series of strokes and heart attacks and had to be hospitalized. He died in a nursing home on December 3, 1978. His music, with its very original style and important message, was his chief legacy. In his career, he also broke new ground in the art music of the United States.

William Grant Still's Afro-American Symphony: **Composition,**
Performance, and Publication

William Grant Still could be considered a Black nationalist composer. He imbued most of his music with the lore or musical style of Afro-American culture, stretching back to roots in Africa and extending forward past the Civil Rights movement. The pinnacle of his development as a Black nationalist came when he composed his *Afro-American Symphony*, because of its high quality and because it expressed the entire sweep of Black American history from the oppression of slave days to the hopes of the mid-20th century. Viewed in this way, the symphony can be placed among the most significant achievements in American music.

According to Still's biography *In One Lifetime* by Verna Arvey, he began composing the *Afro-American Symphony* on October 30, 1930. We are fortunate to have the composer's own words concerning many historical, stylistic, and technical aspects of the work. For its first recording (1965), Still wrote:

> It was not until the Depression struck that I went jobless long enough to let the symphony take shape. … I rented a room in a quiet building not far from my home in New York and began to work. I devised my own Blues theme (which appears in varied guises throughout the symphony as a unifying thread), planned the form, then wrote the entire melody. After that I worked out the harmonies, the various treatments of the theme, and the orchestration.
>
> [Liner notes to "Music in America," MIA 118, © 1965 by The Society for the Preservation of the American Musical Heritage.]

In a 1967 speech before the National Association of Negro Musicians, Still elaborated on the blues element in his symphony:

> Long before writing this symphony, I had recognized the musical value of the *Blues* and had decided to use a theme in the *Blues* idiom as the basis for a major symphonic composition. When I was ready to launch this project, I did not want to use a theme some folk singer had already created but decided to create my own theme in the *Blues* idiom.
>
> [Judith Anne Still, managing ed., *William Grant Still and the Fusion of Cultures in American Music*, 2nd ed. (Flagstaff, AZ: The Master Player Library, 1995), p. 102. Used by permission of William Grant Still Music.]

Sometime in 1931, Still completed the symphony. While writing the work, he considered the music to be absolute, that is, without any programmatic suggestions. However, after completing it, the composer thought to add a program to enable audiences lacking in the Black experience to understand it better. His desire was to present the symphony as

> … a musical portrait of the African Americans of yesteryear: their longings, sorrows, humor, and aspirations. Their day is gone, but what they worked for and hoped for is coming to slow realization in our era. The *Afro-American Symphony* commemorates their dream.
>
> [Liner notes to "Music in America."]

For that purpose, he gave each movement a title and prefaced the music with excerpts from the verses of African-American poet Paul Laurence Dunbar (1872–1906):

Part I.   *Longing* (Moderato assai)

       "All my life long twell de night has pas'

       Let de wo'k come ez it will,

       So dat I fin' you, my honey, at last,

       Somewhaih des ovah de hill."

Part II.   *Sorrow* (Adagio)

"It's moughty tiahsome layin' 'roun'

Dis sorrer-laden earfly groun'

An' oftentimes I thinks, thinks I,

'Twould be a sweet t'ing des to die

An' go 'long home."

Part III.   *Humor* (Animato)

"An' we'll shout ouah halleluyahs

On dat mighty reck'nin' day."

Part IV.   *Aspiration* or *Sincerity* (Lento; Con risoluzione)

"Be proud, my Race, in mind and soul.

Thy name is writ on Glory's scroll

In characters of fire.

High mid the clouds of Fame's bright sky

Thy banner's blazoned folds now fly,

And truth shall lift them higher.

PERFORMANCES. The *Afro-American Symphony* was first presented during the
1931–1932 season of the Rochester Philharmonic Orchestra with Howard Hanson conducting. Still was no stranger to that audience at the time. Toward the end of the previous season,
they had warmly received his choral ballet *Sahdji*. The premiere of the *Afro-American Symphony* took place on an American Composers' Concert at the Eastman School of Music on
October 29, 1931. The audience and critics immediately lauded the work. Hanson repeated the
performance later in that season; this time Still received a standing ovation. When Hanson performed the third movement with the Berlin Philharmonic in January 1933, the audience

Ill. 6-6 African-American poet
Paul Laurence Dunbar,
1872–1906. Photo: Stock Montage, Inc.

demanded an encore before the concert continued. Some years later, a Budapest audience did the same.

In 1934, the publisher George Fischer approached Still concerning the publication of the *Afro-American Symphony*. On a handshake, they made an agreement that Still would receive royalties from the score after publication and Fischer had recouped promotion expenses. This publication enabled Still to join the American Society of Composers, Authors, and Publishers (ASCAP).

Ex. 6-3 Principal theme of William Grant Still's *Afro-American Symphony*, first movement. Elements from this melody reappear in each succeeding movement of the work.

FEATURES OF THE SYMPHONY. The blues theme, which is heard at some point in all four movements, became the principal theme of Part I (first movement), shown in Ex. 6-3.

The yearning quality of the poetry is reflected in this music. In contrast, the secondary theme of this modified sonata form resembles Black spiritual melodies. The development section works out each of the themes, giving them new dimensions.

A "blues-y" principal theme informs Part II also. Later Still wrote that after the subordinate theme "comes an alteration of the principal theme . . . that represents the fervent prayers of a burdened people rising upward to God."

Following the Classical symphonic model, Still put the *Humor* movement in third position, where Beethoven would have placed a scherzo (literally, "joke" in Italian). This movement has received such acclaim that it has been separately recorded and often appears by itself on concert programs under the title, "Scherzo." The spirited music also contains strong touches of the blues. Among the most significant features of the scherzo, however, are not the blue notes, but the featured presence of a banjo in the orchestra. As far as can be determined, Still's symphony was the first serious orchestral work to employ that instrument.

Part IV of the symphony is a free form, which Still explained in his 1967 speech,

> . . . is largely a retrospective viewing of the earlier movements with the exception of its principal theme. It is intended to give musical expression to the lines from Paul Laurence Dunbar, which appear on the score: "Be proud, my race, in mind and soul. . . ."

Summarizing the stylistic feeling of the *Afro-American Symphony*, Still wrote:

> The harmonies employed in the symphony are quite conventional except in a few places. The use of this style of harmonization was necessary in order to attain simplicity and to intensify in the music those qualities which enable the hearers to recognize it as Negro music. The orchestration was planned with a view to the attainment of effective simplicity.

> [Verna Arvey, *Studies of Contemporary American Composers: William Grant Still* (New York: J. Fischer & Bro., 1939), p. 28.]

Exploring the **Afro-American Symphony,** *third movement*

Listen to the entire movement, then listen to just the first 45 seconds. You have heard the introduction and main theme of this movement. The theme, heard in the first violins, is in two parts shown in Ex. 6-4.

Ex. 6-4 Main theme melody of the *Afro-American Symphony*, third movement.

What unusual instrument is strumming chords in the accompaniment to this theme? We hear a banjo, a unique feature of the orchestration.

"Blue" notes are the *lowered third* and *seventh* scale degrees in an otherwise **diatonic** major scale. They are *inflections* of the diatonic notes. In a melody, they may appear close to their diatonic counterparts, yielding the true "blue" effect. *Still's main theme for this movement (Ex. 6-4), in the key of A-flat major, contains three occurrences of "blue" notes. Identify where they occur.* G-flat (lowered seventh degree) is the "blue" note here. We find it in mm. 16, 20, and 21.

Continue listening. At approximately 1 minute 15 seconds into the movement, notice the announcement of a new idea:

diatonicism The principle of constructing scales that employs particular combinations of whole steps and half steps, such as formed by the white keys of a keyboard. Adj.: diatonic.

What section of the orchestra presents this? The brass section plays this passage.

Following this, listen to bits of this idea tossed back and forth between the brass and the strings (doubled by horns and woodwinds). In the present work, this dialogue technique could be termed "call and response," a type of singing employed in Negro work songs of Africa and the Americas.

Listen from this point to the end of the movement. During the last 30 seconds, the main theme returns for the last time. Listen closely to the accompaniment in the trumpets and trombones, playing Ex. 6-5:

Ex. 6-5 Trumpets and trombones, *Afro-American Symphony*, third movement, mm. 88–91.

From what theme has the composer taken this music? To find the answer, you must compare this with the music in Ex. 6-3, above. This idea is derived from the symphony's pervasive blues theme, and here is where Still places this musical idea in the third movement.

The Afro-American Symphony, third movement: A Closer Look

Please refer to the score of the *Afro-American Symphony*, beginning on page 123 of the Score Anthology.

"Blue" notes can also include *raised second (= lowered third)* and *raised fourth/lowered fifth* scale degrees. *Identify the "blue" notes in Ex. 6-5.* A raised fourth degree occurs in m. 88, and a raised second in m. 89.

Look at the first page of the score and notice the larger orchestra required for the Afro-American Symphony, *compared with the final movement of Beethoven's Fifth Symphony. List the additional instruments.*

Woodwinds: English Horn; Bass Clarinet

Brass: Horns 3 and 4

Percussion: Small Cymbal and Large Suspended Cymbal

"Extra" Instruments: Harp and Tenor Banjo (not shown this page)

Studying the score also allows us to observe the structure of this movement. *The following table shows starting measures of the main structural points. Mark them all in your score:*

MEASURE	SECTION
1	Introduction
	Main Theme:
8 (with upbeat)	Part 1
16 (with upbeat)	Part 2
24 (with upbeat)	Part 1, restated
27	*Transition*
39	*Second thematic idea* (motivic)
47 (with upbeat)	*Development*
	Modified Restatements of Main Theme:
69 (with upbeat)	Part 1
75 (with upbeat)	Part 2
88 (with upbeat)	Parts 1 and 2 with "blues-y" variants

Now listen to the movement, following the score and noting the places you have marked.

William Grant Still was a colorful orchestrator, and studying the orchestration of this movement in detail is instructive. However, within the scope of this text, we will only observe his *instrumentation* at certain points. *In mm. 8–15, which instruments carry the melody of the main theme?* The first phrase is sounded in both sections of violins and violas. Then the melody's instrumentation shifts to first violins and one clarinet. *What is the instrumentation of part 2 of the theme, mm. 16–23?* First violins are doubled by two flutes, piccolo, two oboes, two clarinets, and the first trumpet. *On your own, study each of the remaining main structural points, noting the instrumentation of the chief musical ideas.*

When the main theme returns following the development section, it is varied in several ways. *For example, compare the original version of part 1 of the theme (see mm. 8–11 or Ex. 6-4) with the parallel passage, mm. 69–72 (first violins). What is the difference?* The second version changes in the third measure. The melodic shape is different, including a "blue" note (lowered third). *Similarly, find the "blue" note variant in m. 78 (first violins).* Again, we have a lowered third. *Finally, examine the concluding statement of this theme, beginning with the upbeat* _to m. 88. Note all the variants in melody and rhythm. List the measure numbers and types of all "blue" notes in this passage._

MEASURE	"BLUE" NOTE
88, upbeat	Lowered seventh
88	Lowered third, lowered seventh
89	Raised fourth
90	Lowered third, lowered seventh
91	Lowered seventh
92	Lowered third, lowered seventh
93	Raised fourth
94	Lowered third, lowered seventh
95	Lowered seventh

Thus, this statement contains an intense concentration of "blue" notes. In combination with syncopated rhythmic variants and the original blues theme in the brass (m. 88), these notes comment colorfully on the main theme and give the movement's ending a raucous, celebratory feeling.

DEBUSSY: _PRELUDE TO "THE AFTERNOON OF A FAUN"_

Between the eras of Beethoven and Still, orchestral music developed a rich literature of program music. One of the most significant works in this literature is the symphonic poem _Prélude à "L'Après-midi d'un faune"_ (_Prelude to "The Afternoon of a Faun"_) by Claude Debussy. In musical style, this work was a turning point between the Romantic and Modern periods.

Orchestral Program Music of the Romantics

Here is a brief overview of the four types of program music that developed in the Romantic orchestral repertoire.

Program Symphony	This is a symphony that illustrates a specific story. Beethoven's _Pastoral_ Symphony (Symphony No. 6) set an example for program symphonies that followed. The young French composer Hector Berlioz (1803–1869), composed his _Symphonie fantastique_ "Episodes in the life of an artist" in 1830, giving the music a literal story published in the concert program. Franz Liszt, who coined the term "program music," composed two program symphonies named _Faust_ and _Dante_ (1854 and 1857, respectively).
Incidental Music	Nineteenth-century theatrical productions often included music to cover scene changes or underscore dialogue; this became known as incidental music. Famous examples include Beethoven's Overture to _Egmont_; Mendelssohn's Wedding March composed for a production of Shakespeare's _A Midsummer Night's Dream_; and _Peer Gynt Suite_ by Edvard Grieg (1843–1907).

Concert Overture

From the opera overture, composers derived both the incidental-music overture and the idea of the programmatic concert overture. Mendelssohn's *Hebrides (Fingal's Cave) Overture* (1829) describes an adventure on an island off the coast of Scotland. Tchaikovsky based his *1812 Festival Overture* (1881) on Russia's historical defeat of Napoleon's troops. Part of its emotional appeal comes from the inclusion of Russian sacred and patriotic hymns as well as the French national anthem, the "Marseillaise." Actual cannon fire and heavy percussion in the final section make a spectacular impact.

Symphonic Poem

The symphonic poem is a type of programmatic orchestral work in one movement. Liszt was the first use the term *symphonische Dichtung* (symphonic poem), and his dozen works under this designation virtually defined the genre. He achieved unity by limiting the number of themes and by causing new musical ideas to grow out of one main idea through a technique called "thematic transformation." *Les Preludes* (c. 1853) is an example.

Richard Strauss (1864–1949) inherited the mantle of symphonic poetry from Liszt. His *Also sprach Zarathustra* (*Thus Spake Zarathustra*, 1896) based on Friedrich Nietzsche's poetic-philosophical book, sought to represent the loftiest abstract thoughts in music.

The symphonic poem was also an important tool of musical expression for the nationalist composers. Smetana's *The Moldau*, Borodin's *In the Steppes of Central Asia,* and Sibelius's *Finlandia* are well-known examples.

In France, Camille Saint-Saëns (1835–1921) composed some symphonic poems, the most famous of which was *Danse macabre* (1874), which represents a scene at night in a graveyard. A younger generation of French composers, whose lives extended well into the 20th century, sought to develop a truly French sound in their orchestral music. Claude Debussy was the most important pioneer in this new movement, and his *Prelude to "The Afternoon of a Faun"* (1894) was the symphonic poem that led the way.

CLAUDE DEBUSSY

Photograph, c. 1895.

Achille-Claude Debussy was born on August 22, 1862, in St. Germain-en-Laye, just outside Paris. His father, Manuel-Achille Debussy, was variously a printer's assistant, traveling salesman, and merchant; his mother Victorine-Joséphine-Sophie (née Manoury) had been a seamstress but was running the family china shop when Claude was born. The child received piano lessons and advanced so quickly that he was accepted into the Paris Conservatory at the age of ten. Able to play Chopin's F Minor Piano Concerto by the age of 12, Debussy was headed for a career as a concert pianist. However, his poor examinations in 1878 and 1879 dictated a change of direction. In 1880, he joined the composition class of Ernest Giraud and unofficially attended a few of César Franck's classes. He exasperated both teachers with his iconoclastic attitude. (Franck, hearing Debussy play an original piece, blustered, "Modulate, modulate!" to which Debussy calmly replied, "Why? I'm perfectly happy in this key.")

At the recommendation of one of his teachers, Debussy became part of the traveling entourage of Mme. Nadezhda von Meck (patroness to Tchaikovsky; see Chapter 7) during the summers of 1880 and 1881. In Moscow, he became acquainted with Tchaikovsky's music but much preferred that of the forward-looking, intuitive Modest Mussorgsky (1839–1881).

Debussy made his debut as a composer at a concert in 1882. At the Conservatoire, his introverted personality and rebelliousness did not win him friends on the composition faculty, however. Though he was clearly the most gifted composition student, he had to settle for Second Prize in 1883. The following year the committee reluctantly awarded him First Prize, the Prix de Rome, for his cantata *L'enfant prodigue* (*The Prodigal Son*).

Debussy detested the time he spent in Rome, returning to Paris in 1887. The period 1887–1892 was crucial in the formulation of Debussy's musical personality. In 1888 and 1889, he made "pilgrimages" to Bayreuth to hear operas by Richard Wagner, notably *Parsifal* and *Tristan und Isolde*. Although Debussy would later write scathing criticisms about the "excesses" of Wagner's music dramas, these two works deeply influenced his development as an opera composer. Balinese Gamelan music, which Debussy heard at the 1889 Paris World Exposition, impressed his sense of tone color, and he connected its shimmering sound with the qualities of French Symbolist poetry of the time. During this period Debussy obtained a copy of Mussorgsky's opera *Boris Godunov*. He devoured the score, playing and discussing it with anyone who would listen. Mussorgsky's fresh, unschooled harmonic style appealed to Debussy's anti-academic bent.

He also met composer Erik Satie (1866–1925) and Symbolist poet Pierre Louÿs (1879–1925) at this time, and they became his closest friends. Satie, the creator of such satirical trifles as *Three Pieces in the Form of a Pear*, was a decided influence on Debussy. We need only examine the harmonies in such an early work as Satie's *Trois Gymnopédies* for piano (1888)—two of which Debussy later orchestrated—to discover a few of the roots of Debussy's revolutionary harmonic ideas. Also during this time, Debussy gained some public recognition. *La Damoiselle élue* (*The Blessed Damsel*, 1889) was acclaimed at its premiere, and he began to compose music worthy enough to find its way into permanent music literature, notably piano music such as the two *Arabesques* (1888) and "Clair de lune" from the *Suite Bergamasque* (1890–1905).

Debussy was never a prolific composer, but the two decades between 1892 and about 1912 were the most productive time of his life. In the first ten years he composed two of his most famous works: *Prélude à "L'Après-midi d'un faune"* (*Prelude to "The Afternoon of a Faun"*), written in 1892–1894; and his only completed opera, *Pelléas et Mélisande*, begun in 1893. He completed the first version of the opera in 1895. Meanwhile, *Prélude à "L'Après-midi d'un faune"* had premiered in December 1894 at the Société Nationale but went almost unnoticed. Debussy also composed his String Quartet in G Minor at the same time as the orchestral *Prelude*. In 1897, he wrote some of his most famous songs, the *Trois chansons de Bilitis* (text by Pierre Louÿs), and two years later, he finished the final version of his next orchestral masterpiece, the three *Nocturnes*. In 1901, Debussy began sporadically to contribute music reviews to Paris papers. Writing under the thinly disguised pen-name of "M. Croche [Mr. Eighth Note], the Dilettante-Hater," he contributed articles showing a deep intellect and impeccable, sensitive musical judgment.

The first version of *Pelléas et Mélisande* had been finished in 1895, and Debussy immedi-

(continued)

CLAUDE DEBUSSY *(continued)*

ately set about revisions that would last until 1897. Still unsatisfied with his work and at first on the verge of destroying it, the composer continued to tinker with the opera until the beginning of 1902. *Pelléas et Mélisande* premiered at the Paris Opéra Comique late in April of that year. Reactions in the press were divided between praise and censure, and Debussy, as had happened before, became a controversial figure. Nevertheless, that year the French government awarded Debussy the Croix d'Honneur.

Debussy's personal life was *very* personal, and his love life was as free-spirited as his philosophy of the arts. When he returned from Rome in 1887, he began living with Gaby DuPont, who supported him with her labor for over ten years. He married Lily Texier in 1899, whereupon Gaby shot herself (but not fatally). The marriage to Lily lasted only until 1904, when Debussy left her for Emma Bardac, the wife of a banker, whereupon Lily (like Gaby) shot herself (but also not fatally). Emma was older than Claude and had grown children. The following year she bore him his only known child, Claude-Emma, who was called "Chouchou" (pronounced *shoe*-shoe). For Chouchou, Debussy composed the well-known *Children's Corner* Suite for piano. He completed it in 1908, the year Claude and Emma were married.

After *Pelléas et Mélisande*, Debussy concentrated heavily on orchestral and piano music. Composed in 1903–1905, *La Mer* (*The Sea*) is as close as Debussy ever came to writing a symphony. Its intimately related three movements stand in sharp contrast to the three unrelated essays in his next orchestral work. Over the years 1906–1912, Debussy assembled *Ibéria, Gigues,* and *Rondes de Printemps* (*Spring Rounds*) under the general title of *Images*. He also used that title for two suites of piano music written in 1905 and 1907. Perhaps Debussy reached the culmination of his piano literature in the *Préludes*, completed as two sets of 12 in 1910 and 1913. Each prelude's title appears at the end—like an afterthought—and many of them resemble Symbolist poetic imagery, for example *Ce qu'a vu le vent de l'Ouest* (*What the West Wind Saw*) or *La Cathédrale engloutie* (*The Engulfed Cathedral*), both from Book I. Debussy's 12 *Etudes* from 1915, dedicated to Chopin, round out his piano *oeuvre*.

In 1914, Debussy began to suffer from what was to be a painful fatal illness. The following year, the 53-year-old composer was diagnosed with cancer, and in December he underwent a colostomy. Though he was weakened, his creative urge was still strong, and he undertook a project of writing six sonatas for various instrumental combinations. He lived to complete only three of them, but they incorporated new directions in his musical thinking. The Sonata for Cello and Piano (1915); Sonata for Flute, Viola, and Harp (1915); and Sonata for Violin and Piano (1917) were his last works. At the beginning of 1918, Debussy was confined to his room, and he died on March 25.

Impressionism (1) A movement in the visual arts in France during the second half of the 19th century. Impressionism emphasized suggestion rather than depiction and the play of light on a subject rather than its depiction. (2) In music, a set of style characteristics perceived as analogous to (1). Impressionistic harmony tends to be nontraditional and orchestration is transparent. Adj.: impressionistic.

Debussy's Prelude: Background and Aftermath

Debussy's music is usually labeled **Impressionism**, a term taken freely from the French visual arts of his time. However, he considered himself more closely allied with the Symbolist poets than with painters and was irritated when his music was called Impressionistic. He stated, "What I am trying to do is something different … but what some fools call Impressionism, a term that is usually misapplied. …"

His music was actually something apart, spontaneous and intuitive, and possibly the most

Ill. 6-7 Stéphane Mallarmé.
Lithograph by James A.
Whistler, 1894. © The British
Museum.

innovative and original since Beethoven. As Beethoven had stood with one foot in the Classical period and the other in the Romantic, so Debussy straddled the 19th and 20th centuries. His music partook somewhat of both Romanticism and modernism. The programmatic titling of most of his instrumental music was a continuation of the Romantic tendencies of Liszt. Yet his musical language turned away from functional harmony and conventional techniques in orchestration in favor of new directions. For example, in harmony, he often favored "exotic" scales (modes, pentatonic scales, whole-tone scales, etc.), and in orchestration, he emphasized the woodwind section over the strings. In sum, Debussy opened the door to modern tonal music and became its most influential composer.

Since Claude Debussy always connected himself more closely with poets than with painters, both socially and in spirit, it comes as no surprise that he was friendly with Stéphane Mallarmé (1842–1898), the Symbolist poet who wrote "L'Après-midi d'un faune" ("The Afternoon of a Faun"). In 1884, Debussy made a song setting of Mallarmé's poem, "Apparition." By the time Debussy returned home from Rome in 1887, Mallarmé was well established and had a circle of "disciples" with whom he met weekly to discuss poetry. Debussy met with this group from time to time, and by 1892 he was well enough known to bring a guest.

Mallarmé's most famous poem, *L'Après-midi d'un faune,*" went through two preliminary versions over a period of more than a decade before reaching its final form in 1876. That year Mallarmé finally succeeded in publishing his "L'Après-midi d'un faune," subtitled "Eclogue," a term taken from the pastoral poetry of Virgil. It was his first publication, and it did for French poetry approximately what Debussy's *Prelude* did for French music. As a result, during the 1880s the poem virtually made Mallarmé's reputation.

The faun who relates his own experiences in the poem is, of course, a Roman mythological creature, half goat and half man—the counterpart of the Greek figure of Pan. Briefly, the poem's story is that, while the faun is playing his double flute made of reeds, he falls asleep and dreams of two nymphs. He awakens, only to find reality the same as before; then he tries to relive the dream in his mind. This lengthy poem, however, does not start at the beginning of the story, but after the faun has awakened. We glean the preceding story in a series of flashbacks. Here is the poem's opening:

Ces nymphes, je les veuz perpéteur.

Ci clair,

Leur incarnat léger, qu'il voltige dans l'air

Assoupi de sommeils touffus.

Aimai-je un rêve?

Mon doute, amas de nuit ancienne, s'achève

En maint rameau subtil, qui, demeuré les vrais

Bois mêmes, prouve, hélas! Que bien seul je m'offrais

Pour triomphe la faute idéale de roses—

Réfléchissons …

I would immortalize these nymphs

So bright

Their sunlit coloring, so airy light,

It floats like drowsing down.

Loved I a dream?

My doubts, born of oblivious darkness, seem

A tree's self—proving that I have known

No triumph, but the shadow of a rose—

But think back …

[Translation by Aldous Huxley, *The Defeat of Youth, and Other Poems*, (London: Oxford University Press, 1918), p. 44; edited by Michael Fink.]

Like the poem, Debussy's *Prelude* evolved from earlier plans. In 1891, Mallarmé was still nursing the idea of some sort of staged version, and a second-hand story places Debussy in the picture from that time. Nothing came of that idea immediately; however, Debussy did begin work on the *Prelude* sometime in 1892. The *Prelude* years, 1892–1894, represent a turning point in Debussy's musical style, when he shed the last vestiges of German and French academicism in favor of a new, more intuitive approach, which closely paralleled Symbolism in poetry and Impressionism in the visual arts. When finally finished, the *Prélude à "L'Après-midi d'un faune"* would be Debussy's first essay in his new, fully developed style.

An 1893 advertisement promised that Debussy's forthcoming music to Mallarmé's poem would consist of a "prelude," "interludes," and "paraphrase finale." These were to have premiered in a concert in March 1894, but none of the music was performed then. By October 23, the score to the *Prelude* was finished, and Debussy had abandoned the other movements. He had by this time played it for Mallarmé, who was astonished, according to a later report of Debussy's, exclaiming, "I was not expecting anything of this kind! This music prolongs the emotion of my poem and sets its scene more vividly than color." The *Prelude* received its world premiere at a concert of the Société Nationale on December 22, 1894, featuring eight works, mostly the music of contemporary French composers. Debussy's music was played immediately following Saint-Saëns's Third Violin Concerto. The program was repeated the following evening. Mallarmé attended the first at Debussy's invitation.

The conductor, Gustave Doret, felt that the premiere was a complete success. Reports about the audience's response, however, have been mixed. Biographer Léon Vallas claims the audience demanded an encore, whereas an eyewitness quoted in Oscar Thompson's biography reported hisses from the audience. We know that press reviews showed no enthusiasm, and that may also have been the audience's true reaction. Thompson remarks that "at the time it was written, nothing like it existed in music." Some of the well-established, more "academic" musicians in Paris subsequently reacted against this revolutionary piece. For example, as late as 1920, Saint-Saëns still opposed it when he wrote, "The *Prélude à 'L'Après-midi d'un faune'* is pretty sound, but in it you find not the slightest musical idea, properly speaking. It is as much like a piece of music as the palette a painter uses is like a painting."

Despite such opposition, Debussy's *Prelude* caught on in Paris. In late 1895, three performances took place there. Soon the work became a programming "obsession," so that in 1899, when Debussy wished to introduce his new *Trois Nocturnes*, he had to veto his publisher's proposal that the *Prelude* appear on the program ahead of the premiere. Ten years after Debussy penned the first notes of the *Prelude*, its popularity had spread through Europe, and it had even been performed in Boston. Debussy himself conducted the work a few times during the years 1908–1913 in London, Vienna, Turin, and Paris.

In 1912, *Prelude to "The Afternoon of a Faun"* became a ballet at Serge Diaghilev's Ballets Russes. Vaslav Nijinsky, the star of the company, choreographed it and danced the part of the faun with a spotted body stocking as his costume. Six ballerinas danced with him. The production was such a success that it eclipsed a much longer mythological ballet they produced the same season: Ravel's masterpiece *Daphnis et Chloë*.

Justifiably, *Prelude to "The Afternoon of a Faun"* became Debussy's best-known orchestral work and a fixture in the orchestral literature. French composers of the 1920s (e.g., Darius Milhaud, Arthur Honegger, and Francis Poulenc) tried hard to escape the "Debussyism" that had inundated French music, but still they studied the *Prelude* and other Debussy works. As late as the 1960s, French (and other) serialists continued to laud Debussy's music and pay tribute to this piece as a turning point in European musical style. Notably, composer-conductor Pierre Boulez (1925–), who also set some of Mallarmé's poetry to music, wrote that "modern music was awakened by the *Prelude to 'The Afternoon of a Faun.'*"

Ill. 6-8 Vaslav Nijinsky in the title role of his ballet, *L'Après-midi d'un faune* (1912), based on Debussy's music. Photo by Baron Adolf de Meyer.

Exploring Debussy's Prelude to "The Afternoon of a Faun"

MAIN THEME. Listen to the Prelude to "The Afternoon of a Faun" to get a general idea of the piece. Now listen to about the first 30 seconds, attending closely to the famous main theme for solo flute. Does this melody suggest any features in the original poem by Mallarmé? The faun is playing a flute when he falls asleep. That instrument is heard, and we could make a case for the melody having a languid, "sleepy" nature.

FORM. Debussy's adherence only to general principles of thematic and structural form make the analysis of the *Prelude* problematic. At the heart of the difficulty of analyzing Debussy is his blended unity of harmony, tone color, and thematic material. Analysts disagree, for example, on how many sections this movement contains. Here we will take the point of view that the structure is basically in four sections: A–B–C–A' followed by a brief coda.

Listen again from the beginning. Notice that the main theme begins with downward melodic motion. Continue listening until you hear the following theme:

What instrument plays this theme? This entirely new theme, played by a solo oboe, begins with a *downward* motion, as did the main theme. This is the beginning of the B Section of the *Prelude*.

Continue listening until you reach this theme:

What section of the orchestra plays this theme? Performed by the woodwinds, this theme announces the opening of section C. Notice the emphasis, again, on *downward* motion in this melody.

CLIMAX AND RETURN. In writing the *Prelude to "The Afternoon of a Faun,"* Debussy purposely avoided Classical forms such as sonata form or theme and variations. However, he did preserve a few universal principles of form, such as *climax* and *return. In section C, note where the dynamic (and emotional) climax occurs. Following that, identify where the music returns to the main theme (flute solo).* This marks the A' section, which starts the *Prelude* toward its conclusion.

INSTRUMENTATION. On the first page of the score, study the instrumentation, identifying all the instruments you can. The following table translates the French designations that may be difficult to guess:

FRENCH	ENGLISH
Hautbois	Oboe(s)
Cor anglais	English horn
Cors à pistons	Horns (French horns with valves)
Cymbales antiques	Antique cymbals
Altos	Violas

Antique cymbals are a pair of small plates suspended by a thong. Both are tuned to a designated high pitch. This score calls for two pairs tuned to E and B. Modern concert harps have

Prelude to "The Afternoon of a Faun": A Closer Look
Please refer to the score of *Prelude to "The Afternoon of a Faun,"* beginning on page 139 of the Score Anthology.

the ability to tune every diatonic note, either flat, natural, or sharp. The score indicates the tuning for harp I, enabling it to perform the *glissando* notated in measures 4 and 7.

This is the complete orchestra, a very specialized one. What instruments that you would expect in a full orchestra are omitted from this score? The brass section contains neither trumpets nor trombones. Antique cymbals are the only percussion; timpani and other percussion are omitted.

TERMS. This French score contains some terms that might not be familiar. Refer to the following table for clarification.

TERM	DEFINITION	CONTEXT AND EXPLANATION
1ᵉʳ mouvᵗ	First tempo	(m. 51) Tempo marking
Accordez	Tune	(m. 1) Directive to tune the harp
Changez en La	Change to clarinet in A	(m. 89) Directive to clarinetist
Dans le 1ᵉʳ mouvᵗ avec plus langueur	In the first tempo, but with more languor	(m. 94) Tempo marking
Dans le mouvᵗ plus animé	In the more animated tempo	(m. 90) Tempo marking
Deux	Two	(m. 93) Here, asking for two solo first violins
Doux	Sweetly	(m. 37) Expression marking
En animant	Becoming animated	(m. 37) Tempo marking
En dehors	Standing out	(m. 47) Expression marking
Jusqu'à la fin	Until the end	(m. 106) Part of a tempo marking
Légèrement	Lightly	(m. 21) Expression marking
Lent	Slowly	(m. 106) Tempo marking
Même mouvᵗ	Same tempo	(m. 55) Tempo marking
Modéré	Moderate	(m. 1) Tempo marking
Mouvᵗ de Début	Beginning tempo	(m. 79) Directive to return to the tempo of the movement's beginning
Position nat.	Natural position	(m. 17) Bowing returns to normal position
Ôtez	Remove	(m. 21) Directive to remove string mutes
Retenu	Ritenuto	(m. 20) Tempo held back
Sans	Without	(m. 39) Usually applies to mutes
Sourdines	Mutes	(m. 5, 31) Applied to strings or horns
Soutenu	Sustained	(m. 55, 56) Tempo or expression marking
Subito (Italian)	Suddenly	(m. 63) Dynamic directive

(continued)

TERM	DEFINITION	CONTEXT AND EXPLANATION
Sur la touche	Over the fingerboard	(m. 11) Strings draw their bows over the fingerboard for a special mellow effect
Toujours	Even more	(m. 44) Used in tempo markings
Très	Very	(m. 1) Used in tempo and expression markings
Un peu plus animé	A little more animated	(m. 83) Tempo marking
Vite	Quickly	(m. 30) Directive about removing mutes

Ex. 6-6 Main theme of Debussy's *Prelude to "The Afternoon of a Faun,"* with constituent motives bracketed.

MAIN THEME: VARIANTS AND TRANSFORMATION.   Ex. 6-6 shows the *Prelude*'s main theme. The constituent motives are bracketed: a, b, and c. Because Debussy sometimes subdivides motive a, the example shows that division into "a_1" and "a_2." In this work Debussy derived fresh yet familiar material from the main theme by writing *variants* of it and employing *thematic transformation*. In applying these techniques, the composer was able to rework one or more of the motives into a new melodic idea.

Ex. 6-7 lists, in order, each melodic idea derived from the main theme. The motives' sources are labeled. Look through the score carefully and find each of the ideas. Make a table of information about Ex. 6-7(a-i), identifying starting measure number(s) and instrument(s) playing the melody in each excerpt.

Ex. 6-7 *Prelude to "The Afternoon of a Faun"*: new musical ideas derived from the main theme.

When completed, your table should contain this information:

	MEASURE(S)	MELODY INSTRUMENT(S)
a.	5; 8; 9	1 horn
b.	15	1 oboe
c.	17; 18	2 oboes, 2 clarinets; then strings added
d.	28	2 flutes
e.	46; 47	English horn, 2 clarinets; then violins
f.	61	Woodwinds
g.	67; 74	Strings; 1 horn, then 1 clarinet
h.	83	1 oboe
i.	96	Woodwinds

SPOTTING THE FORM. In the "Exploring" exercises above, we observed the basic A–B–C–A' structure. Now we will go through the score to find these structural points and other details: the two transitional passages and coda. Mark each of these important points in your score as we go along.

Section A begins right away, without an introduction, and continues until m. 30. *In the strings, notice the "cadence" on the note B.* In the next measure, the violas introduce a transition (mm. 31–36).

Section B begins in m. 37, where the tempo increases, and Debussy introduces a new theme. *What instrument plays this theme?* The oboe's melody is the theme, partly echoed in the strings at m. 40. A new transition begins in m. 51, as the opening tempo returns.

Section C, beginning in m. 55, is where the *Prelude*'s climax will occur. *What is the instrumentation of the theme introduced at this point?* It is exclusively woodwinds: a flute, an oboe, an English horn, and a pair of clarinets playing in octaves. The woodwind section continues to make its presence known as the strings play the theme at m. 63. *The full orchestra builds to a dynamic climax of ff. In which measure does this occur?* The *Prelude*'s only *ff* appears in the strings at m. 70. *Notice that after that measure, both the dynamic level and the number of instruments diminish dramatically.*

Now find the beginning of section A', where the main theme returns. As at the beginning, a solo flute plays the opening of the theme at m. 79. Its rhythmic values have been augmented, however. *Which instrument next sounds the theme?* In m. 85, the oboe (again in long notes) echoes the opening of the theme. *Now find the entrance of the antique cymbals.* This occurs at m. 94, as the two flutes in unison begin the main theme. Other material from the first section A also returns.

The coda starts in m. 106 with a descending idea in the two harps. *What instruments then play the beginning of the main theme?* Two horns with mutes ("*sourdines*") play this final melody, which then fades away.

CHAPTER SEVEN

The Concerto

When we see a concerto listed on a concert program or hear it performed, we may assume that, like most concertos in the modern repertoire, it was written for one soloist with orchestra. Piano or violin is the most usual solo instrument, although concertos have been composed for virtually every instrument capable of carrying a melodic or rhythmic line. The solo concerto, then, is most familiar to us. However, before the solo concerto developed in the 18th century, a type of *multisoloist* concerto had laid the groundwork for the concerto idea. This was the *concerto grosso* (grand concerto), which originated in Italy and soon spread to other countries during the late Baroque period. In our study we will first focus on a Baroque *concerto grosso* by J.S. Bach, then move on to a Classical piano concerto by Mozart, and, finally, a Romantic violin concerto by Tchaikovsky.

BACH, "BRANDENBURG" CONCERTO NO. 2 IN F MAJOR (BWV 1047), FIRST MOVEMENT

The Concerto Grosso before Bach

The instrumental concerto began in Italy in the late 17th century as a counterpart of vocal music. Mirroring the Baroque practice of contrasting a small group of vocal soloists with an entire choir, Italian *instrumental* composers like Arcangelo Corelli (1653–1713) began to write works in which a group of three string soloists were contrasted with a larger group. The solo group—two violins and a cello—was labeled *concertino* (little concerto). The larger group, called the *ripieno* or *ripieni* (filling or "stuffing"), included parts for four small sections: two violins, viola, and *basso continuo* (which usually included a cello). Together, the two groups made up the *concerto grosso* (large concerto or grand concerto), also called the ***tutti***. Throughout a movement, the concertino played constantly. Often the *ripieno* would be silent, leaving the spotlight on the *concertino*. Thus, the instrumental concerto principle was created: a contrast between soloists and orchestra, but with cooperation and close coordination between them. This genre became known as the *concerto grosso*, and Corelli was its "father."

During the 1680s the German composer Georg Muffat (1653–1704) spent time studying music in Rome, Corelli's home. Years later he recalled hearing string concertos "composed by the gifted Signor Arcangelo Corelli, and beautifully performed with the utmost accuracy by a great number of instrumental players." We know little about the musical forces at Corelli's disposal as he developed his 12 Concerti Grossi, published posthumously as Opus 12. However, Muffat states in the foreword to his own concertos—modeled on Corelli's and published in 1701—that the *ripieno* group could be made up of just one player to a part. If more strings are available, this group could expand to two, three, or more players to a part, with a double bass added to the cellos. The "little choir or trio" (*concertino*), he goes on to say, should always be just one player per part.

tutti Literally, "all" in Italian. The usual meanings are full orchestra or full string section.

Brahms, Double Concerto (1887) •

Tchaikovsky, Violin Concerto (1878) •

Brahms, Violin Concerto (1878) •

Saint-Saëns, Cello Concerto (1873) •

Vieuxtemps, Violin, Concerto No. 5 (1861) •

Mendelssohn, Violin Concerto (1844) •

Paganini, Violin Concerto No. 2 (1827) •

Beethoven, Piano Concerto No. 5, "Emperor" (1809) •

• Beethoven, Violin Concerto (1806)

• Mozart, Piano Concerto in A Major, K. 488 (1786)

• Haydn, Symphonies 6, 7, and 8, *concertante* works (1761)

• Bach, *Brandenburg Concertos,* 1721

• Corelli, 12 Concerti Grossi, Op. 6 published (1714, posthumously)

• Vivaldi, *L'Estro Armonico* (12 concertos) published (1711)

• Muffat, *Ausserlesene Instrumental-Music* (12 concerti grossi) published (1701)

Ex. 7-1 Time line of the Concerto: 1700–1900; 1900 to the present (p. 201).

| 1700 | 1725 | 1750 | 1775 | 1800 | 1825 | 1850 | 1875 | 1900 |

Georg Muffat (1652–1704)

Arcangelo Corelli (1653–1713)

Giuseppe Torelli (1658–1709)

Antonio Vivaldi (1685–1741)

J. S. Bach (1685–1750)

Joseph Haydn (1732–1809)

Wolfgang Amadeus Mozart (1756–1791)

Ludwig van Beethoven (1770–1827)

Niccolò Paganini (1782–1840)

Louis Spohr (1784–1859)

Felix Mendelssohn (1809–1847)

Henry Vieuxtemps (1820–1881)

Johannes Brahms (1833–1897)

Camille Saint-Saëns (1835–1921)

Max Bruch (1838–1920)

Peter I. Tchaikovsky (1840–1893)

ritornello In an Italian opera or chamber cantata of the 17th–18th centuries, an instrumental passage at the end of an aria or following each verse of a strophic aria.

RV Abbreviation for "Ryom Verzeichnis" (Ryom Catalog), a thematic catalog of music by Antonio Vivaldi compiled by Peter Ryom.

The next generation of *concerto grosso* composers, working around 1700 and later, devised forms and procedures to make sharper distinctions between the *concertino* and the *tutti.* Giuseppe Torelli (1658–1709) assigned a recurring theme to *tutti* segments, while writing completely different material in passages for the *concertino* alone. This became known as the **ritornello** form.

Antonio Vivaldi (1678–1741) and Tommaso Albinoni (1671–1751)—both from Venice— further developed the *ritornello* idea. They kept the string orchestra intact for the *ripieno* but sometimes used different instruments in the *concertino.* Vivaldi, for example, who composed more than 40 works in the *concerto grosso* genre, employed pairs of oboes and clarinets in two works (**RV** 559, 560), a flute, oboe, and bassoon in another (RV 570), and mixtures of woodwinds and strings in several others.

Corigliano, Clarinet Concerto (1977) •
Barber, Piano Concerto (1962) •
Schuller, Concertino (1959) •
• Strauss, Oboe Concerto (1948)
• Korngold, Violin Concerto (1947)
• Martin, *Petite symphonie concertante* (1945)
• Bartók, Piano Concerto No. 3 (1945)
• Bartók, *Concerto for Orchestra* (1943)
• Barber, Violin Concerto (1940)
• Rodrigo, *Concerto de Aranjuez* (for guitar, 1939)
• Stravinsky, *Dumbarton Oaks Concerto* (1937)
• Berg, Violin Concerto (1935)
• Prokofiev, Violin Concerto No. 2 (1935)
• Shostakovich, Piano Concert No. 1 (1933)
• Ravel, Piano Concerto (1931)
• Walton, Viola Concerto (1929)
• Nielson, Clarinet Concerto (1928)
• Gershwin, Piano Concerto (1925)
• Bloch, Concerto Grosso No. 1 (1925)
• Elgar, Cello Concerto (1919)
• Prokofiev, Piano Concerto No. 1 (1912)
• Glazunov, Violin Concerto (1905)

```
1900        1925        1950        1975        2000
```

Richard Strauss (1864–1949)
Carl Nielsen (1865–1931)
Maurice Ravel (1875–1937)
Béla Bartók (1881–1945)
Igor Stravinsky (1882–1971)
Alban Berg (1885–1935)
Sergei Prokofiev (1891–1953)
George Gershwin (1898–1937)
Samuel Barber (1910–1981)
Dmitri Shostakovich (1906–1975)
Gunther Schuller (1925–)
John Corigliano (1938–)

The Six "Brandenburg" Concertos: Background

J.S. Bach knew and studied many concertos by Vivaldi, Albinoni, and other Italian composers. During his Weimar years, Bach and the Duke of Weimar's nephew (Johann Ernst) shared an appreciation for Italian concertos, and Bach transcribed for the keyboard 16 concertos (BWV 972–987), mostly by Vivaldi. Besides the six "Brandenberg" Concertos, Bach's original works include two concertos for violin solo (BWV 1041, 1042) and a two-violin concerto (BWV

Be sure you have read Bach's biography, beginning on page 25.

1043). He adapted a concerto for flute, violin, and harpsichord (BWV 1044) from original keyboard and chamber movements. His ground-breaking concertos for one, two, and four harpsichords were actually transcriptions of concertos for other instruments, both his own works and some by others.

Bach's Cöthen period (1717–1723) was his time of concentrated instrumental composition. There Bach put the six "Brandenberg" Concertos into final form, although some music may have originated during the earlier Weimar period. Technically, we cannot call every one of these a *concerto grosso*. By the time they were written, two additional types of multisoloist concerto had evolved:

Orchestral Concerto: No set *concertino*; various instruments (or groups) are treated soloistically at various times.

Chamber Concerto: A small group of players, each functioning as soloist at certain times or as *ripieno* at others.

The following table shows the keys, types, and instrumentation of Bach's six "Brandenberg" Concertos.

NO.	KEY	TYPE	INSTRUMENTATION
1	F Major	Orchestral	2 horns, 3 oboes, bassoon, "violino piccolo," strings, *basso continuo*
2	F Major	Grosso	Trumpet, alto recorder, oboe, violin solo; ripieno strings, *basso continuo*
3	G Major	Orchestral	3 violins, 3 violas, 3 cellos, *basso continuo*
4	G Major	Grosso	Solo violin, 2 recorders; *ripieno* strings, *basso continuo*
5	D Major	Grosso	Flute, solo violin, solo harpsichord (sometimes playing *basso continuo*); *ripieno* strings
6	B-flat Major	Chamber	2 violas, 2 viola da gambas, cello, *basso continuo*

Thus, only Concertos Nos. 2, 4, and 5 fall into the *concerto grosso* category.

Most, if not all, of the "Brandenberg" Concertos could have been performed by the court instrumental ensemble at the court of Anhalt-Cöthen, where Bach was employed. The orchestra included 2 flutists (who could, no doubt, also play the recorder); 1 oboist; 1 bassoonist; 2 trumpeters; 1 timpanist; 1 organist; 2 violinists; 1 cellist; 1 bass **viol** (*Violone*) player; and 3 "ripienists." The last were string players of lesser quality than the other instrumentalists, who filled in the violin and viola sections. Bach himself would have also played the viola when not leading the ensemble from the harpsichord.

The title "Brandenberg" Concertos derives from the Margrave of Brandenburg, Christian Ludwig, to whom Bach sent his magnificent manuscript of six concertos. Bach met the margrave in 1719 in Berlin, where the composer had been sent to purchase and transport a new harpsichord for the Cöthen court. (Concerto No. 5 may have been composed for that particular instrument.) Bach played for the margrave and, as a result, the nobleman asked him to send some music to his court. The six beautifully copied "Brandenberg" Concertos, sent in 1721, were Bach's response.

viols Family of bowed string instruments developed in the Renaissance. Viols were shaped slightly differently from members of the later violin family (violin, viola, violoncello) and were also tuned differently. A modern survivor of the viol family is the contrabass.

Ill. 7-1 Bach's autograph of the "Brandenburg" Concerto No. 2: opening measures of the first movement. Staatsbibliothek zu Berlin — Preussischer Kulturbesitz Musikabteilung mit Mendelssohn-Archiv, Am.B.78.

We have no way of knowing whether the court ensemble at Brandenburg ever performed any of the concertos or whether the margrave ever sent Bach a gratuity for the music. However, Bach must have kept copies of the concertos, for he adapted portions of them in later works. On the death of the margrave in 1734, one of his heirs received the Brandenburg manuscript, and later (perhaps after 1750) it came into the possession of Johann Philipp Kirnberger, who had been a student of Bach's. It then passed to other owners and is presently housed in the Deutsche Staatsbibliothek in Germany. Until 1849, the "Brandenberg" Concertos were neglected and nearly unknown. They were first published in 1850, on the centenary of Bach's death. Today, these masterpieces are Bach's most frequently performed and recorded instrumental ensemble music. Not only are they important among the *oeuvre* of J.S. Bach, but they represent the culmination and perfection of the Baroque multisoloist concerto.

Exploring Bach's "Brandenburg" Concerto No. 2, first movement

The Second "Brandenburg" Concerto is a textbook example of a late Baroque *concerto grosso*. Its clearly delineated *concertino* consists of a trumpet, a recorder, an oboe, and a violin. Four string parts constitute the *ripieno* group; and a cello and a harpsichord provide the *basso continuo*. The whole concerto follows the fast–slow–fast movement plan that had been standardized by Torelli and Vivaldi years before. (This also became standard for solo concertos and early symphonies.)

Listen to the entire movement. This music is cast in a sophisticated adaptation of a Baroque form called the *ritornello*. As the name implies, *ritornello* form features the "return" of a theme or part of it. In a typical *ritornello* movement by, say, Torelli, the *tutti* would present statements of the full theme at the opening and closing. Between free passages for the *concertino*, the *tutti* would play various segments from the theme. Bach takes that idea and develops it by allowing the soloists also to state segments of the theme. Ex. 7-2a shows Bach's *ritornello* theme with its four segments marked a–d. Instead of free material for the *concertino*, Bach writes a distinct "*concertino* theme," Ex. 7-2b, presented at the first entrance of the violin soloist and reiterated several times afterward. As you will hear, the *concertino* is not strictly limited to that material, either. *Concertino* instruments play various organic material quoted or developed from both themes.

(a)

(b)

Ex. 7-2 "Brandenburg" Concerto No. 2, themes: (a) *ritornello* theme; (b) concertino theme.

IDENTIFYING THE RITORNELLO THEME SEGMENTS. *Listen to the entire movement again, perhaps more than once. Referring to the segments marked in Ex. 7-2a, make notes about which segment(s) of the ritornello theme Bach is using as the movement goes along. Try to note also when the music changes from major to minor mode, or vice versa. Start your observations after the opening statement of the main theme, and end them just before the final statement (which occurs at the sudden change of key near the end).*

Your observations may have included:

- Three iterations of segment a between the first entrances by the *concertino* soloists (playing their theme).
- A statement of the rest of the *ritornello* theme (segments b, c, and d).
- More work with segment a (minor mode)
- A statement of segment b and a kind of development of segment c (changing keys) punctuated by a major-mode statement of segment d.
- Following a passage based on the "*concertino* theme," the *tutti* begins segments a and b in the minor mode, then suddenly switches to the major for some work with segment c, then back to minor for some attention to segment a, concluding with segments c and d.
- Overlapping fragments (minor mode) from segment a and echoes of segment b lead again to a segment c–d punctuation and cadence.

DYNAMICS. *As you listened, you probably noticed that sometimes the music became suddenly softer, then suddenly louder. (Crescendo and diminuendo dynamics were not yet in use in Baroque music.)* Dynamics shifted suddenly, analogous to a terrace jutting out of the ground. This musical technique later became known as "terrace" dynamics. The movement under study contains good examples of Baroque "terrace" dynamics, shifting between *forte*, *piano*, and *pianissimo*.

TEMPO AND SCORE LAYOUT. At the top of the score, notice that Bach gives no tempo marking. This is not unusual in some concerto first movements by Bach, Vivaldi, and others. Because the fast–slow–fast movement plan was so well known, performers could assume that the opening movement would be fast, probably an *allegro*.

Look at the score's layout of instruments. How does Bach distinguish between the concertino and the ripieno? At the top of the score system, the *concertino* instruments are braced together. Below that appear the *ripieno* strings. At the bottom is the *basso continuo*: cello and harpsichord (*Cembalo* = harpsichord). *What are the two instruments at the top of the concertino group?* A "*Tromba*" is a trumpet. Bach employed the type of valveless trumpet that was still in use during Beethoven's lifetime. Here, however, probably the trumpeter would have played a small "clarino" trumpet sounding an 11th (one octave plus a perfect fourth) above the written pitch. "*Flauto*" was the Baroque designation not for the flute but for an alto recorder. (*Flauto traverso* would indicate the flute.) Bach even clarified his intention with the French designation, "*Flûte à bec*," flute with a "beak" (or **fipple**).

DIVIDING THE CONCERTINO. In many places during this movement, Bach uses all four of the *concertino* instruments together. However, often he divides them into smaller groupings. Let's examine the first few *concertino* entrances. *In your score, find the first concertino entrance (following the opening statement of the ritornello theme) at m. 9. Which concertino instrument plays at this point? In what measure is the next concertino passage, and which instruments play? Repeat this investigation through m. 22, making a small table of measure numbers and instruments. Can you recognize a pattern?*

Your table should look like this:

MEASURE	INSTRUMENTS
9	Violin
13	Oboe, violin
17	Recorder, oboe
21	Trumpet, recorder

After the first passage (violin), each passage uses the previous instrument to accompany a new instrument, running the whole gamut of the *concertino*.

Which theme does the new instrument play in each of those passages? It is always the "*concertino* theme," shown in Ex. 7-2b. *Study the concertino parts in mm. 60–67. Which theme appears here, and what is the order of instruments playing it?* Again, it is the "*concertino* theme," heard, respectively, in the recorder, violin, oboe, and trumpet.

KEY AREAS. When studying the sonata form, we placed great emphasis on harmonic aspects: the location of different key areas within the structure. In *ritornello* form, the order and placement of keys are also inportant but not so predictable. In fact, the only "rule" is that the opening and closing statements of the *ritornello* theme should be in the tonic key. To learn about Bach's harmonic thinking, we will now examine the movement to discover the pattern of its chief key areas. *Study the places where Bach establishes a new key, and make a new table showing the name of the key and its functional relationship to the tonic, F major. (Hint: In Baroque music, the bass line can be a more important indicator of the key than the upper parts.) Examine each of the following measures:*

Mm. 18, 31, 56, 68, 75, 94

The "Brandenburg" Concerto No. 2, first movement: A Closer Look
Please refer to the score of the "Brandenburg" Concerto No. 2, beginning on page 169 of the Score Anthology.

fipple Mouthpiece of a whistle or recorder in which air is blown across a fixed reed.

Your table should look like this:

MEASURE	KEY	FUNCTIONAL RELATIONSHIP
18	C major	Dominant
31	D minor	Submediant
56	B-flat major	Subdominant
68	C minor	Minor dominant
75	G minor	Supertonic
94	A minor	Mediant

Bach's music traverses a rich variety of keys within the F-major orbit. Other than tonic at the beginning and end, the same key is never touched twice. Most keys are closely related, not deviating from the tonic by more than one flat (plus or minus). Notice, however, the use of C minor (m. 67), a slightly more distant key with a signature of three flats.

During m. 103 the music cadences in A minor, then suddenly drops into the tonic, F major, for the *ritornello* theme's final appearance. *Look over mm. 103–118. Does Bach interrupt the theme at any point?* Mm. 107–112 is a digression away from the theme. *Examine mm. 50–55 to discover the source of this passage.* Bach has transposed and adapted the earlier measures, exchanging some material between oboe and trumpet. Near the end, the digression is a suspenseful anticlimax before Bach's forceful concluding statement, which employs segments c and d of the *ritornello* theme.

Concertante Music and Multisoloist Concertos after Bach

During Bach's lifetime, the orchestral concerto merged with the newly born symphony, and the chamber concerto disappeared entirely. In addition, the *concerto grosso* principle evolved into new orchestral techniques and genres. The earliest was the *concertante* technique: using individual players of the orchestra temporarily as soloists—in the manner of a concerto. Found in certain symphonies and other orchestral music, *concertante* passages could feature any instrument. However, the favorites were the first-chair players of the first and second violin sections. At other times a passage might spotlight a solo woodwind or a pair of wind instruments, such as the horns. Joseph Haydn employed *concertante* technique in fully one-third of his symphonies, the earliest being his 1761 trilogy of Symphonies Nos. 6, 7, and 8 ("Le Matin," "Le Midi," "Le Soir"), where he uses violins, flute, and other instruments soloistically. The *Serenata notturna*, K. 239, by Wolfgang Amadeus Mozart (1756–1791) employs solo violins prominently.

The *symphonie concertante* genre was the other prominent Classical-period development. A *symphonie concertante* was a concerto for two or more soloists, a genre that achieved great popularity after 1770, especially in Paris. Mozart composed his first work of this type for a 1778 Parisian audience: the Symphonie Concertante in E-flat Major, K. 297b. Its *concertino*-like group of solo instruments includes flute, oboe, horn, and bassoon. Haydn's Symphonie Concertante in B-flat, Op. 84, features solo violin, cello, oboe, and bassoon: a high and low instrument from the string and woodwind families.

THE 19TH CENTURY. With the rise of public interest in virtuoso soloists, enthusiasm for multisoloist works faded. Ludwig van Beethoven (1770–1827) composed only one multisoloist work, the Triple Concerto in C Major, Op. 56. In it the solo instruments are violin, cello, and piano—the chamber instrumentation of a piano trio. After Beethoven, multisoloist concertos almost disappeared. Louis Spohr (1784–1859) wrote two works titled *Concertante*, both for two violins, and a concerto for string quartet and orchestra. Robert Schumann (1810–1856) composed a *Konzertstück* (*Concerto-piece*) featuring four horns, and Brahms's contribution was his Double Concerto in A Minor, Op. 102, for violin and cello.

THE MODERN PERIOD. After World War I, European musicians and audiences became interested in the music of the 18th century, especially Bach. This not only resulted in a revival of composers like Bach, Vivaldi, Mozart, and Haydn in the concert hall, but also many 20th-century composers consciously incorporated this trend into the style of their music. The neo-Classical movement in new music of the 1920s–1950s was the chief result. Many composers outside that movement also felt the impact of the revival.

With this trend came a revival of 18th-century forms and genres, now newly clothed in 20th-century sound. The *concerto grosso* genre received significant attention. Igor Stravinsky (1882–1971), the leader of neo-Classicism, composed his *Dumbarton Oaks Concerto* (1937) as a sequel to Bach's "Brandenberg" Concertos. Scored for 15 instruments, Stravinsky's concerto even borrowed a few motives from the Bach works, notably the Third "Brandenburg" Concerto. In response to criticism, Stravinsky referred to Bach's own concerto borrowings, declaring, "I do not think that Bach would have begrudged me the loan of these ideas and materials, as borrowing in this way was something he liked to do himself."

The Swiss neo-Classicist Frank Martin (1890–1974) composed two works that hark back to 18th-century multisoloist music. His *Petite Symphonie Concertante* (1945) is scored for harp, harpsichord, piano, and two string orchestras. Martin followed this four years later with his Concerto for Seven Wind Instruments, Percussion, and String Orchestra. Solo winds include the four main woodwinds (flute, oboe, clarinet, bassoon) and the three main brasses (trumpet, horn, trombone).

Other 20th-century composers wrote works they titled *Concerto Grosso*. Ernest Bloch (1880–1959) composed two, the first (1925) being the more popular. Scored for strings and piano **obbligato**, the first movement contains Baroque-style motoristic rhythm, and the last movement is a fugue. Another example is the *Concerto Grosso* by Ralph Vaughan Williams (1872–1958), composed in 1950. It employs three small string orchestras, the music for each demanding a different technical level.

obbligato Obligatory, usually meaning an accompanying instrument or part that must not be omitted.

In one of his last and greatest works, Béla Bartók expanded the *concertante* idea to every corner of the modern symphony orchestra. This was his Concerto for Orchestra, completed in 1943 for the Boston Symphony Orchestra. In its five movements, this work explores many possibilities of using instruments as *concertante* soloists, grouping them, and spotlighting the various sections.

Toward the end of the 1950s, American composer Gunther Schuller (1925–) wrote a series of compositions in which he fused Western art music with American jazz in a style he called "Third Stream." For much of this music, Schuller focused on the then-popular Modern Jazz Quartet, consisting of a piano, **vibraphone**, contrabass, and drum set. One of the most important "Third Stream" works is Schuller's Concertino for jazz quartet and orchestra (1959) written for jazz quartet and full orchestra. The music is innovative especially in its coloristic combinations and its requirement for occasional group improvisation by the solo quartet. Schuller's Concertino (here, meaning "small concerto") also evokes another aspect of Baroque ensemble music: The combination of a piano and a contrabass remind us of a *basso continuo*.

vibraphone A keyed percussion instrument, similar to a xylophone but using metal bars, a damper, and optionally rotating "propellers" over resonator tubes located under the bars.

MOZART, PIANO CONCERTO NO. 23 IN A MAJOR, K. 488, FIRST MOVEMENT

Birth of the Keyboard Concerto

Around 1700, Torelli and other Italian composers were perfecting the *ritornello* form and were applying it to the *concerto grosso*. At the same time, they were evolving another type of concerto, to which they also applied the *ritornello*. This new genre was the *solo* concerto. At first the violin was the only instrument for which solo concertos were written. The next generation, headed by Vivaldi, continued to favor the violin but broadened the solo concerto idea to include other single-line instruments, such as the oboe, the flute, and so on. Keyboard instruments were not yet considered for a solo role, however, probably because of their traditional place as part of the *basso continuo*.

It remained for J.S. Bach—as a performer, primarily a keyboardist—to experiment with the world's first keyboard concertos. In his "Brandenburg" Concerto No. 5 in D Major, Bach included a part marked *cembalo concertato*, that is, "solo harpsichord." This instrument is part of a *concertino* that also includes a flute and a violin. However, in the concerto's fast movements, the harpsichord receives the lion's share of attention. In fact, the first movement includes an extended cadenza for the harpsichord by itself (see Ill. 7-2)—historically, (1) the first keyboard cadenza, and (2) the first cadenza ever written out by a composer. This concerto was composed no later than 1721.

Ill. 7-2 Part of the cadenza for harpsichord solo in Bach's "Brandenburg" Concerto No. 5, first movement. The print is from an 1871 volume of the Bach-Gesellschaft (Bach Society) edition.

Bach built on the idea of *concertante* harpsichord parts while working in Leipzig. When he took over the town's Collegium Musicum for concerts in the local coffeehouse, his harpsichord concertos formed an important part of the group's repertoire. Bach contributed 14 concertos for one, two, three, or four harpsichords and strings. However, research has revealed that most of these works were not originally harpsichord concertos, but were adaptations of concertos for the violin or other instruments. Others were adaptations from church cantatas. Bach succeeded in establishing a keyboard-concerto idiom, which became a legacy to his sons.

Wilhelm Friedemann Bach composed about a half-dozen keyboard concertos, and Carl Philipp Emanuel Bach wrote more than fifty, including a famous one in D minor. However, the most influential keyboard concertos before Mozart's were the work of Johann Christian Bach, often called "the London Bach." J.C. Bach learned about Italian concertos firsthand as he worked and studied in Bologna and Milan around 1760. After he moved to London in 1762, he enjoyed great success with his 40 keyboard concertos written 1763–1777.

When young Mozart visited London during 1764–1765, he met J.C. Bach and absorbed some of his music, which impressed him. *Form* was the most powerful feature of Bach's keyboard concertos passed on to Mozart, especially in the first movements. Invariably, a concerto's first movement would begin with a big orchestral *tutti* presenting the main musical ideas. The function of this *tutti* was like that of the opening statement in a *ritornello* form. The soloist would then enter, reiterating previous ideas and adding new material (in the key of the dominant). This procedure was like the repeated exposition in a sonata form. Another *tutti* might introduce a short development section, leading to a recapitulation of the soloist's exposition followed by a cadenza. Again, in the manner of a *ritornello* form, the movement would end with a *tutti* statement. When we study the first movement of Mozart's A Major Piano Concerto, K. 488 further along, we will we see this prototype that J.C. Bach provided for Mozart's first-movement form.

Mozart as a Composer of Piano Concertos

The first piano concertos by Wolfgang Amadeus Mozart were not original works. When he was 11, his father, Leopold, felt it was time that his son should learn to write keyboard concertos. To that end, he hit on a clever composition assignment: a set of "pastiche" concertos—arrangements of movements from published keyboard sonatas. Among the composers tapped were two famous Bachs: C.P.E. and Johann Christian. Mozart pieced together seven such concertos between 1767 and 1771, only four of which were known when the Breitkopf & Härtel catalog set the numbering system "in stone." Thus, of the 27 *numbered* solo piano concertos, the first completely original work is No. 5.

SALZBURG CONCERTOS. Two years after the last "pastiche" concerto, Mozart composed his first original Piano Concerto, in D Major, K. 175. Completed in 1773, the work was still a popular part of his repertoire during his Mannheim/Paris tour of 1777–1778. He also used it during his first year in Vienna, 1782, for which he composed a new rondo finale.

Probably Mozart's most significant Salzburg concerto is No. 9 in E-flat Major, K. 271. Mozart wrote it for a "Mlle. Jeunehomme," a touring artist who gave a concert in Mannheim in 1777. In the first movement, Mozart broke with the tradition of holding off the soloist until after the opening orchestral exposition. Boldly he had the piano soloist immediately share the first theme with the orchestra, a move that would not be replicated until Beethoven's Fourth Piano Concerto (1808).

CONCERTOS OF THE VIENNA YEARS. Within months of settling in Vienna in 1781, Mozart was becoming one of its most popular composers. In a letter home he wrote, "Truly

Be sure you have read Mozart's biography, beginning on page 61.

this is the land of the piano!" Mozart composed three piano concertos in late 1782 and early 1783 (Nos. 11–13), his first for Vienna. Around the Lenten season of 1784, Mozart composed a series of four piano concertos (Nos. 14–17), reflecting his activity as a composer-performer and as a teacher.

The next four piano concertos, written between September 1784 and March 1785, show Mozart at the height of his popularity. Leopold was with him during Lent of 1785, when Mozart almost certainly would have also premiered his F Major Piano Concerto (No. 19, K. 459). However, its fame derives more from Mozart's performing it again at the coronation celebration for Emperor Leopold II (Frankfurt, 1790). The last two concertos in this group are a closely related pair. No. 20, K. 466, is special for being Mozart's first piano concerto in the minor mode: D minor. Almost exactly a month later, having entertained his father and taught all that time, Mozart completed the C Major Concerto (No. 21, K. 467) and premiered it the next night.

Just as Mozart had begun his brilliant Viennese period of piano concerto composition with three works, so he reached the zenith of that run with a piano-concerto trilogy. The first of the group, No. 22 in E-flat Major (K. 482), however, seems a prelude to a pair of major/minor works, the Concertos No. 23 in A Major (K. 488) and No. 24 in C Minor (K. 491). Both were completed in March 1786, as Mozart was working on *The Marriage of Figaro*. Mozart's C Minor Concerto (one of only two in the minor mode) was very likely premiered during his "academy" (concert) of April 2. The darkness and Storm-and-Stress qualities of this concerto set it off from the others and made it a favorite among 19th-century piano virtuosos.

After the Lenten season of 1786, Mozart's production of piano concertos declined sharply. He composed only three more in his lifetime. This reflects the general trend he experienced during that time: extreme difficulty in obtaining performances of his music in Vienna. Mozart composed his Piano Concerto No. 25 in C Major (K. 503) toward the end of 1786. More than a year passed before Mozart composed his next piano concerto, No. 26 in D Major, K. 537. This work derives its nickname, "Coronation," from Mozart's 1790 Frankfurt performance of it for the installation of Leopold II as Holy Roman Emperor. Mozart completed his final concerto, No. 27 in B-flat (K. 595) on January 5, 1791, exactly 11 months to the day before his death. Its melancholy mood reflects the composer's feelings in those last days. The theme of the concerto's finale is the same as his song written at the same time: "Longing for Spring" (K. 596). Perhaps Mozart knew that would be his last spring.

One of the briefest yet best summaries of the significance of Mozart's piano concertos was written by Alfred Einstein, who also revised the Köchel catalog of Mozart's works. Einstein's words are loaded with personal opinion, but their enthusiastic spirit is worthy of reflection:

> Splendid as are the examples of the concerto form for string and wind instruments, it was only in the piano concertos that Mozart achieved his ideal. They are the peak of all his instrumental achievement, at least in the orchestral domain. … It was in the piano concerto that Mozart said the last word in respect to the fusion of the *concertante* and symphonic elements—a fusion resulting in a higher unity beyond which no progress was possible. …
>
> [Alfred Einstein, *Mozart, His Character, His Work*. Trans. Arthur Mendel and Nathan Broder (New York: Oxford University Press, 1945), pp. 287–288.]

INFLUENCE ON BEETHOVEN. Reportedly, Mozart met Beethoven in spring 1787 during the latter's first stay in Vienna, and a few lessons in music theory followed. As a young composer, Beethoven was enthralled with Mozart's music. In Bonn and later Vienna, Beethoven had easy

MOZART, PIANO CONCERTO
NO. 23 IN A MAJOR, K. 488,
FIRST MOVEMENT

Ill. 7-3 The final measures of Mozart's Piano Concerto in D Major ("Coronation"), K. 537: (a) Mozart's manuscript; (b) the 1879 edited publication in *Wolfgang Amadeus Mozart's Werke*. The order of instruments in (a) differs from the modern layout. From top to bottom, Mozart's score shows violins I, violins II, violas, flute, oboes, bassoons, horns, trumpets, timpani, piano, and *bassi* (cellos and contrabasses). The printed score (b) shows flute, oboes, bassoons, horns, trumpets, timpani, piano, and strings. Source for (a): The Pierpont Morgan Library/Art Resource, NY.

access to Mozart's publications. When establishing his career in Vienna, first as a pianist, Beethoven employed Mozart's music to advantage. He knew, admired, and possibly played the C Minor Concerto, K. 491. The D Minor Concerto, K. 466, was a special favorite, and he performed it at a musical event organized by Mozart's widow in 1795. Beethoven composed original cadenzas for this work, which he later wrote out for one of his own students.

Mozart's Vienna piano concertos provided models for Beethoven's five piano concertos. In matters of the plan of movements, first movement form, placement of cadenzas, and symphonic balance between soloist and orchestra, Beethoven inherited many ideas and techniques from Mozart. Mozart also anticipated some important innovations attributed to Beethoven. For example, Beethoven brings in the soloist at the opening of his Fourth and Fifth Piano Concertos, yet decades earlier Mozart had tested that idea in his Salzburg concerto in E-flat Major (K. 271). Some scholars credit Beethoven's Piano Concerto No. 5 ("Emperor") with being the first in history to *contain* a cadenza prescribed by the composer. However, in Mozart's C Minor Concerto (K. 491), the composer wrote his first-movement cadenza into the score itself.

The A Major Piano Concerto: Background

Mozart's personal thematic catalog shows that he completed the Piano Concerto in A Major on March 2, 1786. However, we have evidence that the composer sketched some of it one or two years earlier. In 1784, when he began to keep his thematic catalog, he also started a file of musical sketches—portions of works to be finished later, when he needed them. Among these were ideas for three or four piano concertos, one of which was the Concerto in A Major.

THE CADENZA. In Mozart's day, the place in the score marked "Cadenza" in the first movement (and often also the last) was the soloist's moment to shine. Unaccompanied, he or she would play a passage based loosely on thematic material already heard, but shaping it in new, virtuosic ways. Usually the performer would prepare the cadenza ahead of time and write it out. Mozart was able to keep so much music in his head at once that he had no need to do that. However, he did write out some cadenzas. As mentioned above, Mozart included a cadenza in the score to his C Minor Piano Concerto, K. 491. For a few other concertos, he wrote out cadenzas separately. These were for either his sister, Nannerl, who often performed his concertos, or ostensibly for students. Fortunately for us, Mozart wrote out a cadenza for the first movement of his A Major Piano Concerto (see the Score Anthology, p. 204).

PERFORMANCES. We have no record of a premiere for the concerto. However, since it was completed during Lent of 1786, we may assume it was played at that time during an "academy" (concert) with Mozart at the piano. At the end of the following September, the composer offered it (and two other concertos, among other works) to the court of Prince von Fürstenberg in Donaueschingen. However, it was 1800 before the A Major Piano Concerto was published. The previous year, Anton André, an Offenbach publisher, purchased Mozart's musical legacy from his widow. He then published the composer's musical catalog and brought out many works listed in it, including the Piano Concerto in A Major.

Exploring Mozart's A Major Piano Concerto, first movement

Listen to the entire movement. Listen from the beginning again, this time only until the piano enters. Mozart composed this movement in a type of sonata form. As you have learned, the exposition section of a Classical-period sonata form was normally repeated. What you have just heard is the exposition, the first time through. *Listen to just this much again, and now identify its themes or theme groups: P (principal), T (transition), S (secondary), K (concluding), and C (codetta).* You probably noted the themes shown in Ex. 7-3.

Ex. 7-3 Exposition themes in the
first movement of Mozart's A
Major Piano Concerto, K. 488.

TWO EXPOSITIONS. Part of Mozart's method of adapting sonata form to the concerto medium is to write two closely related versions of the exposition: the first for the orchestra by itself; the second for the piano soloist with the orchestra. The orchestra exposition is also a continuation and an expansion of the idea of the Baroque *ritornello*, a theme for orchestra *tutti* that appeared at the opening of a movement in *ritornello* form. In Mozart's concertos, later orchestral *tutti* entrances also parallel the older *ritornello* form by bringing back prominent themes.

Now we will study the second exposition. *Begin listening at the point where the piano enters. Keep listening until you have heard P, T, S, and K, ending in a V$_7$–I cadence with a trill in the piano.* You have just heard the soloist-orchestra exposition, including all the themes introduced in the orchestra exposition. You may have noticed the lyrical style of the P and S themes despite the *allegro* tempo. Analysts call this style "singing allegro."

DEVELOPMENT. *Begin listening where you left off. An orchestral* tutti *announces the beginning of the development section. Which theme appears here, and what happens next?* First the orchestra sounds the T theme. This breaks off suddenly, and Mozart now presents a *new theme*:

Introducing a new theme in the development section was a little unusual in Mozart's time but still within the "rules." (Recall that in the Mozart piano-sonata movement studied in Chapter 3, an × motive not heard before appeared in the development. Later in history, Beethoven sometimes introduced a new theme in the development—or even later in the movement!) We will call Mozart's new theme the "development theme." *Keep listening until you hear the return of the P theme.* This constitutes the development section. *Notice that the entire development is based on the new development theme.*

Ex. 7-4 Diagram of the first movement of Mozart's A Major Piano Concerto, K. 488.

RECAPITULATION. *Listen from this point to the end of the movement.* This is the recapitulation. *Does the development theme return in this final section?* Twice we hear this theme: first following the K group and then just before the piano's cadenza (piano alone, no orchestra). *After the cadenza, what theme concludes the movement?* We hear the C theme slightly extended to bring the movement to its conclusion. The diagram in Ex. 7-4 summarizes the form, instrumentation, themes, and key areas of the entire movement.

Section:	ORCHESTRA EXPOSITION					SOLOIST & ORCHESTRA EXPOSITION				‖
Measure:	1	18	31	47	63	67 82 99			115	‖
Instrumentation:	Orch. (tutti)...					Piano, Orch...				‖
Theme Group:	P	T	S	K(K₁K₂)	C	P	T	S	K	‖
Key Area:	Tonic					(Tonic)		Dominant		‖

Section:	DEVELOPMENT				‖
Measure:	137	143	178	197	‖
Instrumentation:	Orch.	Orch., Piano			‖
Theme Group:	T	Development Theme			‖
Key Area:	Dominant	Modulating...	(V of Tonic)		‖

Section:	RECAPITULATION											‖
Measure:	198	213	229	245	261	284	290	297	298	300	306	‖
Instrumentation:	Orch., Piano								Piano solo	Orch., Piano		‖
Theme Group:	P	T	S	K	Dev. Th.	T	Dev. Th.		(cadenza)	K₂	C	‖
Key Area:	Tonic							$(I_4^6$		...$V_7 I$)		‖

Mozart's A Major Piano Concerto, first movement: A Closer Look

Please refer to the score of the A Major Piano Concerto, beginning on page 182 of the Score Anthology.

Open your score to the first page of the concerto and study the instrumentation. Notice that just one Flauto (flute) is required. The rest of the woodwinds and horns are in pairs. However, *what pair of woodwind instruments is absent?* This work omits oboes. (At the time, oboists often doubled on the clarinet, so the presence of clarinets might explain the absence of oboes.) Note that the Clarinetti and Corni (horns) are pitched in the key of A, the key of the concerto.

FORM. Following the diagram in Ex. 7-4 (above), go through your score and mark the beginning of each large section of the movement. Now listen to the orchestra exposition, following your score. Find each theme and mark its beginning in your score. Do the same for the soloist-orchestra exposition. Check your markings against the measure numbers in Ex. 7-4. (The S and K₁ themes begin with an upbeat to the identified measures.)

THE TWO EXPOSITIONS: KEY AREAS. As you have previously learned, the S theme in a sonata form's exposition is normally heard in the key of the dominant. *Find the S theme in the* orchestra exposition and study the melody and bass line at the beginning. In what key is this theme? Mozart presents this theme in A major, the key of the tonic.

Examine the cadence at the end of the orchestra exposition, mm. 65–66. In what key is this cadence? Again, we find a confirmation of A major, the tonic key. Thus, Mozart has kept the entire orchestra exposition close to the movement's home key.

Examine the S theme as it appears in the soloist-orchestra exposition (m. 99 with upbeat). Also, look at mm. 136–137, the conclusion of this section. What key is established or confirmed at each of these points? Mozart has moved to the key of the dominant for the S theme and has maintained that key area through the rest of the soloist-orchestra exposition. This, of course, is the usual way for an exposition section to proceed.

DEVELOPMENT AND RECAPITULATION. Listen to the development section, following your score. As you discovered before, the T theme begins the development section (in an orchestral tutti), but the new development theme appears soon. Find this theme, beginning in m. 143. Notice the novel character or mood of this theme. Analyst Donald Tovey writes that this theme "brings a deeper and graver mood to add to the grace of the whole work." Find some later appearances of the theme and note how Mozart develops it.

These are some examples:

MEASURE	TECHNIQUE
156	Woodwinds in dialogue with piano
166	Piano inverts the theme, then strings do the same
170	Melodic intervals are altered; the theme overlaps itself (clarinet, flute)
178	Melodic shape is altered; rhythm is kept the same

Find the beginning of the recapitulation section in your score. Listen to the recording to the end of the movement, following the score. At the point where the piano's cadenza appears, turn momentarily to p. 204 of the Score Anthology and follow the music.

TUTTIS. Passages in the score that the composer has marked tutti focus on the orchestra. They either play down the importance of the solo instrument or omit it entirely. Find the following tutti passages in the score, and make a table showing which theme the orchestra is playing each time: mm. 82, 137, 156, 198, 213, 284, and 299/300.

Your table should contain this information:

MEASURE	THEME
82	T
137	T—then development theme
156	Development theme
198	P
213	T
284	T—then development theme
299/300	K_2—then C

The table shows that all themes except S are represented in this movement's tutti passages.

MOZART'S CADENZA. Finally, examine Mozart's cadenza on p. 204 of the Score Anthology. The brevity and simplicity of this music probably do not represent the full range of

Mozart's famed genius for improvisation at the keyboard. However, it does show us the type of music a piano soloist might play as the cadenza to a concerto.

A cadenza may include references to one or more themes or other material heard in the movement. Does this one refer to any previously heard material? Mozart quotes only one of his themes. *Compare the cadenza's mm. 12 (with upbeat) to 15 with the orchestral score at mm. 62–66. From which theme does the composer derive this portion of the cadenza?* He has altered an idea from the C theme. Mozart also makes subtle references to one brief passage from the development section. *Compare the cadenza's mm. 3, 5, and 7 with the orchestral score at mm. 158–159 and 162–163.* The quotation is free material from a piano-orchestra exchange involving the development theme. *In the score, following the cadenza, notice that a tutti featuring the K_2 and codetta themes closes the movement.*

TCHAIKOVSKY, VIOLIN CONCERTO IN D MAJOR, OP. 35, THIRD MOVEMENT

Concertos for the violin have a longer history than those for any other instrument. Beginning in Corelli's generation, violins were the first *concertino* instruments, and in the works of Torelli and Vivaldi, solo violin concertos figure prominently. Bach composed two solo violin concertos, Mozart composed five, and Haydn wrote four. A new chapter in the development of violin concertos began early in the 19th century. By that time virtuoso soloists had reached a higher plateau of technical accomplishment than ever. Technique and interpretation grew even more brilliant during the Romantic century, as audiences came to expect performances that incorporated both showy display and sensitive emotional values. Composers from Beethoven to Brahms and Tchaikovsky served this demand with works high in artistic quality yet heavily demanding in technique.

PETER I. TCHAIKOVSKY

Anonymous photograph.

On May 7, 1840, Pyotr (Peter) Ilich Tchaikovsky was born in Kamsko-Votkinska in the Vyatatka province of Russia. He was the second son of a mining engineer, Ilya Petrovich Tchaikovsky, and his second wife (of French extraction), Alexandra Andreyevna (née Assier). The boy grew up in an upper-middle-class home, where he had many cultural advantages. When young Peter showed an early interest in music, his family responded by providing him with piano lessons from the age of five.

When Peter was eight, the family moved to St. Petersburg, and in 1850, they enrolled him in preparatory studies at the School of Jurisprudence. Hearing a performance that year of Glinka's *A Life for the Tsar* impressed the boy deeply. In June 1854, the death of his mother distressed him to the point of seeking an emotional outlet: musical composition. Having improvised at the piano for years, he now wrote down a waltz. Gradually now, he sought more musical instruction, studying privately in music theory, voice, and piano.

After completing his studies at the School of Jurisprudence in 1859, Tchaikovsky took a job as clerk in the government's Ministry of Justice. At the age of 21, he began music theory studies and enrolled at the newly established St. Petersburg Conservatory the following year. After a one-year excursion through Europe, he resumed his studies, joining the composition class of the conservatory's director, Anton Rubinstein (1829–1894). By the end of 1863,

Tchaikovsky had resigned his government job and was a full-time music student, supporting himself by teaching piano and theory. In 1865, the precocious student began gaining public recognition through performances of his music under the baton of Johann Strauss and himself. Tchaikovsky's interest in Russian folk songs stemmed from this period, and he began incorporating them into some of his music.

After graduation, Tchaikovsky was invited to join the faculty of the newly founded Moscow Conservatory in 1866. The liberal atmosphere of Moscow and the encouraging support of conservatory director Nicolai Rubinstein (1835–1881, brother of Anton) gave Tchaikovsky an environment in which his compositional abilities could develop. That year, he completed the initial drafts of his First Symphony ("Winter Daydreams"). The following year and a half saw him engrossed in writing the first of his ten operas, *Voyevoda*. In Moscow, Tchaikovsky also made several important contacts. In 1867, he was introduced to Mily Balakirev (1837–1910). Around Balakirev gathered the circle of composers called "The Mighty Five," who were deeply committed to developing Russian nationalism through their music. While Tchaikovsky often lent sympathetic support to their cause, he was never a member of their group. Balakirev mentored Tchaikovsky, notably in the composition of the famous *Romeo and Juliet* fantasy overture (first version, 1869).

In the early 1870s, Tchaikovsky composed his Second Symphony, posthumously nicknamed the "Little Russian" because he had included some Ukrainian folk tunes. Its Moscow premiere in 1873 was received enthusiastically. Mozart was Tchaikovsky's favorite composer, and during the mid-1870s, he himself became interested in neo-Classicism. The most overt expression of this came in his *Variations on a Rococo Theme* for cello and orchestra (1876). Other music from that time is heavily Romantic. An example is his famous Piano Concerto No. 1 in B-flat Minor (1874–1875), which begins in the "wrong" key and presents a wonderful opening theme, which is never played again. Also from this period came the Third Symphony and the first of his three ballets, *Swan Lake* (both works 1875–1876). While working on these scores, he also completed his best-known solo piano work, the suite of 12 pieces titled *The Seasons* (Op. 37b). Hearing the opera *Carmen* by Georges Bizet (1838–1875) in 1876 fired him to compose his symphonic poem *Francesca da Rimini*.

In 1877, Tchaikovsky made the most disastrous blunder of his life: He married. Antonia Mlyukova, a former conservatory student, had written him unexpectedly, declaring her love for the composer. Under her threats of suicide, he visited her but felt no deep attraction. Tchaikovsky was a homosexual who kept the fact a secret. At the time, he was working on the scenario to his next opera, *Eugene Onegin*, and, moved by Eugene's rejection of Tatanya in the story, Tchaikovsky proposed to Antonia with the proviso that their relationship never be a physical one. Deceptively, she accepted. In July, after he had finished sketching his Fourth Symphony and much of the new opera, he married Antonia, and his nightmare began. He soon made excuses to stay away, but the fall term at the conservatory compelled him to return to her in September. Within days he had attempted suicide and soon fled to St. Petersburg, where his family cared for him and dispatched a brother to arrange for a separation from Antonia. To recover, Tchaikovsky took an extended vacation in western Europe.

The counterbalance to that disaster came from another woman, Mme. Nadezhda von Meck, a wealthy widow who idealized Tchaikovsky and wished to become his patron, but at a distance. They never met and only occasionally glimpsed each other in public, but their writ-

(continued)

ten correspondence is probably our clearest and most important window into the composer's heart. When he wrote to her asking for a loan with which to flee his marriage, she responded with an annuity of 6,000 rubles, enabling him to be financially independent and no longer in need of his conservatory position. Their unique relationship lasted for 14 years. Mme. von Meck was the dedicatee of Tchaikovsky's Fourth Symphony, which he finished in January 1878; he completed *Eugene Onegin* the following month. The Violin Concerto (which we will be studying in this chapter) was also composed during this turbulent year.

Over the next several years, Tchaikovsky experienced a creative dip equal to the rise he had just completed. Part of the problem is attributable to the divorce proceedings, which dragged on for three years, during which time Antonia purposely aggravated him. Only in a few works, for example, the famous *1812 Festival Overture* (1880) or his *Pezzo elegiaco* (1882) written for von Meck's resident piano trio, did the old inspiration return temporarily.

In 1884, Tchaikovsky's muse began to rejuvenate. He probably felt more at ease socially because of the Tsar's awarding him the Order of St. Vladimir. The great success of *Eugene Onegin* in the fall also bolstered his self-confidence. Around that time he renewed contact with Balakirev, and his old mentor now gave him a new idea, which resulted in the *Manfred* Symphony (1885) based on Byron's legend. The year 1888 saw the creation of a significant orchestral work: the Symphony No. 5 in E Minor.

The momentum of Tchaikovsky's renewed creativity reached a peak with his return to the ballet theater. The score to *The Sleeping Beauty* (1889), which the composer considered one of his best works, fully revealed his gift for colorful theatrical music. In opera, *The Queen of Spades* (1890) took a place next to *Eugene Onegin*. Following this opera, Tchaikovsky capped his sparse chamber-music catalog with his famous *Souvenir de Florence* for string sextet, a memoir of his many Italian sojourns.

The spring of 1891 saw him on a new sort of sojourn—in the United States conducting his own music. Four concerts in New York were triumphant, and Tchaikovsky wrote in his diary that "the enthusiasm was greater than anything I have experienced, even in Russia." Returning home, he set to work that fall and winter on one of his most beloved scores, *The Nutcracker* ballet. It was produced in 1892, and the composer quickly extracted a concert suite.

In February 1893, an idea for his Sixth Symphony (*Pathétique*) came to him: the duality of life and death for the outer movements, love and disappointments for the inner two. Deeply pessimistic—reflecting his frequent bouts with depression—this music became, arguably, his most profound, sincerest, and possibly his greatest. Finished on the last day of August 1893, the *Pathétique* Symphony received its premiere under the hands of the composer October 28 in St. Petersburg.

The next nine days were the last of Tchaikovsky's life, and the exact course of events leading to his death have been a matter of heated controversy. Researchers have advanced two theories. The first and "official" one comes from the words of Modest, the composer's brother. He wrote that Tchaikovsky carelessly drank a glass of unboiled water in Modest's home at a time when cholera was rampant and died as a result. The other theory is that Tchaikovsky was showing overt homosexual attention to his nephew, and that his former schoolmates convened a "court of honor," convincing him to commit suicide to save the School of Jurisprudence's reputation (and theirs, too). This theory concludes that Tchaikovsky took his own life by arsenic poisoning in conspiracy with Modest and the family doctors.

Both theories are questionable. Regarding the first: Why did Modest have unboiled water on the table at mealtime when its dangers were so obvious? And why did Tchaikovsky lie in state in the open air of Modest's apartment for days, exposing thousands of visitors to the disease, when the law required a closed coffin? Regarding the second theory, much of its data is from second- or third-hand hearsay brought forward decades after the composer's death. Further, Tchaikovsky carefully kept his homosexual preference a secret, which his family and many others helped to protect. The strongest evidence pointing to suicide (whether from bad water or poisoning) comes from Tchaikovsky's perennial state of depression and his previous suicide attempt in 1877.

Tchaikovsky died on November 6, 1893, in St. Petersburg. For days afterward, a constant stream of mourners paid respects, and several Requiem Masses were said. His subsequent funeral in the Kazan Cathedral was attended by a capacity crowd of 8,000, and more than 50,000 were refused admission. Memorial concerts soon followed, beginning with a second performance of the *Pathétique* Symphony.

Tchaikovsky's Violin Concerto: Genesis and Premieres

In certain ways, the year 1878 was one of the worst in Tchaikovsky's life, and in other ways it was one of the best. The composer spent most of the year in western Europe (notably Italy and Switzerland) recovering from a shattered marriage and a near breakdown. During March

Ill. 7-4 Photo of Mme. Nadezhda von Meck, Tchaikovsky's ardent patroness. Though they never met face-to-face, their lengthy correspondence is famous for revealing the composer's inner thoughts and feelings.

and April, he stayed in the Swiss resort town of Clarens, and it was there, in a sudden burst of inspiration, that he wrote one of the most brilliant and cheerful of all his works, the Violin Concerto.

On March 13, only four days after arriving at Clarens, Tchaikovsky began composing a piano sonata. However, from the start, work on it did not go well. Fortunately, March 14 brought his dear and close friend, Iosef Kotek (1855–1885), who had been a student at the Moscow Conservatory and now was a touring violin soloist. Kotek arrived from Berlin, where he had amassed a pile of violin-piano duet music. Eagerly, he and Tchaikovsky began playing through it, and the composer grew increasingly enthusiastic about writing a violin work instead of the piano sonata; the following day he dove into work on his Violin Concerto in D Major. It was a labor full of joy, the more so since Kotek was there to advise him on the finer points of violin technique. By March 23, Tchaikovsky had finished sketching the first movement, and three days later he finished the second and began the finale. By March 28 sketches of the entire concerto were complete.

Tchaikovsky's brother, Modest, was also with them at Clarens. Both he and Kotek were enthusiastic about the outer movements but had doubts about the slow movement. Tchaikovsky agreed, and on April 5 he composed an entirely new movement titled *Canzonetta*. (The discarded movement, *Méditation*, became the first of three pieces for violin and piano published as Op. 42.) Six days later Tchaikovsky put the finishing touches on the concerto's orchestration.

A TALE OF THREE VIOLINISTS. Tchaikovsky's love for Kotek—homosexual in nature—played strongly into the creation of the concerto. This love was returned in Kotek's devotion to

Ill. 7-5 Photo of Tchaikovsky and Kotek taken in St. Petersburg in 1877, the year before the Violin Concerto's creation.

the new work. Tchaikovsky wrote to his other brother, Anatoly, "How lovingly he occupies himself with my concerto! ... Without him, I would have been able to do nothing. He plays it marvelously!" Obviously, Tchaikovsky would have wished to dedicate the concerto to Kotek and have him play its premiere in St. Petersburg. However, he feared that linking their two names would cause gossip, possibly damaging to both of their careers. So instead he dedicated the concerto to Leopold Auer (1845–1930), a popular virtuoso and the chief violin professor at the St. Petersburg Conservatory. (He would later become the teacher of such 20th-century notables as Mischa Elman and Jascha Heifetz).

However, when Tchaikovsky came to Auer to go over the music and formally ask him to play the premiere (scheduled for March 1879), he was met with a devastating blow. According to Tchaikovsky's diary from 1888, Auer deemed the concerto "too awkward to play." The St. Petersburg premiere had to be canceled. In his autobiography, published 30 years after Tchaikovsky's death, Auer presented a different version of the story. He wrote that Tchaikovsky brought the score to him one day, showing the violinist the dedication. Auer claimed that he was "profoundly touched" by the dedication, and that he was "struck by the lyric beauty" of the work. However, on later study of the score, he determined that "in spite of its great intrinsic value, it called for a thorough revision, since in various portions it was quite unviolinistic."

Meanwhile, Auer had just accepted an important conducting post with the Russian Musical Society, a job that absorbed his time in rehearsals and administrative details. He postponed giving the concerto his attention for a long time, but he coveted the privilege of premiering it in St. Petersburg, scaring off one violinist but not carrying off the honor in the end. Finally, Adolf Brodsky (1851–1929), Auer's counterpart at the Moscow Conservatory, courageously committed himself to premiering the work during his 1881 tour of western Europe. (Following Tchaikovsky's death, Auer published his "version" of the Violin Concerto, played it often, and taught it to his advanced students.)

Brodsky had previous connections in Vienna, so that musical capital was, naturally, a stop on his tour. There, during a Philharmonic Society concert on December 4, 1881, with Hans Richter conducting, Brodsky presented the first public performance of Tchaikovsky's Violin Concerto in D Major. During the concerto, the audience became disruptive. Given the work's distinct Russian character, the Austrian audience's reaction may have been more political indignation than artistic aversion. Most reviews following the concert echoed the audience's rejection of the work. Despite this negative reaction, Brodsky continued performing it, notably in Germany, where it rapidly gained acceptance, and Tchaikovsky eventually changed the concerto's dedication from Auer to Brodsky.

No doubt Tchaikovsky would have wished for Iosef Kotek to play the Russian premiere of the concerto in St. Petersburg. However, the severe criticism from Auer, Hanslick, and others added to the young violinist's fear that performing the work might be harmful to his career. The matter apparently became an issue between Tchaikovsky and Kotek, and they broke off relations at the end of 1881. On August 20, 1882, Adolf Brodsky gave the Russian premiere in Moscow. There the audience was completely enthusiastic, and Tchaikovsky's triumph was complete.

Exploring Tchaikovsky's Violin Concerto, third movement

Tchaikovsky's Violin Concerto in D Major begins impressively with two grand movements. After a modest introduction, the first movement presents three ingratiating themes. The development section does not discuss the themes thoroughly but instead drives toward the brilliant violin cadenza. A majestic recapitulation and applause-stirring coda complete the movement. The *canzonetta* slow movement reveals what Tchaikovsky scholar David Brown terms "Tchaikovsky's burning love of Russia" and his melancholy yearning to return there. Here the composer's great gift for lyrical melody comes to the fore with tunes of unmistakable folk flavor.

Without a pause, the finale's athletic opening begins. *Listen to the entire finale. Now listen to the beginning up to the main theme that follows the unaccompanied violin passage.* What you have heard is the movement's introduction. *What is the correct term for the unaccompanied violin passage?* We call it a cadenza.

Next comes the main theme. Notice its quick tempo and distinct rhythmic character. This is based on a folk dance called a *trepak* traditionally associated with Russian cossack soldiers. *Listen to the music from the beginning of this theme until it returns (about halfway through the movement). Take note of other themes along the way. How many themes did you hear in all?* Tchaikovsky presents three themes, shown in Ex. 7-5.

Ex. 7-5 The three themes in Tchaikovsky's Violin Concerto finale.

We might call the main theme (a) the "cossack" theme. The second theme (b) has a rustic quality reminiscent of Russian peasant celebrations. We could call this the "rustic" theme. The third theme (c) is slower and more sentimental/nostalgic. We might call this the "sentimental" theme.

Listen from this point (the second appearance of the cossack theme) to the end of the movement. What has Tchaikovsky done with the three themes? He has cycled back through all three themes and then has restated the cossack theme one last time. *Then what happens?*

From this final statement, the composer derives an extended coda section, where the music becomes increasingly excited, driving to an exhilarating finish.

Listen to the entire movement again, this time following the score. In what measure begins the section that introduces the rustic theme? In what key is this section? The section begins in m. 145 and is in the key of A major, the key of the dominant. *Notice the accompaniment in the cellos (second staff from the bottom). What harmonic interval do the cellos play?* It is a perfect fifth. In folk music, continuing open fifths like these are called a *drone*. They are reminiscent of folk instruments such as the **bagpipe** or the **hurdy-gurdy**.

Continue to look at the score. In what measure does the cossack theme begin? Which instruments are involved with the melody at first? The theme begins with the upbeat to m. 197 with a solo oboe answered by a solo clarinet:

bagpipe A folk instrument, notably from Scotland or Ireland but also found in several other European countries.

hurdy-gurdy A string folk instrument originating in the Middle Ages.

Tchaikovsky's Violin Concerto, third movement: A Closer Look

Please refer to the score of Tchaikovsky's Violin Concerto, beginning on page 205 of the Score Anthology.

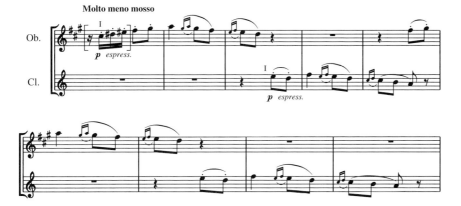

Study the rhythm of the sentimental theme. Does it bear any relationship to either of the other themes? Yes, it is clearly derived from the beginning rhythm of the rustic theme, as shown in Ex. 7-6.

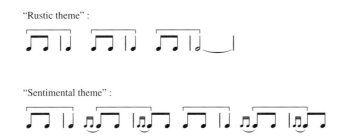

Ex. 7-6 Rhythm in two themes compared.

Notice, however, that the *character* of the two themes is distinctly different. In the cossack theme section, the character is magnified as the tempo goes through a gradual *rallentando* (mm. 227–230).

Simultaneously, what is happening in the solo violin's tessitura? The working range of the violin solo part descends gradually. Notice that the tessitura goes even lower as the violin reintroduces motives from the cossack theme, beginning in m. 235. *In what measure does the cossack theme actually return?* A brief transitional passage marked *stringendo* leads to a "Tempo I" marking and a key-signature change back to D major. Here the theme returns in m. 243.

Where does the rustic theme next appear? In what key? The rustic theme returns in m. 349, this time in G major, the key of the subdominant. Just one whole-step lower than its first appearance, this statement of the theme gives the solo violin part a more "deep-throated" sound, including the long-held note on an open G string (the lowest note on the instrument):

rallentando Gradually slowing the tempo.

stringendo Quickening the tempo. See also *accelerando*.

Find the cossack theme after this. In what measure does it begin, and in what key? M. 400 marks the final return of this theme, continuing in the key of G major.

Does the cossack theme return after this? In what measure? In m. 460 the theme appears for the last time.

Beginning in this measure, trace the solo violin part, comparing it with the parallel passage that began in m. 53. How far does the latter passage repeat the former one before deviating from it? The two passages are identical until mm. 133 and 540. At that point, the former passage begins to prepare for the rustic theme section by modulating, but the latter stays more firmly around the key of D major. *What would we call this last section of the movement?* This is the coda. In summary, Ex. 7-7 shows the thematic and harmonic layout of the entire movement.

Measure:	1		17		53		145		196		
Theme/Section:	Introduction (motives from "Cossack Theme")			‖	"Cossack Theme"	‖	"Rustic Theme"	‖	"Sentimental Theme"	‖	
Instrumentation:	Orchestra (tutti)		Violin solo (cadenza)	‖	Vln., Orch.	‖	Vln., Orch.	‖	Vln., Orch.	‖	
Chief Key Area:	Tonic (V ...)			‖	Tonic	... ‖	Dominant	‖	Dominant	‖	

(handwritten: A   B   C)

Measure:	235		243		349		400		450		
Theme/Section:	Transition (1)	‖	"Cossack Theme"	‖	"Rustic Theme"	‖	"Sentimental Theme"	‖	Transition (2)	‖	
Instrumentation:	Vln. solo	‖	Vln., Orch.	‖	Vln., Orch.	‖	Vln., Orch.	‖	Vln. solo	‖	
Chief Key Area:	(Tonic: V ...)	‖	Tonic	... ‖	Subdominant	‖	Subdominant		‖ (Tonic: V ...)	‖	

(handwritten: A   B   C)

Measure:	460		540		564		
Theme/Section:	"Cossack Theme"	‖	Coda			‖	
Instrumentation:	Vln., Orch.	‖	Orch.		Vln., Orch.	‖	
Chief Key Area:	Tonic	... ‖	Tonic (V ... I)			‖	

(handwritten: A)

Ex. 7-7 Diagram of the finale to Tchaikovsky's Violin Concerto.

(handwritten: ✳ Rondo Form)

♭ CHAPTER EIGHT

Opera

Originally an Italian invention around 1600, opera became a popular part of musical culture in Europe within its first century of existence. By 1700 serious Italian opera was played regularly in France, England, and the German-speaking countries. During the second half of the 17th century, France had developed its own style of opera, *tragedie lyrique*. England and Germany were more sporadic in their attempts at establishing a national opera, making Purcell's *Dido and Aeneas* (1689, see Chapter 2) a somewhat isolated work.

Comic opera arrived later. During the 1720s, a type of Italian opera called *intermezzo*—a pair of comic scenes—began to be played during the intermissions of an **opera seria**. About the same time, French comic pastiches, called *vaudevilles*, began to be performed at parish fairs. English comic opera ("ballad opera") came about suddenly in 1728 with *The Beggar's Opera* by John Gay and Samuel Pepusch. By mid-century, Italian *opera buffa* and French *opéra comique* had evolved from the *intermezzo* and *vaudeville* into full-length genres of opera. Successful English ballad operas were exported to Germany at that time with great success—so much that German composers began composing their own type of comic opera. Modeled on the ballad opera with its folksy tunes and spoken dialogue, the German type, called the *Singspiel*, soon gained widespread popularity.

In Austria, the Singspiel was a farcical type of entertainment containing influences drawn from the opera buffa. Before the 1780s, much Singspiel was frivolous, lowbrow musical theater not considered on a level with Italian comic opera. Many composers and connoisseurs viewed the German language as too guttural to be sung with the refinement of Italian. It remained for Mozart to bring German comic opera to a high cultural level, infusing his Singspiels with the same high culture and psychological insight he brought to his operas in the Italian language.

opera seria 18th-century Italian opera based on "serious" or tragic plots. Handel's Italian operas are examples.

MOZART, *THE MAGIC FLUTE*, TWO EXCERPTS

Mozart's Singspiels before The Magic Flute

BASTIEN UND BASTIENNE. Mozart is most famous in the field of opera for his three mature opera buffas: *Le nozze di Figaro* (*The Marriage of Figaro*); *Don Giovanni* (*Don Juan*); and *Così fan tutte* (*So Do All Women*). Mozart's earliest full-length opera was also on an Italian comic libretto. At the tender age of 12, he composed *La finta semplice* (*The Pretended Simpleton*), K. 51 (46a), which apparently was not performed immediately. Mozart's first full-length operatic performance was of a German-language comedy, *Bastien und Bastienne*, K. 50 (46b), which he completed in 1768—the same summer that he had written the opera buffa. *Bastien und Bastienne* was a one-act Singspiel on a libretto that parodied Jean-Jacques Rousseau's opéra comique, *Le Devin du village* (*The Village Soothsayer*, 1752). Mozart's little opera involved only three singers—a pair of country lovers (named in the title) and the soothsayer—and a small orchestra. The story is a mere vignette in which the lovers squabble and are reconciled.

Be sure you have read Mozart's biography, beginning on page 61.

Wagner, *Lohengrin* (1850) •
Verdi, *Nabucco* (1842) •
Meyerbeer, *Les Huguenots* (1836) •
Donizetti, *Lucia di Lammermoor* (1835) •
Bellini, *Norma* (1831) •
Weber, *Der Freischütz* (1821) •
Rossini, *Il Barbiere di Siviglia* (1816) •
Beethoven *Leonore* [later, *Fidelio*] (1805) •
Mozart, *Die Zauberflöte* (1791) •
Mozart, *Don Giovanni* (1787) •
Mozart, *Le nozze di Figaro* (1786) •
Mozart, *Die Entführung aus dem Serail* (1781) •
• Gluck, *Orfeo ed Euridice* (1762)
• Rousseau, *Le devin du Village* (1752)
• Pergolesi, *La Serva Padrone* (1733)
• Pepusch and Gay, *The Beggar's Opera* (1728)
• Handel, *Giulio Cesare* (1724)
• Handel, *Rinaldo* (1711)

Ex. 8-1 Time line of Opera History. The year associated with a work is its premiere: 1700–1850; 1850–1999 (p. 227).

| 1700 | 1725 | 1750 | 1775 | 1800 | 1825 | 1850 |

George Frideric Handel (1685–1759)
Giovanni Battista Pergolesi (1710–1736)
Christoph Willibald Gluck (1714–1787)
Wolfgang Amadeus Mozart (1756–1791)
Ludwig van Beethoven (1770–1827)
Carl Maria von Weber (1786–1826)
Giacomo Meyerbeer (1791–1864)
Gioacchino Rossini (1792–1868)
Gaetano Donizetti (1797–1848)
Vincenzo Bellini (1801–1835)
Richard Wagner (1813–1883)
Giussepe Verdi (1813–1901)

Die Entführung aus dem Serail. Mozart always knew that the road to fame as a composer was paved with successful operas. So we are not surprised to find him pursuing operatic goals when he moved to Vienna in 1781. The composer first encountered the libretto to *Die Ent-führung aus dem Serail* (*The Abduction from the Seraglio* [harem]), K.384, in July 1781. He was excited about its prospects and wrote to his father, "I am going to compose the sinfonia [over-ture], the chorus in the first act, and the closing chorus with Turkish music." "Turkish" music was all the rage in Vienna at that time. The Ottoman Empire was at Austria's back door, and Turkish janizary bands, with their brash array of percussion, could even be heard on Vienna's street corners.

Corigliano, *The Ghosts of Versailles* (1991) •
Adams, *Nixon in China* (1987) •
Schönberg, *Les misérables* (1980) •
Henze, *The Bassarids* (1966) •
Poulenc, *Dialogues des Carmelites* (1956) •
Stravinsky, *The Rake's Progress* (1951) •
Menotti, *The Consul* (1950) •
Britten, *Peter Grimes* (1945) •
Hindemith, *Mathis der Maler* (1938) •
Gershwin, *Porgy and Bess* (1935) •
Shostakovich, *Lady Macbeth of Mtsensk* (1934) •
Berg, *Wozzeck* (1925) •
• Debussy, *Pelléas et Mélisande* (1902)
• Puccini, *La bohème* (1896)
• Verdi, *Otello* (1884)
• Massenet, *Manon* (1884)
• Wagner, *Der Ring des Nibelungen* completed (1876)
• Bizet, *Carmen* (1875)
• Mussorgsky, *Boris Godunov* (1874)
• Wagner, *Tristan und Isolde* (1865)
• Gounod, *Faust* (1859)
• Verdi, *La Traviata* (1853)

1850	1875	1900	1925	1950	1975	2000

Richard Wagner (1813–1883)
Giussepe Verdi (1813–1901)
Charles Gounod (1818–1893)
Georges Bizet (1838–1875)
Jules Massenet (1842–1912)
Giacomo Puccini (1858–1924)
Alban Berg (1885–1935)
George Gershwin (1898–1937)
Gian-Carlo Menotti (1911–)
Benjamin Britten (1913-1976)
Hans Werner Henze (1926–)
John Adams (1947–)

Another trendy aspect of *The Abduction from the Seraglio*'s libretto was its rescue plot. At first fashionable in France, rescue plots had become popular throughout Europe by this time. This story is set in the 16th century. It deals with an attempt by the noble Belmonte, assisted by his servant, Pedrillo, to rescue his betrothed Constanze and her maid, Blonde, from a Turkish harem into which they have been sold. The Turkish pasha who owns the harem is trying unsuccessfully to gain Constanze's love. The would-be rescuers are captured, and all four fear that they will be put to death. However, the pasha (with humanistic benevolence) frees them all.

The Abduction from the Seraglio was like nothing heard before in German-language opera. The Emperor's comment, made famous in the film *Amadeus*, was "too beautiful for our ears, and an enormous number of notes, my dear Mozart." To which the composer answered, "Only as many as are needed, Your Majesty." This quotation from an early Mozart biography reflects the high artistic level Mozart had brought to German opera in this work. Emotion in the arias and other numbers is on the level of Mozart's Italian operas, and an aura of nobility covers the entire score. In one stroke, *The Abduction from the Seraglio* proved the artistic possibilities of the Singspiel medium and placed it on an equal footing with comic opera in other languages.

Der Schauspieldirektor. In the midst of composing *The Marriage of Figaro* in early 1786, Mozart received a commission—really more of a command—from Emperor Joseph II to compose a short German opera. The occasion was a dinner party the emperor was about to give for his sister, who helped rule the Austrian Netherlands. The emperor also selected a librettist, one Gottlieb Stephanie, Jr., the librettist of *The Abduction from the Seraglio*. Together he and Mozart turned out a charming one-act piece, *Der Schauspieldirektor* (The Impresario), K. 486. This comedy was a spoof on the backstage lives of actors, singers, and an **impresario** trying to put together a traveling company. The entire act included only an overture and four sung numbers interspersed among spoken dialogue. The brief scenario involves rivalries among actors and singers, mainly dealing with issues of money and who will be billed as the *prima donna*. When the impresario threatens to abandon the project, the would-be prima donnas agree to make monetary sacrifices for the sake of their art and their audience. The finale sums up the little Singspiel's message: "Every artist strives for recognition, wants to be unique; if it were not so, Art would be as common as beer."

> **impresario** Producer and promoter of theatrical, balletic, and operatic productions; often the manager of a company.

The Magic Flute: *Conception, Composition, and First Run*

The Abduction from the Seraglio had been a great success in Vienna's Burgtheater. Over the next several years, it was performed widely throughout Germany and became very popular. (Because the country lacked good copyright laws at the time, however, Mozart received little or no money for the later performances.) In 1788, the Burgtheater ceased performing German-language operas in favor of an all-Italian repertoire. Thus Mozart had no further opportunity to mount a new Singspiel inside Vienna proper. A chance to write a Singspiel for a suburban theater came up in 1791, however, through a friend. Emanuel Schikaneder (1751–1812) had taken over the directorship of the Theater auf der Wieden in 1789. Schikaneder was a very successful manager-director-writer-actor who could also sing tolerably. He and Mozart were both Freemasons, though not members of the same lodge. He caught the composer at a fortuitous time. Since the death of Emperor Joseph II in 1790, Mozart's music had become unpopular at court, and by 1791 he found it difficult to support his wife, Constanze, and their child; another baby was due in July. So Schikaneder's proposal that the two collaborate on a popular-level Singspiel was welcomed in the Mozart household. It was to contain "magical" subject matter and effects—all the rage among German-speaking audiences. Schikaneder's main source was *Lulu, or the Magic Flute*, a pseudo-oriental fairy tale by A.J. Liebeskind. The story went through many transformations before the libretto was complete. Shifts and inconsistencies suggest that Mozart and Schikaneder changed the plot during composition. By June 1791, Mozart was well into composing *The Magic Flute*, and by the birth of Mozart's new son on July 26, it was nearly complete. Now, however, the composer needed to take time to finish another commission, the *opera seria* titled *La Clemenza di Tito*. Reluctantly, he did so and traveled to Prague in late August to oversee its production. About mid-September he was back in Vienna to supervise final rehearsals of *The Magic Flute*.

Mozart's Singspiel premiered on September 30. Schikaneder himself played Papageno, the work's central character. Mozart's sister-in-law, Josepha Hofer (Constanze's oldest sister) played the role of the Queen of the Night. The composer himself conducted the first performances, which were immensely successful. To Constanze, who was in Baden, he wrote on October 7,

> I have this moment returned from the opera, which was as full as ever. As usual, the duet, "Mann und Weib" and Papageno's **glockenspiel** in Act I had to be encored and also the trio of the boys in Act II. But what always gives me most pleasure is the *silent approval*! You can see how this opera is becoming more and more esteemed.

[Emily Anderson, *The Letters of Mozart and His Family* (New York: W.W. Norton, 1985), pp. 966–967.]

glockenspiel A set of tuned metal bars laid out on a frame like a piano keyboard.

Connoisseurs and the general public attended performances and enjoyed *The Magic Flute*. Antonio Salieri (1750–1825, unfortunately maligned in the play and film of *Amadeus*) was Mozart's guest at the October 13 performance. In his last letter, Mozart wrote to his wife, "Salieri listened and watched most attentively, and from the overture to the last chorus there was not a single number that did not call forth from him a bravo!" By November 6, the Theater auf der Wieden had presented 24 performances of *The Magic Flute*, and subsequent Viennese publications of pieces from the opera suggest that it ran even longer. This was Schikaneder's most successful project, and it became a fixed part of his company's repertoire. By October 1792, nearly a year after Mozart's death, he had given more than 80 performances of the Singspiel. At that point, Prague—always enthusiastic about Mozart's music—mounted the first production of *The Magic Flute* beyond Vienna. During the next two years, about forty cities saw the opera, mostly in German-speaking areas, but Pest (Hungary) and Warsaw (Poland) are also on the list. The early performances of this, Mozart's last comic opera, took a central role in the spread of his fame during the decade following his death.

Synopsis of the Opera

ACT I. (*A rocky region with trees overgrown and hills on both sides near a round temple*) Enter the hero, Tamino, an Egyptian prince. He is pursued by a huge serpent and is unable to defend himself. He falls to the ground unconscious, and Three (veiled) Ladies armed with javelins kill the serpent. They are impressed by Tamino's handsome looks and reluctantly leave to report the incident to their mistress, the Queen of the Night. As Tamino awakens, the bird catcher Papageno, enters singing "Der Vogelfänger bin ich ja" ("Yes, I Am the Bird Catcher"). He tells Tamino that he killed the serpent himself. The ladies return and punish Papageno for lying by placing a padlock on his mouth. They leave Tamino with a portrait of Pamina, daughter of the Queen of the Night. Immediately Tamino falls in love with her and sings the aria "Dies Bildnis ist bezaubernd schön" ("This Portrait is Bewitchingly Beautiful"). The Queen of the Night now appears and promises Tamino that if he rescues her daughter from the "evil magician," Sarastro, she will give him Pamina's hand in marriage. The Ladies remove the padlock from Papageno's mouth after he hums his pleas in the Quintet "Hm! Hm! Hm!" As protection against danger, the ladies give Tamino a magic flute, and Papageno, who is to be his guide, receives a miraculous glockenspiel. Three Boys will guide them to Sarastro's palace.

(*A Magnificent Egyptian chamber*) Monostatos, Sarastro's servant, attempts to seduce the

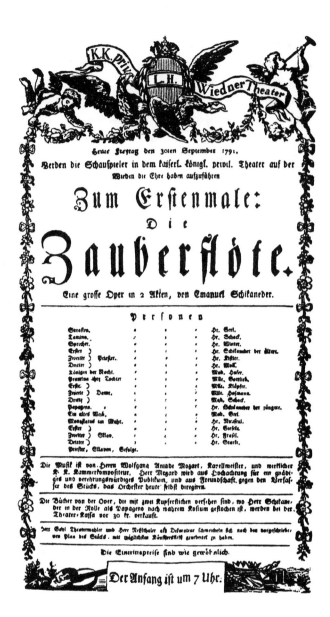

Ill. 8-1 Playbill from the premiere performance of *The Magic Flute*, September 30, 1791. The large print reads, "For the first time: The Magic Flute, a grand opera in two acts by Emanuel Schikaneder."

beautiful Pamina, but Papageno comes to the rescue, frightening both the slave and himself. Monostatos runs away, and Papageno persuades Pamina to flee with him to find Tamino. The scene closes with their duet, "Bei Männern, welche Liebe fühlen" ("In Men Who Feel Love"), which speaks of the comforting power of love.

(*A grove with three temples bearing the words "Temple of Wisdom," "Temple of Reason," and "Temple of Nature"*) In the big musical finale, Tamino is led in by the Three Boys, who counsel him to maintain silence, patience, and perseverance. Tamino attempts to enter The Temples of Nature and Reason but is driven away by voices within them. In the third temple, a priest informs him that the Queen has deceived him. Sarastro is not evil, but rather is the chief priest of the Temple of Wisdom. Tamino, consoled by a mysterious voice saying that Pamina still lives, begins to play the magic flute and sings praises to its power. At this point, Papageno and Pamina hear the music and rush in hoping to find Tamino but just miss him. Monostatos and some slaves pursue them, but Papageno plays his magic bells for protection. Sarastro enters, and Tamino is brought before him. The two lovers, Tamino and Pamina, meet now for the first time. Sarastro orders Monostatos to be punished, and Tamino and Papageno are led into the temple for their trial.

ACT II. (*The Temple*) In a solemn scene, Sarastro explains to his priests that he abducted the daughter of the Queen of the Night to keep her for Tamino, for whom she was destined by the gods. He intends to admit him to their priestly fraternity and invokes the gods' protection for Tamino in the moving aria, "O Isis und Osiris" ("O Isis and Osiris"). Tamino must now prove himself worthy.

(*A vault of the Temple*) Left alone in darkness, Tamino and Papageno are visited by the Three Ladies. In the Quintet, "Wie? Wie? Wie? Ihr an diesem schreckens-ort?" ("What, What, What? You in this Frightful Place?) the Three Ladies try to persuade the men to turn away from their purpose for fear of the Queen's anger. They remain steadfast, however, and the priests drive off the Three Ladies. The two men have passed their first trial.

(*A garden*) Monostatos finds Pamina asleep and attempts to steal a kiss. He is prevented by the entrance of the Queen of the Night, who gives Pamina a dagger, commanding her to kill Sarastro and secure the all-powerful sevenfold shield of the sun, which is in Sarastro's possession. She vows revenge through Pamina in her famous aria, "Der Holle Rache kocht in meinem Herzen" ("The Wrath of Hell Boils in my Heart"). The Queen of the Night leaves, and Monostatos, who has overheard all, threatens to tell Sarastro the plot and even kill Pamina if she does not yield to his lustful desires. Pamina refuses and he threatens to kill her just as Sarastro enters. Hearing of the plot, he dismisses Monostatos. In the aria, "In diesen heil'gen Hallen" ("In These Hallowed Halls"), he demurs from taking revenge, because it would be contrary to the principles of the Temple of Wisdom.

(*A Hall in the Temple*) During the trial of silence, Papageno cannot resist talking to an old woman. The Three Boys bring in a table with food, drink, and the previously confiscated magic flute and bells. Pamina enters, but both Tamino and Papageno refrain from speaking to her. Pamina interprets this as a sign that Tamino no longer loves her, and she leaves in despair. Tamino is then brought before the assembly of priests.

(*The Temple*). Papageno, left alone, reflects that the only thing missing in his life is a woman, singing the very popular aria, "Ein Mädchen oder Weibchen" ("A Little Girlfriend or a Little Wife"). He speaks again with the old woman, who is now magically transformed into his female counterpart, Papagena. However, a priest takes her off. Now both Papageno and Tamino are torn from their loves.

(*A Garden*) The Act II finale begins as Pamina, convinced that Tamino has deserted her, attempts suicide. The Three Boys prevent the deed. (*Gateway to the Temple*) Tamino is subjected to the third trial, that of fire and water. Pamina now joins him by permission of the Two Men in Armor. The lovers pass the trial with the help of the magic flute and are welcomed into the temple as initiates. (*A Garden*) Papageno reappears and, like Pamina, is prevented from killing himself by the Three Boys, who tell him to summon his Papagena with his magic bells. He does so, and they are happily reunited in the comic duet "Pa-pa-pa." (*Outside the Temple*) The Queen of the Night with her Ladies and the traitor, Monostatos, attempts to overtake the temple but fail. (*The Temple*) Having succeeded in all trials, Tamino and Pamina come together with Sarastro and the priests to thank Isis and Osiris and sing a chorus of praise to beauty and wisdom.

Symbolism and Meaning in The Magic Flute

Many features in the libretto and score to *The Magic Flute* are related to Freemasonry. As practiced in the 18th century, the secret organization of Freemasons was a part of the Enlighten-

Ill. 8-2 Emanuel Schikaneder as Papageno, an illustration for the first publication of *The Magic Flute*'s libretto, 1791.

ment movement that reflected its humanistic motives. Symbols and implements used during Masonic ceremonies related to the "craft," which for Freemasons echoed the great stonework accomplishments of antiquity, such as Solomon's temple and the architectural wonders of Egypt.

Masonic lodges were found in most European cities during Mozart's time. Officially, the Roman Catholic Church banned the fraternity. Some members of the ruling class (e.g., Maria Theresa in Austria) also opposed it, while others (notably, Austria's Emperor Joseph II) tolerated it as long as it was kept "underground." Vienna had several Masonic lodges at various times. Mozart had become a Freemason in 1784, and Haydn joined that lodge the following year. Another member of Mozart's lodge was Haydn's patron, Nicolaus Esterházy, illustrating Freemasonry's opportunities for members of different social classes (also employers and employees) to fraternize on equal terms. Eighteenth-century proponents of personal freedom and equality such as François Voltaire were Freemasons, and in the United States of America, George Washington and John Hancock were Freemasons also.

The Magic Flute contains many references to the ideals, symbols, and ceremonies of Freemasonry. Since Mozart and Schikaneder were both Masons, these held special meanings to them and other Masons who saw the opera. Some references were secret, Masonic messages. However, the librettist and composer also used their theatrical vehicle to spread some positive propaganda about important universal Masonic ideals. One is the happy resolution and union of apparently conflicting (but complementary) opposites through purification. In his book *The Magic Flute, Masonic Opera*, Jacques Chailley explores and explains the many symbols by relating them to this dualism, which he relates to the two concrete or marble columns ("Jakin" and "Booz") at the entrance of a Masonic temple. These are examples from his table of dualisms:

JAKIN	*BOOZ*
Osiris	Isis
Masculine	Feminine
Sun	Moon
Day [Sarastro]	Night [Queen of the Night]
Fire [Tamino]	Water [Pamina]
Gold	Silver
Active	Passive
Number 3	Number 5
Red	Black or White
Elucidation	Discourse

We cannot discuss all of these here, but we can easily relate some to the opera's synopsis. The libretto contains many references to the number three: Three Ladies, Three Boys, three temples, and so on. Mozart's score also holds some groups of three. For example, the predominant key of *The Magic Flute* is E-flat major, the signature of which is three flats. In that key, the overture opens with a threefold fanfare:

On closer inspection, this fanfare contains not three but five rhythmic attacks—five, the number opposite to three in the table above. Symbolically, Mozart has joined the two symbolic numbers in this brief musical space.

Papageno, the opera's central character, seems at times to be merely a silly comedian. However, he also symbolizes something deeper. Since he is a catcher of birds, he represents the Kingdom of Air opposite to the Kingdom of Earth, whose representative is Monostatos. The Queen of the Night is a vengeful character, symbolizing chaos in a spirit deprived of the Sun (symbol of wisdom).

Aspects of actual Masonic ritual in Act II elucidate the deeper underlying meaning of the opera. The trials by water and fire are obvious references to purification rites. The highest (33rd) degree of the Scottish Rite in Freemasonry is represented in a triangle, the meaning of which is "wisdom, beauty, strength," as stated in the words of the libretto. Aspects of Christianity are also mixed into the purification trials. Most obvious is the ancient Lutheran chorale, "Ach, Gott, vom Himmel sieh' darein" ("O God, Look Down from Heaven"), which the two Men in Armor sing in a Bach-like contrapuntal setting.

Finally, at the opera's happy ending, we have the symbolic union of complementary opposites. In 1791, this would have resonated with all the enlightened, revolutionary ideas of the time and with the ideals of the French Revolution itself, which had begun two years earlier. Also, at the end, the forces of darkness (Queen of the Night, Monostatos, etc.) have been vanquished, allowing the light of wisdom to shine. This is the universal message of *The Magic Flute*, which is also the motto of the 33rd Masonic degree: *Ordo ab Chao*, order out of chaos— or, darkness into light.

Exploring Two Excerpts from The Magic Flute

PAPAGENO'S SONG. Although Tamino is the "hero" of *The Magic Flute*, Papageno is really the central character. In theatrical terms, he derived from the traditional German stock character, Hanswurst, who, in turn, had grown out of the Italian *commedia dell'arte* comic part, Arlecchino. Through Mozart's music, Papageno is still traditional but certainly not "stock." Mozart gave him a heart and a personality besides making him very funny.

Listen to Papageno's song (No. 2 in the opera). Now listen again to the instrumental introduction that precedes the voice's entry. This is Papageno's lengthy entrance music, during most of which he is offstage. *Notice the recurring high piping on the motive:*

This sound is Papageno playing his panpipes, with which he attracts birds to catch. (See Ill. 8-3.)

Now listen again to the complete song, beginning where Papageno starts singing. These are the words:

Das Vogelfänger bin ich ja,	Yes, I am the bird catcher,
stets lustig, heisa hopsasa!	and very merry, hopsasa!
Ich Vogelfänger bin bekannt	A well-known bird catcher I,
bei alt und jung im ganzen Land.	by old and young in every land.
Weiß mit dem Locken umzugehn,	I'm good at decoying them, and they
und mich aufs Pfeifen zu verstehn!	come to the sound of my pipe.
Drum kann ich froh und lustig sein,	So I can be happy and jolly,
denn alle Vögel sind ja mein.	for all the birds are surely mine.
Der Vogelfänger bin ich ja	Yes, I am the bird catcher,
stets lustig, heisa hopsasa!	and very merry, hopsasa!
Ich Vogelfänger bin bekannt	A well known bird catcher I,
bei alt und jung im ganzen Land.	by old and young in every land.
Ein Netz für Mädchen möchte ich,	I wish I had a net for girls,
ich fing' sie dutzendweis für mich!	I'd surely catch them for myself!

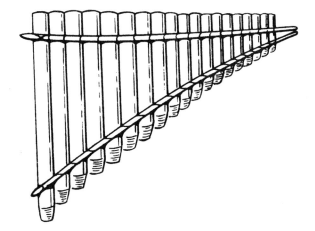

Ill. 8-3 Panpipes, as used by
Papageno. This instrument was
named for the god Pan in
ancient Greece.

Dann sperrte ich sie bei mir ein,	I'd close the net on them,
und alle Mädchen waren mein.	and all the girls would be mine.
Wenn alle Mädchen wären mein,	If all the girls were mine,
so tauschte ich brav Zucker ein,	I'd trade some for sugar,
die welche mir am liebsten wär',	and the one who is my favorite,
der gab' ich gleich den Zucker her.	I'd give her the sugar.
Und küßte sie mich zärtlich dann,	And if she kissed me sweetly,
wär sie mein Weib un ich ihr Mann.	She'd be my wife and I her man.
Sie schlief an meiner Seite ein,	She'd sleep by my side, and
ich wiegte wie ein Kind sie ein.	I'd rock her like a child.

[Translation by Michael Fink]

Does the panpipe motive recur in the song? Yes, we hear it just before and just after the last phrase of each verse. *Notice the simple, folk-song style of the melody.* This was typical in the Viennese Singspiel of Mozart's time—just as typical as the character of Papageno himself. In Austria, this tune even achieved the status of a folk song. Its musical style is just one of several that Mozart combined successfully in the score of *The Magic Flute.* As you will hear, the other excerpt under study shows an entirely different style.

The Queen of the Night's Aria. In opera, an aria often occurs at a high point of emotion. In this case the Queen of the Night is intensely angry because her evil plans have been foiled. She can regain her power only if Sarastro is killed, and she hands her daughter, Pamina, a dagger to murder him. Here are the words of her aria:

Der Hölle Rache kocht	The wrath of Hell boils
in meinem Herzen,	in my heart,
Tod undVerzweiflung	death and despair
Flammet um mich her!	blaze within me!
Fühlt nicht durch dich	If you do not cause

Sarastro Todesschmerzen,	Sarastro a painful death,
so bist du meine Tochter nimmermehr!	then you are my daughter
	no more!
Verstoßen sei auf ewig,	Abandoned you'll be forever,
Verlassen sei auf ewig,	forsaken you'll be forever,
Zertrümmert sei'n auf ewig,	shattered forever shall be
alle Bande der Natur,	all natural ties abandoned,
verstoßen, verlassen und zertrümmert	abandoned, forsaken, and
alle Bande der Natur,	all natural ties shattered,
wenn nicht durch dich Sarastro	if Sarastro does not meet his death
wird erblassen!	through you!
Hört Rachegötter,	Heed a mother's oath!
Hört der MutterSchwur!	

[Translation by Michael Fink]

Listen to the Queen of the Night's Aria from Act II (No. 14 in the opera), following the words. Aside from differences in vocal range, what is the main stylistic difference between this aria and Papageno's song? This sounds more like "real opera." Any singer attempting to perform this aria would need extensive professional training and preparation. On the other hand, Mozart designed Papageno's music for an actor who could also sing. For the Queen of the Night's aria, Mozart has brought in some of the style of Italian opera. The Queen herself is like an *opera seria* character, and her aria of vengeance is like something that could have come from an Italianate opera by Mozart (either an *opera seria* or a serious portion from the tragicomedy *Don Giovanni*).

Do the Queen's words of vengeance always fit the mood of the melody? Some of the melody may be in the aria purely for showy entertainment and not to express the aria's emotion. This is especially true of the two passages on the syllable "mehr" of "nimmermehr" ("no more"). (See Ex. 8-2.) The passage also involves the flashiness of twice singing a high F.

Ex. 8-2 Flashy coloratura passage in the Queen of the Night's Aria from Mozart's *The Magic Flute*, Act II.

Two Excerpts from* The Magic Flute: *A Closer Look

Please refer to the score to *The Magic Flute* excerpts, beginning on page 242 of the Score Anthology.

PAPAGENO'S SONG. *Listen to Papageno's song, following along in your score. Can you identify the vocal form Mozart is using for these three verses?* It is *strophic form*, introduced in Chapter 4 of this text. *How can you tell it is strophic form?* Each verse of the text is set to the same melody.

THE QUEEN OF THE NIGHT'S ARIA. *Follow your score (starting on p. 244) as you listen to the Queen of the Night's aria. Now look through the vocal part and identify the lowest pitch and the highest pitch.* The Queen's lowest pitch is F (first space on the staff) and the highest is the F an octave above the staff. You probably also observed that most of the melody's range (its tessitura) was above the C on the staff—a high soprano vocal tessitura.

In contrast with Papageno's songs, this aria is through-composed. Mozart's form is sectional, held together mainly by the recurrence of a melodic idea shown near the end of Ex. 8-2. The five sections of the aria are as follows:

1. mm. 1–24 (third beat)

2. mm. 25 (with upbeat) to 52

3. mm. 53 (with upbeat) to 67

4. mm. 68–82 (third beat)

5. mm. 83 (with upbeat) to 99

Examine each section and describe it briefly. You might observe:

1. Declamatory vocal style, many leaps.

2. Coloratura mostly; a bell-like figure precedes broken chords that include the famous high F; the section ends with an orchestral interlude.

3. A second declamatory section containing many downward octave leaps.

4. A second coloratura passage, but this one is more like a cadenza; m. 74 begins a melodic reference (now in the minor mode) to mm. 41–42 from the previous coloratura section.

5. Recitative-like ending and orchestral codetta.

Oddly, instead of beginning the aria with a recitative, Mozart ends with one. Take a guess at why. Dramatically, swearing and oaths might work better in recitative style. However, could the recitative at the end also be Mozart's joke? After all, the Queen of the Night is a villain and a parody on the historical Maria Theresa, who opposed Freemasonry.

VERDI, *LA TRAVIATA*, ACT I EXCERPT

The traditions of Italian opera—serious and comic—continued from the Classical into the Romantic period. With the rise of the middle classes, however, tastes shifted. Audiences were larger and less educated than before. Therefore, the subject matter of serious opera shifted from the kings and queens of Greco-Roman antiquity to mostly fictional characters of drama and literature. With this trend came a simpler, more popular style. An emphasis on solo-voice virtuosity grew after the turn of the 19th century, ushering in a period of applause-getting vocalism called *bel canto* (literally, "beautiful singing").

Before the first successes of Giuseppe Verdi (1813–1901), three composers dominated early Romantic Italian opera: Gioacchino Rossini (1792–1868); Gaetano Donizetti (1797–1848); and Vincenzo Bellini (1801–1835). Rossini wrote both serious and comic opera, but he excelled in comedy. His masterpiece is *Il Barbiere di Siviglia* (*The Barber of Seville*, 1816), which ranks with Mozart's *The Marriage of Figaro* and Verdi's *Falstaff* as a superlative example of Italian comic opera. In 1824 Rossini settled in Paris, where his operas enjoyed continuing success. Trying his hand at opera in French, he wrote the comic *Le Comte Ory* (*Count Ory*, 1828) and the grand opera *Guillaume Tell* (*William Tell*, 1829), which was his last work for the operatic stage.

Donizetti's reputation rests equally on his serious and comic operas. *L'elisir d'amore* (*The*

237

VERDI, LA TRAVIATA,
ACT I EXCERPT

Elixir of Love, 1832) and *Don Pasquale* (1843) are opera buffas, and the tragic melodramas *Lucia di Lammermoor* (1835) and *Mary Stuarda* (Mary Queen of Scots, 1832) are examples of his serious side. In all his music, Donizetti knew well his public's taste, and he gave people what they wanted. Bellini's work, by contrast, was more highbrow and aristocratic. He composed only serious or semi-serious operas, among the most famous of which were *Norma* (1831) and *I Puritani* (*The Puritans*, 1835). Bellini's flowing, highly ornamented vocal lines represent the epitome of the *bel canto* style.

Giuseppe Fortunino Francesco Verdi was born on October 9 or 10, 1813 in the village of Roncole near Busseto, Italy. His father, Carlo, and mother, Luigia, were tavern owners. Besides Giuseppe, they had a daughter, Giuseppa Francesca, three years younger than their son. Almost from infancy, Giuseppe showed remarkable musical talent, which his family fostered eagerly. When he was only three years old he began studies with the local organist. His father gave him a spinet piano, which he kept throughout his life. At the age of nine, he took over some of his teacher's playing duties. His formal education began in Busseto at the age of 11 at the *ginasio* (high school). Simultaneously young Giuseppe received lessons in counterpoint and composition from Ferdinando Provesi, the town's *maestro di musica* (music director).

Until 1832, Verdi remained in Busseto, where he composed sacred and secular music. During his last year there, he lived in the home of music patron Antonio Barezzi. Verdi's father applied for a scholarship for Giuseppe's further musical education, but none was available until the next year. Barezzi then volunteered to finance the boy's education. When the Milan Conservatory turned down the 18-year-old, he became a private student of counterpoint and composition under Vincenzo Lavigna, a minor opera composer. That lasted until 1835, when Verdi was invited back to Busseto to head the city's secular music. His salaried duties included giving free instruction, composing, and conducting the local philharmonic orchestra. Financially secure, Verdi now married Barezzi's oldest daughter, Margherita, with whom he was to have two children.

Verdi spent the years 1836–1839 as Busseto's *maestro*. In 1838, some songs were published in Milan. About that time, he began work on his first opera, *Oberto*. In February 1839, he moved his family to Milan, where La Scala produced *Oberto* that November. Its moderate success led to publication and to commissions from La Scala for three more operas. The first of these, the comedy *Un giorno di regno* (*King for a Day*, 1840), was a failure. (Verdi did not turn again to comedy until his last opera more than 50 years later.) Three months before its premiere Margherita died, the two children having predeceased her. Alone and rejected, the composer fell into a deep depression and vowed never to compose again.

His state and his vow were broken when La Scala's impresario persuaded him to consider the libretto to *Nabucco*, which would become his third opera and his first real masterpiece. What attracted Verdi first to *Nabucco*'s libretto was the touching chorus of Israelite exiles, "Va, pensiero, sull'ali dorate" ("Go, Thought, on Gliding Wings"). This patriotic chorus also became the most popular moment in the opera when it was produced in spring 1842. It resonated in the hearts of the Milan audience, who for years had lived under the tyrannical occupation of Austria. They wanted their country back, and beginning with *Nabucco*, Verdi's music became a rallying point. La Scala repeated *Nabucco* 57 times that autumn, launching Verdi's initial reputation in Italy and soon throughout Europe and the New World. His librettist, Temistocle Solera, provided the vehicle for his next triumph, *I Lombardi* (1843). It, too, contained a moving patriotic chorus—by Italian crusaders this time—which stirred feelings of patriotism among its audiences. The composer continued with more operas containing outward or symbolic calls to patriotic action: *Ernani* for Venice (1844); *I Due Foscari* for Rome (*The Two Foscaris*, 1844); *Alzira* for Naples (1845); and *Attila* again for Venice (1846). The movement to rid Italy of foreign powers and unify it under the monarchy of Vittorio Emanuele was about to come into full swing, and the name Verdi was part of it. By the late 1850s, the unification movement's slogan was, "Viva VERDI" (the name being an acronym for *Vittorio Emanuele, Re D'Italia*"—Vittorio Emanuele, King of Italy). As late as *Aida*, drafted even as the movement was achieving its goal in the Italian *Risorgimento* (Resurgence) of 1870, Verdi still infused his operas with deep sentiments of patriotism.

Verdi composed three operas based on Shakespearean plays. The earliest was *Macbeth*, produced in 1847. Its librettist was Francesco Maria Piave, who had already written *Ernani* and *I Due Foscari* with Verdi. Piave now became the composer's principal librettist, a relationship that lasted nearly 20 years. Early on, Verdi had hit upon a winning dramatic structure, which he required Piave and his other librettists to use in many of his operas. The plan called for four main divisions—usually either four acts or a prologue and three acts. Important ensembles are found in the middle divisions, usually including a big duet. The fourth division often opens with a meditative scene featuring the heroine.

The operas of the late 1840s culminated with *Luisa Miller* (1849). In this work Verdi began to depict his characters with greater psychological distinction, refining their emotional expression. His orchestration and textures also became distinctively individual for each particular opera, reflecting aspects of the characters, the story, and the opera's general mood. Unfortunately, *Luisa Miller* was not successful. However, between 1851 and 1853, Verdi brought forth a triad of operas that formed the culmination of his first creative period and would thereafter remain high in the permanent world repertoire of opera: *Rigoletto* (1851); *Il Trovatore* (1853); and *La Traviata* (1853). *Rigoletto* is famous for the aria "La donna è mobile" ("Woman Is Fickle"), sung by the lustful Duke of Mantua, and for the Quartet—both from Act III. *Il Trovatore* (*The Troubadour*) contains many famous melodies, notably the "Anvil Chorus" from Act II. In this work Verdi continued to perfect his smooth transitions between dialogue and lyrical expansion, blurring the distinctions between the opera's "numbers." *La Traviata* (*The Fallen Woman*) failed at first. However, later productions placed this work high in the pantheon of Verdi's operas.

Unlike Verdi's earlier operas, none of these three premiered in Milan's La Scala opera house. That audience had rejected *Un giorno di regno* in 1840, and now he rejected Milan until 1869, instead focusing on other Italian centers. Paris also beckoned. Since 1839, Verdi had maintained a close professional relationship with soprano Giussepina Strepponi. She retired from the stage in 1846, moving to Paris to teach singing. Verdi joined her there the following year, and they lived together from that time. When they returned to Italy in 1849 to live near Busseto, there was considerable gossip, which persisted even after they were married in Savoy in 1859. Like Violetta in *La Traviata*, Giussepina often considered herself unworthy of the man she loved, yet she was a stabilizing influence on him.

After Verdi's initial visit to Paris, he and Giussepina returned several times for productions of his operas at the internationally renowned Paris Opéra. In 1854, that company commissioned

(continued)

a new opera from Verdi, a grand opera that would take advantage of the lavish production style of the biggest French grand operas. The composer settled on *Les vêpres siciliennes* (*The Sicilian Vespers*) to a libretto by Eugène Scribe. With a story concerning the massacre of a group of French by Sicilians at Palermo in 1282 and with Verdi's compelling music, the opera was a resounding success when it premiered in June 1855. This was the first of a half dozen operas Verdi composed or revised over the next 15 years, all of which were marked by experimentation—mostly under the influence of French grand opera. Not all met with success at first. *Simon Boccanegra* (1857) was received poorly at its Venetian premiere. Verdi had problems with censors in Naples over the historical/political subject matter of *Un ballo in maschera* (*A Masked Ball*) in 1858, and the composer reassigned the premiere to Rome for the following year.

In 1861, Verdi accepted an offer from St. Petersburg, Russia. This commission became *La forza del destino* (*The Force of Destiny*), based on a French grand opera scenario. Delays in production allowed Verdi and his wife to visit London in spring 1862, where he scored *La forza* for its November premiere in St. Petersburg. Verdi had done something new in this opera. In his words, it was the first of his "operas made with ideas" rather than arias, duets, etc. Verdi took the expansive style of French grand opera and compressed it into a fast-moving drama in which spectacle and big musical effects (orchestral, choral, ensemble, etc.) are essential to the drama. In his next opera, *Don Carlos* (1867, written for Paris), Verdi took the typically bigger-than-life hero of a historical grand opera and focused on the intimacy of his private life, setting it against a sweeping background of military and dynastic problems. During the grand-opera period, Verdi completed a new work every two to three years. Besides his exploration of new material, he often occupied himself with revising earlier operas.

Verdi's next opera, *Aïda*, brought his middle period to a close. The Suez Canal and a new opera house in Cairo had both opened in 1869. For the next season, the Cairo opera wished to commission Verdi to write a new work. Twice he resisted, but when he received the scenario for *Aïda*, he was intrigued with several of its "situations." Cairo offered him a very large sum of money and the freedom to produce the opera outside Egypt. The composer accepted and signed the contract in June 1870. The extravagant settings were designed and built in Paris, but French wartime problems delayed their completion. Thus, the world premiere did not take place until Christmas Eve of 1871. However, the European premiere at La Scala was only seven weeks later. In *Aïda*, Verdi could realize the full potential of grand opera, especially in the heroic first act and the spectacular second with its gold sets, processions, choruses, and ballet. In Acts III and IV, a more personal drama unfolds, exposing also the theme of patriotic loyalty to an occupied fatherland. The touching tragic ending poignantly blends the personal with the spectacular.

When Rossini died in November 1868, Verdi conceived a grand project to commemorate the anniversary of his death. It was to be a Requiem Mass for which the most prominent Italian composers of the time would each contribute one movement. Unfortunately, Verdi's plan fell through due to lack of cooperation by officials in Bologna. He had already sketched one movement but had put it aside, since *Aïda* occupied his efforts. Then, in May of 1873 another Italian artistic giant passed away: the novelist-poet Alessandro Manzoni. He, like Verdi, had been an activist in the movement for Italian unification, which had triumphed in 1870. Following Manzoni's death, Verdi hit on the idea of completing the *Requiem* by himself in memory of the great writer. He finished the score in Paris between the summer of 1873 and spring 1874. On May 22, the anniversary of Manzoni's death, the composer conducted the *Requiem* in the Church of San Marco, Milan. Public acclaim prompted three more performances of the work, and these were given at La Scala. Perhaps that venue raised some questions in the press and elsewhere about the *Requiem*. Certain portions, notably the "Dies irae," contain an operatic style of composition. Some reviewers rebelled against such music in a religious context, calling it "tawdry," "cheap," "sensational," "unreligious," and "melodramatic." Verdi took it all in stride, for words of criticism rarely fazed him. Soon a "*Requiem* tour" followed, in which the composer conducted the work in Paris, London, and Vienna.

Functionally, Verdi had retired from the theater after *Aïda*. During the 1870s and early 1880s, his only operatic activities were revisions of *Simon Boccanegra* and *Don Carlos*. Through his publisher, Giulio Ricordi, Verdi had become acquainted with composer-librettist Arrigo Boito (1842–1918), who then helped him to revise *Boccanegra*. As early as 1879, Boito sent Verdi his libretto for *Otello*, based on the Shakespearean tragedy. Verdi had laid it aside but did not forget it. Beginning in March 1884, the 71-year-old composer set to work, collaborating with his best and most compatible librettist. Composition on *Otello* took close to three years (including some long interruptions). In February 1887, La Scala gave the premiere of *Otello*, and the audience heard a new Verdi in it. Certainly the arias, duets, choruses, and other numbers were structured in the usual ways. However, the composer now used a freer style of declamation, and some numbers—Iago's "Credo," for example—had more impact because they stressed dramatic more than lyrical values. Also, Verdi made more use of recurring themes in the orchestra than before, making his own adaptation of Richard Wagner's **Leitmotiv** procedure. Verdi had topped himself again.

Two years after *Otello*'s premiere Boito sent Verdi a sketch of his libretto for *Falstaff*, based on Shakespeare's comedy *The Merry Wives of Windsor* with elements of *Henry IV*. The composer was delighted, and, though he worried that he might not live to complete it, he set to work on *Falstaff* immediately. During its two years of composition, the opera was kept a secret. In February 1893, La Scala presented the first performance of *Falstaff*. Again, Verdi was full of surprises. His only previous comedy had been a failure, but now the master of Italian tragic opera was crowning his career with an *opera buffa*. Far from showing any signs of the composer's advanced age, *Falstaff* bounds and bubbles along in impeccable comic timing. The sparkling ensembles are among the best Verdi ever wrote. Harking back to his student days of fugue writing, Verdi surprisingly provides a great fugal finale to the opera, signing off with Falstaff's words, "Tutto nel mondo è burla" ("Everything in the world is a joke"). Verdi turned 80 the year of *Falstaff*'s premiere.

Though he wrote no more operas, Verdi did not stop composing completely. Before and between *Otello* and *Falstaff*, he had composed three sacred choral works: *Ave Maria*; *Laudi alla Vergine Maria*; and *Stabat Mater*. To these he added a *Te Deum* completed in 1897, the year of Giussepina's death. Together the *Quattro pezzi sacri* (Four Sacred Pieces) were published in 1898. Boito, Ricordi, and other friends were close by during Verdi's last few years. He spent Christmas of 1900 with them in Milan, but he suffered a heart attack on January 21 and died six days later. The bodies of Verdi and his second wife were laid to final rest on the grounds of the Casa di Riposo, a retirement home for musicians in Milan, which the composer had founded and endowed. On that day, February 28, 1901, Italy observed general mourning. Later the same year, the Milan Conservatory, which had once refused Giuseppe Verdi entry as a student, was officially named after him.

Leitmotiv (German, "leading motive) A short musical idea in an opera related to some aspect of the drama. Richard Wagner (1813–1883) used leitmotivs systematically in his late operas, notably the four operas of *Der Ring des Nibelungen* (1853–1874).

La Traviata: Background

In 1848, during Verdi's first stay in Paris, a new novel was published and became an instant best-seller. It was *La Dame aux camélias* (The Lady of the Camellias) by Alexander Dumas the younger (whose father had authored *The Three Musketeers*). The new book was the story of Marie Duplessis, a famous courtesan (upper-class prostitute) whom Dumas had known personally. She had died the previous year of "consumption" (tuberculosis) at the age of 23. Most of her patrons had been wealthy aristocrats, who kept her in sumptuous living quarters and an exciting (but dissolute) lifestyle. However, among her clientele were also men of the arts like Franz Liszt and poor nobodies like Dumas before the fame of his novel. The book caused such a stir that Dumas turned it into a play in 1849. However, the censors kept it off the stage for three years.

Verdi was in Paris during February 1852, when the play of *La Dame aux camélias* finally premiered. He and Giussepina saw it, and the composer was immediately taken with the story of the beautiful courtesan. Doomed to an early death, she falls in love with a penniless young man, giving up her life of luxury to live with him, but finally sacrificing their relationship for his sake. It was a perfect story for his next opera. At the time, he had two commissions in his pocket. The first was for *Il Trovatore*, which would be premiered in Rome the following January. The second was an opera for Teatro Fenice in Venice the following month, but the subject was unspecified. Verdi got the production postponed. Not until October 1852 did he commit to an opera on the Dumas play, but it was a bold and firm commitment, and he set to work on it with concentration. On New Year's Day 1853, he wrote to a friend:

> For Venice, I have written *La dame aux camélias*, which will probably be called *La Traviata*. It is a contemporary subject. Another composer would perhaps not have done it because of the costumes, the period, or a thousand other foolish scruples, but I did it with great pleasure. Everyone complained when I proposed putting a hunchback on the stage. Well, I wrote *Rigoletto* with great pleasure.

> [Charles Osborne, *Letters of Giuseppe Verdi* (New York: Holt, Rinehart and Winston, 1972), p. 89.]

At the time, Verdi had not yet completed *La Traviata*. In fact, he was still finishing *Il Trovatore*. However, after *Il Trovatore*'s January 19 premiere in Rome, Verdi directed all his energies toward *La Traviata*. Unfortunately, he had to spend some of that energy arguing with the management of La Fenice. They wished to use their plump *prima donna*, Fanny Salvini-Donatelli. Verdi knew she was physically wrong for the part, which Dumas had described as "tall" and "very thin." Working through the librettist, Piave, the managers finally wore down Verdi (but in the end he was correct). Another problem was the period setting of the opera. During the Romantic age, a play about a prostitute set in "modern" times was considered *scandalous*—an attractive idea to the daring Verdi, but anathema to the financially savvy theatrical management. The premiere was originally to be done in modern dress according to the composer's directions, but at the last minute the management outvoted him, and the setting became "around 1700," creating a tradition that would linger until after the turn of the 20th century.

"*La Traviata* last night—fiasco. Was the fault mine or that of the singers? Time will be the judge." Verdi wrote these words the morning after the March 6, 1853, premiere. Act I had actually gone well, and the audience had called Verdi to take a bow three different times. In the remaining acts, however, the disaster built. The *prima donna*'s voice began to fail, the tenor became hoarse, and the baritone began to sulk. The "fiasco" peaked in the final act, when the doctor pronounced the corpulent *prima donna* to be wasting away from consumption. The audience broke into uproarious laughter. The production closed after only one more performance.

For the next 14 months nothing more was heard of *La Traviata*. However, neither Verdi nor his loyal circle lost faith in the opera. Antonio Gallo, a Venetian admirer of his, sponsored a revival of *La Traviata* at the San Benedetto Theater. On May 6, 1854, the opera's revival opened with a hand-picked cast. Verdi could not be present, but Piave reported that this was the greatest Verdi triumph ever in Venice, with "an indescribable storm of applause." Now, Verdi could write, "Last time it was a fiasco; this time it is a furore [fashionable craze]. Draw your own conclusion!"

The popularity of *La Traviata* has never wavered. From 1854 it became Verdi's most universally beloved opera. Paris first saw it that year in a pirated production given by the Théâtre des Italiens. Ten years later Verdi was looking for alternative venues to the famed Paris Opéra and found it in the Théâtre Lyrique, where *La Traviata* was performed in French. By then, New York and the major cultural centers of Europe had already mounted the opera. It even became a personal favorite of the composer himself. When asked years later which of his

Ill. 8-4 Engraving of Verdi conducting an opera in Paris, 1876.

operas he considered the best, he replied, "Speaking as a professional, *Rigoletto*; as an amateur, *La Traviata*."

Synopsis of the Opera

ACT I. (*A drawing room in the Paris home of Violetta Valery sometime in the 1840s*) A festive party is in progress. Among the guests is the young, handsome Alfredo Germont, who is presented to Violetta. Wine is served and all sing the brilliant *Brindisi* (Drinking Song), "Libiamo" ("Let's Drink"). As a waltz begins in the adjoining ballroom, Violetta suggests that they dance. She becomes weak and almost collapses but pretends that she is all right. The guests leave except for Alfredo. Thinking she is alone, Violetta looks in the mirror, remarking how pale she has become. She now realizes that Alfredo is with her. He confesses that he has been in love with her for a year and expresses his desire to take care of her. In a duet, Violetta tells him that he should forget her because she does not know such innocent love. She gives him a camellia, saying she will see him when the flower wilts, that is, tomorrow. The guests return to bid goodnight to their hostess. As they depart and Violetta is left alone, she thinks about how empty her life has been and how strangely she is affected by Alfredo's expression of his love for her. In her big scene "Ah, fors'è lui," ("Ah, Perhaps He Is the One"), she speculates on the possibility of this new romance but then decides it would be folly in the aria "Sempre libera" ("Forever Free"). She suddenly hears Alfredo singing of his love from the street below. She is moved but wonders whether a woman like her can ever find lasting love.

ACT II. SCENE I. (*A country house near Paris*) Alfredo has been living with his beloved Violetta and sings of his happiness in "De' miei bollenti spiriti" ("Of My Ardent Spirits"). From the maid, Alfredo learns that Violetta is in dire financial straits from paying all their bills and has had to sell her jewels. Alfredo leaves for Paris to raise money. Violetta enters, appearing happy and very different from the courtesan in the first act. She finds a letter from her friend Flora. It is an invitation to a ball, but Violetta is no longer interested in such events. The maid announces a visitor, Alfredo's father, Germont. He informs Violetta that Alfredo has a younger sister who is engaged. However, Alfredo's scandalous relationship with Violetta is jeopardizing the girl's marriage. He begs her to give up Alfredo. She begs him not to ask her to make such a sacrifice, but she finally agrees. Germont steps into the garden, and Violetta writes a note of farewell to Alfredo. He returns, believing his father is yet to arrive. As Violetta prepares to leave, she asks Alfredo for an expression of his love, then runs from the room. Shortly, a servant brings Alfredo Violetta's note. He feels betrayed. As Alfredo reads, his father enters and offers him consolation, reminding him of their Provençal home in the great aria, "Di Provenza il mar" ("The Sea at Provence"). He begs Alfredo to return home, but finding Flora's invitation, Alfredo dashes off to Paris to avenge what he takes to be Violetta's insult.

SCENE II. (*The salon in Flora's Parisian house*) Flora is entertaining her guests with a Spanish costume ball. Entertainers include Spanish Gypsies. Alfredo enters alone, pretending he does not care where Violetta is. He plays cards and wins. As Violetta arrives with Baron Duphol, she is distressed to see Alfredo. Soon the baron and Alfredo exchange words. They gamble, and Alfredo nearly breaks him. As the guests move to another room, Violetta takes Alfredo aside and begs him to avoid trouble by leaving. He refuses to leave without her and wants to know whether she loves the baron. Violetta remembers her promise to Alfredo's father and says yes. Infuriated, Alfredo calls the guests together and denounces Violetta, throwing his

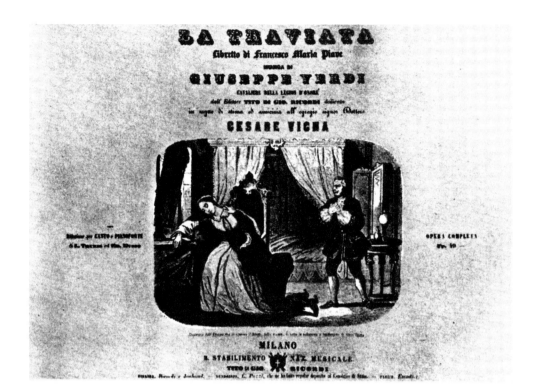

Ill. 8-5 Cover of the first edition
score to *La Traviata*. Characters
in the graphic image are dressed
in late 17th-century costumes
instead of mid-19th-century
garb, which would have been
true to the original story.

winnings at her feet. She faints. Germont now appears and reprimands his son, who is ashamed. Amid a grand ensemble, the baron challenges Alfredo to a duel.

ACT III. (*Violetta's bedroom*) The curtain rises on the scene of Violetta dying in poverty. Some time has passed, and her illness has been aggravated by her longing for Alfredo. As the doctor enters, he informs the maid privately that Violetta will not live long. When he and the maid leave, Violetta reads a letter from Germont informing her that in the duel the Baron was wounded. Alfredo has left the country, but his father has written him of Violetta's sacrifice. Alfredo will return to ask her forgiveness, and Germont, too, will come. In "Addio del passato" ("Farewell to Past Dreams"), Violetta hopes she will live long enough to see Alfredo one last time. Sounds of the Parisian carnival celebration can be heard from the street. Preceded by the maid's breathless announcement, Alfredo rushes in, and Violetta falls into his arms. They sing a beautiful duet, "Parigi, o cara" ("Paris, O Love"), in which they plan to live again in the countryside. He begs her forgiveness and says that now that he has returned, everything will be fine. Violetta tries to dress, but she collapses. With the doctor, Alfredo's father enters, coming to release her from her promise. Violetta imagines herself to be feeling better, as the love music from Act I returns in the orchestra. Then she falls back on the couch. The doctor pronounces her dead as the curtain falls.

Exploring La Traviata, *Act I Excerpt*

The excerpt from *La Traviata* under study begins with the Act I "Drinking Song." It continues through Violetta and Alfredo's first scene together in which he declares his love and she becomes intrigued with him and the thought of his innocent caring. Although the score to this music consists of two "numbers" (No. 3, "Libiamo" [Drinking Song] and No. 4, "Un di felice" [Valse and Duet]), the music to No. 4 consists of more than one section. *Listen to the entire excerpt and identify the large main divisions. Changes in the tempo are your main cues.* Here are the four main divisions, showing libretto dialogue for each:

[1] Drinking Song:

Alfredo:	Libiamo ne' lieti calici	Let's drink from joyful goblets
	Che la bellezza infiora,	That flourish in beauty,
	E al fuggevol ora	And in the fleeting hour
	S'inebrii a voluttà.	become drunk with lust.
	Libiam ne'dolci fremiti	Let's drink to the sweet thrills
	Che suscita l'amore,	that love follows,
	Poichè quell'occhio al core,	For those eyes
	Onnipotente va.	Go right to your heart.
Alfredo, then all:	Libiamo, amor fra i calici	Let's drink, for from the goblets
	Più caldi baci avrà.	come warmer kisses of love.
Violetta:	Tra voi saprò dividere	Among you I can divide
	Il tempo mio giocondo;	my joyous time;
	Tutto è follia nel mondo	All of life is folly
	Ciò che non è piacer.	except for pleasure.
	Godiam, fugace e rapido	Let's revel, for quick and fleeting
	È il gaudio dell'amore,	is love's pleasure,
	È un fior che nasce e muore,	It is a flower that is born and dies,
	Nè più si può goder.	Never more to be enjoyed.
	Godiam, c'invita un fervido	Let's revel, as an alluring, ardent
	Accento lusinghier.	impulse invites us.
All:	Ah! godiam—la tazza e il cantico	Ah! Let's revel—drink and song
	La notte abbella e il riso;	Adorn the night and our laughter;
	In questo paradiso	In this paradise
	Ne scopra il nuovo dì.	The new days will find us.
Violetta (to Alfredo):	La vita è nel tripudio.	Life is in the reveling.
Alfredo (to Violetta):	Quando non s'ami ancora.	When one does not also love.
Violetta:	Nol dite a chi l'ignora.	Speak not to one who knows it not.
Alfredo:	È il mio destin così.	Such is my destiny.
All:	Ah! Godiam—la tazza e il cantico	Ah! Let's revel—drink and song
	La notte abbella e il riso;	adorn the night and our laughter;

	In questo paradiso	In this paradise
	Ne scopra il nuovo dì.	The new day will find us.

[2] Waltz & Dialogue:

All:	Che è ciò?	What is that?
Violetta:	Non gradireste ora le danze?	Wouldn't you like to dance now?
All:	Oh, il gentile pensier! Tutti accettiamo.	Oh, a lovely thought! We all accept.
Violetta:	Usciamo dunque.	Let's go in then.
	Ohimè!	Ohhh!
All:	Che avete?	What's wrong?
Violetta:	Nulla, nulla.	Nothing, nothing.
All:	Che mai v'arresta?	What is the problem?
Violetta:	Usciamo.	Let's go in.
	Oh Dio!	Oh, God!
All:	Ancora!	Again!
Alfredo:	Voi soffrite?	Are you ill?
All:	O ciel! Ch'è questo?	Heavens! What is this?
Violetta:	Un tremito che provo. Or là passate—	Just a little chill. Now, go on in—
	Tra poco anch'io sarò.	I'll join you in a little while.
All:	Come bramate.	As you wish.
Violetta (looking into a mirror):	Oh, qual pallor!	Oh, how pale!
Alfredo:	Cessata è l'ansia Che vi turbò?	Has the anxiety that disturbed you now gone?
Violetta:	Sto meglio.	I am better.
Alfredo:	Ah, in cotal guisa V'ucciderete—aver v'è d'uopo cura Dell'esser vostro—	Ah, in such a way you could kill yourself—you must take care of yourself—
Violetta:	E lo potrei?	But can I?
Alfredo:	Oh, se mia Foste, custode io veglierei pe' vostri Soavi dì.	Oh, if you were mine, I would watch over you every day.
Violetta:	Che dite? Ha forse alcuno Cura di me?	What are you saying? Is there anyone then to care for me?
Alfredo:	Perchè nessun al mondo V'ama	That's because no one in the world loves you.

Violetta:	Nessun?	No one?
Alfredo:	Tranne sol io.	No one but me.
Violetta (laughing):	Gli è vero! Sì grande amor dimenticato avea.	That's true. I had forgotten such a great love.
Alfredo:	Ridete? E in voi v'ha un core?	You laugh? Have you no heart?
Violetta:	Un cor? Si, forse—e che lo richiedete?	A heart? Yes, perhaps—and why do you ask?
Alfredo:	Ah, se ciò fosse, non potreste allora celiar.	Ah, if that were so, you could not joke with me this way.
Violetta:	Dite davvero?	Are you serious?
Alfredo:	Io non v'inganno.	I do not deceive you.
Violetta:	Da molto è che mi amate?	Have you loved me for a long time?
Alfredo:	Ah, sì; da un anno.	Oh, yes, for a year.

[3] **First Duet:**

Alfredo:	Un dì felice, eterea,	One happy, ethereal day,
	Mi balenaste, innante,	You flashed before me,
	E da quel dì tremante	And from that trembling day
	Vissi d'ignoto amore—	I lived by a love never known before—
	Di quell'amore ch'è palpito Dell'universo intero.	A love that is the breath of the whole universe.
	Misterioso, altero,	Mysterious, proud,
	Croce e delizia al cor.	Both sorrow and delight to my heart.
Violetta:	Ah, se ciò è ver, fuggitemi.	Oh, if that is true, then leave.
	Sola amistade io v'offro:	I offer you only friendship:
	Amar non so, nè soffro	I neither know how to love, nor
	Un così eroico amore.	do I bear such a heroic love.
	Io sono franca, ingenua;	I am frank and ingenuous;
	Altra cercar dovete;	You should find another;
	Non arduo troverete	It will not be difficult then
	Dimenticarmi allor.	To forget me.
Alfredo: [together]	Oh amore!	Oh, love!
Alfredo:	Misterioso, altero *etc.*	Mysterious, proud, *etc.*
Violetta:	Non arduo troverete, *etc.*	It will not be difficult then, *etc.*

[4] Waltz Reprise and Second Duet:

Gaston:	Ebben? Che diavol fate?	Everything all right? What the devil are you doing?
Violetta:	Si folleggiava—	We were joking with each other.
Gaston (at the door):	Ah, ah! Sta ben—restate.	Ah, ah! Good—don't get up. [He leaves.]
Violetta:	Amor dunque non più. Vi garba il patto?	Now, no more of love. Agreed?
Alfredo:	Io v'obbedisco. Parto.	I obey. I'll leave.
Violetta:	A tal giungeste? Prendete questo fiore.	Just like that? Take this flower.
Alfredo:	Perchè?	Why?
Violetta:	Per riportarlo—	To bring it back—
Alfredo:	Quando?	When?
Violetta:	Quando sarà appassito.	When it has wilted.
Alfredo:	O ciel! Domani—	O heavens! Tomorrow—
Violetta:	Ebben. Domani.	Good. Tomorrow.
Alfredo:	Io son felice!	I am happy!
Violetta:	D'amarmi dite ancora?	Do you still say you love me?
Alfredo:	Oh, quanto, quanto v'amo!	Oh, how much, how much I love you!
[together:]	Oh, quanto …	Oh, how much …
Alfredo:	V'amo, oh, quanto!	I love you, oh, how much!
Violetta:	D'amarmi …	You love me …
Violetta:	Partite?	You're leaving?
Alfredo:	Parto.	I'm leaving.
Violetta:	Addio.	Good-bye.
Alfredo:	Di più non bramo.	I desire no more.
Violetta and Alfredo:	Addio. Addio.	Good-bye. Good-bye.

[Translation by Michael Fink]

Listen to the First Duet again. Can you hear differences in melodic style between the two characters' parts? Do these reflect personality differences?

Ex. 8-3 shows the opening phrase of each character in this duet. In Alfredo's melody (Ex. 8-3a), note the rhythmic hesitancy at first. The unadorned, smooth line that follows could signify his fervent, innocent sincerity. By contrast, Violetta's answer (Ex. 8-3b) contains wide leaps followed by a richly ornamented line. We could interpret these to show Violetta's sophistication, superficiality, and frivolous attitude toward men who approach her romantically.

Ex. 8-3 *La Traviata*: differences
in melodic style between (a)
Alfredo and (b) Violetta.

Notice how Verdi weaves these two melodic styles together by the end of this duet:

VERDI, LA TRAVIATA,
ACT I EXCERPT

La Traviata, Act I Excerpt:
A Closer Look
Please refer to the score of *La Traviata*, beginning on page 248 of the Score Anthology.

   Listen to the entire excerpt, following the music, words, and singing translation in the score. Listen again to the "Drinking Song" only. In what key does it begin? To what key does it change, and where? Beginning in the key of B-flat major, the "Drinking Song" remains in that key through Alfredo's and Violetta's verses. When all the others begin a verse of their own in m. 124 (with upbeat), the key shifts to E-flat major, key of the subdominant. *When does the music return to the home key?* Verdi cleverly works the music back to B-flat major during the exchange between Violetta and Alfredo (mm. 143–151):

This could symbolize the rapport between them, and it prepares for the full-ensemble ending of the "Drinking Song."

In opera frequent changes in the music are necessary to maintain dramatic momentum. In the "Drinking Song" we saw how the music changed keys and then shifted back. You also noted the effect of contrasting changes between solo and choral textures. *Now study the Valse and Duet (No. 4) for changes in:*

- *Key*

- *Tempo*

- *Meter*

- *Vocal Texture (chorus, solo, etc.) and Instrumentation (band or orchestra).*

Make a chart showing the status and changes in these parameters throughout the number. Your chart should look something like this:

MEASURE	KEY	TEMPO	METER	TEXTURE; INSTRUMENTATION
1	E-flat major	Allegro brillante	3/4	Chorus with solos; Offstage Military Band
51	C minor			Band alone
	G minor			
	E-flat major			

(continued)

MEASURE	KEY	TEMPO	METER	TEXTURE; INSTRUMENTATION
85				Solo (Violetta, Alfredo); Band continues
97	A-flat major			
133	D-flat major			
148	C major			
163	F major			
181	(F major)	Andantino	3/8	(Solos continue, then duet); Orchestra
251	C min/G min/ E-flat major (Remains near E-flat major until end)	Tempo I. (Allegro brillante)	3/4	(Solo and duet); Band

𝄢 C H A P T E R   N I N E

Choral Music

The history of choral literature is the longest in Western music. Beginning with the unison chants of the Middle Ages (codified by Pope Gregory I around the year 600, subsequently called Gregorian Chant), the idea of ensemble singing expanded during the later Middle Ages, culminating in the *Nostre Dame Mass* by Guillaume de Machaut (c. 1300–1377). Renaissance Masses and motets by composers such as Josquin des Prez

Ex. 9-1 Time line of Choral Music: 900–1800; 1800 to the present (p. 255).

Haydn, *The Creation* (1798) •
Mozart, *Requiem* (1791) •
Bach, *Mass in B Minor* completed (c. 1747–1749) •
Handel, *Messah* (1742) •
Bach, Cantata No. 140 (1731) •
Vivaldi, *Gloria* (1725) •
Neumeister's first cantata librettos (1700) •
Praetorius, *Musae Sionae* (1605–1610) •
Nicolai's chorale *Wachet Auf* published (1599) •
Palestrina, *Pope Marcellus Mass* (1567) •
Earliest Lutheran chorales (1620s) •
Des Prez, *"Pange lingua" Mass* (c. 1514) •
• Machaut, *Nostre Dame Mass* (c. 1350)

• Gregorian Chant codified (c. 900)

| 900 | 1000 | 1100 | 1200 | 1300 | 1400 | 1500 | 1600 | 1700 | 1800 |

_____ Guillaume de Machaut (c. 1300–1377)
_____ Josquin Des Prez (c. 1440–1521)
_____ Martin Luther (1483–1546)
Giovanni P. da Palestrina (c. 1525–1594) _____
Giovanni Gabrieli (1554/1557–1612) _____
Michael Praetorius (1571–1621) _____
Heinrich Schütz (1585–1672) _____
Giacomo Carissimi (1605–1674) _____
Erdmann Neumeister (1671–1756) _____
J. S. Bach (1685–1750) _____
George F. Handel (1685–1759) _____
Joseph Haydn (1732–1809) _____
Wolfgang Amadeus Mozart (1756–1791) ___

Pärt, *Miserere* (1989) •
Pärt, *St. John Passion* (1982) •
Penderecki, *St. Luke Passion* (1965) •
Britten, *War Requiem* (1961) •
Poulenc, *Gloria* (1959) •
Stravinsky, *Threni* (1958) •
Orff, *Carmina Burana* (1936) •
Walton, *Belshazzar's Feast* (1931) •
Stravkinsky, *Symphony of Psalms* (1930) •
Honegger, *King David* (1921) •
Vaughan Williams, *A Sea Symphony* (1910) •
• Elgar, *The Dream of Gerontius* (1900)
• Mahler, Symphony No. 2 ("Resurrection," 1894)
• Fauré, Requiem (first version, 1887)
• Verdi, Requiem (1874)
• Brahms, *A German Requiem* (1868)
• Liszt, *Dante* and *Faust* Symphonies (1856, 1857)
• Berlioz, *L'Enfance du Christ* (1854)
• Mendelssohn, *Elijah* (1846)
• Berlioz, Requiem (1837)
• Beethoven, Ninth Symphony (1824)
• Beethoven, *Missa Solemnis* (1823)

1800   1825   1850   1875   1900   1925   1950   1975   2000

Ludwig van Beethoven (1770–1827)
Hector Berlioz (1803–1869)
Felix Mendelssohn (1809–1847)
Franz Liszt (1810–1886)
Giuseppe Verdi (1813–1901)
Johannes Brahms (1833–1897)
Edward Elgar (1857–1934)
Gustav Mahler (1860–1911)
Ralph Vaughan Williams (1872–1958)
Igor Stravinsky (1882–1971)
Arthur Honegger (1892–1955)
Carl Orff (1895–1982)
Benjamin Britten (1913–1976)
Krystof Penderecki (1933–)
Arvo Pärt (1935–)

Ill. 9-1 Woodcut from Hermann Finck's *Practica musica* (Part V, 1556), showing a chapel choir accompanied by two cornetts and a sackbut. At that time, boys sang the soprano parts.

a cappella Vocal music, especially choral, performed without instrumental accompaniment.

(c. 1440–1521) and Giovanni Pierluigi da Palestrina (c. 1525–1594) were intended for church choirs embodying the full range of human voices: soprano, alto, tenor, and bass (SATB). These four ranges became the standard sections of a choir. In Renaissance choral music, improvised organ accompaniment was common as well as *a cappella* performance. Where available, wind or string instruments might also be used to double and reinforce the choral parts (see Ill. 9-1). During the 16th and early 17th centuries, music for double or triple choirs also developed, particularly under the leadership of Giovanni Gabrieli (1554/1557–1612) and Heinrich Schütz (1585–1672).

The influence of opera in the early Baroque period shifted some attention away from purely choral music in favor of music for solo singers, and the religious wars of the 17th century also took their toll on many choirs. The Baroque penchant for *contrast* led to "sacred concertos" involving various combinations of soloists, small and large choirs, and instrumental ensembles. Thirty or more voices were common among the major choirs in the Renaissance and Baroque periods, although smaller organizations also thrived. In Roman Catholic countries, the Mass and the sacred concerto were the preferred genres. Protestant England adapted the Catholic Mass into a genre called the service, and motetlike anthems also developed. In Lutheran Germany, a new type of hymn, the *chorale,* came into practice (see below), providing basic material for sacred concertos and, later, sacred cantatas.

Modeled on opera, sacred oratorios, which told Biblical stories, evolved during the mid-17th century in Rome. Led by Giacomo Carissimi (1605–1674), Latin oratorios developed, using the choir for crowd scenes and to comment on the drama. Then, during the 1730s, George Frideric Handel virtually reinvented the oratorio, making it a truly choral genre, which also included soloists and important orchestral participation. The popularity of *Esther*, the first of these, led to Handel's famous oratorios, for example, *Messiah* and *Judas Maccabaeus*. Emulating Handel, Joseph Haydn completed his oratorio, *The Creation*, in 1798.

Apart from opera and related secular forms, choral music was reserved exclusively for church use until the 18th century. Handel, besides his sacred oratorios, composed some mythological and allegorical ones, notably *Hercules* and *The Triumph of Time and Truth*. Again, Haydn emulated him with a secular oratorio, *The Seasons* (1801).

J.S. BACH, CANTATA NO. 140: "WACHET AUF, RUFT UNS DIE STIMME," THREE MOVEMENTS

Lutheran Chorales

When Martin Luther (1483–1546) started the Protestant Reformation and formed his new church in the 1520s, music played an important role. One basic precept of Luther's liturgical reform was strong *congregational* participation in the service, a function that differed sharply with the practices of the Church of Rome. Luther stated, "I wish to make German psalms for the people, that is to say sacred hymns, so that the Word of God may dwell among the people." To that end, the musically literate Luther himself, along with his chief musical advisor, Johann Walther (1496–1570), set about creating the first Protestant hymnbook, *Geystlich Gesangk Buchleyn* (*Little Sacred Song Book*, 1524). In this publication Luther and his group established the basic traits for *chorales* (Lutheran hymns) appropriate to congregational singing:

- Simple language in the vernacular (German, not Latin)
- Rhymed metrical verse
- Strophic forms
- Easily singable melody

Over the next several years, more chorales were added to the repertoire. The idea was to form a collection that would cover the **liturgy** for every Sunday and feast in the Lutheran church calendar, together with some chorales appropriate generally to some part of the calendar such as Advent, Christmas, and Easter.

liturgy The authorized texts for services within a particular religion. Adj.: liturgical.

TEXTS AND MELODIES. For texts, Luther relied on German translations of Biblical passages (notably Psalms) and Latin liturgical passages, some reaching back to the Middle Ages. Similarly, many chorale melodies were adaptations of Roman Catholic hymns. Thus, for example, the Latin Easter melody "Victimae paschali laudes" ("Praise to the Paschal Victim") became the German chorale "Christ lag in Todesbanden" ("Christ Lay in the Bonds of Death"). Other melodies were adaptations of secular folk songs or melodies from the German Meistersinger tradition. Later, a few Renaissance secular **part songs** were given new sacred words. The most famous early chorale is "Ein feste Burg ist unser Gott" of 1529, the music and text of which are attributed to Luther himself (see Ill. 9-2). He wrote this chorale, a religious "battle hymn," for the Feast of the Reformation in the Lutheran Church.

part song A choral composition in which the highest part carries the melody and the lower parts provide support.

WACHET AUF. After Luther's death, poets and composers augmented the central corpus of chorales. A major contributor was the poet-composer Philipp Nicolai (1556–1608), creator of two famous Lutheran chorales, "Wie schön leuchtet der Morgenstern" ("How lovely shines the morning star") and "Wachet auf, ruft uns die Stimme" ("Wake Up, the Voice Calls to Us"), both published in 1599. "Wachet auf," which has been called the "king of chorales," became the basis for Cantata No. 140 by J.S. Bach (1685–1750) more than 130 years later.

Like many chorales written during Luther's time, "Wachet auf" was cast in a form known as bar form. Originating in 13th-century Germany, bar form became the established and predominant form among the *Meistersinger* (Mastersingers), who were active during the early Reformation. Meistersinger songs, especially those by Hans Sachs (1494–1576), were an important influence on Lutheran chorales; thus, many were composed in bar form. The bar form consists of two sections called the *Stollen* and *Abgesang*, respectively. The Stollen consisted of two strophes of text sung to the same melody, and the Abgesang was a continuing chain of phrases that followed. We can represent the whole bar form as:

A–A–B

Ill. 9-2 Melody of Martin Luther's chorale "Ein feste Burg ist unser Gott" in its first printing, *Geistliche Lieder* (Sacred Songs), 1533. Note the alto clef and key signature of F major.

Usually, the final melodic phrase of the Abgesang was a reprise of the last phrase from the Stollen. Ex. 9-2 shows the melody of the chorale "Wachet auf," with sections and phrases marked. Notice that phrase a$_3$ from the Stollen returns at the end of the Abgesang.

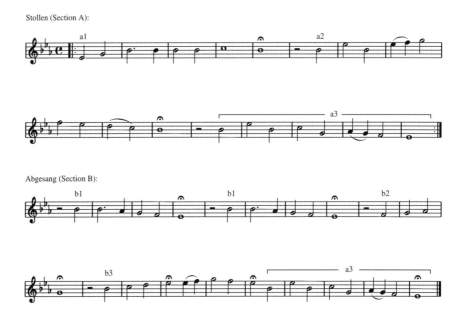

Ex. 9-2 Melody of Nicolai's chorale "Wachet auf, ruft uns die Stimme" with sections and phrases labeled.

LATER SACRED SONG. As the Baroque period developed, Lutheran church composers grew less interested in writing chorales in the formal melodic-rhythmic molds of the past. Similarly, religious poets progressed from the formality of traditional texts to a new, more personal style, increasingly marked with mysticism and religious emotionalism. Thus, the traditional Lutheran chorale evolved into the 17th-century German devotional song—still simple enough for congregants to sing. The style of Italian operatic arias was also an influence. Flexible melody, declamatory rhythm, and sometimes freer forms characterized the newer sacred songs. Promoted chiefly by a large sect of Lutherans known as the Pietists, vast numbers of devotional songs were coming into print by the year 1700. Later J.S. Bach wrote only three such pieces, but in 1736 he provided the *basso continuo* part for a publication of 48 existing devotional songs.

The Sacred Cantata before Bach

From the outset, chorales had an important function besides congregational singing. They provided professional Lutheran church composers with familiar material on which to base new sacred works. We call this procedure *cantus firmus* technique. As defined by *The New Harvard Dictionary of Music*, a *cantus firmus* is "a preexistent melody used as the basis of a new polyphonic composition." Beginning in the 16th century, chorales were used as *cantus firmi* in polyphonic "chorale motets" for two or three voice parts. In these, the chorale melody appeared in one part, while the others contained newly composed counterpoint. This was the first step toward full-length cantatas using a chorale as a *cantus firmus*.

One composer of chorale motets was Michael Praetorius (1571–1621). He also took the chorale *cantus firmus* idea a step further in his *Musae Sioniae* (*Muses of Zion*, 1605–1610). In some compositions from this monumental series, each verse of the chorale is treated as a separate section or movement. There the chorale *cantus firmus* would appear in one part or another with the remaining parts harmonizing or in counterpoint with the main melody. In miniature, these multimovement works were the forerunners to Bach's sacred cantatas.

The Thirty Years' War (1618–1648) disrupted the development of Lutheran church music, but notable advances followed it. In addition to chorales, music for services included new settings of Biblical texts. The influence of Italian opera and its chamber-music counterpart, the cantata, was now heard in solo arias based on chorale melodies as shown in Ex. 9-3. Gradually composers also introduced recitative and aria settings of newly written sacred texts. The personal nature of these reflected the Pietist approach.

Ex. 9-3 Excerpt from the chorale aria "Wachet auf, ruft uns die Stimme" by Franz Tunder (1614–1667). For a translation, see p. 262.

The organization of these varied elements—as well as the resolution of Pietist and Ortho-dox liturgies in the Lutheran Church—came in the year 1700 from poet-theologian Erdmann Neumeister (1671–1756). Each of his librettos for sacred cantatas effectively coordinated the verses of a seasonal or weekly chorale with interspersed original texts for recitatives, arias, and other numbers. These usually dwelt on scriptural material associated with the chorale text. Neumeister wrote many cantata librettos, the success of which led to the work of several fol-lowers. Soon every slot in the Lutheran calendar was filled with a cantata text.

Before Bach perfected the Lutheran sacred cantata, composers in the preceding generation defined the genre. Johann Philipp Krieger (1649–1725) working in Weissenfals and Johann Kuhnau (1660–1722), Bach's predecessor in Leipzig, did significant work. The most important foreshadowings of Bach's cantatas, however, came from Friedrich Wilhelm Zachow (1663–1712), Handel's teacher in Halle. Zachow was an undeniable influence on Bach in the variety of forms, emphasis on instrumental participation, and focus on chorale melodies.

Ill. 9-3 Performance of a can-tata in a South German church. Singers are unseen. Frontispiece to Johann Gottfried Walter, *Musikalisches Lexicon* (Leipzig, 1732).

Bach as a Composer of Sacred Cantatas

J.S. Bach was a mere 15 years old when Neumeister introduced his first librettos to the church. Although all the cantata texts Bach later set follow the Neumeister model, only five have been authenticated as Neumeister originals. Many others can be identified as the work of one or another of his emulators. Bach's main librettist in Leipzig, where he composed most of his sacred cantatas, was Christian Friedrich Henrici (1700–1764), who used the pen name "Picander." Most likely he was the librettist of Cantata No. 140.

Bach composed more sacred cantatas than any other type of music. He wrote about 300 in all, but the music to only about 200 has survived. The traditional numbering of Bach's cantatas is not chronological. When the Bach-Gesellschaft (Bach Society) began publishing the master's complete works in 1851, it printed the cantatas as they came to hand, which led to an arbitrary numbering. Thus, *Wachet auf, ruft uns die Stimme* is not Bach's 140th cantata but closer to his 300th!

MÜHLHAUSEN AND WEIMAR. Bach's earliest sacred cantatas came from his Mühlhausen period and are datable around 1707–1708. These include the famous Easter cantata *Christ lag in Todesbanden* (*Christ Lay in the Bonds of Death*, No. 4) and *Gottes Zeit ist die allerbeste Zeit* (*God's Time is the Best Time of All*, No. 106), which was written for a memorial service. The early Weimar years saw no sacred cantatas from Bach, but when he was promoted to concertmaster in 1713, a flow of cantatas began. Bach planned to write a one-year cycle of Sunday and feast-day cantatas, but he had completed only about two dozen works when he moved to Cöthen in 1717. Among them was *Nun komm, der Heiden Heiland* (*Come Now, the Heathen's Savior*, No. 61), one of Bach's few cantatas based on a Neumeister text. During his Cöthen period (1717–1723), Bach composed only secular cantatas for special occasions such as birthdays.

LEIPZIG. The Leipzig appointment in 1723 prompted Bach's most intensive period of sacred-cantata composition. His position required sixty cantatas per year for the liturgy of Sundays and feast days. However, the liturgical cycle of weekly scriptural readings ran three years, requiring at least 180 new cantatas in all. Most were original works, but the pressure of short deadlines sometimes compelled Bach to adapt movements from other works or even to refashion one of his secular cantatas into a sacred one. Bach completed the three cycles of sacred cantatas during his first three years in Leipzig and wrote a fourth cycle in 1726–1727. From that time until the mid-1730s, Bach occasionally added new sacred cantatas to the Leipzig repertoire. Among them was *Wachet auf, ruft uns die Stimme,* composed in the early 1730s.

Besides the cantata cycles connected with the church year, Bach also contributed sacred cantatas for weddings, funerals, town-council inaugurations, and organ dedications. In addition, his monumental *St. John Passion* (1724), *St. Matthew Passion* (1727), and *Mass in B Minor* (c. 1749) crowned his output of choral-orchestral masterpieces.

Bach's Cantata No. 140: Background, Meaning, and Structure

Cantata No. 140, *Wachet auf, ruft uns die Stimme,* was written for the 27th Sunday after Trinity. This comes at the very end of the church calendar and occurs only when Easter falls very early. That accounts for Bach composing the cantata in 1731, later than most of his other cantatas. The 27th Sunday after Trinity occurred only twice during Bach's life in Leipzig: in 1731 and 1742. Bach conducted the cantata's premiere on November 25, 1731. Although he did not show a completion date on his manuscript, it was his habit to finish most cantatas the week that they were to be first performed.

J.S. BACH, CANTATA NO. 140: "WACHET AUF, RUFT UNS DIE STIMME," THREE MOVEMENTS

Be sure you have read Bach's biography, beginning on page 25.

The Gospel reading for this Sunday is the parable of the wise and foolish virgins (Matthew 25:1–13), a teaching on the spiritual marriage between Christ and his Church. Since this passage was the inspiration for the text of the chorale "Wachet auf, ruft uns die Stimme," it is important to read it at this point. Jesus tells the story:

> "Then the kingdom of heaven will be comparable to ten virgins, who took their lamps, and went out to meet the bridegroom. And five of them were foolish, and five were prudent. For when the foolish took their lamps, they took no oil with them, but the prudent took oil in flasks along with their lamps. Now while the bridegroom was delaying, they all got drowsy and *began* to sleep. But at midnight there was a shout, 'Behold, the bridegroom! Come out to meet *him*.' Then all those virgins rose, and trimmed their lamps. And the foolish said to the prudent, 'Give us some of your oil, for our lamps are going out.' But the prudent answered, saying 'No, there will not be enough for us and you *too*; go instead to the dealers and buy *some* for yourselves.' And while they were going away to make the purchase, the bridegroom came, and those who were ready went in with him to the wedding; and the door was shut. And later the other virgins also came, saying, 'Lord, lord, open up for us.' But he answered and said, 'Truly I say to you, I do not know you.' Be on the alert then, for you do not know the day nor the hour."

[Scripture taken from the NEW AMERICAN STANDARD BIBLE®, Copyright © 1960, 1962, 1963, 1968, 1971, 1972, 1973, 1975, 1977, 1995, by The Lockman Foundation. Used by permission.]

The first two verses of the chorale "Wachet auf, ruft uns die Stimme" are a paraphrase of the parable without reference to the foolish virgins:

VERSE 1

Wachet auf, ruft uns die Stimme	"Wake up," the watchmen's voice
der Wächter sehr hoch auf der Zinne,	calls to us from high on the tower,
wach auf, du Stadt Jerusalem!	"Wake up," you city of Jerusalem!"
Mitternacht heisst diese Stunde;	Midnight is this very hour;
sie rufen uns mit hellem Munde:	they call to us with a clear voice:
wo seid ihr klugen Jungfrauen?	"Where are you, wise virgins?"
Wohl auf, der Bräut'gam kömmt,	Be happy, the Bridegroom comes,
steht auf, die Lampen nehmt!	get up and take your lamps!
Alleluja!	Hallelujah!
Mach euch bereit zu der Hochzeit,	Make yourselves ready for the wedding,
ihr müsst ihm entgegengehn!	you must go to meet him!

VERSE 2

Zion hört die Wächter singen,	Zion hears the watchmen singing,
das Herz tut ihr vor Freuden springen,	her heart leaps for joy at it,
sie wachet und steht eilend auf.	she wakes and rises quickly.
Ihr Freund kommt vom Himmel prächtig,	Her friend comes splendidly from heaven,
von Gnaden stark, von Wahrheit mächtig,	Strong in grace, mighty in truth,
Ihr Licht wird hell, ihr Stern geht auf.	Her light is bright, her star ascends.

Nun komm, du werte Kron,	Come now, you honored crown,
Herr Jesu, Gottes Sohn,	Lord Jesus, Son of God,
Hosianna!	Hosanna!
Wir folgen all'	We all follow
Zum Freudensaal	to the joyful hall
Und halten mit das Abendmahl.	and celebrate with the [Lord's] Supper.

Verse 3 draws the chorale to a conclusion with rejoicing from the church and its members:

Gloria sei dir gesungen	May *Gloria* be sung to you
mit Menschen- und englischen Zungen,	with human and angelic tongues,
mit Harfen und mit Cymbeln schön.	with harps and with fine cymbals.
Von zwölf Perlen sind die Pforten	Made of twelve pearls are the gates
an deiner Stadt; wir sind Konsorten	of Thy city; we are consorts
der Engel hoch um deinen Thron.	of the angels high around Your throne.
Kein Aug' hat je gespürt,	No eye has ever perceived,
kein Ohr hat je gehört	no ear has yet heard
solche Freude.	such joy.
Des sind wir froh,	We rejoice in all of this,
io, io!	io, io!
ewig in dulci jubilo.	ever *in dulci jubilo.*

[Translation by Michael Fink.]

The librettist of Bach's cantata devised a plan that maximizes the chorale text by making it the "pillars" of a symmetrical structure. Cantata No. 140 contains seven movements. The three chorale verses appear at the beginning, middle, and end of the work, and Bach makes a choral movement of each of them. Between these, recitatives are coupled with vocal duets, which meditate or comment on the parable. The following table shows the layout and content of the cantata's seven movements.

MVT	VOCAL FORCES	INSTRUMENTAL FORCES	TEXT
1	Choir: SATB	Horn, 3 double reeds, violino piccolo, strings, *basso continuo* with organ and bassoon	CHORALE, Verse 1
2	Tenor soloist	*Basso continuo*	Recitative ("He comes, He comes, the Bridegroom comes! Ye daughters of Zion, come out!", etc.)
3	Soprano, bass soloists	Violino piccolo, *basso continuo*	Duet (Soul: "When comest thou, my salvation?" Jesus: "I am coming, thy portion." etc.)

(continued)

MVT	VOCAL FORCES	INSTRUMENTAL FORCES	TEXT
4	Choir: tenor section (or solo)	Violins and violas (unison), *basso continuo*	CHORALE, Verse 2
5	Bass soloist	Strings, *basso continuo*	Recitative ("Come, go in with me, my chosen bride! I have betrothed thee eternally." etc.)
6	Soprano, bass soloists	Oboe, *basso continuo*	Duet (Soul: "My Friend is mine!" Jesus: "And I am thine!" Both: "Love shall divide nothing." etc.)
7	Choir (and congregation): SATB	Full ensemble	CHORALE, Verse 3

Exploring Bach's Cantata No. 140

FIRST MOVEMENT. *Listen to the entire first movement of the cantata. Now listen to approximately the first minute of the music. Does the choir enter immediately?* No, the orchestra plays an opening statement before we hear the choir. *If this music were a Baroque concerto grosso, what would we call that opening statement?* It would be the *ritornello*. Like a *ritornello*, this statement contains more than one motive or musical idea. In addition, it may contain programmatic suggestions related to the chorale's first verse. The opening idea is in dotted rhythms. Its character might symbolize either (1) a wedding processional or (2) the watchmen's announcement:

Immediately after this comes a running, syncopated motive:

Possibly this suggests the virgins' hurried preparations for the bridegroom's arrival. Also, the melodic rise to a peak might reflect the chorale text, "from high on the tower."

The choir, by its delayed entrance and its sound (which contrasts with the orchestral **timbres**), also calls to mind the concerto idea. In fact, we often call this movement a choral concerto. *What melody does the choir sing at its entrance?* It is the chorale melody's first phrase. *Verify this by referring to Ex. 9-2 on p. 258.*

As you continue to listen, notice that the sopranos alone sing that melody. The lower parts provide supporting music. The chorale melody in this movement is an especially good example of a *cantus firmus* (described above), particularly since it is intoned in long note values. *Notice the gaps between choral phrases, allowing the orchestra to restate* ritornello *material.*

FOURTH (MIDDLE) MOVEMENT. This is one of the most famous movements in all of Bach's cantatas. The composer himself was so fond of it that he placed an organ arrangement

timbre Tone color, as in the difference in tone color between instruments. Adj., timbral.

of it at the head of his *Schübler Chorales* for organ published during the 1740s. In fact, this choral movement is in the style of an organ *chorale prelude*. In Bach's chorale preludes, one part sounds the chorale melody as a *cantus firmus* in long note values, while the other parts play new, original lines created by the composer.

Listen to the entire movement. Which part of the choir (or voice type) sings the chorale melody? It comes in the tenor part. We also hear two nonchorale lines, which begin this movement and then continue: the *basso continuo* and a melodic violin-viola part. *Notice the interplay between the melodic line for strings and the vocal chorale melody.* If we were looking for an interpretation of the **cantabile** string melody, we might consider it to represent the watchmen's song itself. One writer, however, has described it as the "mystic swaying dance of the Bridesmaids."

SEVENTH (FINAL) MOVEMENT. Here Bach harmonizes the third verse of the chorale as a church hymn in four parts: SATB. *In which part do we hear the chorale melody?* It comes in the sopranos, the usual placement in harmonized hymns. *Notice that the full orchestra joins the choir, each instrument playing a part appropriate to its range.*

FIRST MOVEMENT: INSTRUMENTS. *Study the lineup of parts on the first page of the cantata.* (Clefs to the left of the brace are the ones used in Bach's original score.) *Where has Bach placed the choral parts (soprano, alto, "tenore," and "basso")?* These appear just above the lowest line, the *basso continuo*. The reason is that in the Baroque period, the keyboardist/organist was usually also the conductor, who had to direct all vocal entrances. Playing in the *basso continuo* from a full score, this musician needed to see the vocal/choral parts conveniently—near the *basso continuo* line.

Next look over the instrumentation, starting at the top of the score. From Chapter 6, you already know that the *corno* is a horn. Here the part is represented at **concert pitch**. Next come the upper woodwinds. Bach identified the third part in that section as a *taille*. This was a Baroque tenor oboe pitched in a range similar to the English horn. Bach wrote its part in the alto (viola) clef, and the instrument often doubles the violas.

The highest instrument among the strings is the *violino piccolo*, which usually doubles the violin I part. *The editor shows the violino piccolo's first note, a C. By comparing this note with the instrument's first note shown at concert pitch, in what key was this early instrument pitched?* It was an E-flat instrument. *Look now at the lowest line of music on the score, the Continuo [basso continuo]. Which woodwind instrument do you find included in that part?* The score reads *fagotto*, which, as we have learned (Chapter 6), means bassoon. The inclusion of this double-reed instrument provides a bass-line balance to the oboes and *taille*.

FIRST MOVEMENT: FORM. *Listen to the entire first movement, following the score.* Example 7-2 shows the form of the chorale, a normal bar form. The first movement follows this form exactly—with the addition of instrumental *ritornellos*. Instead of using a repeat mark, however, Bach has written out everything. By following the chorale melody in the score, we can find the various sections of the form and mark them. *The choir's entrance after the first* ritornello *is obviously the first strophe of the Stollen, so mark "Stollen: Strophe 1" over m. 17. In the soprano part, trace the chorale's phrases (comparing them with Ex. 9-2) until you reach the end of the Stollen melody. In what measure does that occur?* You should be at m. 53. In that measure, the initial *ritornello* also returns. *Looking ahead, find a return of the Stollen's first phrase in the soprano. In what measure does this occur?* The second strophe ("Mitternacht …") begins in m. 69. *Mark that measure as "Stollen: Strophe 2."*

Now your job is to find the end of the Stollen and the beginning of the Abgesang. Again, com-

cantabile In a singing manner; lyrical.

Cantata No. 140: A Closer Look
Please refer to the score of Cantata No. 140, beginning on page 277 of the Score Anthology.

concert pitch Untransposed; the key in which the piano and all other "C" instruments are pitched.

pare the phrases with Ex. 9-2 until you find the end of the a₃ phrase in the score. In what measure does that phrase finish. The movement reaches this point in m. 105. Then a *ritornello* introduces the Abgesang. *In what measure does the chorale's Abgesang begin?* The chorale melody of the Abgesang starts in m. 118, although the supporting parts begin one measure earlier.

At one point in the Abgesang, the supporting choral parts (alto, tenor, and bass) come to the fore in a florid imitative passage on the word "Alleluja." In which measure and in what part does this begin? Starting in m. 135, the altos lead off. *In m. 137, can you identify a similarity between the alto's melody and an idea from the movement's opening* ritornello? The syncopated rhythm and rising melody are the clues:

Finally, compare the opening ritornello *(m. 1 to the downbeat of m. 17) with the closing* ritornello *(m. 189 to the end). What do you find?* The two passages are identical.

FOURTH (MIDDLE) MOVEMENT. *Look at the instrumentation at the beginning of the fourth movement. The instrumental line requires all the upper strings except which instrument?* The *violino piccolo* has been omitted, undoubtedly because its higher range would not allow it to play low notes in unison with the violins and violas. *Follow this melody for the first four measures. A two-measure phrase repeats melodically, but what happens in the dynamics?* Lacking an indication to the contrary, we can assume a beginning dynamic of *forte* in a Baroque movement. Bach then calls for a sudden drop to *piano* when the phrase repeats. This is an excellent example of two Baroque techniques: (1) "terrace" dynamics, discussed in Chapter 7, and (2) an echo effect. Dynamics return to *forte* on the upbeat to m. 5. *Look further along in this part. Does an echo effect take place in the strings during the first phrase of the sung chorale?* Yes, but the entire dynamic level has now been lowered. Now *piano* is echoed by *più piano*.

Listen to the fourth movement, following the score. The phrasing differences between the chorale melody and the string melody are interesting. *Find the end of the chorale's first phrase in m. 15. Does the string melody reach a phrase ending at the same time?* No, the strings had just begun a new phrase on the upbeat to that measure. *Scan the rest of the movement, noting where and how phrases overlap between vocal and string parts.*

SEVENTH (FINAL) MOVEMENT. The three choral movements of Cantata No. 140 move from the complex to the relatively simple. Movement 1 is a heavily contrapuntal "choral concerto," and Movement 4 is a "chorale prelude" featuring two independent melodies. Now the cantata's final movement is a simple four-part homophonic setting with a sharp focus on harmony. However, like the first movement, the final one employs the full orchestra. *Notice which instruments Bach has assigned to double each choral part.* Instruments are spread among the parts according to their ranges and functions. (For example, the function of Oboe II and Violin II here is to play the part immediately below that of Oboe I and Violin I.) *Which choral part does the basso continuo double?* It is an exact replica of the choir's bass part.

The first page of the movement is the Stollen. (Note the repeat at the end.) The second page is the Abgesang. Notice the unusual arrangement of bar lines: Some are complete, running

through the four choral parts, while others are only partial strokes on each staff. Find the proce-
dure used to distinguish between the two types of markings. Full bar lines appear only at the
end of each phrase (except in mm. 46 and 48, where the phrases end on the first part of the
measure). Partial strokes divide all other measures according to the meter.

HANDEL, *MESSIAH*, TWO EXCERPTS

Handel's *Messiah* is by far his best known work and his most beloved oratorio. Each year—at
Christmas, Easter, and other times—thousands of church choirs and community choruses
around the world perform part or all of this masterpiece of choral literature. For that reason
alone, any inquiry into oratorios should begin with *Messiah*. In this study, we will focus on
excerpts of the score that show two styles Handel used in writing for the chorus: dramatic and
anthem-style.

Be sure you have read Handel's biography, beginning on page 38.

Handel as a Sacred-Oratorio Composer

When George Frideric Handel arrived in Rome in 1706, the oratorio genre had been flourishing there for about half a century. As composed by Italians, oratorios were like unstaged
operas, using all its forms: arias, recitatives, instrumental sinfonias, etc. The subject matter of
an oratorio was usually Biblical; however, moralistic or allegorical topics were also employed.
Handel's first oratorio, produced in Rome in 1707, was of the latter type. *Il Triofo del Tempo e
del Disinganno* (later adapted for English performance as *The Triumph of Time and Truth*) was
based on a "morality" libretto. Easter Sunday of the following year saw the premiere of
Handel's first sacred oratorio, *La Resurrezione* (*The Resurrection*). The libretto involved events
between the crucifixion and resurrection of Christ, who does not appear in the oratorio at all.
Instead the work is mainly a dialogue between Lucifer and an angel of the Lord. Similar to
operas and oratorios by Italian composers, Handel's Italian oratorios devoted great attention
to the solo voices and little to choruses.

Ten years passed before he composed his next sacred drama. It was a masque titled *Haman
and Mordecai* (story drawn from the biblical Book of Esther), produced privately in 1718. The
composer's interest in sacred drama dissolved for another 14 years, while he became deeply
involved in composing, producing, and conducting Italian operas for his company. Then
Handel gave birth to the English oratorio in one stroke by revising and enlarging the masque
of 1718, presenting it under the title *Esther*. Three completely staged performances of *Esther* in
its new form were presented in a fashionable London meeting place during spring 1732. This
was the first oratorio the London public had ever heard. *Esther* was so successful that Handel
enlarged it further and transferred it to the King's Theatre. The Bishop of London, however,
objected to staged theater performances involving sacred subject matter. Thus the three new
performances that Handel presented were unstaged—a dignified practice he would follow in
all his succeeding oratorios. Several of Handel's additions to *Esther* were anthem-style choruses, which established the Handelian oratorio as a choral-vocal genre rather than a strictly
solo vocal affair. The following year the King's Theatre presented Handel's new *Deborah*, and
he also completed a third oratorio, *Athalia*. He conducted all three at Oxford that year to high
acclaim.

In 1738, the year following the demise of Handel's opera company, the composer began a
new spurt of oratorio composition. Collaborating with Charles Jennens (later the librettist of
Messiah), Handel wrote *Saul* between July and September. Immediately he began another oratorio, *Israel in Egypt*, to a libretto also possibly by Jennens. These two works, premiered the fol-

lowing year, are among Handel's greatest oratorios. The new features in *Israel in Egypt* were its sparse solos and its predominance of choral movements to tell the story and comment on it. Appropriately, this oratorio is about an entire people rather than individuals.

Messiah, first heard in Dublin and London in 1742, represents a turning point in Handel's career. His retirement from the opera theater was now complete. All his new major compositions would be oratorios (mostly on sacred subjects) or instrumental music to be performed with them.

In Dublin, Handel had probably intended to premiere a second new oratorio, *Samson*, but it was not heard until the following year. In this work, the composer used the chorus to represent, alternately, two masses of people: the Israelites and the Philistines. By contrast, the next oratorio, *Joseph and his Brethren* (1743), is mostly for soloists and contains only ten choruses. Handel gave greater emphasis to choruses in *Belshazzar* (1744, text by Jennens), often linking the movements in groups of two or three.

England's defeat of Charles Edward Stuart ("The Young Pretender") in 1746 prompted Handel to compose a trilogy of victorious Biblical oratorios. In *Judas Maccabaeus* (1746) he explored three types of choral writing: anthem style, a chordal declamatory method, and an expressive chamber style. *Alexander Balus* and *Joshua* were both composed in the summer of 1747. The former is somewhat operatic with few choruses, but Handel compensates in the latter by introducing each of its three "acts" with a choral movement.

For the next year's season, Handel composed another pair of sacred oratorios, *Solomon* and *Susanna*. A wide variety of choral writing appears in *Solomon*, including big, anthem-style double choruses, as Handel had used in *Israel in Egypt* and elsewhere. *Susanna*, on the other

Ill. 9-4 Page from Handel's original manuscript of *Messiah*: opening measures of the chorus "Glory to God in the highest."

hand, is unique among Handel's oratorios for the contemplative nature of its choruses. For example, choral prayers appear in the third part.

Handel composed only two more sacred oratorios. *Theodora* (1749) concerns a martyrdom and uses the chorus in a limited way. *Jephtha* (1751) is characterized by grand choruses in a variety of textures and functions (narration, commentary, reflection, etc.). A consensus of critics considers this to be among Handel's greatest oratorios, others being *Saul, Israel in Egypt, Messiah,* and *Judas Maccabaeus.* Through these works, the composer explored the choral medium thoroughly, bringing out its aspects of grandeur, expressiveness, and dramatic declamation. As the late works of Handel's maturity, these also show us the most accomplished music of his career.

Messiah: *Composition and Early Performances*

By 1741, Handel had collaborated with Charles Jennens in one successful oratorio, *Saul* (1738). Jennens, a gentleman of independent means, was enthusiastic about what Handel was accomplishing in the field of the oratorio and was anxious for the composer to set another of his "scripture collections," as he called sacred oratorio librettos. By July 1741, he had sent Handel a new libretto. As he mentioned in a letter to a friend, "I hope he will lay out his whole Genius and Skill upon it, that the Composition may excell all his former Compositions, as the Subject excells every other Subject. The Subject is Messiah." The new text was timely, for Handel had been invited to give a series of concerts in Dublin later in the year, some of which would be charity benefits.

The amazing speed with which Handel composed *Messiah* is legendary, but it was not unusually fast for him. His composition method was first to write a skeleton draft of each of the movements (choruses, recitatives, arias, etc.). Then he made a second pass, filling in his outline and completing the orchestration, an operation that usually took just a few days. Officially, he began work on *Messiah* on August 22, 1741. The work was completed thus:

August 28:	Draft of Part I
September 6:	Draft of Part II
September 12:	Draft of Part III
September 14:	Filling in and orchestrational completion

The pressure of the upcoming journey to Ireland and the urge (or need) to immediately write another oratorio, *Samson* (draft completed October 29), must have influenced his speed. The astonishing thing is that a work written in such haste should be such a consistent, peerless masterpiece. One might even consider divine inspiration, for Handel once declared, "When I composed the 'Hallelujah' Chorus, I did think I did see all Heaven before me and the great God Himself."

Less than three weeks after completing *Samson,* Handel departed for Dublin. Arriving there, he set up a subscription series of six concerts spread between December and February. These performances in a new concert hall featured his established music, such as *Esther,* rather than the new oratorio, which he was saving for the Lenten season. A second similar series concluded on April 7, 1742. Then, on April 13, 1742, Dublin heard the premiere of *Messiah* in a charity benefit concert, and the reception was enthusiastic. The newspaper reported:

> Words are wanting [i.e., lacking] to express the exquisite Delight it afforded to the admiring crouded Audience. The Sublime, the Grand, and the Tender, adapted to the most elevated, majestick and moving Words, conspired to transport and charm the ravished Heart and Ear.

By popular demand, Handel conducted *Messiah* again on June 3, and by early September, he was back in London. However, the first hearing of *Messiah* in that city would not occur until Lent of the following year. Handel conducted six performances of the now-completed *Samson* beginning March 16, 1743. On March 23, London heard *Messiah* for the first time. Despite a few attacks from the puritanical element concerning the "impropriety" of presenting this subject matter (Jesus Christ) in a theater, portions of the new work captivated the London audience. Tradition has it that during the performance, the entire audience, which included King George II, rose to its feet on hearing the words, "For the Lord God Omnipotent reigneth" during the "Hallelujah" Chorus, initiating the custom of audiences standing when that movement is sung.

Messiah as a whole was not immediately a success, however, and was even attacked in the press. Jennens, too, did not care for the music and for some time prodded Handel to make drastic revisions. The composer followed some of the librettist's suggestions, but the many changes and alternate versions he prepared over the next several years were mainly to accommodate different groups of soloists and choruses. (Thus, arriving at a single "authoritative" version of *Messiah* is difficult.) The oratorio was revived in 1745 for two performances during Holy Week, then it was not heard until 1749. Handel presented it again during Holy Week in 1750 at Covent Garden but without much notice. However, on May 1, he gave a performance to inaugurate the chapel of London's Foundling Hospital, an event that changed *Messiah*'s reputation forever. The chapel was packed with nearly 1,400 listeners. As in Dublin, a connection between *Messiah* and a charitable cause seemed to ensure success. Also, as in Dublin, the oratorio was soon repeated by popular demand.

From that point, a yearly performance of *Messiah* at Covent Garden with a repeat performance in the Foundling Hospital chapel became traditional. Interestingly, in 1759, Handel died between the two presentations, and that year's Covent Garden *Messiah* was the last time he heard his own music.

A full score of *Messiah* was not published until 1767, after which performances and adaptations proliferated. In 1784, London held a commemoration of Handel in Westminster Abbey and the Pantheon—a five-day festival of Handel's masterpieces, including music from the oratorios. Two complete performances of *Messiah* figured prominently in the proceedings, given by a chorus of 250 voices and about the same number of instruments. Music critic/historian Charles Burney published a detailed account of the commemoration in 1785. Movement by movement, Burney reviewed the music of *Messiah* as performed on the third concert. The following is his critique of the two choruses under study here:

> The magnificent Chorus, *"Glory be to God in the highest! and peace on earth, good-will towards men!"* … in which the *pianos* and *fortes* were admirably marked and observed, never had so great an effect before, in any performance within my knowledge. There is more *claire obscure* in this short Chorus than perhaps had ever been attempted at the time it was composed. The answers to the fugue succeeding each other so clearly and closely at the words *"good-will towards men,"* must always please artists, who know the ingenuity and merit of such contrivances; but the general effects of this Chorus want nothing in the ignorant, but attention and feeling, to afford them unaccountable delight.

* * *

> … I hasten to speak of the Allelujah, which is the triumph of HANDEL, of the COMMEMORATION, and of the musical art. The opening is clear, chearful [sic], and bold. And the words,

"For the Lord God omnipotent reigneth," … set to a fragment of canto fermo [i.e., *cantus firmus*], which all the parts sing, as such, in unisons and octaves, has an effect truly ecclesiastical. It is afterwards made the subject of fugue and ground-work for the Allelujah. Then, as a short episode in plain counter-point, we have *"The kingdom of this world"*—which being begun *piano*, was solemn and affecting. But the last and principal subject prosed, and led off by the base [i.e., bass]—*"And he shall reign for ever and ever,"* is the most pleasing and fertile that has ever been invented since the art of the fugue was first cultivated. It is marked, and constantly to be distinguished through all the parts, accompaniments, counter-subjects and contrivances, with which it is charged. And, finally, the words—*"King of Kings, and Lord of Lords"* … always set to a single sound, which seems to stand at bay, while the other parts attack it in every possible manner, in *"Allelujahs—for ever and ever,"* is a most happy and marvelous concatenation of harmony, melody, and great effects.

[Charles Burney, *An Account of the Musical Performances in Westminster Abbey and the Pantheon … in Commemoration of Handel.* London, 1785. (Reprint edited by Peter Kivy, New York: Da Capo Press, 1979, pp. 77 and 83.)]

Notable among early adaptations of *Messiah* was Mozart's reorchestration for the 1789 Vienna premiere.

Exploring Handel's Messiah, *Two Excerpts*

(Note that the term "Messiah" is derived from *Mashiach* from the Hebrew scriptures meaning "anointed one." The Greek equivalent is *Christos*, from which the Latin *Christus* and the English *Christ* have derived. Thus, "Messiah" and "Christ" are synonymous.)

For the 1743 performance of *Messiah*, Charles Jennens prepared a "word book," which was distributed to the audience. It showed the oratorio divided into its three parts, each corresponding roughly to an act of opera. In essence, the parts represent:

I. Prophesies concerning the Messiah; their fulfillment in his life.

II. The Messiah's last days, his death and resurrection; the triumphant second coming.

III Resurrection of the faithful at the Last Judgement; the Messiah's final enthronement.

Jennens also divided each part into numbered components like the scenes of an opera. We can easily grasp *Messiah*'s layout by viewing his outline:

PART ONE

1. Isaiah's prophesy of Salvation: the Gospel or "good news"

2. The judgement that will accompany the appearance of the Savior

3. The specific prophesy of Christ's birth

4. The Incarnation, announced to the shepherds near Bethlehem

5. The redemption and healing brought by the Savior

PART TWO

1. Christ's passion, scourging, and crucifixion

2. Christ's death and resurrection

3. Christ's ascension

4. Christ's reception in Heaven

5. Whitsun [Pentecost], and the subsequent preaching of the Gospel

6. The world's hostile reception to the Gospel

7 God's ultimate victory

PART THREE

1. The promise of eternal life and the triumph over Original Sin, through Christ's victory

2. The general resurrection that will accompany the Day of Judgement

3. The final conquest of sin

4. Acclamation of the Messiah

FIRST EXCERPT: MESSIAH'S BIRTH ANNOUNCEMENT. In our study, we focus on two excerpts from the oratorio. The first comes from Part One and corresponds to Jennens's "scene" four. He drew its text from Luke 2:8–11, 13–14 (King James Version). Handel designated a soprano soloist as a narrator (singing a recitative), and the chorus portrays the "heavenly host":

Recitative: There were shepherds abiding in the field, keeping watch over their flocks by night. And lo, the angel of the Lord came upon them, and the glory of the Lord shone round about them, and they were sore afraid. And the angel said unto them, Fear not; for behold, I bring you good tidings of great joy, which shall be to all people. For unto you is born this day, in the city of David, a Saviour, which is Christ the Lord. And suddenly there was with the angel a multitude of the heav'nly host, praising God, and saying,

Chorus: Glory to God in the highest, and peace on earth, goodwill towards men.

Now listen to the recitative portion of the excerpt. Notice that it is in four sections. The first and third use an accompaniment of *basso continuo* only (as in the Baroque recitative preceding "Dido's Lament," studied in Chapter 2). In the second and fourth sections, the upper strings join the accompaniment as a special effect that heightens the words. *Listen again and identify the texts where the string accompaniments occur.* The text begins, "And lo, the angel of the Lord …" and "And suddenly, there was with the angel." *Why would Handel increase the excitement of these texts by adding strings?* One thing the two texts have in common is the startling appearance of heavenly beings: first an angel by itself, then a "multitude of the heavenly host." ("Host" here means "army.")

Now listen to the chorus that follows. How does the choral sound differ between the lines, "Glory to God in the highest" and "and peace on earth"? The former, which mentions "God" and "highest," uses a high register. The latter, about "earth," uses lower pitches and only men's voices (a distinctly darker tone color). *In setting the words "goodwill towards men," what contrapuntal technique is Handel using?* This is an example of *imitation* (despite Burney calling it a fugue).

SECOND EXCERPT: THE "HALLELUJAH" CHORUS. *Messiah*'s famous "Hallelujah" Chorus forms the conclusion to Part Two of the oratorio. Its text is based on Revelation (19:6; 11:9; and 19:16):

Hallelujah, for the Lord God Omnipotent reigneth, Hallelujah! The Kingdom of this world is become the Kingdom of our Lord and of His Christ, and He shall reign for ever and ever. King of Kings, and Lord of Lords.

Perhaps the most striking feature of this chorus is the frequent recurrence of what we could consider its "motto":

Handel introduces this near the opening. Then he brings it back often—as a punctuation following a line of text or as a counterpoint against a line of text. *Listen to the entire movement and identify as many recurrences of the "motto" as you can.* You may have noted these later appearances:

- Punctuation to "for the Lord God Omnipotent reigneth."
- Counterpoint in the following *fugato* passage on those words.
- Counterpoint against the longer notes of "King of Kings, and Lord of Lords."
- Punctuation at the end of that passage.
- Punctuation at the end of the entire movement.

The following example shows two melodies: (a) the second phrase of the chorale "Wachet auf, ruft uns die Stimme," and (b) Handel's melody for the text, "and He shall reign for ever and ever."

(a)

(b)

In his book on Handel's *Messiah*, musicologist Jens Peter Larsen asserts that Handel based his melody on this chorale phrase (which he undoubtedly knew from his formative years in Germany). *Examine and sing the two phrases. Can you find some similarities? In what ways do they differ?* The first two notes of each ascend from the fifth to the first scale degree, and both melodies begin with three leaps, up-down-up. Both melodies end with downward scalar motion. However, the melodic details in between are different. The chorale moves up to a high point before its stepwise descent to the *fifth* scale degree. Handel's melody continues leaping up and down, then its descending scale (including a lower auxiliary tone on E) finishes on the *first* scale degree. *Do you feel that Larsen is justified in comparing these melodies?*

With your score in hand, listen to the soprano recitative sequence at the beginning of the first excerpt, noticing the changes in instrumentation among the four sections. With each section also comes a change of key. Make a brief table of the four sections, giving for each (1) its key, (2) its instrumentation, and (3) the opening text. (Hint: for the key of the third section: look at the final cadence.) Your table should show:

Ex. 9-4 Melodic phrases from (a) Nicolai's Lutheran chorale, "Wachet auf, ruft uns die Stimme," and (b) Handel's "Hallelujah" Chorus.

***Messiah, two excerpts:
A Closer Look***

Please refer to the score of the *Messiah* excerpts, beginning on page 304 of the Score Anthology.

KEY	INSTRUMENTATION	TEXT
C major	*Basso continuo*	"There were shepherds …"
F major	Upper strings and *basso continuo*	"and the Glory of the Lord …"
F-sharp minor	*Basso continuo*	"And the angel said to them …"
D major	Upper strings and *basso continuo*	"And suddenly …"

What is the **practical** *reason for concluding the fourth section in D major?* The following choral movement begins in D major, and the chorus must enter without hearing an instrumental introduction that would establish the key.

Now listen to the chorus "Glory to God," following along in your score. Note the two trumpets in the instrumentation. In the original manuscript of *Messiah*, Handel marked these "*ad lontano ed un poco piano*" (from a distance and somewhat quietly). Probably he meant them to be played from offstage, a theatrical device.

Notice that in each phrase from the opening through m. 17, the upper strings begin with voices but continue to play after the chorus cuts off. Take a guess at what Handel might have wished to illustrate with this technique. We could interpret this several ways. One might be that the upper strings represent a glorious "halo" of sound that continues to "shine." Another is that the composer desired an effect like a comet at night, whose long tail follows the main mass.

Study the imitative passage in the choral parts, beginning in m. 18 on the word "Goodwill":

good will to - wards men,

Make a brief table of the entrances of this idea, showing (1) measure number, (2) choral part, and (3) names of the first two pitches, for example: 18 / Bass / D, G. Your table should read:

MEASURE	CHORAL PART	PITCHES
18	Bass	D, G
18	Tenor	A, D
19	Alto	E, A
20	Soprano	A, D
21	Alto	D, G
21	Bass	A, D
22	Tenor	E, A
22	Soprano	D, G

Notice that the entrances of this phrase run through all four choral parts twice. Now look in the score at the first four entrances (mm. 18–20). Do you perceive a pattern of pitch levels and voice ranges? The passage shows an *ascending* pattern of pitches and voice ranges. Later in the movement (m. 33), another passage begins with this musical idea. Notice that the instrumental postlude beginning in m. 42 also makes use of it.

THE "HALLELUJAH" CHORUS. This movement contains some marvelous contrasts in choral writing between block-chord (homophonic) and contrapuntal styles. *Listen to the entire movement, following the score, and note passages in each of these styles. Where does the first contrapuntal section begin?* We find it starts in m. 22: a melody in long notes ("for the Lord God …") against many interpolations of the Hallelujah "motto." *Can you identify a true fugue exposition in the movement?* The passage beginning in m. 41 on ("and He shall reign …") is a fugue exposition:

m. 41	Bass	Subject
m. 44 (with upbeat)	Tenor	Answer
m. 46	Alto	Subject
m. 49 (with upbeat)	Soprano	Answer

(The shorter similar passage beginning in m. 69 is freer and not genuinely fugal.)

Handel begins setting the words "King of Kings, and Lord of Lords" in m. 52. After an initial statement by sopranos and altos in unison (mm. 52–56), sopranos restate this musical idea by themselves beginning in m. 57. Each succeeding repetition rises in pitch—a stirring effect. *In this passage, trace all iterations of the text line and document the starting pitch of each.* You will have four in all, beginning, respectively, on D, E, F-sharp, and G.

The chorus "Glory to God," as we noted, uses offstage trumpets. In "Hallelujah," the trumpets return, this time onstage and with timpani (the usual coupling in the 18th century). *In mm. 1–28, how would you describe the rhythmic function of these instruments?* They play only the Hallelujah "motto," adding emphasis to it.

The text line, "for the Lord God Omnipotent reigneth" is sung in long note values four times, beginning in m. 12—

for the Lord God Om-ni - po-tent reign - eth,

—and again in mm. 17, 22, and 29. Each time a different choral sound is used for the melody, and each time the orchestration calls for a different instrumental sound loosely doubling the choral line (at the unison or octave). *Make a brief table, showing the chorus parts and doubling instruments in each of these passages.* Your table should look like this:

MEASURE	CHORUS PART(S)	DOUBLING INSTRUMENT(S)
12	Full chorus	2 oboes, 2 bassoons, all strings
17	Alto, tenor, bass	2 bassoons, all strings
22	Soprano	2 oboes, violin I
29	Alto	Trumpet solo

In this chorus Handel sometimes uses the orchestra to play counterpoint against the chorus. Note the upper string parts in mm. 81–85, for example. At other times he uses it to add subtle rhythmic excitement to the choral parts. *Study the movement's ending, mm. 67–94, and notice the small rhythmic differences between the chorus, the upper strings, and the trumpets.*

STRAVINSKY, *SYMPHONY OF PSALMS*, FIRST MOVEMENT

Major Choral-Orchestral Music Between Handel and Stravinsky

During the 18th century, many rulers and wealthy noblemen maintained an orchestra and singers on permanent staff. An important function of these musicians was to perform in church or private chapel services. Thus, the Masses that Mozart composed for his Salzburg employer, the archiepiscopal court, employed a mixed chorus (SATB), soloists, and a small orchestra. Some members of the nobility kept only a small group of musicians on the payroll and expanded the ensemble for special occasions. For example, Haydn, after his second trip to England, wrote a half dozen Masses for special occasions in the Esterházy family. These required his patrons to bring their small musical ensemble up to a full choral-orchestral complement plus vocal soloists. The six choral-orchestral Masses by Franz Schubert were also part of this liturgical tradition.

Handel's oratorios of the first half of the 18th century had effectively brought choral music out of the church and into the English concert hall. Haydn's *Creation*, performed in the final years of the century, did much the same for central Europe. At that time, another trend also worked in favor of making choral music more universal than before. This was the rise of amateur music making. Focused chiefly on music in the home, the trend also spawned public amateur choruses. The idea intensified during the following century, resulting in many *choral societies*. Partially as a result, the Romantic period saw the development of a new type of choral literature—either sacred or secular in nature—written for the concert hall rather than the church. Many works of this type took full advantage of the enlarged choir by matching it with a full orchestra. The following table shows a small sampling of a much vaster choral-orchestral literature:

III. 9-5 Choral-orchestral performance in Exeter Hall, London. Woodcut from *The Illustrated News*, London, 1848.

TYPE OF CHORAL-ORCHESTRAL MUSIC	NOTEWORTHY COMPOSITIONS
Oratorio. Modeled after Handel's *Messiah*, these are large-scale works that tell a biblical or mythological story.	Beethoven, *Christ on the Mount of Olives* (1803) Mendelssohn, *St. Paul* (1836); *Elijah* (1846) Berlioz, *L'Enfance du Christ* (1854) Lizst, *Christus* (1867) Elgar, *The Dream of Gerontius* (1900) Honegger, *King David* (1921)
Concert Mass and Concert Requiem. These are usually settings of texts from the Roman Catholic liturgy performed in concert halls. Requiems were originally written to immortalize a recently deceased person, but came to include an solemn work commemorating a loss.	Bach, *Mass in B Minor* (1747/1749) Beethoven, *Missa Solemnis* (1823) Berlioz, *Requiem* (1837): a memorial to patriots Brahms, *A German Requiem* (1868): based on Scriptures rather than liturgy. Verdi, *Requiem* (1874) Fauré, *Requiem* (1887)
Choral Symphony. Influenced by the success of Beethoven's Ninth Symphony (1824), a large-scale symphonic work incorporating choral forces and usually expressing a lofty philosophical ideal.	Berlioz, *Romeo and Juliet* (1839): two choruses representing the dual feuding families Mendelssohn, Symphony No. 2 in B-flat Major (1840): finale is a self-contained cantata, "Song of Praise" Lizst, *Dante* (1856) and *Faust* (1857) Mahler, Symphony No. 2 (1894, subtitled "Resurrection") and Symphony No. 8 (1907, nicknamed "The Symphony of a Thousand") Vaughan Williams, *A Sea Symphony* (Symphony No. 1, 1910) Stravinsky, *Symphony of Psalms* (1930)

Igor Feodorovich Stravinsky was born on June 17, 1882, in Oranien-baum (later, Lomonosov), Russia. He was the third of four sons born to Feodor and Anna Stravinsky. Feodor had a fine bass voice and was a prominent soloist with the Imperial Opera in St. Petersburg. Anna came from a well-to-do family. Igor first attended school during adolescence and was exposed to much opera and ballet by way of his father's occupation. From the age of nine he received piano lessons, but his parents had no intention of allowing him to pursue a career in music. Instead, they insisted that he study law at St. Petersburg University. He was a poor student, uninterested in his subject, but he was fascinated with counterpoint, which he began to teach himself at the age of 18. He also improvised at the piano and dabbled at writing short piano compositions.

(continued)

IGOR STRAVINSKY

Anonymous photograph from the 1930s. Photo: Stock Montage, Inc.

The Stravinsky family spent the summer of 1902 near Heidelberg, Germany, where Nicolai Rimsky-Korsakov (1844–1908) was staying with his family. One of Rimsky-Korsakov's sons was a fellow student of Igor's, who introduced him to his father, the famous composer of operas and orchestral music. Rimsky-Korsakov was unimpressed with Stravinsky's piano pieces but recognized his potential. He advised the youth to study harmony and counterpoint formally with his own students. After Stravinsky's father died in December 1902, Rimsky-Korsakov became the young man's mentor. In 1905, Stravinsky left the university to study music full-time with Rimsky-Korsakov. That autumn he became engaged to his first cousin, Katerina Nossenko, whom he married the following January.

Stravinsky soon produced some significant orchestral works. He completed a Symphony in E-flat Major and a *Scherzo fantastique* in 1907. The next year he composed another orchestral piece, *Feu d'artifice* (*Fireworks*), for the wedding of Rimsky-Korsakov's daughter. Unfortunately, the old master died before seeing the score. On hearing these two short orchestral pieces in a St. Petersburg concert, Sergei Diaghilev, producer of the famed Ballets Russes in Paris, engaged Stravinsky to make some orchestrations for his 1909 season. Then, for the 1910 season, he commissioned the 27-year-old composer to write a full-length ballet, which would become his first masterpiece, *The Firebird*.

The Firebird was very successful, and the composer now lived in Paris during each ballet season, continuing his association with Diaghilev. During 1910–1911, Stravinsky wrote his second ballet, *Petrushka*, in which his personal musical style developed further. Its 1911 premiere was as successful as the first ballet.

The last of the three early ballets took longer to compose and produce. Stravinsky composed Part One of *The Rite of Spring* during the second half of 1911. However, a production delay gave the composer the entire year of 1912 to finish Part Two. About that time, he established friendships with prominent Parisian composers such as Debussy and Ravel. The night of May 29, 1913—the premiere of *The Rite of Spring*—made musical history. Its folk melodies, jagged rhythms, and dissonant chords shocked the Parisian audience. Early in the performance, members of the audience unexpectedly began protesting and counterprotesting the sound of Stravinsky's music and the look of Vaslav Nijinsky's choreography. A near-riot followed, during which Stravinsky went backstage for his own safety. Far from harming the composer's career, the scandal created publicity for him as a "bad boy" of music and generated world interest in *The Rite of Spring*.

During 1913–1914, Stravinsky completed his first opera, *The Nightingale*, begun during 1908–1909 and based on a Chinese legend. Diaghilev produced the opera in May 1914, the year the Stravinsky family settled in Switzerland. When World War I broke out later that year, Stravinsky was safe but also isolated from the Parisian culture of which he was now an important part. He was also cut off from Russian income and from his publishers, who were mostly in Germany. Nevertheless, the composer maintained a moderate level of productivity. His main project during 1914–1917 was a scenic cantata titled *Les Noces* (*The Wedding*), which celebrated Russian peasant marriage customs. (It then took him another six years to choose the right instrumentation.) In 1915, Stravinsky debuted as a conductor for a Red Cross benefit performance in Geneva, leading the concert suite from *The Firebird*.

At the beginning of 1918, Stravinsky and a writer friend, C.F. Ramuz, conceived the idea of an unpretentious theater piece that could easily tour around Switzerland. The result was *L'Histoire du soldat* (*The Story of a Soldier*), "a piece to be read, played, and danced," which was successfully premiered in Lausanne that year but not toured. For this low-budget production, Stravinsky used a miniature orchestra: clarinet, bassoon, cornet, trombone, violin, contrabass, and one percussionist. It was also his first work to employ the sound of American jazz (ragtime).

Following the war's end in 1918, Stravinsky did not return to France, and the Russian Revolution made it nearly impossible to return to his homeland. Instead he remained in Switzerland until 1920. During that time, Diaghilev reestablished the Ballets Russes and sought a new ballet from Stravinsky. In 1919, he brought the composer some 18th-century manuscripts he had picked up in Italy: chamber music and arias thought to be the work of Giovanni Battista Pergolesi (1710–1736). Diaghilev imagined that Stravinsky would merely orchestrate the music as he had done with Chopin's piano pieces for the 1909 pastiche *Les Sylphides*. Instead Stravinsky "re-composed" (Stravinsky's own expression) the music, peppering it with 20th-century dissonances, yet maintaining the essence of the music's rococo style. The resulting ballet, *Pulcinella*, became Stravinsky's bridge between his own century and the 18th, opening the door to an entirely new aesthetic and a new stylistic direction for him: neo-Classicism.

Stravinsky's neo-Classical period, which was to last about 30 years, was as much a reaction against Romanticism as it was a new direction. His new style rejected 19th-century emotionalism in favor of restraint, objectivity, style consciousness, and other ingredients of 18th-century musical aesthetics. In his autobiography published in 1935–1936 (two volumes), Stravinsky wrote:

> The need for restriction, for deliberately submitting to a style, has its source in the very depths of our nature, and is found not only in matters of art, but in every conscious manifestation of human activity. It is the need for order without which nothing can be achieved, and upon the disappearance of which everything disintegrates. Now order demands restraint. But one would be wrong to regard that as any impediment to liberty. On the contrary, the style, the restraint, contribute to its development, and only prevent liberty from degenerating into license. At the same time, in borrowing a form already established and consecrated, the creative artist is not in the least restricting the manifestation of his personality. On the contrary, it is more detached, and stands out better when it moves within the definite limits of a convention.
>
> [Igor Stravinsky, *An Autobiography* (New York: Simon & Schuster, 1936), p. 207.]

Stravinsky did not embrace neo-Classicism all at once. Between 1919 and 1923, he completed several "transitional" works and works that were already in progress. An important transitional score (and one of Stravinsky's most original) was the *Symphonies of Wind Instruments*, finished in 1920. Its focus away from strings in favor of the drier sound of woodwinds and brass pointed the way to a full-blown neo-Classical aesthetic. Stravinsky's neo-Classicism came to full flowering in his Octet, another work for winds, written in 1923. This music not only revived Classical forms such as sonata, variations, and rondo, it also indulged in a semihumorous parody of 18th-century mannerisms such as trills and suspenseful half-cadences.

During the 1920s, Stravinsky's career took a new direction: He became a concertizing pianist performing his own works. For his concerts, he composed a rich variety of piano music, ranging from his Sonata (1924) and Serenade (1925), both for piano solo, to the Concerto (1924) for piano, winds, timpani, and contrabass, and a *Capriccio* (1929) for piano and orches-

(continued)

tra. Stravinsky also continued to work with the Ballets Russes, even going on tour with them, but he was now beginning to accept commissions from other patrons for ballets, including *Apollo* (1928) and *The Fairy's Kiss* (1928, based on songs and piano pieces by Tchaikovsky).

The 1927 "opera-oratorio" *Oedipus Rex*, a collaboration between Stravinsky and Jean Cocteau, extended the idea of neo-Classicism into the realm of ancient Greco-Roman classicism. Based on the play by Sophocles and written to a libretto in classical Latin, Stravinsky's score maintained the ritualistic qualities of Greek tragedy, while it drew on operatic traditions ranging from Handel to Verdi. Diaghilev died in 1929 a few months after his concert presentation of *Oedipus Rex*.

The next decade began with the composition of perhaps Stravinsky's most significant neo-Classical work, the *Symphony of Psalms*, commissioned for the 50th anniversary of the Boston Symphony Orchestra. Gone from this score were the self-conscious 18th-century parodies and posturing found among other neo-Classical works. In the *Symphony of Psalms*, Stravinsky summarized the sweep of choral and instrumental traditions from the Renaissance to the 20th century. This work, along with Stravinsky's tours with violinist Samuel Dushkin, spread the composer's reputation through the United States and created increased demand for his music. One result was the ballet *Jeu de cartes* (*Card Game*, 1936), choreographed by George Balanchine for the American Ballet Company. Another was the "Dumbarton Oaks" Concerto (1938), which owes much to Bach's "Brandenburg" Concertos.

American interest in Stravinsky's music came at a crucial moment in his life. Within one year, his wife and eldest daughter died of tuberculosis, and his mother also passed away. Simultaneousiy, war in Europe was becoming inevitable. In September 1939, shortly after the outbreak of World War II, Stravinsky sailed to the United States, where he would reside the rest of his life.

Immediately on his arrival, Stravinsky went to Harvard University to deliver a series of lectures; later these were published under the title *The Poetics of Music*. In January 1940, Vera de Bosset, Stravinsky's secret love since 1913, arrived in America. They were married two months later and settled in Los Angeles, California. Stravinsky now completed and premiered the *Symphony in C*, which he had begun in the months before leaving France. Some shorter dance and orchestral works followed. Commissioned by the New York Philharmonic, Stravinsky then wrote the *Symphony in Three Movements* during 1942–1945. It incorporated elements of American "swing" music, and its second movement included music Stravinsky had salvaged from an aborted film project. While composing the symphony, he took time to work at other music, notably his liturgical Latin *Mass* (1944–1948) for choir and wind instruments. His last neo-Classical ballet, *Orpheus* (1948), showed the placid restraint of the Classical period alongside the reedy qualities of Baroque music.

A turning point in Stravinsky's development began in 1948. He began a three-year project: *The Rake's Progress*, an opera in English, and his only full-length theatrical piece. W.H. Auden and Chester Kallman provided the libretto, based on a series of moralistic engravings by William Hogarth (1697–1764). When Auden delivered the libretto in March 1948, he introduced the composer to Robert Craft, a conductor of contemporary music who had had some correspondence with Stravinsky. This began a relationship of inestimable importance, because Craft became a close collaborator with Stravinsky on a series of published memoirs in the form of dialogues. Craft also introduced Stravinsky to the 12-tone music of Anton Webern (1883–1945) and newer serial European composers such as Pierre Boulez (1925–). Craft's discussions of *avant-garde* music piqued the composer's interest, leading eventually to his serial period. For now, however, Stravinsky worked at *The Rake's Progress*, his last truly neo-Classical work, which employed forms from 18th-century opera and a "Classical" orchestra (including a harpsichord).

After *The Rake's Progress* premiered in 1951, Stravinsky's musical style veered abruptly. The *Cantata*, written in 1951–1952, experimented with complex canons in the manner of Webern. Stravinsky then began experimenting with works drawing closer and closer to pure serialism, most notably the choral work *Canticum sacrum* (1955), and his abstract final ballet *Agon* (1957). Finally, *Threni* (1958), a 35-minute choral-orchestral work based on the Lamentations of Jeremiah, was Stravinsky's first strictly 12-tone work.

The decade between 1952 and 1962 was devoted to touring and conducting. Craft was valuable to Stravinsky for these performances, as he could conduct the arduous rehearsals, leaving the final run-through and performance to the aging master. The two also used this routine to make the many Stravinsky recordings for Columbia Records.

The celebration of Stravinsky's 80th birthday in 1962 was on a worldwide scale. In addition to countless all-Stravinsky concerts, honors from President John F. Kennedy led those from other heads of state. In that year, Stravinsky also returned to Russia for the first time in nearly a half century and conducted concerts in Moscow and St. Petersburg (then called Leningrad). The early 1960s also saw the production of a Stravinsky trilogy on religious texts. *A Sermon, A Narrative, and a Prayer* (1960) was a Biblical cantata; *The Flood* (1962) was a "musical play" for TV based on the Bible and medieval mystery plays; and *Abraham and Isaac* (1962) was a "sacred ballad" in Hebrew dedicated to the people of Israel.

As Stravinsky approached the end of his life, he considered composing a Requiem Mass. A commission from Princeton University gave him the opportunity to compose his last substantial work, *Requiem Canticles,* in 1965–1966. Written for vocal soloists, choir, and orchestra, these excerpts from the Requiem liturgy were in reality his own Requiem.

Failing health soon made every activity an effort. The Stravinskys moved from Los Angeles to New York in 1969, and the following year they spent time in Switzerland. On April 6, 1971, Stravinsky died quietly in his New York apartment. Nine days later, the music for his funeral service in Venice was the *Requiem Canticles*. Stravinsky's gravesite is not far from that of Sergei Diaghilev on the cemetery island of San Michele in Venice.

Greatly pampered during his lifetime and voluminously written about since his death, Igor Stravinsky was undoubtedly the preeminent composer of the 20th century. Lauded as possibly the greatest ballet composer of all time, he also contributed significantly to the literatures of opera, orchestral music, choral music, and the piano.

Stravinsky's Choral Music

Igor Stravinsky composed choral music during every phase of his stylistic development. This body of music extends from the period of the early ballets to his last substantial work, *Requiem Canticles*. His initial efforts in choral music were essentially miniatures. These completely secular pieces stand in sharp contrast with the spiritual nature of most of his later choral music. Stravinsky had been baptized in the Russian Orthodox Church as baby, but when he was 18 years old he ceased practicing his faith. Then, in 1926, he had a deeply moving religious experience while in Padua, Italy, attending the 700th anniversary of St. Anthony. Between that year and 1934, Stravinsky composed three short *a cappella* pieces on texts drawn directly from the liturgy: *Our Father* (1926); *Credo* (1932); and *Hail Mary* (1934). The midpoint of these years saw the creation of the *Symphony of Psalms* (1930).

Stravinsky's later choral music also focused on spiritual texts with the single exception of the *Cantata* (1952). During the 1940s, the important choral work was the quasi-medieval-sounding *Mass*, which Stravinsky intended for actual church services, but it has rarely been performed that way. When Stravinsky entered his serial period, the choral medium played an important role. *Threni*, one of his longest works, was also his first completely serial one. The Judeo-Christian textual link through the Book of Lamentations lends a universal aspect to this work, which also has strong ritualistic qualities.

Stravinsky's last two substantial works were choral music based on the traditional Latin text of the Requiem Mass. In all, 15 choral works represent all of his main periods (early ballets, neo-Classical, and serial); they appear in four languages (Russian, Slavonic, Latin, and English); and they were written for all the chief choral performance venues (church, theater, and concert hall).

Creation of the Symphony of Psalms

The 1930–1931 season was the 80th anniversary of the Boston Symphony Orchestra. To celebrate, its conductor (and an old friend of Stravinsky), Serge Koussevitzky, commissioned several prominent composers to write new works, which would be premiered that season. Stravinsky received an invitation, and he accepted. He wished to compose a work of some weight and length but not a conventional 19th-century type symphony. Simultaneously, he was in the throes of a spiritual revival and viewed this commission as an opportunity to glorify God. As a result he planned a symphony built on biblical songs—the Psalms—which in places uses the choir to symbolize the human and the orchestra the divine.

In his *Autobiography* of 1935, Stravinsky explained the impulse and planning considerations that preceded the composition of his *Symphony of Psalms*. Among "masters of contrapuntal music," he undoubtedly included Bach and Handel:

> Symphonic form as bequeathed to us by the nineteenth century held little attraction for me, inasmuch as it had flourished in a period the language and ideas of which were all the more foreign to us because it was the period from which we emerged. As in the case of my *Sonate* [for piano], I wanted to create an organic whole without conforming to the various models adopted by custom, but still retaining the periodic order by which the symphony is distinguished from the suite, the latter being simply a succession of pieces varying in character.
>
> I also had under consideration the sound material with which to build my edifice. My idea was that my symphony should be a work with great contrapuntal development, and for that it was necessary to increase the media at my disposal. I finally decided on a choral and instrumental ensemble in which the two elements should be on an equal footing, neither of them outweighing the other. In this instance my point of view as to the mutual relationship of the vocal and instrumental sections coincided with the masters of contrapuntal music, who also treated them as equals, and neither reduced the role of the choruses to that of a homophonous chant nor the function of the instrumental ensemble to that of an accompaniment.

[Igor Stravinsky, *An Autobiography* (Simon and Schuster, 1936), pp. 254–255.]

The first text Stravinsky chose was Psalm 150, which exhorts us to praise God both verbally and on instruments. This would become the final movement. In his initial sketches, the composer set the words of the Slavonic version, "Gospodi Pomiluy" ("Praise the Lord"), but he later switched to Latin, changing the words to "Laudate Dominum." The Latin Vulgate Bible became the text source for the three movements of the *Symphony of Psalms*. The first two movements were based on Psalm 38:13–14 and Psalm 39:1–4 (Vulgate numbering), respectively. The progress of ideas among the three movements is intentional according to a program note by the composer—a planned "periodic scheme" that builds logically and emotionally and makes the work a symphony.

MVT.	ORIGINAL TITLE (LATER REMOVED)	SOURCE
I.	Prelude	Ps. 38, ending: "Prayer of the sinner for divine pity"
II.	Double Fugue	Ps. 39, beginning: "Recognition of grace received"
III.	Symphonic Allegro	Ps. 150 (lacking verse 4): "Hymns of praise and glory"

Stravinsky began the *Symphony of Psalms* early in 1930, but his heavy schedule of concerts prevented him from finishing the music until August 15. The first performance took place in Brussels on December 13 with Ernest Ansermet conducting, and the American premiere followed six days later in Boston under the baton of Koussevitzky. Stravinsky heard only the Brussels performance. The work was received favorably on first hearings. In his review for *Modern Music* (January–February 1931), Walter Piston began with the words, "The *Symphony of Psalms* by Stravinsky will undoubtedly take ultimate high place among that composer's works." With this music, Stravinsky had reached the pinnacle of neo-Classicism. In the symphony, we hear no mannerisms of 18th-century music; no aping of Bach, Mozart, or Haydn; and few anti-Romantic tactics. The work successfully assimilates and combines elements of the polyphonic music tradition, reaching back historically, and synthesizing them into a new 20th-century creation of high seriousness and inspiration.

Exploring the Symphony of Psalms, *first movement*

Years after writing the *Symphony of Psalms*, Stravinsky reflected that he had composed the first movement "in a state of religious and musical ebullience." Here is the text he chose, with an English translation:

Exaudi orationem meam, DOMINE,	Hear my prayer, O Lord, and
Et deprecationem meam.	give ear to my cry;
Auribus percipe lacrimas meas.	Do not be silent at my tears;
Ne sileas.	For I am a stranger with Thee,
Quoniam advena ego sum apud te	A sojourner like all my fathers.
et peregrinus, sicut omnes patres mei.	Turn Thy gaze away from me,
Remitte mihi ut refrigerer	that I may smile *again*,
Prius quam abeam et amplius non ero.	Before I depart and am no more.
(Latin Vulgate, Ps. 38:13–14)	

Listen to the entire movement. Now listen again from the orchestral beginning through the first phrase sung by the alto section of the choir:

How many different pitches are involved in this phrase, and what melodic interval is emphasized? The entire phrase is built on two pitches, E and F, lying a half step apart. Thus, the *only* interval in the phrase is a minor second. *Can you perceive a relationship between this restrictiveness and "the need for restriction" in the Stravinsky quotation on page 279? Now listen to the movement's opening again. Does the composer preview this melody in the orchestra?* Yes, just before the altos enter, we hear a form of the phrase played by a solo cello and a horn.

Keep listening after the choir enters. Notice that the melodic compass in the choral melodies is narrow for a while. On what words does Stravinsky break away from this restrictive trend with a melodic phrase that begins with an octave leap? The phrase begins, "Quoniam advena ego sum … " in the altos and basses:

Notice that the instrumentation also changes suddenly at this point. Does the half-step melody return? What are the words at that point? On a repetition of the words, "Remitte mihi," the narrow melody returns in the tenor section against repeated notes in the altos.

Listen now to the ending. What chord type does Stravinsky use to conclude this movement? It is a major chord.

We begin again by examining the instrumentation of Stravinsky's symphony. Look first at the woodwind section and notice how strongly it stresses double-reed instruments. Name these instruments. We find four oboes, English horn, three bassoons, and contrabassoon. This combination helps to lend the music a specially reedy ancient quality. *Which woodwind instrument usually found in the modern orchestra is missing?* The score omits the clarinet. *Look now at the string section. Which instruments are missing?* This section has no upper strings—neither violins nor violas. Choral authority Percy Young submits that by omitting clarinets, violins, and violas, Stravinsky had "the intention of reducing the purely emotional temperature" of the orchestra's tone colors. Stravinsky himself revealed that in 1930, when first considering writing his *Symphony of Psalms*, his first sound image was of "an all male chorus and *orchestre d'harmonie*" (symphonic wind ensemble). *Note the large brass section, including five trumpets.* The final instrumentation does resemble a symphonic wind ensemble combination with its large woodwind and brass sections. *Between the choir and the cello parts, which "extra" instruments do you find?* The score calls for a harp and *two* pianos. Later (rehearsal no. 2, etc.), the pianos and low strings will combine to give something of the effect of a *basso continuo*.

OPENING CHORD. *Examine the chord in m. 1 and identify it.* The work begins with an E minor chord. *Looking in the piano part, describe the spacing of this chord:*

The Symphony of Psalms, *first movement: A Closer Look*

Please refer to the score of the *Symphony of Psalms,* beginning on page 333 of the Score Anthology.

Spacing in the right hand is like a mirror of the left. Triad formations are bunched at the top and bottom with additional doublings of the third of the chord in between (played by the thumbs). This symmetrical spacing plus the four thirds give the chord a unique, ringing sound.

A BAROQUE EFFECT. Listen to the entire movement, following the score. Listen again from the beginning to the choral entrance at rehearsal no. 4. What happens in the orchestra at this point? When the altos begin, the orchestration shifts abruptly from horns, pianos, and low strings to double-reed woodwinds. This resembles Baroque "terrace" effects (such as those found in Bach's "Brandenburg" Concerto No 2).

INTERVALS. From rehearsal no. 5 to no. 6, examine the oboe 1 line. Do you find one interval type predominating? The pair of eighth notes on each beat spells a minor third. *Look at the first two measures, between beats 1 and 2 of each. How are these intervals paired?* They *interlink*, that is, the former and latter interval overlap:

Now turn to rehearsal no. 7. In the first measure, cellos and contrabasses, do you find a similar pattern? Yes, it is a pair of interlinked minor thirds—in fact, the same four pitches (written three octaves lower) as the beginning of rehearsal no. 5. *What happens to this bass line in subsequent measures, and what is the term for it?* The same four notes repeat in the next several measures. We call this an *ostinato*.

At rehearsal no. 7, the interlinked minor thirds in the orchestral bass part plus the half-step predominance in the choral part provide the crux of the movement's raw musical materials:

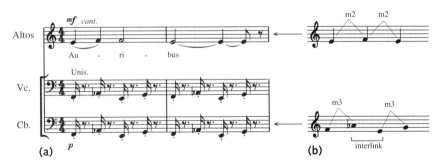

Ex. 9-5 Fundamental interval materials in the first movement of the *Symphony of Psalms*: (a) choir and orchestra at rehearsal no. 7; (b) interval content abstracted.

In the score, you can find several other instances of patterns built on minor thirds. *Look further ahead in the low string parts. Can you spot a return of the interlinked minor-third ostinato?* In the fourth measure of rehearsal no. 12, the ostinato returns for a few repetitions.

MODALITY. Hear and examine the music at rehearsal no. 10, particularly the trombones and bassoon 1. Does the music seem to be in one of the "church" modes? The trombones' emphasis on a key center of E and the scales in the bassoon strongly suggest the Phrygian mode, one of the Medieval-Renaissance "church" modes:

Since composers revived these scales in the 20th century, this occurrence is a connection between the remote past and Stravinsky's personal musical language.

   HARMONIC UNITY. Examine the final measure of the movement. What chord is sounded? It is a G major chord. *Does this chord bear a relationship to the movement's opening chord?* They are relative major and minor chords. If we consider the movement to end in G major, the E minor chord at the beginning would function as vi (submediant) in that key. We have seen tertian (third) relationships used as widely as Fauré (*Après un rêve*) and Bach ("Brandenburg" Concerto No. 2). Thus, even this subtle feature of the *Symphony of Psalms* is drawn from one of the strongly established traditions of the past.

Glossary

absolute music Music that is completely free from nonmusical implications; "music for music's sake." Ant.: **program music**.

a cappella Vocal music, especially choral, performed without instrumental accompaniment.

accelerando Accelerating the **tempo** of the music.

acousticon A device used in "harmonic analysis" to determine the relative volume of **partials** (harmonics) above a fundamental pitch.

action Part of a piano's mechanism consisting of a system of levers that throws the hammer against the string(s).

aleatory. See **indeterminacy**.

alla breve A duple **meter** equivalent to 2/2 time, with a time signature of ¢.

alto (1) The lowest vocal range for women or children; (2) French designation for the viola.

anthem An English sacred choral composition, either accompanied or unaccompanied. Verse anthems include sections for vocal soloists.

appoggiatura A Baroque ornament; a relatively accented non-**chord** (non-**consonant**) tone.

arch form (German, *Bogenform*) (1) A roughly symmetrical movement, such as A-B-A form. (2) A plan of roughly symmetrical movements in which the first movement balances the last, the second balances the penultimate, etc., bisected by one central movement.

aria, air Literally, **song**. In opera, a set piece for solo voice where action stops so that a character can **lyrically** reflect or emote. An aria can be **through-composed** but more often follows an established form. Arias also appear in other vocal genres such as cantatas (chamber or sacred) and oratorios.

arioso A style of writing for the voice less tuneful than an **aria** but more melodic than a **recitative**. Ariosos, like recitatives, are **through-composed**.

arpeggio Broken **chord**.

arrangement (1) Elaboration of a simple melody resulting in a full composition; (2) adaptation or transcription of a composition for a performance medium different from the one originally intended. "Transcription" is sometimes a synonym. Adj.: **arranged**. Verb: **arrange**.

art song A song of serious artistic intent as distinct from a folksong or a popular song.

art music The cultivated composed music of a culture, as distinct from folk, vernacular, or popular music.

atonality Literally, "without tonality." In 20th-century music, the conscious avoidance of tonalities (keys) in a piece of music, usually accomplished by avoiding traditional **harmony** and traditional treatment of **consonance** and **dissonance**. Adj.: **atonal**.

avant-garde Literally, "advance guard": Relating to new or experimental trends in the arts and people associated with those trends.

bagpipe A folk instrument, notably from Scotland or Ireland but also found in several other European countries. Wind for its reed pipes is stored in a bag, which the player inflates and keeps full. One pipe is fingered to produce a melody, and other pipes sound steady pitches (often a perfect fifth or octave), called a drone.

ballad An early Romantic type of German **Lied** based loosely on popular ballads of England and Scotland. Besides Schubert, Johann Zumsteeg (1760–1802) and Carl Loewe (1796–1869) excelled at ballad composition.

bass (1) The lowest men's voice range; (2) the lowest range in a family of instruments; (3) in a musical **texture**, the lowest-sounding part.

basso continuo A style of accompaniment employed in most music of the Baroque period. It consists of a bass **line** and **chords** built up from the bass line. The chords are usually symbolized by numbers and other signs, collectively called "figured bass." Technically, at least two players are required to "realize" a basso continuo: (1) a single-line bass instrument such as a viol or cello and (2) a **harmony** instrument such as a lute or keyboard instrument. In certain situations, such as early monodies and operas or organ continuo playing, a single instrument suffices.

beam A thick line that joins two or more **melodic** notes of equal value. That value must be an eighth note or less, since the beam replaces the flags of all the notes.

binary In two parts. A binary form consists of two sections, each of which is repeated.

bitonality, polytonality The presence or impression of more than one key (tonality) in a single musical passage. Bitonality has two keys at once; polytonality contains more than two simultaneous keys.

blues A song form based on a 12-measure harmonic pattern, originating among African Americans around 1900.

bohemian A old slang term for alternate life styles, often associated with the **avant-garde** in the arts. "Bohemia" in this context, therefore, did not mean the central European country but any bohemian neighborhood, such as Greenwich Village in the first half of the 20th century.

bravura Technical skill, often referring to compositions requiring great technical skill.

cadence A **melodic** or **harmonic** formula at the end of a **phrase**, section, or **movement** that conveys the feeling of momentary or permanent repose.

cadenza In a solo **concerto**, a **virtuosic** passage for unaccompanied soloist in free tempo. Occasionally, such displays occur in **sonatas** and **chamber music**.

canon (1) A technique of **counterpoint** wherein an extended **melody** stated in one part is restated (**imitated**) in its entirety after a time interval in another part; (2) a more complex **contrapuntal** puzzle in which one part is given and other parts must be deduced from it. Adj.: **canonic**.

cantabile In a singing manner; **lyrical**.

cantata A composition for soloists or chorus or both with instrumental participation. In the Baroque period, chamber cantatas contained **recitatives** and **arias** for one or two soloists. Sacred cantatas contained these and chorus **movements**.

cantilena A **song**-like melody.

chamber music Music composed for a small group of instruments (fewer than ten), one instrument to a part.

"chance" music. See **indeterminacy**.

character piece A composition intended to convey a **programmatic** idea or a mood.

choir In church music, a large ensemble of voices (usually mixed: soprano, alto, tenor, and bass). See also **chorus**.

chord Three or more tones sounded simultaneously, usually a **consonance**.

chorus (1) A **movement** for a large ensemble of voices; (2) a large ensemble of voices (usually mixed: soprano, alto, tenor, and bass) performing theatrical or concert music. See also **choir**.

chromaticism In **melody** or **harmony**, the organic use of the chromatic scale containing 12 **pitches** per octave. Adj.: **chromatic**.

circle of fifths An arrangement of the 12 **tonalities** starting with C major, in order by ascending fifths, symbolized as clockwise points along a circle. Moving through the sharp signatures, the keys turn to flat signatures (F-sharp = G-flat), returning to C.

clavichord A small keyboard instrument in early music, mostly for practice in the home. Pressing a key causes a metal tangent to strike one of its strings.

coda A section at the end of a **movement** that brings the music to a conclusion.

codetta A short **coda**, usually located at the end of a section or a **movement**.

coloratura A passage of rapid notes (often on a single syllable) designed to express emotion, show off the voice, or both.

concert pitch Untransposed; the key in which the piano and all other "C" instruments are pitched.

concerto (1) Since the Classical period, a work for one soloist and **orchestra**; (2) in the Baroque period, a work for orchestra with one or a group of soloists; (3) an early Baroque sacred **movement** involving voice(s) and instruments.

conservatory A high school or college of music; originally (Baroque period), an orphanage where music was usually taught vocationally.

consonance, dissonance In Western music before the 20th century, a combination of tones that serves as a point of momentary repose. Adj.: **consonant**. Ant.: **dissonance**.

consort A chamber ensemble of the 16th–17th centuries, made up either of instruments from the same family (whole consort) or different families (broken consort).

countermelody A **contrapuntal** part designed to accompany another part to which the countermelody is only slightly subordinate.

counterpoint The craft of composing in **polyphony**. The principal techniques of the craft include imitation, canon, and fugue. Adj.: **contrapuntal**.

crescendo Becoming louder.

D. Abbreviation for "Deutsch," meaning Deutsch's catalog of works by Schubert.

da capo Literally, "from the top." A *da capo* aria is in A-B-A form, where the final "A" section is a literal reprise of the aria's opening section.

damper In a piano mechanism, a felt pad that prevents the string(s) of a key from sounding. It is released when the key is pressed. The piano's damper pedal releases all the dampers at once.

declamation In text setting, the technique of making textual accent patterns coincide with musical accent patterns at the levels of syllable, word, phrase, and sentence.

decrescendo See **diminuendo**.

development (1) The application of various techniques to exploit musical material already exposed (chiefly, **themes** or **motives**), also termed "working out"; (2) the central section of a **sonata** form, where these techniques are commonly found.

diatonicism The principle of constructing scales that employs particular combinations of whole steps and half steps, such as formed by the white keys of a keyboard. Adj.: **diatonic**.

digital In audio, a method by which sound waves are produced or recorded by numerical representation.

diminuendo Becoming softer (quieter).

dissonance In Western music before the 20th century, a combination of tones not in repose, requiring resolution. Adj.: **dissonant**. Ant.: **consonance**.

divertimento A multimovement **chamber-music work** of the Classical period, usually intended as background music at parties, banquets, etc.

dodecaphonic See **12-tone**.

dolce Sweet, sweetly.

dynamics, dynamic markings Gradations of loudness in music. The most common markings are *pp* (*pianissimo*, very softly), *p* (*piano*, softly), *mf* (*mezzo-forte*, medium-loud), *f* (*forte*, loud), *ff* (*fortissimo*, very loud), *crescendo* (becoming louder), and *diminuendo* or **decrescendo** (becoming softer).

electronic music Music generated by an electronic **synthesizer**, usually preserved on tape or other magnetic storage medium.

encore From the French for "again," (1) *n.* either an immediately repeated performance of a **work**, **aria**, or **movement** or a short **piece** added at the end of a program; (2) *v.* to repeat a work, aria, or movement.

enharmonic In an **equal-tempered** scale, the equivalency of two notes of different names or spellings, such as C-sharp = D-flat.

equal temperament A method of tuning keyboards in which the interval between every semitone is exactly equal. Adj.: **equal-tempered**.

escapement Part of a piano's mechanism allowing a hammer to fall back to an intermediate position after striking the string(s), preventing it from striking a second time.

ethnomusicology The study of music outside European **art music**, including the traditional music of any particular culture.

Expressionism A movement in the arts during the early 20th century in which distortion, exaggeration, and symbolism were purposely used to evoke nightmarish feelings. Adj.: **expressionistic**.

fantasy, fancy, fantasia, fantaisie, phantasy (1) A Renaissance-Baroque **contrapuntal** form, forerunner to the fugue; (2) A free, rhapsodic, improvisatory-style **movement** of the 18th–20th century.

fermata A symbol placed over a note or **chord** to show that it is to be held longer than normal. a *fermata lunga* (long fermata) in 20th-century music may appear between notes and may be measured in seconds.

figure, figuration In music of the 17th and 18th centuries, a short, stereotyped melodic pattern used repeatedly, especially in keyboard accompaniment textures. Adj.: **figural**.

finale (1) The final movement of a multimovement instrumental work, usually fast and climactic. (2) The last piece in an operatic act, usually long and elaborate.

fipple Mouthpiece of a whistle or recorder in which air is blown across a fixed reed.

flamenco A style and repertoire of dance and song found in Andalusia (southern Spain). Its origins are attributed to a combination of Arabic traditions and European gypsy music.

forte Loud.

fortissimo Very loud, one **dynamic** level above *forte*.

fugato A section of a movement composed in the manner of a **fugue**.

fugue A **contrapuntal** form or procedure involving statements of a subject, called "expositions" alternating with relatively free sections called "episodes." Adj.: **fugal**.

gigue A dance of the Baroque period in triple or compound duple meter and in a quick, lively tempo.

glockenspiel A set of tuned metal bars laid out on a frame like a piano keyboard.

grace note An ornamental note printed smaller than its context. Its value is quick but indefinite, usually taking time from an adjacent note.

ground bass A continually repeating **ostinato** in the bass part that supports varying music above it, usually throughout a **movement**.

gruppetto An ornamental group of notes.

harmony The aspect of music resulting from a progression of **chords**, either sounded or implied. Adj.: **harmonic**. Verb: **harmonize**.

harmonic series A fundamental pitch together with a series of natural pitches above it (overtones) formed from multiples of the fundamental. See **partial**.

harpsichord The most popular Baroque keyboard instrument. Pressing a key causes a plectrum to pluck one or more of its strings.

heterophony Usually improvised, the simultaneous performance of a melody and an elaborated (or ornamented) version of that melody. The two musical sources often are a singer and an instrument.

homophony Music in which one melody leads or predominates, while supported by the rest of the **texture**, which is of secondary importance. In some homophony, the supporting parts move in the same **rhythm** as the melody. Adj.: **homophonic**.

horn Brass instrument, circular shaped with a flared bell. The modern instrument is called a French horn.

hurdy-gurdy A string folk instrument originating in the Middle Ages. Strings are activated by a rosined wheel, turned by a crank, which scrapes against them. Some strings produce the melody while others sound steady pitches (often a perfect fifth or octave), called a drone.

imitation A technique of **counterpoint** wherein a short **melody** stated in one part is restated (imitated) after a brief time interval in another part. Adj.: **imitative**.

impresario Producer and promoter of theatrical, balletic, and operatic productions; often the manager of a company.

Impressionism (1) A movement in the visual arts in France during the second half of the 19th century. Impressionism emphasized suggestion rather than depiction and the play of light on a subject rather than its depiction. (2) In music, a set of style characteristics perceived as analogous to (1). Impressionistic **harmony** tends to be nontraditional and **orchestration** is transparent. Adj.: **impressionistic**.

improvisation Spontaneous music making, often based on an existing **theme** or **harmonic** pattern.

indeterminacy, aleatory, "chance" music A 20th-century compositional technique in which the composer purposely leaves certain features of the music incomplete for the performer(s) to determine at the moment of performance. The result is unpredictable, and usually no two presentations of an indeterminate work sound the same.

intermezzo (1) A two-scene Italian light musical theater piece of the early 18th century, forerunner to the full-length *opera buffa* (comic opera); (2) a lightweight instrumental **movement** or **character piece** sometimes placed between more serious movements.

K. Abbreviation for "Köchel" (Ludwig Köchel, 1800–1877), meaning Köchel's chronological catalog of the works of Mozart, first edition, 1862. The catalog number follows "K." In the third edition, Alfred Einstein (1880–1952) adjusted the chronological position of many works, resulting in new numbering for them. Whenever a work is so affected, the adjusted number appears in parentheses following the original number.

key. See **tonality.**

Leitmotiv (German, "leading **motive**) A short musical idea in an opera related to some aspect of the drama. Richard Wagner (1813–1883) used leitmotivs systematically in his late operas, notably the four operas of *Der Ring des Nibelungen* (1853–1874).

libretto The script or "book" of an opera (or oratorio). A libretto includes dialogue, stage directions, and texts of the "set pieces" such as arias and ensembles. A **librettist** is a poet who writes librettos.

Lied A solo **art song** in German with keyboard accompaniment. Plural: **Lieder.**

line A particular **melody** in a particular musical context. Sometimes synonymous with **melody.**

liturgy The authorized texts for services within a particular religion. Adj.: **liturgical.**

lute A plucked string instrument popular from the Middle Ages through the Baroque period. It was one of the forerunners of the guitar.

lyric, lyrical Melodious or **song**-like.

lyrics Words, usually poetic, set to music.

madrigal Renaissance **secular** vocal ensemble genre popular in Italy and England.

Mass Service in the Roman Catholic Church commemorating the Last Supper. In music, usually a setting of the text to the sections of the sung "ordinary," those performed daily. These sections include Kyrie, Gloria, Credo, Sanctus, and Agnus Dei.

mediant In harmony, a triad whose root lies a third above the tonic. The term can be generalized to mean the relationship of any two chords lying a major or minor third apart.

melody A succession of single tones, usually expressing a musical idea. Adj.: **melodic.**

meter The division of musical time into groups of pulses (beats). Simple meters (2/4, 3/4, and 4/4) and compound meters (6/8, 9/8, and 12/8) are divisible into groups of two or three pulses. Asymmetrical meters (e.g., 5/4 or 7/8) combine groups of two and three pulses. Adj.: **metric, metrical.**

mezzo-forte Medium loud.

mezzo-soprano A women's voice range between **soprano** and **alto.**

microtone Any interval smaller than a semitone. Splitting semitones into quarter-tones is the most common microtonal application.

minimalism A postmodern movement in the arts that stresses simplicity and repetition of small elements. In music it also stresses a single, obvious tonality. Adj.: **minimalist.**

mode, modality (1) A **diatonic** scale, such as one of the eight Church modes used in the Middle Ages. (2) A major or minor scale.

modulate To make a transition from one key to another. N.: **modulation.**

monody Accompanied solo vocal **song** that developed in the last quarter of the 16th century in reaction to Renaissance **polyphonic** vocal ensemble music (e.g., madrigals).

monophony A musical texture consisting of a single melodic **line**; unaccompanied **melody.** Adj.: **monophonic.**

motet In sacred music of the Renaissance and later, an individual **polyphonic** choral piece, usually a setting of a Biblical passage.

motive A short melodic/rhythmic idea, sometimes constructed from shorter **figures.** Motives are sometimes derived from longer **themes** or fugue **subjects.**

moto perpetuo Perpetual motion, a type of composition in which constant rhythmic motion persists, usually based on a single note value throughout.

movement A comparatively independent portion of a larger instrumental composition such as a sonata, symphony, or suite. In performance, movements are usually separated by brief pauses (during which the audience does not applaud).

MS Manuscript (as opposed to a published print).

musicology The scholarly study of music. By itself, the term often means "historical musicology." Someone who studies musicology is called a **musicologist.**

nationalism A trend in music in which the folk songs, dances, and lore of a particular country provide the basis for works of **art music** that express national feeling or personality. Adj.: **nationalistic, nationalist.**

neo-Classicism An anti-Romantic movement in 20th century music that revived many of the practices and aesthetics of the 18th century. Adj.: **neo-Classical.**

obbligato Obligatory, usually meaning an accompanying instrument or part that must not be omitted.

oeuvre In French, "work," normally used to mean an individual composer's entire body of **works** (collectively).

opéra comique French comic opera originating in the 18th century, employing spoken dialogue. A serious/tragic operatic type developed from it, also called *opéra comique*.

opera seria 18th-century Italian opera based on "serious" or tragic plots. Handel's Italian operas are examples.

operetta A type of light opera that grew out of *opéra comique* in the 19th century, developing primarily in Vienna and London.

opus Literally "work," used to indicate the chronological position of a composition within a composer's *published* output. Thus, an opus number is part of a publisher's cataloguing system, rather than an entry in the log of a composer's output. Abbr., **Op.**, (pl.) **Opp.**

oratorio A quasidramatic, unstaged, vocal-choral work. Originating in the Baroque period, oratorios were usually based on stories from the Old Testament.

orchestra A large ensemble of instruments, as distinct from a small **chamber music** group. In an orchestra, more than one player performs each string part. Adj.: **orchestral.**

orchestration The art of combining instruments in an orchestral composition or arrangement. Adj: **orchestrational.**

ornamentation Embellishments added usually to **melody** (sometimes to **rhythm**), most frequently employed in the 17th–18th century.

ostinato A continually repeating melodic/rhythmic **phrase, motive,** or other pattern.

overtone See **partial.**

overture (1) An orchestral movement that precedes a theatrical work, such as an opera, a ballet, or a play. (2) An independent orchestral concert piece, related to the **symphonic poem.**

part song A choral composition in which the highest part carries the melody and the lower parts provide support.

partial, upper partial One of several **pitches** above a fundamental pitch, the intensities of which determine the fundamental's **tone color.** Other terms sometimes used interchangeably with "partial": harmonic, overtone.

passacaglia A Baroque **variation** form using a repetitive **ground bass.**

pedal point A long note, usually in bass part, which is sustained while harmonies above it change.

periodic (1) A natural division of a **melody** into regular, equal lengths; (2) the grouping of even-length **phrases** or subphrases.

perpetuum mobile. See **moto perpetuo.**

phantasy. See **fantasy.**

phrase Part of a melody that conveys a partial or whole musical thought, analogous to a clause or sentence in prose.

phonograph Forerunner to the compact disc player. A stylus traced the wavy grooves in a disc (**record**), producing vibrations that were amplified into audible sound.

pianissimo Very softly.

piano Softly.

Picardy third In the final chord of a **movement** or piece in a minor key, raising the third a half step to form a major chord.

piece An individual **movement, song,** or **aria** that is part of a larger **work,** or a work written as a single movement.

pipe and tabor A pair of instruments for one player. The **recorder**-like pipe had only three holes and, thus, a limited range. While the left hand played the pipe the right would tap out rhythms on the tabor, a cylindrical drum.

pitch Any point on the continuum of our perception of the relative depth or height of a sound. Pitch is a function of frequency, usually measured in Hertz (Hz), meaning vibrations per second.

pizzicato The technique of plucking a string instrument that is normally bowed.

pitch class Any one of the 12 tones of the chromatic scale without regard to octave position.

pointillism A term borrowed from painting meaning, in music, a texture with sparsely placed notes and many rests. Adj., **pointillistic**.

polychoral style A method of choral composition where the ensemble is divided into two (sometimes three) distinct groups performing both singly and together. The term also implies spatial separation between the groups.

polymeter The simultaneous use of more than one **meter**.

polyphony A musical **texture** consisting of two or more melodies heard simultaneously. Adj.: **polyphonic**.

polytonality. See **bitonality**.

posthumous Literally, after death, usually referring to music published or discovered after the composer's death. Adv.: **posthumously**.

prelude A piece of music originally intended to introduce one or more other movements, such as a fugue or a **suite**. Later, an independent movement.

primitivism A style tendency in some artworks of the 20th century that purposely evokes a primeval atmosphere.

program music Instrumental music inspired by or based on something nonmusical, e.g., a piece of literature, a painting, or a legend. Adj.: **programmatic**. Ant.: **absolute music**.

prosody The pattern of natural stresses (accents) in a text when spoken or sung; versification.

quarter-tone An interval half the size of a semitone, usually produced by special tuning or intonation.

rallentando Gradually slowing the tempo.

recitative In an opera, oratorio, or cantata, a section of dialogue or monologue. Recitatives imitate the **rhythms** and rise-fall patterns of heightened, dramatic speech. Thus they are not usually very **melodic**, in contrast with more **lyrical** "set pieces" (e.g, **arias**).

record A vinyl or shellac disc on which grooves have been scribed, which contain sound material playable on a **phonograph**.

recorder An end-blown (mouthpiece) flute in use from the Middle Ages through the Baroque period.

register A segment of the total **pitch**-range of a voice or an instrument.

reprise (1) The return of a **theme** or section of music after intervening material. (2) Repetition. (3) To bring back or recollect.

Requiem Mass for the Dead, which differs from a Solemn Mass in the texts of several sections.

rhapsody Free **fantasy**, often employing **virtuosic** techniques. Adj.: **rhapsodic**.

rhythm The aspect of music related to time; specifically, the durations of sounds and silences in relation to the pulse (beat) of the music. Adj.: **rhythmic**.

ritornello In an Italian opera or chamber **cantata** of the 17th–18th centuries, an instrumental passage at the end of an **aria** or following each verse of a **strophic** aria.

rondo A form, often the final movement in a sonata plan, consisting of a main theme (A) alternating with digressive sections (B, C, …). Typical rondo forms are A–B–A–C–A and A–B–A–C–A–B–A.

rubato A style of interpretation in which the tempo is slowed expressively at times and may be slightly rushed at others.

RV Abbreviation for "Ryom Verzeichnis" (Ryom Catalog), a thematic catalog of music by Antonio Vivaldi compiled by Peter Ryom.

salon The drawing room of an aristocratic or wealthy person's home. In Paris or Vienna during the 19th century, it was often the gathering place for intellectuals, poets, artists, and musicians. The "appointments" of a salon usually included a piano.

Sarabande A dance of the Baroque period in triple meter and in a slow, dignified tempo.

secular Worldly, rather than sacred.

scherzo A quick **movement** in triple meter in a form derived from the minuet. In a **sonata** plan, it is usually positioned immediately before the final movement.

score A musical work in visible, notated form, thus, the basic material of music literature.

sequence The immediate repetition of a **figure** or **motive** at another pitch.

serenade A multimovement **work**, usually instrumental, originating in the 18th century, performed outdoors in the evening for the benefit of a specific individual.

serial music, serialism In the 20th century, music organized by a predetermined series. Most commonly, **pitch** is organized by serializing the 12 tones of the **chromatic** scale. Called "12-tone music," this system provides an organizational alternative to **tonality**, resulting in **atonal** music. A composer who writes serial music is called a **serialist.**

set piece In an opera, a distinctly **lyrical** portion (e.g., **aria**, ensemble, or chorus) set off from **recitatives.**

sforzando, sforzato A strong **dynamic** accent on a single note or **chord.**

shawm A double-reed woodwind instrument used in Europe during the 13th–17th centuries; forerunner to the oboe.

sinfonia (1) An orchestral movement preceding an early Italian opera; (2) an instrumental **prelude** to an essentially vocal work; (3) the Italian term for **symphony.**

Singspiel An opera in German from the 18th or early 19th century. Singspiels were usually comic and used spoken dialogue between musical numbers.

sonata (1) A plan of three or four movements applied to works for piano, **chamber music** ensembles, or **orchestra** (the **symphony**); (2) a form usually employed for the first movement in a sonata plan; it consists of three sections (exposition, development, recapitulation) within a **binary** type of structure.

song Music for one solo voice, usually accompanied by a single instrument. The text may be secular or sacred (but nonliturgical). For this study, music for two or more voices is not considered song but vocal ensemble literature (considered in Chapter 9). Songs accompanied by more than one instrument belong in the literature of either **vocal chamber music** or orchestral song.

song cycle A group of songs unified by a literary theme or story line. A song cycle is, therefore, distinct from a collection or anthology of songs.

soprano Highest vocal range for a woman's or child's voice.

spatial music Music in which performing forces are separated rather than grouped together traditionally. The most common spatial effects are splitting ensembles within the hall and the offstage instrument(s) or voice(s). In 20th-century music, spatial effects have been used to add "dimension" and special "imaging" to sound.

staccato Articulation that shortens notes or detaches them from each other.

stop (1) In an organ, the manual control that opens and closes a rank of pipes. (2) In a **harpsichord**, the manual control that activates and deactivates a set of strings.

Storm and Stress A tendency in some music by Haydn and, to a lesser degree, Mozart during the early 1770s. Its main characteristics were turbulent fast movements in minor keys and poignant slow movements.

string quartet (1) A **chamber music** ensemble consisting of two violins, one viola, and one cello; (2) a composition intended for a string quartet ensemble, usually consisting of four **movements.**

stringendo Quickening the tempo. See also *accelerando.*

strophic The form of **song** composition where each verse (or strophe) of text is set to the same music.

subject A **theme** in a **fugue.**

suite A loosely organized series of movements related either by key or by subject matter (as in a ballet suite).

Symbolism A movement in French poetry during the second half of the 19th century. It employed free verse and conveyed impressions by suggestion rather than by direct statement. Counterparts in the visual arts and in music were called **Impressionism.**

symphonic poem A one-movement orchestral composition; the epitome of **program music.**

symphony A composition for orchestra, usually in four **movements.**

syncopation A shifting of rhythmic accentuation that causes a momentary contradiction of natural **metric** accentuation.

synthesizer An instrument that generates sound electronically, permitting independent and exact control of waveforms, frequencies, durations, etc. Adj.: **synthesized.**

system Two or more staves joined on the left by a vertical line.

tablature A type of graphic notation for lute or guitar in which letters, numbers, or symbols show fingering positions rather than pitches.

tempo The speed at which the music is performed.

tenor A high men's vocal range. In the Middle Ages, the term "tenor" or "contratenor" referred to instrumental parts roughly in that range but usually extended downward into the baritone range.

tessitura The portion of a **pitch** range used most consistently in a passage or a work, as opposed to the total range.

texture (1) The pattern of sound created by the interplay of the music's constituents, such as melody, rhythm, and tone color; (2) one of the common textures of music: **monophony**, **polyphony**, **homophony**, or **heterophony**.

theme A musical idea used as a basis for a composition or a **movement** within a multimovement composition. A composition, movement, or song may employ more than one theme.

theme and variations. See **variation**.

through-composed A method of **song** composition where regular, strophic repetition is avoided. The effect is a continuous unfolding of the song, although fleeting, unpredictable references to earlier sections may occur.

timbre Tone color, as in the difference in tone color between instruments. Adj., **timbral**.

toccata A piece for keyboard (organ or harpsichord) in a free, quasi-improvisatory style. Around 1600, the term was also applied to fanfares.

tonality, key Nearly synonymous terms. A system in which one **pitch class** at a time (called the "tonic") is central or nuclear to the music. The system has dominated Western music from the Middle Ages to the present, with a system of tonal harmonic "common practice" prevalent from the late 17th to the early 20th century. Adj., **tonal**.

tone cluster A **chord** with notes spaced very close, usually produced on the piano by striking a group of keys with the hand, fist, or forearm. The effect is very **dissonant**.

tone color Also called "timbre," the quality, nature, or type of sound produced by one instrument as distinct from that of another.

transposition The rewriting or performance of music in a key other than its original. Verb: **transpose**.

treble The highest range among voices or families of instruments. In vocal music, synonymous with **soprano**.

tremolo On a string instrument, the rapid and continuous repetition of a single note. On a piano, the rapid and continuous alternation of notes in a **chord**, meant to resemble several string instruments playing the chord using tremolo technique.

tutti Literally, "all" in Italian. The usual meanings are full orchestra or full string section.

12-tone, dodecaphonic A method of composition in which all 12 tones of the **chromatic** scale are preordered serially and treated equally without regard to any key or to **consonance** and **dissonance**.

upbeat One or more notes that come before the first full measure of a **phrase**. More technically termed an anacrusis; sometimes called a "pickup."

variant A varied presentation of previously exposed musical material. See also **variation**.

variation, variations, theme and variations Variation technique modifies or transforms a musical idea in a way that retains some essential features of that idea. Theme and variation form uses a stated **theme**, which is then modified/transformed differently in each succeeding variation.

vibraphone A keyed percussion instrument, similar to a xylophone but using metal bars, a **damper**, and optionally rotating "propellers" over resonator tubes located under the bars.

vibrato Slight, rapid fluctuations of **pitch** and/or intensity applied to sustained notes.

vihuela Renaissance plucked string instrument, forerunner to the guitar. It was shaped like a guitar but tuned like a Renaissance lute.

viola da gamba Bass member of the family of **viols**, held between the legs; often employed in a Baroque *basso continuo*.

viols Family of bowed string instruments developed in the Renaissance. Viols were shaped slightly differently from members of the later violin family (violin, viola, violoncello) and were also tuned differently. A modern survivor of the viol family is the contrabass.

virtuoso A musical performer possessing highly developed technical abilities. Adj.: **virtuosic**.

vocal chamber music A **song** or group of songs accompanied by a small group of instruments, one instrument to a part.

vocalise A wordless vocal composition or passage in a composition.

whole-tone scale A scale consisting of whole tones only (no half tones), six tones to the octave. Only two such scales are possible.

woodwind A family of instruments (all originally made from wood) that includes the **recorder**, saxophone, flute, oboe, clarinet, and bassoon.

work A whole composition of **art music**, possibly including more than one **movement** or act.

WoO In Beethoven's catalog, an abbreviation for *Werke ohne Opuszahl* (work without Opus number).

Index